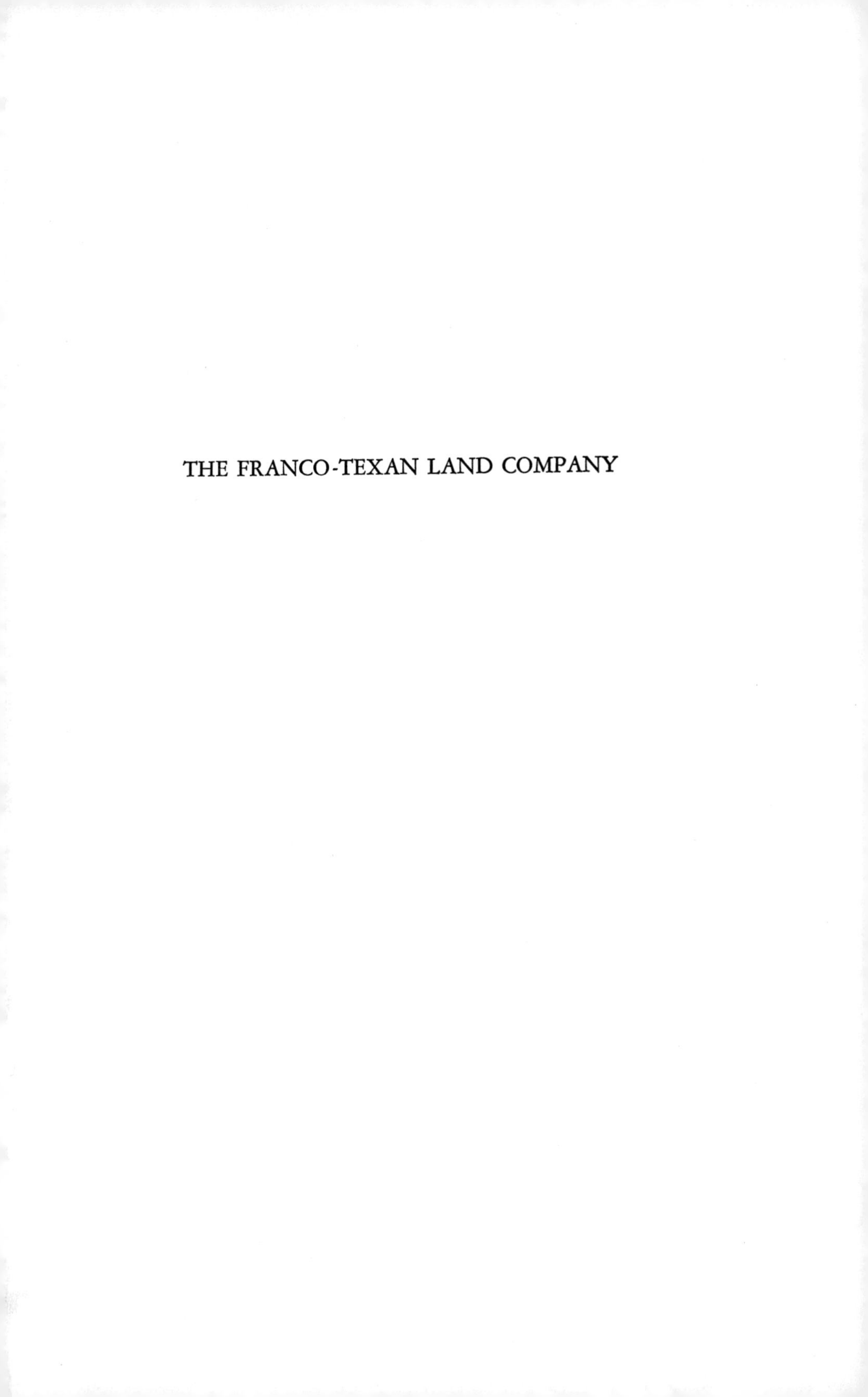

THE FRANCO-TEXAN LAND COMPANY

Number 7

M. K. Brown Range Life Series

The Franco-Texan Land Company

By VIRGINIA H. TAYLOR

UNIVERSITY OF TEXAS PRESS
AUSTIN & LONDON

Standard Book Number 292–78417–1
Library of Congress Catalog Card No. 70–79540

Type set by G&S Typesetters, Austin
Printed by The Steck-Warlick Company, Austin
Bound by Universal Bookbindery, Inc., San Antonio

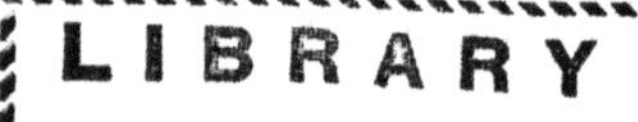

PREFACE

In 1948, while serving as Spanish translator for the General Land Office of Texas, I found ten letters, written in French, tucked away in a box of old deeds, manumissions, and affidavits. The letters formed no part of the official records of the Land Office but had obviously been the property of Xavier Blanchard Debray, who was the Spanish translator from October, 1856, to January, 1857, and from August, 1877, until the spring of 1895. They were in an unsealed envelope addressed to General G. T. Beauregard, New Orleans, Louisiana, with Debray's name in the upper left-hand corner. The letters themselves had been written to General Beauregard by P. Pecquet du Bellet of Paris, France, in 1877–1878, and each was labeled "Relative to the affairs of the Franco-Texan Land Company." Debray was a close friend of Beauregard, and both had been Confederate generals and were directors of the Franco-Texan Land Company. Doubtless, Debray intended to return the letters but failed to do so before his death in 1895.

In 1961, serving once again as the Spanish translator, I came across the Beauregard letters in a storage box in the bottom drawer of a file cabinet, and this time I read them. The affairs of the Franco-Texan Land Company proved interesting and, on further inquiry, somewhat of a mystery in the field of Texas history. A laborious search for clues revealed a cold, cold trail, but at length, as my search became an obsession, a connected story began to unfurl. That story is presented here, compiled without benefit of the company's records, since none were left, and with noticeable gaps and nagging little mysteries remaining. It is to be hoped that the still elusive details may some day be brought to light.

The resurrection of the Franco-Texan Land Company has required special assistance. Edwin Lanham, now living in Clinton, Connecticut, but formerly of Weatherford, Texas, the local headquarters of the Franco-Texan Land Company, suggested numerous sources and contributed firsthand information obtained from his grandfather, Associate Justice I. W. Stephens, who was at one time a director of the company. George Huddleston of the Pan American Petroleum Corporation searched his historical papers for references and facts and gathered material from Weatherford and the Federal Records Center in Fort Worth. Fred Cotten of Weatherford made available his books and numerous items concerning Parker County. Mrs. Evelyn Beavers, the district clerk of Parker County, patiently searched for old files in the vault and made other district court records readily accessible. Mrs. Alfred Hammond of Weatherford, a native of France and the last surviving member of the French colony, contributed not only pictures but private letters, and these, along with her recollections, breathed life and reality into the story and provided a number of the missing links as well. Chester Kielman, University of Texas archivist, facilitated the reading of the Epperson Papers and above all discovered an original Franco-Texan stock certificate. James Day and Mrs. Mary Osburn gave me daily access to the newspapers and other valuable material in the Texas State Archives. Mrs. Frances Horton of the Texas Supreme Court Library graciously lent her assistance during many lunch hours. R. A. Malone of the Texas and Pacific Railway Company sent the pictures of the presidents of the Texas and Pacific Railway Company and of Engine No. 20, the little woodburner which pulled the first train into Fort Worth. J. J. Bowdoin of Arlington, being familiar with railroad history, directed me to the Epperson Papers and other essential sources. These and many faithful library staff members have been indispensable.

CONTENTS

ILLUSTRATIONS

(following page 146)

MAPS, FIGURES, AND CHARTS

INTRODUCTION

Buried in the records of Parker County, Texas, is the final chapter of a story not generally known. It is international in scope; it is the subject of an historical novel, aptly entitled *The Wind Blew West*; and it had its origin in the old and persistent search for a direct passage across the American continent.

No. 3a rue de la Bruyère was the Paris address of the Franco-Texan Land Company. This name and address, in fluid script, formed the engraved letterhead of the company's stationery. In the years 1878 and 1879, Paul Pecquet du Bellet, stockholder and officer, wrote a series of extraordinary letters to his friend, General Pierre Gustave Toutant Beauregard, then holding the position of commissioner of the Louisiana State Lottery, that being the only employment available to a Southern general and military engineer in the aftermath of the Civil War.

Paul Pecquet du Bellet of New Orleans was an attorney, born in Louisiana.[1] He and his wife, a Virginian, and his son Henry P. du Bellet had resided in Paris since 1856. In 1869 the Du Bellets and thousands of French citizens invested in the Memphis, El Paso, and Pacific

[1] *New Orleans Directory for 1842* lists Paul Pecquet as a "Student-at-Law, 70 Royal Street." Cohen's New Orleans Directory, 1851–1855, lists Paul Pecquet du Bellet as an attorney, 45 Camp Street, residence at 42 Rampart Street. In 1871, in *Le Salut des peuples europeens*, Paul Pecquet du Bellet states that he had been living in France for fifteen years. He was the author of *The Diplomacy of the Confederate Cabinet of Richmond and Its Agents Abroad* and also of two other books, and numerous essays and newspaper articles, some of which were translated into English and reprinted in the New York *Herald* in 1861 (editor's introduction by William Stanley Hoole in *The Diplomacy of the Confederate Cabinet of Richmond and Its Agents Abroad*).

Railway bonds offered for sale in France by John C. Frémont. When General Frémont's railroad collapsed under a dark cloud of suspicion, the French bondholders became the owners of the 640,000 acres of Texas land which secured their bonds. It was doubtful security for the French in their remote position, for they soon found themselves at the mercy of the New York lawyers who had implemented General Frémont's ruin, sold his railroad to the Texas and Pacific Railway Company, and organized the Franco-Texas Land Company in order to reap the final rewards of the fraudulent bond sale.

Judge Du Bellet had one hope. He believed the French investors could be saved by his trusted friend in New Orleans, that is, if the New Yorkers could be ousted and Beauregard could be made president of the land company. He staged the *coup d'état*, but the General decided not to accept the offer. The stockholders, having rid themselves of Yankee domination, then elected a Texan as president. And Judge Du Bellet recorded it all in graphic style, leaving no little suspense as to the outcome of the ill-conceived enterprise. It was clear, though, that the author himself would have a hand in it, as he did when he sent his son Henry to live in Weatherford, Texas, until he had garnered a large share of the company's profits. The field was wide open until a fellow Frenchman and rival appeared on the scene. Texans, too, cooperated in riddling the coffers of this lucrative company which had fallen like manna into their midst. The losers were the French peasants who had invested their life savings in the Memphis, El Paso, and Pacific bonds.

THE FRANCO-TEXAN LAND COMPANY

CHAPTER 1

JOHN C. FRÉMONT AND THE MEMPHIS, EL PASO, AND PACIFIC RAILWAY COMPANY

The events which led to the creation of the Franco-Texan Land Company were no less extraordinary than Judge Du Bellet's letters. United States Army explorations in 1849 under Captain Randolph B. Marcy and Lieutenant William H. Emory had disclosed that the southern transcontinental route, near the 32nd parallel, presented few obstacles to the construction of a railroad from the Mississippi River to the Pacific coast. There was not yet one foot of railroad in Texas, but the state, having retained possession of her vast public domain on annexation to the Union, was able to make liberal land grants for railway construction. On February 9, 1850, the State Legislature passed a resolution providing that the federal government would be given a right of way through Texas, plus ten sections (640 acres each) for every mile of track constructed, if it would adopt the southern route for a national transcontinental railroad by March 5, 1851.[1] Because of rivalry over the location of the eastern terminus, the offer was not accepted. The Legislature then looked with favor on private proposals, and in 1852 and 1853 it incorporated five Pacific railroads, agreeing to donate eight

[1] H. P. N. Gammel, *The Laws of Texas, 1822–1897*, III, 589.

sections of land for every mile constructed.[2] Two of these railroad companies were the Memphis and El Paso and Pacific and the Vicksburg and El Paso, or the Texas Western, subsequently known as the Southern Pacific.[3]

In 1853 and 1854 the United States Army Corps of Topographical Engineers reported four feasible routes to the Pacific coast.[4] With eastern connections the southern route would be the shortest road between the two oceans; it had a snow-free pass over the Continental Divide and the least elevation to overcome. All routes except the southern crossed unorganized Indian territory. The federal government therefore hastened to conclude the Gadsden Purchase, by which it acquired 45,535 square miles of land from Mexico and provided an almost level roadbed for the southern route through New Mexico and Arizona.[5] Jefferson Davis, Secretary of War, recommended the natural advantages of this same route in his report to Congress in February, 1855.

When no immediate steps were taken to build the transcontinental railroad, the Texas Legislature decided to be more liberal. Its Act of December 21, 1853,[6] offered charter privileges to the company which would give the most satisfactory proof of its ability to build a railroad on the 32nd parallel, to be known as the Mississippi and Pacific. The proof required was a deposit of $300,000 in gold, silver, or good par stocks. The land donation was more than doubled, and all unappropriated lands within thirty miles of the line were to be reserved for selection by the company. The accepted bidder for this concession was the Atlantic and Pacific Company, a New York corporation, which lured Anson Jones, Thomas J. Rusk, and Thomas J. Green into its speculative scheme. However, Governor Elisha M. Pease refused the questionable

[2] *Ibid.*, III, 1184, 1231, 1245, 1268, 1433.

[3] Not the Southern Pacific of today.

[4] "Report of Explorations and Surveys to Ascertain the Most Practicable and Economical Route for a Railroad from the Mississippi River to the Pacific Ocean," *Senate Documents*, 33rd Congress, 2nd Session, Document 78 (Vol. 3).

[5] The Gadsden Treaty was signed on December 30, 1853, and ratified on June 30, 1854.

[6] Gammel, *Laws of Texas*, IV, 7.

stocks offered for the company by Jeptha Fowlkes of Memphis, Tennessee, and solicited new proposals. None was received and the offer ultimately expired.[7]

The Atlantic and Pacific quietly withdrew its papers, but it had already begun construction at Marshall under the charter it had expected to receive. Meanwhile, hoping to acquire the exclusive right to build on the 32nd parallel, it purchased four other trans-Texas railroad charters: the New Orleans, Texas, and Pacific; the Texas and Louisiana; the Vicksburg and El Paso (or Texas Western); and the Memphis and El Paso and Pacific. The company soon began to operate under its Texas Western charter. In 1856 it reorganized and changed its name to the Southern Pacific.[8]

The sale of the Memphis and El Paso and Pacific had been made subject to ratification within sixty days. The Atlantic and Pacific did not ratify the purchase contract, so the Memphis and El Paso and Pacific Company continued to exist. In 1855, after doing nothing but hold a few railroad meetings in counties south of the Red River, its directors petitioned for a new charter. On February 4, 1856, the Legislature gave them new corporate privileges under the name of the Memphis, El Paso, and Pacific. The act authorized the construction of a railway from a point on the eastern boundary of the state between Sulphur Fork and the Red River[9] to a point on the Rio Grande opposite or near the city of El Paso in the Mexican Republic and granted the company sixteen sections (10,240 acres) for every mile of road constructed and placed in running order, on the completion of a minimum of ten miles, and allowed certificates for eight sections of land per mile for the grading of a minimum of twenty-five miles of roadbed. All the lands located on each side and within eight miles of the center line constituted the Memphis, El Paso, and Pacific Railroad Company reserva-

[7] *Ibid.*, IV, 474–475, 879, 902, 1024–1025, 1381–1382, 1384.

[8] *Ibid.*, IV, 622–624; Andrew Forest Muir, "The Thirty-Second Parallel Pacific Railroad in Texas to 1872" (Ph.D. dissertation), pp. 62–63, 73, 80.

[9] To be at the western terminus of either the Cairo and Fulton Railroad or the Mississippi, Ouachita, and Red River Railroad, sometimes called the Gaines Landing Road.

The seal of the Memphis, El Paso, and Pacific Railroad Company

tion.[10] According to Section 17 of the charter, the certificates to be received for grading were conditional, because no title could vest in the company until track had been laid upon the roadbed for which they had been issued.

The company reorganized under this charter in Paris, Texas, on May 9, 1856.[11] All the directors were Texans—a group of earnest men who truly desired to build a railroad. They elected Travis G. Wright president, N. W. Townes secretary, and Stephen D. Rainey treasurer. F. S. Mosby was employed as chief engineer on October 7, 1856.[12] One of the early subscribers was Benjamin H. Epperson of Clarksville, Texas, who took eight shares of unpaid stock at $25.00 per share. In the au-

[10] Gammel, *Laws of Texas*, IV, 377, 378–385.

[11] Clarksville *Standard*, May 17, 1856; Dallas *Herald*, May 24, 1856. The board of directors of the original company—composed of President Travis G. Wright and Directors Simpson H. Morgan, George W. Wright, John D. Thomas, and Stephen D. Rainey—dissolved their organization, and a stockholders meeting was held. The new directors elected were Travis G. Wright, Simpson H. Morgan, John D. Thomas, George W. Wright, John T. Mills, Stephen D. Rainey, Benjamin S. Walcott, Thomas Ragsdale, H. G. Hendricks, Samuel Bogart, and Josiah W. Fort.

[12] Wright, Townes, and S. F. Mosby to E. M. Pease, Paris, May 9, 1857, Railroad Papers, Texas State Archives.

tumn of 1856, a call of 5 per cent, due on January 1, 1857, was made on the stockholders. This was the second call, the first having been for 2 per cent of the company's capital stock of $1,056,000, as required by the charter. With the money collected from these assessments, James Mitchell Daniel,[13] assistant engineer, began work December 15 very near the future site of Texarkana[14] and made substantial progress in spite of the company's limited finances.[15] In May, 1858, Travis G. Wright resigned as president and was replaced by Simpson H. Morgan.[16] At that time there were forty-seven employees drawing salaries: fifteen engineers, two contractors, and thirty laborers. One contractor

[13] Daniel came to Texas from Virginia in 1854 at the age of twenty-one. He married Emma Wright, whose father, George W. Wright, came to Pecan Point with his family and his brother Travis G. Wright, in 1816 (Alexander White Neville, *History of Lamar County,* pp. 91–92, 239). Daniel had five brothers, one of whom was a journalist on the *New York Herald*; another, John Moncure Daniel, was editor of the *Richmond Examiner* and Minister to Italy for eight years, under Pierce and Buchanan.

[14] The junction point was decided on by the Memphis, El Paso, and Pacific, the Cairo and Fulton, and the Gaines Landing roads. It was known as Nash and was located about ten miles north of the Sulphur Fork and five west of the Red River. Texarkana was not established until December 8, 1873, when the Texas and Pacific connected with the Cairo and Fulton at the river.

[15] In the annual report of 1859, the capital had been reduced to $557,625 on which calls of 22 per cent had been made, but only $48,303.38 had been paid in. A fifth call, for 10 per cent, was made on July 25, 1859 (Morgan, Townes, and James M. Daniel to H. R. Runnels, Paris, May 9, 1859, Railroad Papers; Stock Certificate 201, Epperson Papers, The University of Texas Archives).

[16] T. G. Wright to H. R. Runnels, Paris, May 17, 1858, Railroad Papers. At the first annual meeting R. D. King replaced H. G. Hendricks on the board of directors. Travis G. Wright was reelected president; N. W. Townes, secretary. J. D. Thomas was elected treasurer. At the second annual meeting, the same officers were elected, and the number of directors was increased from eleven to fifteen: P. T. Andrew, Sam Bogart, James P. Dumas, J. W. Fort, Calvin J. Fuller, John D. Thomas, B. S. Walcott, Edward West, Thomas Ragsdale, S. H. Morgan, S. B. Skidmore, James C. Moore, John T. Mills, George W. and Travis G. Wright (*Proceedings of the First Biennial Meeting of the Stockholders of the Memphis, El Paso, and Pacific Railroad Company, Held at Paris, May 10, 1858,* File 4, Railroad Contracts, General Land Office).

was John B. Ives of Syracuse, New York, and the other was Thomas C. Bates of Rochester, New York, employed to speed up the grading.

Later in 1858, Daniel succeeded Mosby as chief engineer and went to work with a vengeance. He was young and energetic, and both he and the president were being paid in land certificates. On March 27, 1860, a contract was made with Bates for the delivery of railroad iron and rolling stock at Moore's Landing on Sulphur Fork, and on May 7, 1860, a construction mortgage for $350,000 was executed to William M. Harrison of Paris, Texas,[17] to secure Bates's contract. Bonds were issued and deposited in the Canal Bank in New Orleans but were not offered for sale. By the fall of 1860, using funds secured through small loans and additional assessments on stock, the company had designated the center line of its route as far as the Colorado River, surveyed the vacant land within its reservation from the east boundary of the state to the Brazos River, and graded forty-five miles of roadbed west from Texarkana. For grading the roadbed it received 360 certificates for 230,400 acres of land.[18]

On March 20, 1861, the Legislature passed a relief act which allowed the Memphis, El Paso, and Pacific and other companies 10 certificates per mile for each five-mile segment which was graded and ready for superstructure.[19] The grading of five miles of roadbed on the Jefferson branch was completed, and 50 certificates were received, making a total of 410 certificates covering 262,400 acres.[20]

Acting under a contradictory section of the original act of incorporation (Section 16), the state issued patents on about one-fourth of these certificates. Later it claimed that Section 17 was the binding provision and refused to issue further patents until twenty-five miles had been completed and put in running order. The patents issued went to purchasers of the certificates and to creditors of the Memphis, El Paso, and

[17] Harrison, formerly a merchant at Clarksville, married Elizabeth Anne Epperson on January 18, 1855 (Marriage Records of Red River County).

[18] Miscellaneous Scrip, 263–271, issued December 4, 1860, General Land Office.

[19] Gammel, *Laws of Texas*, V, 361.

[20] Miscellaneous Scrip, 272–273, issued December 16, 1861.

Pacific, many of whom were directors and officers of the company. But most of the remaining Memphis, El Paso, and Pacific certificates had already been located by innocent purchasers. In this case the locations were respected by the Land Office though patents were not issued until 1874 and afterward, when rails had been laid upon the roadbed by the Texas and Pacific Company.

Sixty-five miles of grade had been completed when the Civil War suddenly halted all construction. The iron purchased for the graded section between Jefferson and Moore's Landing was seized in New Orleans by the Confederate government, and a locomotive which had arrived at Shreveport could not be put into operation because no track had been laid.[21] The most the company could do was to retain its corporate form for the duration of the war. Handley S. Bennett became president when Simpson H. Morgan was elected to the Confederate Congress. Other company officers of record at that time were Samuel Long, deputy surveyor, and Zenas B. Tyler, resident engineer.[22] Daniel was then in charge of the Lamar Artillery, 9th Texas Brigade, stationed at Paris.[23]

Since the unforeseen delays and hardships caused by the Civil War jeopardized the charters and grants of many railroad companies, the Texas Legislature, on November 13, 1866, passed another relief act extending the limitations on most of them for ten years.[24] Interest in the Memphis, El Paso, and Pacific revived, and the Texas directors, in

[21] *Memorial of the Memphis, El Paso and Pacific Railway Comp'y of Texas, Praying for a Grant of Public Lands, and a Loan of United States Bonds, to Aid in Constructing a Continuous Line of Railroad and Telegraph from Jefferson, in Texas, to San Diego, in California, by Way of El Paso, with Authority to Make Such Railrod Connections as to Reach San Francisco, Guaymas, Memphis, and Virginia City on the Harbor of Norfolk in Virginia, or Any Other Point on the Atlantic Coast, and Washington City, under the Title of Southern Transcontinental Railroad*, pp. 37–38; J. M. Daniel to President and Directors, Paris, December 1, 1866, Railroad Papers.

[22] Certificate of H. L. Bennett, January 28, 1863, File 20, Railroad Contracts; Neville, *History of Lamar County*, p. 152.

[23] Confederate Army Service Records, Texas State Archives.

[24] Gammel, *Laws of Texas*, V, 1130.

search of capital, brought John Charles Frémont into the company. It happened in this way. Benjamin H. Epperson, then president of the company, belonged to a group of Texans who believed that prosperity was to be achieved through industrial progress; and, as a delegate to the state constitutional convention, he succeeded in securing passage of an ordinance inviting foreign immigration and capital to the state.[25] He and the other principal stockholders, Daniel, James C. Moore, and J. H. Pratt, went to Philadelphia, where they became acquainted with Thomas C. McDowell of Harrisburg, Abraham Rex of Philadelphia, and Roger Fowler of Chicago. Being convinced that these men could acquire capital to build the railroad, they opened the stock books, and $4,160,000 was subscribed by Epperson, Daniel, Pratt, Moore, Fowler, McDowell, Rex, and Vice-President W. H. Johnson of Paris, Texas, who declared themselves equal partners for the purpose of constructing the Memphis, El Paso, and Pacific. On the same day, August 8, 1866, they transferred $556,700 of unpaid stock to Thomas C. McDowell. This stock represented a one-half interest in the enterprise, to be held in trust by McDowell & Company for their mutual benefit and to be disposed of to secure the necessary capital for the construction of the railroad; any person who would pay McDowell all or a portion of the sum of $556,700, would acquire an interest in said undivided first half in proportion to such payment, and such person or persons would become co-partners in the firm of Thomas C. McDowell & Company.[26] McDowell then introduced two other parties by the names of Wainwright and Kibbie, and a draft, drawn on these two for $50,000, payable at Jefferson, Texas, where the work on the road was to begin,[27] was handed to Epperson. This was earnest money, to be credited to McDowell as part payment on his stock. However, payment of the

[25] *Convention Journal*, 1866, p. 232.

[26] Articles of Co-Partnership and Articles of Agreement, August 8, 1866, Epperson Papers.

[27] During the spring of 1860 an overflow on the Red River added a mile to the Raft, and this blocked the upper waters of the river at the point where the railroad had begun construction. It was therefore impossible to get materials on the grade although one load of iron had been delivered to Moore's Landing before the overflow (Clarksville *Standard*, April 14, 1860).

draft was refused. Wainwright and Kibbie turned out to be straw men or bogus capitalists, wholly irresponsible and known by other names. When Daniel took the check to their place of business, he found it vacant. He finally located Kibbie, who laughed and said that the whole deal was a hoax, that Wainwright's real name was Dr. Wilson and he had moved to Ohio.[28]

On October 16, 1866, Thomas McDowell & Company entered into a subcontract with John C. Frémont, who agreed to furnish the money to build the road. Under this contract Frémont, Epperson, and Leonidas Haskell formed the executive committee. Frémont became an equal partner when he transferred to McDowell an undivided fourth of all rights and privileges in a certain grant from Jesús González Ortega, so-called Constitutional President of Mexico, for a railway from Guaymas, on the waters of the Pacific in Mexico, to El Paso or any other point on the United States boundary.[29]

A transcontinental railroad from Norfolk, Virginia, to San Diego, California, had long been the dream of John C. Frémont, the "West's Great Adventurer." He had made his last two western explorations for the purpose of selecting a route between the 37th and 38th parallels. Not only was his name indissolubly linked with the project of a Pacific railroad—he had also married a daughter of Thomas Hart Benton, the great Senator from Missouri; he had been the Republican candidate for the presidency of the United States; and in the Civil War he had filled one of the highest positions in the United States Army. This favorite of the government and the people could not help but be a great asset to the company.

After settling his property deficits in California and disposing of his final interest in the famous Mariposa mine, Frémont had purchased

28 Affidavits of Benjamin H. Epperson and James M. Daniel, Epperson Papers.

29 "Forbes et al. v. Memphis, El Paso, and Pacific Railroad Company, Cross Bill," *Memphis, El Paso, and Pacific Railroad Company Records, 1856–1877.* On July 12, 1867, McDowell sold to George W. Gerrish one-eighth of an undivided one-half of the Memphis, El Paso, and Pacific Company and the copartnership estate of the firm of McDowell & Company for $5,000 in cash and property consisting of twenty-one lots (Articles of Agreement in Cross Bill).

shares in the Kansas Pacific and the Southwestern Pacific roads. He then acquired franchises from the legislatures of California, Arizona, and Arkansas, sold his Kansas Pacific stock, and, at the time McDowell contacted him, was vice-president of the Southwestern Pacific.

Early in 1867, under Frémont's guidance, the Memphis, El Paso, and Pacific Company executed two mortgages. One was a land-grant mortgage, dated February 14, on the first 150 miles, covering the section from Jefferson to Paris, Texas. The lands yet to be received after the track was laid were the security for $5,000,000 in bonds at 6 per cent, subject to recall in 1890. The other was a construction mortgage bearing the same date for $2,400,000, independent of the land grant and secured by the railroad itself on the same 150 miles. The land-grant mortgage was made to Svante M. Swenson and Paul S. Forbes of New York and to Governor Andrew G. Curtin of Pennsylvania; the construction mortgage, to Swenson, Curtin, Forbes, and James Pollock of Pennslyvania. These men were trustees under the mortgages, and the bonds issued were to be made payable to John C. Frémont and Thomas C. McDowell or bearer.[30]

Pending the sale of these securities, the Memphis, El Paso, and Pacific acquired terminal facilities on the Atlantic and Pacific coasts, planned to survey the San Diego and Fort Yuma line and do some work in the mountain passes of Southern California under the supervision of Morton C. Hunter, and prepared to petition Congress to charter the road from El Paso to San Diego. Two directors were added: Dr. William Schmoele of Pennsylvania and Worthington G. Snethen of New Jersey. Dr. Schmoele was elected treasurer and Snethen soon succeeded Ed Reilly as secretary. There was also a shift in the company's management. The control passed to an executive committee of which Frémont was chairman, the other three members being Epperson, Schmoele, and Snethen. The central office was moved to New York in violation of both the charter provision and the general railroad laws of Texas. Dr. Schmoele purchased 1,023 acres on Norfolk harbor and

[30] Cardinal Leonidas Goodwin, *John Charles Frémont: An Explanation of His Career*, p. 244; Transcript, Supreme Court of the United States, No. 532: "E. J. Davis v. John A. C. Gray," *Memphis, El Paso, and Pacific Records.*

began to develop Virginia City, envisioned by Frémont and his new partners as a second New York.

Frémont proposed to sell his securities in Europe. For this purpose he enlisted the help of his brother-in-law, Baron Gauldrée Boilleau, who had been the French consul in New York for the past ten years. Boilleau introduced him to Henry Probst, most recently employed to supply the French army of occupation in Mexico. Seemingly, that experience qualified Probst to negotiate the bond sale, and Frémont engaged him as his general agent. A contract was drawn up on March 29, 1867, giving Probst a debit account to draw on and a 6 per cent commission on all money realized through his negotiations. He was authorized to proceed to Europe and sell the bonds in England, Germany, or France. As a bonus, contingent upon effecting the sale, the executive committee voted Frémont a 16 per cent commission on the gross proceeds of all bonds sold.[31]

The members of the executive committee made two other grandiose deals. They purchased two hundred land certificates, at $128 each, to be paid for in cash but delivered a few at a time, from A. M. Gentry, a contractor and president of the Texas and New Orleans Railway Company; and they entered into a contract of consolidation with the Memphis and Little Rock Railroad by which the Memphis, El Paso, and Pacific assumed that road's construction obligations.

While all this was taking place, the railroad languished. Frémont and his associates refused to honor Epperson's drafts, and it was impossible for him to continue construction, much less pay the company's accumulating debts. He spent the winter and spring of 1867 in New York, trying to get help from Frémont, who finally sent Daniel $3,500, which was borrowed on the company's Texas securities. In the summer of 1867 Epperson was served with a notice that Thomas C. Bates had entered suit for $300,000 against the company, in Rochester, New York, claiming nonpayment of his former contract. Bates had offered to compromise for a large amount of stock, but Epperson was unwilling, thinking that he had no real case against the company. In an inter-

[31] Copy of Memphis, El Paso, and Pacific Company Minutes, signed by W. G. Snethen on September 24, 1868, Epperson Papers.

view with Bates in New York, after receiving notice of the suit, Epperson told him the company had nearly failed but could go for six more months. In the event that it became a dead project, a judgment would do Bates little good. When Bates suggested a foreclosure, Epperson surmised that nothing could come of that because he did not believe Frémont and his friends had any credit, though they had control, and he could not get clear of them. However, they professed to think they could go on, and the news from France about the prospect of selling the bonds was good. As for Bates's "ring," Epperson doubted if they had any money either; and all he (Epperson) wanted to do was to build the railroad.[32]

Epperson talked with Frémont again in Washington, where the General was marshalling his forces to put the Memphis, El Paso, and Pacific bill through Congress, but he received not even a promise of money and came away in a despondent mood. Local people along the line had subscribed land and securities, and these could not be redeemed. James C. Moore, a director and devotee of the railroad, needed money at Jefferson. Agents would not work without cash, and there was none in the treasury. Moore said he was paying some of the bills himself, and if he only had $3,000, he could get along.[33] Ex-Governor Throckmorton, a close friend, wrote Epperson from McKinney, "I see by the paper that you are at home and that you are working on the railroad still. I fear the devilish thing will break you up . . . Let me suggest that you get out as easy as you can and let it go to the devil. Unless large capital or Congress can be interested in its behalf, it will fail."[34]

Since Frémont's contract had not been carried out, William Schmoele proposed to construct the railroad by an agreement made on November 14, 1867, but not signed until some time in February, 1868. The subscription books were reopened and the capital stock fixed at $40,000,000 and divided into 600,000 shares at $25.00 each. Schmoele took 200,000 shares, and Frémont, Epperson, and McDowell took

[32] Memorandum of Conversation with Thomas C. Bates in New York, July 23, on Notice of Constitution of Suit for $300,000 against the Company, *ibid.*

[33] Moore to Epperson, August 22, 1867, *ibid.*

[34] Throckmorton to Epperson, December 19, 1867, *ibid.*

100,000 shares. For a commission and expenses, both not to exceed 25 per cent of the gross proceeds, Schmoele agreed to issue and sell:

I. 200,000 certificates of $100 each, entitling the purchaser, when paid in full on monthly installments of $5.00 each, to
   1. A land warrant for twenty acres of agricultural land,
   2. One building lot in any town or city laid out by the company,
   3. A certificate for two shares of fully paid stock ($25.00 each),
   4. A free travel pass over one hundred miles of road for five years.

   The holder was to have the privilege of selecting two additional building lots instead of twenty acres of agricultural land, and the free pass would in such case apply to the area in which the lots were located.

II. 50,000 certificates of $200 each payable in monthly installments and entitling the purchaser to:
   1. A warrant for forty acres of agricultural land,
   2. One building lot, the holder to have the privilege of selecting four additional building lots instead of agricultural land.
   3. Two shares of stock,
   4. One free pass for five years.

III. After disposing of the second series of 50,000 certificates Schmoele would issue and sell 50,000 certificates at $200 each, payable in suitable monthly installments and entitling the purchaser to
   1. A warrant for forty acres of agricultural land,
   2. One building lot, with privilege of converting the forty acres into four additional town lots,
   3. One free pass for five years.

The foregoing plan required (1) 8,000,000 acres of agricultural land (2) 300,000 building lots (3) $12,500,000 in stock (4) 300,000 local free passes for five years. It would realize $40,000,000 or, after deducting 25 per cent for expenses, $30,000,000 in net proceeds for the treasury of the company.[35] Schmoele was to have all these certificates printed in Philadelphia.

[35] Copy of Schmoele's contract, *ibid.*

Meanwhile, in New York, debts were mounting and lawsuits were springing up on all sides. Among other things the company had to clean up the footsteps of Haskell and Naumann, two directors who had resigned and left town after "working" a double pay-off on some bonds they had contracted to sell. Snethen spent all the winter of 1868 preparing the Memphis, El Paso, and Pacific memorial and bill, petitioning for a charter with land grant and subsidy under the new title of "Southern Transcontinental." He was in desperate need of money to push it through Congress. "You can't get anything through on a promise any more," he wrote to Epperson; "they want cash."[36]

The executive committee, on March 2, 1868, resolved to issue construction certificates, Series A, at the rate of $16,000 per mile on the first 150 miles of the road: 5,500 of these certificates in nominal value of $1,000 each were placed in the hands of Frémont to be used by him as the committee might direct. The McDowell interests, having been ignored, immediately restrained the company by injunction from delivering or issuing any more bonds or certificates until their petitions for relief were heard.

The Memphis, El Paso, and Pacific bill was finally introduced into both houses on April 13, 1868, and referred to the Pacific Railroad committees. Hopes revived somewhat, and McDowell, Fowler, and Gerrish discontinued their suit and moved in unison with the Frémont crowd. Snethen wrote Epperson, "With the would-be King of the Cannibals [President Andrew Johnson] out, the goose will hang high. Then our subsidy will be a sure thing . . ."[37] Edward Gilbert, the company's counsel for the state of New York, thought otherwise. He, too, wrote Epperson,

By the way, have you seen the pamphlet memorial of the Southern Transcontinental (a *Transcendental*) Railroad got up by Schmoele and Snethen to

[36] Snethen to Epperson, February 17, 1868, *ibid.* In 1868 the company had nine directors (elected in 1867): B. H. Epperson, James M. Daniel, Samuel Hancock, William H. Johnson, James C. Moore, and Travis G. Wright of Texas; John C. Frémont of New York, Dr. William Schmoele of Pennsylvania, and Worthington G. Snethen of Maryland. (*Memorial of the Memphis, El Paso, and Pacific*, p. 4). Leonidas Haskell and A. Naumann resigned November 15, 1867 (Memorandum, Epperson Papers).

[37] Snethen to Epperson, April 13, 1868, Epperson Papers.

pass around in Congress . . . I hope everything goes well but frankly between you and me in strict confidence, I don't believe these parties have any money whatever. I believe a very limited amount would energize the enterprise but . . . they have just exactly *nill*, neither more or less. The prospect of a subsidy with a lobby of paupers you can imagine as well as myself . . . No spade has been struck on the line of the Memphis, El Paso, and Pacific under the new management yet.[38]

In May Gilbert and Snethen went to Philadelphia to get some help from Schmoele. Besides an advance, they wanted the long-promised certificates which they could sell or dispense in lieu of money, but Schmoele offered only strong expressions of confidence in the subsidy. There had been a delay. The engraver was ill. Gilbert regretted he had wasted $10 and a day's time just to be convinced that any money they got would have to come from the enterprise itself.[39]

In July Epperson was busy settling fourteen immigrant laborers he had brought from Sweden with Swenson's help. He heard nothing from New York until September 29, when he had a ten-page letter from Snethen informing him of the "successful sale of their loan." It was done, Snethen said, through the French consul, Baron Boilleau, and the contract had been sold for 62 per cent to M. J. Paradis, a prominent banker in Paris, conditional upon getting the bonds on the Bourse, where they were not to sell for less than 75¾ per cent.

Frémont, thinking someone should go to Paris at once, sent William Auferman to represent the company. Auferman had been elected assistant treasurer on August 29, 1868, with a 10 per cent commission on the par value of all bonds sold; and Frémont had been elected second vice-president on August 31, "to get around Epperson's absence" and "to make use of Fremont's name, which carried weight in France." Auferman was to take 228 bonds with him in order to get proceeds at once for meeting debts in New York and Texas. Other bonds would be sent to Paris brokers, without the intervention of bankers, as soon as Auferman telegraphed for them. Governor Curtin had consented to serve on the next mortgage. Swenson had hesitated at first but yielded. If they did nothing to prejudice their case, Snethen said, the loan was

[38] Gilbert to Epperson, April 28, 1868, *ibid.*
[39] Gilbert to Epperson, May 7, 1868, *ibid.*

sure to come, and the company expected to net at least $7,500,000 in currency.[40]

Snethen wrote again two days later, saying that Frémont wanted very much to be president and was maneuvering for Epperson's resignation. Snethen advised him not to resign—it would be dangerous because Frémont had all the bonds in his possession at his country seat on the Hudson. The best move would be for Epperson to come sign the bonds himself so Frémont would not have an excuse to press for his election as president, but "let me beg of you," he said, "not to resign under any possible circumstances. Keep the power you have." Snethen did advise Epperson to resign as presidential elector from Texas. Grant and Colfax would certainly be elected and Epperson's name heading the Texas list would hurt the bill.[41]

The Bates suit was then being heard in Rochester, and Gilbert felt sure he could defeat it. The plea set up by the plaintiff was that the company had conspired to produce the rebellion in order to prevent the delivery of the iron! Gilbert said if that was all of it, the case must fail. Bates, however, had given out on Wall Street that he held the company's obligations in part payment of his contract.[42]

Epperson heard from Gilbert again on October 8, 1869: "Apologies for not writing. Reason is we have all been so engrossed with the French loan affair that I have thought of little else." It was of such magnitude that great care, attention, and hard work would be needed if anything was attempted, as Epperson would realize when he had all the official information from Snethen. The chance of a subsidy looked good for the winter. The Bates suit was still undetermined. Auferman had arrived the day before in Paris and telegraphed that things looked hopeful.

The main problem in France at that time was to get the bonds quoted on the Bourse. The permission of the French government was necessary, and four imperial ministers stood in the way. Furthermore, the laws of France prohibited the offering of securities for sale on the Bourse unless they were regularly sold on the exchange of the country

[40] Snethen to Epperson, September 29, 1868, *ibid.*

[41] Snethen to Epperson, October 1, 1868, *ibid.*

[42] Snethen to Epperson, *ibid.*

of their origin. To meet this requisite a simple scheme was devised. First, the following advertisement was placed in the New York *Tribune* on October 1, 1868:

> Memphis, El Paso & Pacific Railroad Company's six per cent First Mortgage land bonds, principal and interest payable in coin, for sale at 105, and accrued interest in currency, by Hodgskin, Randal, and Hobson, No. 14 Broad St., Corn & Auferman, No. 30 Broad St.[43]

Snethen explained this misleading advertisement to Epperson by saying that they couldn't get the bonds quoted in New York unless the railroad was built and trains were running, so they had advertised them "as the next best thing." Then when Auferman arrived in France one week later, he presented forged certificates with signatures and gold seals as conclusive proof that the bonds were being sold on the New York Stock Exchange.[44] Also provided were numerous reports and recommendations, including the number of railroads owned or controlled, the statement of the chief engineer on the amount and character of work done on the road, and a description of the nature and condition of the country traversed. All this was submitted along with the opinion of one of the soundest lawyers in the country, Judge G. W. Paschal of Texas, as to the validity and value of the Memphis, El Paso, and Pacific charter and franchises. Finally, after commitments were made for the purchase of large quantities of rails and rolling stock from French industrial firms, to the extent of 100 engines and 45,000 tons of rails, the government authorized the sale of the bonds. These were the first American securities except government bonds which had ever been accepted for quotation in France.[45]

Auferman remained in France for sixty days, returning on or about December 7, 1868, and on December 10, Epperson received the following telegram from Roger Fowler in New York: "Bonds negotiated in Europe. Telegraph Fremont authority to close transaction."

[43] Cardinal Goodwin, *John Charles Fremont*, p. 245.

[44] *Ibid.*, p. 246.

[45] "Speech of the Honorable Jacob M. Howard in the Senate of the United States, June 22 and 23, 1870," *The Transcontinental, Memphis and El Paso Railroad.*

On December 23, 1868, the third mortgage was executed for another $5,000,000 bond issue, secured by the land along the second 150 miles of the prospective road and made to Swenson, Curtin, and James Pollock of Pennsylvania. When the delivery of this new issue was delayed, Auferman, then back in New York, grew impatient. On January 27, 1869, he wrote Epperson,

It is now *4 weeks* since I was first assured that the bonds of the 2nd series were contracted for, which I duly reported to Paris in order to show progress on this side. Your letter of yesterday does not justify the delay . . . I hope you will attend personally to the necessities of your company. Otherwise you will regret it when it is too late.

He wrote again on February 6,

Your letter in which you say that a power of attorney to sign *coupures* [notes] will not be sent to Probst is astounding and fatal for Mr. Probst and the whole transaction. I must presume you do not understand the full consequence of that act . . . On July 31, 1868, Probst was authorized by dispatch to make and sign *coupures provisoires* of one hundred dollars, signed J. C. Fremont, W. Schmoele, W. Snethen . . . It is your sacred duty to inform him at once by cable of your action which will be looked upon in Paris as a breach of trust and may be ruinous for all of us.

The Congressional part of the RR has been stated with great care and prudence in all pamphlets and papers in Paris. I am sorry to learn that you mailed copies of a new bill[46] without knowing what damage you may have created.

Is it so difficult for you to comply with the request of all friends in Paris to pass all papers through my hands.

And on February 8:

. . . The authority to sign and issue them [*coupures*] was given August 3, 1868, by cable and formally confirmed by a proper document. How can you then cancel such a power and transfer it for discretionary purposes to Mr. Boilleau who would suddenly be exposed as being connected with this business. Who gives you the right to commit Baron Boilleau in his delicate

[46] The 2nd session of the 40th Congress had adjourned on November 10, 1868, without taking any action on the Memphis, El Paso, and Pacific bill, and a new one was to be introduced in the next session.

official position in such a way and how can you justify the distrust towards Mr. Probst by withdrawing a power already conferred on him . . . It is expensive and troublesome to sign 48,000 such things (we were told in every letter the bonds would be here next week) but if necessary it was our duty to sign them . . . I went there to settle differences of opinion and misunderstandings and for the purpose of preparing and furnishing such papers as were required in Paris. Among these documents was the power of attorney for Mr. Probst to sign *coupures*. You suddenly find it convenient to change promises and contracts and expose other parties to disagreeable consequences.

On February 12, Auferman wrote that since he had not heard from Epperson about Probst's power of attorney and had not seen Mr. Snethen, it was his duty to inform Probst by cable of this complication and to warn him. The *coupures*, it seems, were not issued, and it was quite clear from Auferman's correspondence that Epperson disapproved of this method of raising money before the bonds were offered for sale and also that he considered Baron Boilleau a responsible party.

Ten days later, on February 22, 1869, the Memphis, El Paso, and Pacific bill passed the House of Representatives, but Congress adjourned on March 3, without any action taken thereon by the Senate. Undaunted, Frémont immediately put a larger staff to work in France. He employed Frederick Probst as an assistant agent and Emanuel Lissignol as a consulting engineer. A banker by the name of Crampton vouched for the bonds and invented countless preposterous claims. The names of two other agents, Pompinel and General G. Cluseret, also appear in the records. And besides Auferman, there was Charles Mayer, one of the company's New York agents, who broke his contract and came to Paris to sell one hundred of the land-grant bonds. A Texas newsaper later said that Frémont, in making such selection, displayed a subtle ingenuity and capacity for the estimation of human character never equalled until Oakes Ames, of Credit Mobilier fame, came upon the financial stage.[47]

In Paris, Henry Probst and Lissignol set themselves up for business in a luxurious office at 51 rue de la Chaussée d'Antin. They published a semimonthly magazine called *The Transcontinental,* reporting on the

[47] San Antonio *Daily Herald,* April 4, 1873.

condition of the company and the progress of the railroad. They published and circulated pamphlets, one with map attached, which stated that the Memphis, El Paso, and Pacific Railroad Company owned 8,000,000 acres of land in Texas and a continuous line from Norfolk to San Diego, shown in red on the map, and that the principal and interest on the construction bonds were guaranteed by the United States government, all of which was patent deception. Paid ads appeared in the leading newspapers, and notices announcing the dates of the subscription were posted all over Paris and the provinces. One such notice read: "Thirty-eight thousand mortgage bonds of $100 each have been placed at the disposal of the public by the administration of the Moniteur des Tirages Financiers. Price, 410 fr., payable on subscription; yearly interest, 30 fr. 90c. ($6), payable semiannually, at Paris on the 1st January and 1st July; reimbursement at 515 fr. ($100) in 1890; interest from January, 1869." A series of twelve hundred $1,000 bonds had also been issued, and the same notice advertised that each $100 bond was secured by thirty acres of land and each $1,000 bond by three hundred acres, all worth $14 or $15 an acre.[48] James P. Newcomb, Texas Secretary of State, later wrote a French stockbroker that the land was worth scarcely one-sixth that amount.[49]

Suddenly, in March, came a belated objection on the part of French officialdom. When Probst attempted to comply with the necessary formalities, certain departments were unwilling to accept the data submitted. The Department of Public Works, continuing to doubt the security of the bonds since the company had given no evidence of its capital stock, threatened to withdraw them from quotation; an officer in the Revenue Department refused to place the stamps on the bonds; and one director said that for him the quotation did not exist. Probst ironed out this difficulty by explaining the peculiar nature of U.S. railway titles and intimating, in an appeal to the Ministry, that the commercial contracts could be made in Germany or England, to the detriment of French industry and commerce. He also offered a nota-

[48] *Senate Miscellaneous Documents*, 41st Congress, 2nd Session, Serial No. 1408, Document No. 96.

[49] *Senate Executive Documents*, 41st Congress, 2nd Session, Serial No. 1406, Document No. 59.

rized statement certifying to the value of Texas land as already advertised. This statement was signed by three members of the Texas Constitutional Convention: F. W. H. Plimmg (William H. Fleming) of Red River County; Fred M. Sumner of Grayson County; and M. L. Armstrong of Lamar County, also a director of the company.[50]

The advertising continued. French citizens may well have been captivated by so romantic a description as

> Entering the territory of New Mexico, the Transcontinental meets the great commercial route from Guaymas and the interior of Mexico . . . It then reaches California, after receiving at Arizona City the traffic of the great River Colorado. It will in the future suppress the dangerous caravan marches from Santa Fe to San Francisco, New Orleans, and St. Louis . . .

However, a conscientious American living in Paris offered the press a different opinion: "From El Paso to Los Angeles the road traverses one of the most God-forsaken countries in the world, without wood or water. Everything is yet to be created. There are no roads after leaving El Paso; no towns, no cities, but, in fact, almost a barren wilderness, without inhabitants other than Apache Indians. San Diego is a town of only two thousand inhabitants." A well-informed financier of London, England, also communicated his distrust of the American securi-

[50] *Ibid.* Seven directors were added in 1869: James W. Throckmorton, Andrew J. Hamilton, Frederick Butterfield, M. L. Armstrong, J. J. Donaldson, James L. T. Sandford, and John Van Nest, according to Henry V. Poor (ed.), *Manual of the Railroads of the United States for 1869–1870,* p. 439. The New York *Sun,* in a broadside on February 1, 1875, listed the following directors for 1869, in addition to those named above: William M. Harrison of Jefferson, Texas; John T. Robertson of South Carolina; William B. Duncan, and Edward Locke of New York. They were elected at a convention of stockholders held in New York on January 7, 1869, on motion of General Frémont. Frémont, in a press interview on May 20, 1869, added the name of Mr. Dodge of Jay Cooke & Company, New York, to the list and stated that Memphis, El Paso, and Pacific bonds were selling at $79 in gold in Paris: $79 in gold equaled $112 in greenbacks at the rate of exchange. In the United States it was expected, therefore, that the Memphis, El Paso, and Pacific would make enough money to build and equip about three hundred miles of railroad (Clarksville *Standard,* July 3, 1869).

ties, discreetly suggesting that some remedy should be applied to "this evil emanating from Paris."[51]

These first rumors led to investigation and a glimmer of the truth. On the basis of the little information they could get, mainly from the U.S. press, French newspapers, in May of 1869, accused the speculators of fraud and warned their readers not to invest their savings in any stock quoted under the title of "Transcontinental Memphis, El Paso, and Pacific Railroad Company." Henry Probst, the general agent, immediately denied all accusations and instituted a suit for slander against the editors of *La Réforme* and *La Presse Libre*. A. Malespine, of *La Réforme*, replied that Probst seemed to have made a profound study of the French penal code since he knew that proof was not admitted in a libel suit and the law prohibited the publicity of debates, "two very precious and indispensable benefits for the Honorable Mr. Henry Probst." *L'Eclaireur Financier* attacked M. J. Paradis, who headed the Bourse, and continued to warn the public to beware of the American bonds. Paradis answered through his financial journal, *Le Moniteur des Tirages Financiers*, saying only that all the original documents relating to "this company" and authentic translations thereof had been deposited in the office of the trustee of the exchange agency.[52]

As the newspaper war raged on with insistent demands for facts, the United States minister, Elihu B. Washburne,[53] began to view the affair with alarm. On June 2, he commented that "this Transcontinental matter" had inflicted a terrible blow on United States credit abroad. On June 4, he sent Secretary of State Hamilton Fish copies of numerous articles, letters, advertisements, and documents. He wrote: "Many inquiries have been made of me by persons who have invested in these

[51] *Senate Miscellaneous Documents*, 41st Congress, 2nd Session, Serial No. 1408, Document No. 96.

[52] "Speech of the Honorable Jacob M. Howard in the Senate of the United States, June 22 and 23, 1870," *The Transcontinental, Memphis and El Paso Railroad; Senate Executive Documents*, 41st Congress, 2nd Session, Serial No. 1406, Document No. 59.

[53] Washburne presented his credentials to Louis Napoleon on May 29, 1869, replacing General John Adams Dix, the second president of the Union Pacific (Galveston *Weekly Civilian*, June 3, 1869).

bonds, but I am unable to answer them with the exactitude I would wish. I have my own opinion touching the whole business, but I shall guard myself in expressing it until I have correct information as I do not wish to do any injustice to the Company." The Secretary of State requested an investigation by the Department of the Interior with instructions to send the results to the legation in Paris where they might be made known to anyone who requested information on the subject.[54]

In June, while Washburne was receiving reports on the true status of the Memphis, El Paso, and Pacific, Frémont and his chief engineer, James M. Daniel, arrived in Paris.[55] They came, Frémont said, to assist in selling the bonds.

Both Frémont and Daniel were in communication with Epperson all the time they were in Europe. Frémont's vague, almost cryptic letters revealed little that actually transpired there. Daniel, on the other hand, saw, heard, and told all, or at least as much as he could see and hear. He was astounded to learn that the intentions of the "Fremont Ring" extended to the negotiation of all the company's bonds and involved millions. He was enterprising and ambitious and, like Epperson, consumed by his desire to build the Memphis, El Paso, and Pacific Railroad, but this was more than he had bargained for. With each day that passed he grew more suspicious of Frémont's motives and more uneasy about the way the company's money was being squandered. He set out to make the General come down to business and promise to send Epperson $500,000 or $1,000,000 for the road. With his limited authority he found it difficult to pin Frémont down, but the money was there: at least $3,000,000 in gold had already been collected by the time of their arrival.

Daniel found Probst and Lissignol ensconced in superb gilded and frescoed chambers, "finer than anything ever conceived of in America." He was impressed with Lissignol although he belonged to the "Probst, Boilleau, Fremont Ring." Lissignol, he said, was very smart,

[54] *Senate Executive Documents*, 41st Congress, 2nd Session, Serial No. 1406, Document No. 59.

[55] General Frémont and his wife and family sailed on June 17 on the *Ville de Paris*, accompanied by James M. Daniel (Galveston *Weekly Civilian*, June 24, 1869).

spoke English fluently, and was well versed in his profession. He had full and detailed drawings of the rails, fixtures, and engines, but having been unable to find out from Frémont what was wanted in regard to the gauge or whether the engines burned wood or coal or what pattern of rail was used—subjects Frémont would never discuss even with Daniel in America for fear he would investigate matters too closely—Lissignol had designed the engines to burn coal and to run on a gauge of five feet. Therefore, since they would have to burn wood and since the gauge was five feet six inches, all the work done on the five engines under construction would have to be altered at the expense of the company. Lissignol's rails were excellent, however, and would make a much better road than any in the United States.[56] What Daniel failed to see was that these engines were meant not for the Memphis, El Paso, and Pacific road but for the Memphis and Little Rock.

Even though Daniel proved to be a bit gullible at times, he learned more and more of the true state of affairs each day. Mayer had turned out to be a perfect shyster. He lived at 32 rue Vivienne in a miserable little den ten by eight feet, was without standing or credit, and had been written up a while back in the New York *Police Gazette* as a thief and a swindler. These facts were fully known in all banking houses in Paris. If it were known that he was the company's agent in New York, they would be ruined in France. Their ruin had nearly been accomplished in any case by the publication of false claims that the road was consolidated from Norfolk to San Diego, that the company owned the line from Norfolk to Little Rock and that it had been in running order for years; that the Memphis, El Paso, and Pacific was the richest company in the United States; and that the bonds from Memphis west were guaranteed by Congress. These false statements had caused the bonds to be sold at about $800 per thousand and also caused the railroad bonds of good American roads to lie dormant. Many bankers having the latter to negotiate made war on the Memphis, El Paso, and Pacific in earnest. To keep from being sued, Henry Probst had sued them. He had cleaned out ten suits and five more remained. Daniel feared that if the facts were put to a strict test, the government

[56] Daniel to Epperson, June 24, 1869, Epperson Papers.

would seize the money and cause every cent to be refunded. Crampton and Paradis complained bitterly of the way the matter had been managed in New York by the "President" and "Directors," and Lissignol said they had letters from Snethen and Frémont to substantiate everything they had published.

> If this matter fails [Daniel wrote Epperson] F and myself will be arrested on serious charges—and tho innocent on my part of anything, the law of this country will make no allowance for my ignorance of the transactions—which have been sent here officially as coming from the Directors—with all this Auferman holds two boxes of the 100 Bonds sent by that "SNETHEN" to him from New York . . . we must do the best we can to get them out of his hands—He has been paid all his commission and like a thirsty sandbank calls and strikes at every point for more—and don't care a damn if the Road go to Hell—He is very dangerous . . . be very careful and *for God sake dont let Snethen write any more.* Dont write yourself to anybody but me & use careful language—Acknowledge nothing. Deny nothing. My whole aim & F's now is to change the $— to N.Y. & carry on the work. But I am afraid it is too late . . . I think ten days will decide matters. But I run a great risk in writing this letter and dare not send it through the mail. It must go by hand. The Commissioner of Finance at one time last week started to seize the money at the earnest and urgent request of the *Bondholders.* But Probst assured him through high parties that the Company had boldly put the matter in Court and it would be investigated. In the meantime compromising with some suits—Bulling with others—and in some way the matter must be fixed or all is lost . . .[57]

The greatest trouble stemmed from the war of rivals and bankers, Daniel said. They had slandered the company in Paris newspapers and posted placards all over the city calling the Memphis, El Paso, and Pacific agents swindlers and rascals. A wrong move either in New York or Paris would destroy everything. Bergholtz (one of the company agents) was staying in the office of a man whom Daniel considered very dangerous. He was always making trouble, was unscrupulous, and would say anything against the company. Daniel thought he worked with the gang at 22 Broad Street in New York and with their clique in Paris and would have to be arrested and punished if he did not leave.

[57] Daniel to Epperson, June 26, 1869, *ibid.*

"Paris," he added, "is as far ahead of New York in splendor, cooking & beauty as N.Y. is ahead of Clarksville, Texas, and in rascality and robbing the same great differance . . ."[58]

Daniel believed it necessary for Epperson to come to Paris. About $4,600,000 had been realized from the sale, of which amount $3,000,000 was in the Bank of France credited to Probst. If he should die the company would have trouble drawing the money and transferring it to New York, except what was required to pay for the iron and locomotives, interest for January next, and the company's office expenses in Paris. Probst might turn it over to them if it were not for the engineer Lissignol who seemed to control everything, with Frémont and all of them yielding to whatever he said. Lissignol belonged to the Engineering Corps of France, and all the engineers worked as a unit in all matters. They had great influence, and whatever they endorsed they guaranteed as a body, which was one of the principal reasons for the success of the bond sale. Daniel asked for authority to bring the executive committee in New York a full statement of the accounts of Probst and the Paris office, but he preferred for Epperson to come. "Come with every possible paper," he said, "to legalize any action. If you were here, you could stop all this nonsense such as Mayer and Haskell contracts . . . The General is incompetent as a business man and no matter how hard we work he will undo a year's work in one hour."[59]

Day by day Daniel sent his dispatches to Epperson, though he was certain the government was reading all the mail from France as well as that coming into the kingdom.[60]

F is called upon by high parties for the proof of what has been written by him and what has been published by P. I don't know how he will manage. I shall keep my mouth shut . . . If our affairs come out of this tangle we may succeed provided you take charge of all matters yourself with a single will, but if F continues in power with Probst & Lissignol and their complement of parisites, it would be much easier for a camel to go through the eye of a needle than for us to succeed. Keep all matters strictly confidential as I must

[58] Daniel to Epperson, June 27, 1869, *ibid.*
[59] Daniel to Epperson, July 2, 1869, *ibid.*
[60] Daniel to Epperson, July 2, 1869, *ibid.*

not be compromised with F . . . You must see Mr. Swenson and tell him whatever you may see fit about matters. He has written to me for information.[61]

To give Epperson the main reason for the rapid success in realizing the $4,600,000 Daniel said he would have to commence at the start.

A certain *great man* in France advocated the policy of free trade on grounds it would cause French industry to advance and they could then compete with England and Belgium in manufacture of iron, *etc.* for foreign countries. This was his argument and when matter was submitted to popular vote (election of member of Parliament) the people voted it down, but the Army carried it. After it was carried as a state policy it was necessary to show something of its practical workings to the masses so a certain Baron saw the opening for our securities provided they appear to have been taken by iron manufacturers of France, and thus the application for their introduction on the market was made under this garb, and so they have been carried and sustained by Minister of State but opposed by Minister of Finance who does not know the truth and smells there is something he does not understand. If Washburne should say we are not consolidated from Norfolk to Pacific then the Minister of Finance would order the seizure of the money on the ground there is fraud . . . We must have papers of consolidation. A suit comes off in three or four weeks in which that is a point . . . Get some kind of paper to cover that gap.[62]

Of course, Daniel said, Lissignol and Probst and all the rest were concerned with the profit of the iron contracts and hung together, all working hard to sustain the loan. The Baron, he thought, had his money and had got off from any trouble. Auferman had his commission. Probst had his, and he would not be surprised if the iron men had theirs and Frémont his—so if the government should seize the money, these people would all get out of the way and leave the railroad president and directors to hold the bag. But nothing could be done unless they turned the money over to the company. Daniel had not used his authority with Probst and Lissignol because they would only show him what they wanted to and would be afraid of him so he had

[61] Daniel to Epperson, July 4, 1869, *ibid.*
[62] Daniel to Epperson, July 6, 1869, *ibid.*

only played his cards against the General, urging him each day to send Epperson money and to give them both their commission, and each day he promised to do it the next. He was not telling Daniel anything he could help and was playing the same loose game he did in New York.[63]

When Daniel heard that Washburne had written the Secretary of State asking for information on the Memphis, El Paso, and Pacific, he called on him in Hamburg, Prussia, to try to persuade him to abandon his investigation. Washburne said he would not meddle with the company's affairs in Paris unless the Secretary of State instructed him to do so. Hurriedly, Daniel wrote Epperson that it was imperative for him to see Secretary Fish and get others to see Dent and guard against any such move being made from that side of the water.[64]

Meanwhile, the first cargo of iron was about ready to ship, and the workmen were planning a fete for the occasion. The bond sale, however, had stopped. The public would take no more with matters as they were. Frémont had sent Epperson $40,000 on July 3 and $50,000 on July 13, to be credited to his name on the books. He wanted to get rid of Mayer if possible but said he had good reasons for hesitating to take police measures against Auferman. He would return as soon as he closed up the most pressing points there—more money and an emigration contract.[65]

Daniel, still in Hamburg, wrote Epperson that Probst had a seal of the company in his office, the exact counterpart of the one in New York.

> Who authorized him to use our seal—Answer—the General, Baron, Snethen, or Schmoele—which one—& did anyone of these gentlemen ever have such power. I say no. Sooner or later you will be forced to come over here to get this money & open up these *sub rosa* contracts. I will find out all I can & will keep you advised by telegraph and you may reply on my statements . . . I shall go back to Paris tomorrow—distance of 750 miles—15 hrs. travell & no sleeping cars or water closets—Yours, D.[66]

[63] *Ibid.*

[64] Daniel to Epperson, July 7, 1869, *ibid.*

[65] Frémont to Epperson, July 12, 1869, *ibid.*

[66] Daniel to Epperson (n.d.), *ibid.*

But just before leaving on July 17, Daniel reported the following bad news:

Colonel Washburne has sent to the Press of Paris his official statement that our Company is without a national charter, without land grant or guarantee to our bonds from U.S. Government. This is all true but it ruins us and kills the road. All these statements have been published by Paradis and Probst, and they say they have letters from the Board of Directors of the Company attested by seal and secretary's signature claiming all these things. I have not seen such papers but have asked for them. The French government will seize our material and funds on the ground we have obtained it under false pretenses, and we all will be branded as swindlers. Our project is honest and solid if they had only stuck to the truth. Curtin tried his best to move Washburne but without success. I have exhausted myself on him. You must prepare for the worst, which I expect to telegraph you in three days, and I hope to be out of France in that time for everyone connected with this matter will be subject to arrest or detention for investigation. Leaving for Paris, goodbye. D.

Bitter about Washburne's decision, Daniel claimed he was using his official position to injure the company in every possible way.[67] He urged Epperson to see that he was attacked in all American papers—especially in the New York *Herald*, whose favor he courted—and to make him feel the "full recoil" of his action. "Do this promptly," he said, and "why did you and Bergholtz let Greeley publish Cluseret's article calling us a swindle in New York? Have these papers attended to or they will ruin us. Everything they publish comes here and is magnified into French by our enemies." Another thing worried Daniel very much. Probst had copies of letters furnished him by Auferman and authorizing the latter to sell any and all bonds he could get posses-

[67] The House Investigating Committee of which Washburne was a member had found Frémont incompetent and unscrupulous in his management of the Department of the West during the Civil War. Major R. M. Corwin, a Memphis, El Paso, and Pacific attorney and a law partner of Rutherford B. Hayes, had been his chief aid in executing fraudulent contracts (*House Reports of Committees*, 37th Congress, 2nd Session, Serial No. 1142, Vol. 1, No. 2; Serial No. 1143, Vol. 2, No. 2). Washburne abstained from voting when the Memphis, El Paso, and Pacific bill came before the House in February, 1869.

sion of and make his commission. The letters were written by Snethen and signed by Epperson, and this seemed very strange as he doubted that Epperson would ever give Auferman such authority.[68]

Daniel received three letters from Epperson at one time, dated July 1, 7, and 9, all urging him to control Frémont, and to which he replied:

Now I ask you in all reason what can I do with the General alone when the whole Board in N.Y. with yourself at its head, gave way to him and granted him full power . . . Any authority I should show would not be sufficient to reach him over here. My authority says I am to *act in concert* with the General and I am doing so, but at the same time I have guarded the interests of the company as far as it was possible . . . I do not believe he will be hard to control *if he is forced* to account to the Bd. of Directors. But as the matter now stands it is vastly different. We have a good, honest, enterprise and it is the duty of each one connected with the project to see that proper disposition is made of the funds & that the funds go to building the road as soon as possible. As soon as matters can be arranged or placed in your hands I shall return & pursue the work in Texas . . . I am going to see Fremont & will make the same urgent appeal which has been made, I believe, each time I have met him the last month. But I am desperate by your letter for it is not my fault.[69]

Both Daniel and Frémont went to London on Friday, July 22, just before the "Warren suit" began on Saturday, the 23rd. They returned the night of the 23rd but gave no reason for such a brief trip. They may have wanted to avoid being called as witnesses in this important suit on which their future seemed to rest, or they may have wanted to get out of France until they saw what turn the suit would take. Daniel wrote from London that he had just come from a long conversation with the General and had been told that Probst and Lissignol would not turn the money over to him until the suits were decided. At Daniel's point-blank question—how much money had they turned over to him—Frémont seemed confused, and after long thinking with his hands before his face, said about $400,000, but Daniel believed he had about $3,000,000 in his possession and as a blind to bankers was going

[68] Daniel to Epperson, July 21, 1869, Epperson Papers.

[69] Daniel to Epperson, July 22, 1869, *ibid.*

to deposit the money in England. Frémont added that $1,000,000 had gone to buy bonds to sustain the market and he would account for every dollar of the rest.

> This matter [Daniel continued] will never be cleared up until Probst, *etc.* are forced to show to daylight their books and papers . . . but we have the consolation to know they have done what looks like a miracle—raised something for nothing in our hands. The General has the idea to make the whole road or none. He does not think of our local line to Paris [Texas]. His idea is to fight this out and make our credit look like it did two months ago and sell all our bonds. I said the way to make bonds sell was to build some road & send you 2,500,000 to sustain operations as they should be. He said that was correct but he couldn't get the money from Probst. He also said he couldn't exist in France without Probst and Lissignol. I think there maybe some reason in that . . . I go to Paris tonight and so does the General. Have patience with me. I'm doing my best and it's a hard task.[70]

Daniel was preparing to leave France by the end of the first week in August and still had much to tell Epperson. He had found out by hanging around the office and hearing conversations in French, which he could speak and understand though he had been careful not to let anyone know it, that Probst and Lissignol were turning all the money over to Frémont; armed with the facts he brought the matter home to the General and asked him to send the money immediately to Epperson in New York. To his surprise Frémont said that this was not his plan, that he was going to keep the money in Europe and build up the credit of the company. It was impossible to sell the bonds in New York, but with the money deposited in London, Frankfort, Brussels, and Paris in the hands of banking houses such as Baring Brothers in London, Rothschild in Frankfort, and Drexel in Paris, the company would gain strength in Europe, sell all its bonds, and raise any amount of money. Only the funds needed as work progressed would be sent to America. In other words, Daniel said, he would keep all the money raised by his association with the road in his name and under his control. Frémont had also told him in London that it would be impossible

[70] Daniel to Epperson, July 22, 1869, *ibid.* The date of this letter probably should be the 23rd as Frémont and Daniel could hardly have gone to London on the 22nd and returned to Paris that night.

for the company to get along with the president living in America, and since Epperson had intimated that he would give up his office when the Texas debts were paid, Frémont was expecting to be the president very soon. Daniel had agreed that if Frémont would give Epperson enough money to pay the Texas debts and his and Epperson's portions as previously arranged, he would return to America and Epperson would resign. Daniel, however, had objected to the money being kept in Europe. The only way to build up the credit of the company was to build the road and make it a substantial reality—which would give them credit anywhere without bankers' influence. Without such credit the road would fail. The money was needed in America where the foundation of the whole scheme rested. The cost of this money, the delay and wasted time which amounted to interest on the money, would destroy them if they did not act with judgment and make proper use of the funds.

But I had just as well talk to a post [Daniel said] . . . the same mystery exists here about all transactions that existed with you in N.Y. I am not allowed to investigate the company books or contracts & whenever I see & learn anything I am told there was & is full authority from N. Y. . . . It is necessary to have the Jefferson, Paris, and Clarksville papers publish the *facts—that we have 1000 hands at work & the matter is rapidly progressing in Texas*—Can't you do this & send copies over. One thing is fixed. Fremont has the necessary funds under his control at present . . . You must write for money all the time & see it is spent in Texas only . . . Colonel, I give you all the information it is possible for me to obtain, and you must act or advise me to act for you as you think best. I judge you would prefer putting the whole matter into F's hands if he will comply with my terms—Thereby you would be free from the killing annoyance—But you must choose one of two things—the above, or assert your power & come over here & fight the matter in France, England & Germany to get control of it.[71]

On that same day, the 24th, Daniel dropped by the Paris office at an unusually early hour to see what was going on. He found Lissignol alone and extremely polite, but he felt sure he was not wanted. Presently Probst arrived and then two other Frenchmen, each with port-

[71] Daniel to Epperson, July 24, 1869, *ibid.*

folios. They all went into another room, obviously to make a settlement prior to placing the money in Frémont's hands, as Daniel was able to make out from their conversation. He thought one of them might have been Paradis, but he didn't know as he wasn't introduced. "It was evident," he said, "that I was the skeleton at their feast." He did manage to see a memorandum on Lissignol's desk which listed the unsold bonds by number and series—the total was $5,214,000, which meant that half of them had been sold.[72]

On August 5 Daniel left for the United States by way of England, and Epperson was bombarded with cablegrams for three days in succession, from Frémont, Daniel, and Lissignol. Just before leaving Daniel discovered that Frémont had made a secret contract with O. Tamin Despalles for the sale of the remaining bonds—a contract unratified and without the seal of the company, which gave Frémont unlimited power and relieved him of all accountability. Daniel immediately cabled Epperson to refuse ratification, and on the same day, August 5, Lissignol cabled the following: "Has Company authorized contract with Despalles for selling 2nd series bonds at 62. I find contract irregular and ruinous. Lissignol."

On August 6 Daniel cabled from London: "Inform General no contract unless ratified. He has money and wont send it. Come immediately. No delay or we are all ruined. Dont let him know you are coming. Answer immediately Baltimore."

Frémont, who wrote Epperson the same day, did not mention the contract. He said, "Will have 100,000 gold sent you today. Pray make that do for 5 or 6 weeks." After that 50,000 monthly would be sent regularly until more bonds could be sold. Daniel had left for England on his way to N.Y. Auferman had left the day before. "Have him arrested on his arrival," Frémont said, and "See Gould[73] in whose name he collected money on the 128 bonds."

Daniel cabled on the 7th, saying again that if Epperson did not come the company was ruined, and on the 8th, saying that facts proved the

[72] Daniel to Epperson, July 24, 1869 (two letters the same day), *ibid.*

[73] A man by the name of Gould was treasurer of the Memphis, El Paso, and Pacific in 1867 and had contracted to sell the company's bonds. He may have been Jay Gould or his brother Abel.

General could not be trusted and Epperson must stand the consequences.

Epperson did not come. Distraught, Daniel explained the details of the Despalles contract by letter and concluded, "I have telegraphed you to annul the illegal action and come with Schmoele and get the money. You answer that you trust the General and you cant come. Do you forget Haskell, Mayer, Auferman, Hays, Caldwell affairs. I think I shall go by next steamer to America."[74]

On August 9 Frémont cabled Epperson he was sending $100,000 and had annulled the Despalles contract. He would send $500,000 upon ratification of new contract with Probst and Lissignol. On August 10 he wrote Epperson that he was afraid to send any money to New York because Hodgskin, Randal and Hobson would try to attach it. They had already demanded $100,000 in gold. And on the same day, in a letter marked "Confidential," he told Epperson to buy the Memphis and Little Rock and make a strong demonstration at San Diego, saying "Pray, Colonel, work hard at your end of the line." He thought he could dispose of some bonds in Belgium and Germany; there would be 40,000 for the road, and he had 600,000 in gold in hand (to induce Jay Cooke to advance money on construction bonds). The annulment of the Despalles contract was agreed on the day before. At the time it was made—in June before he sailed for France—it was considered in New York that their affair had broken down upon the Exchange and would remain so for many months. On August 26 Frémont sent $200,000 to Epperson and told him to purchase the Shreveport-Marshall road. Then on August 31 he wrote from Prague that in his judgment they should negotiate all their securities from Paris and build the road from there—not from America. He had received Epperson's telegram and had wired for the half-million to be sent at once.

On his return to Paris, Frémont openly accused Washburne of unpatriotic motives and hostility to a great American enterprise, doubtless inspired by the envy of its rivals, the Central Pacific and the Union Pacific. More pamphlets appeared in defense of the "Pathfinder" and "Companion of Humboldt," who made a public denial in *Le Phare de*

[74] Daniel to Epperson, August 7, 1869, Epperson Papers.

la Loire on September 5: "It is completely false," he said, "that we have ever declared that our mortgage bonds enjoy a Federal guarantee of six per cent interest." On September 27 another publication appeared, which corroborated previous statements and falsehoods and even went so far as to say that if a double track was built, "the land grant would be doubled and instead of 8,320,000 acres, it would be 16,640,000. What surer pledge could capital desire."[75] O. Tamin Despalles, who had been retained on the staff to work on an emigration project, was the author of some of these pamphlets and probably of *The Transcontinental*, which ran for fifteen months.

On September 30, in a long letter of explanation, published by *Le Temps*, General Frémont declared:

1. That the concession had been regularly and definitely accorded to the Memphis, El Paso, and Pacific Company by the following laws of the Texas Legislature: February 4, 1856; February 5, 1856; February 19, 1858; March 20, 1861; January 11, 1862; March 30, 1866; and November 13, 1866.
2. That General Hunter, manager, and M. Sedgwick, engineer, were at San Diego, ready to commence the building of that section.
3. That the company owned, in addition to and independently of the lands mortgaged:
   A. 1,023 acres at the port of Norfolk;
   B. 9,000 acres at the port of San Diego;
   C. 600,000 acres in Texas.
4. That the company had acquired by purchase and by consolidation the following concessions which would henceforth form an integral part of the principal line:
   A. The concession of the San Diego and Gila, 160 miles long;
   B. The concession of the Arizona Line, about 500 miles long;
   C. The Memphis and Little Rock Line, the greater part of which was in operation.
5. That the whole of these properties gave the bondholders a general

[75] "Speech of the Honorable Jacob M. Howard in the Senate of the United States, June 22 and 23, 1870," *The Transcontinental, Memphis and El Paso Railroad.*

security and they could be assured that the directors, aware of their duties, would employ all their energies to defend the interests of the company and the bondholders.

He concluded, "I hope that these declarations, as categorical as they are sincere, will put an end to the persistent calumnies of which the Memphis, El Paso, and Pacific Railroad is the object. J. C. Fremont. President of the Committee of Management."[76]

Again Frémont wrote Epperson to buy the Shreveport-Marshall road and told him to send the papers because he had already published a pamphlet saying he owned it.[77] Epperson had tried but failed because the Southern Pacific stockholders went up to $340,000—$140,000 above the $200,000 originally asked—before he could complete the transaction. However, he did contract for 10,100 shares of Memphis and Little Rock stock at $25.00 a share; and, curiously enough, on September 10 he had written Probst and Lissignol that the Cairo and Fulton Railway Company, which would constitute an important link in the Transcontinental road, wanted their state of Arkansas bonds negotiated in Europe. He asked if they could negotiate them without interfering with the sale of the Memphis, El Paso, and Pacific bonds, and if so, in what denominations and what rates. This was not done, probably because Probst and Lissignol had their hands full and already considered their position unsafe. At any rate, things seemed to be closing in on them all just then. Old lawsuits were still pending, and new ones were threatened. The government was not quite so friendly as before. Despalles instituted suit against the company in October, and Frémont did not leave for New York until December. Whether or not he was forcibly detained, as has been claimed, he failed to get the last $500,000 out of France.

French investors, meanwhile, had purchased the "puffed up" bonds in the amount of some 35,000,000 francs which realized at least $5,000,000 for the company. The disposition of this money did not become a matter of public knowledge until the following year when it was exposed by Frémont's enemies. It first appeared in the affidavit

[76] *Flake's Semi-Weekly Bulletin*, October 16, 1869.

[77] Frémont to Epperson, September 30, 1869, Epperson Papers.

of Stephen Sartre, a French broker, who crossed the Atlantic and filed suit against Frémont, Daniel, Probst, and Lissignol in the Supreme Court of the City and County of New York in March, 1870. Sartre had purchased 148 bonds for $116,430 in gold, for which he demanded remuneration. He charged the company with fraud and reported $4,500,000 in gold expended as follows:[78]

Commission to J. Paradis, A. G. L. Crampton, and other bankers in Paris		$ 900,000
Commission to Fremont and William Schmoele		550,000
Commission to F. Probst and E. Lissignol		215,000
Commission to B. H. Epperson, J. M. Daniel, W. G. Snethen, and other directors		150,000
Commission to G. Boilleau, brother-in-law of J. C. Fremont for services in Paris		150,000
Advertisements, maps, pamphlets in France		200,000
Office expenses and salaries in Paris, New York, and Texas		60,000
Old debts		150,000
Coupons on bonds	90,000 July, 1869	
	180,000 January, 1870	
	180,000 To be paid July, 1870	450,000
Stamps and taxes		75,000
Lawyers fees		60,000
Miscellaneous expenses		90,000
Road construction		300,000
Stock purchased in Memphis to Little Rock Line		250,000
Purchase charter of S. D. and Arizona Railroad Co.		100,000
7,000 rails from Europe, freight and duty unpaid		280,000
Locomotives and tenders, freight and duty unpaid		200,000
		$4,200,000
Cash on hand		300,000
		$4,500,000

[78] "How the Money Was Obtained in France under False Pretenses and How It Was Squandered," *The Transcontinental, Memphis and El Paso Railroad,* pp. 5–16. (The total, added correctly, is $4,180,000.)

The amazing thing about this account is that it seems to be approximately correct—that is, when compared with memoranda which appear in B. H. Epperson's papers and with the later findings of a French court. The latter showed a total of $5,200,000 received from Probst and, with slight variations, expended in much the same manner, the chief exception being the additional amount of $786,000 covering the purchase of bonds by the company.[79] Among Epperson's several copies of the company's receipts and expenditures in France is Probst's account up to August 31, after payment of his 6 per cent commission, which confirms the same general pattern of distribution:

By 248 bonds paid Fremont	$ 148,000
.. Amt. paid Daniel	12,718
.. Fremont	1,042,615
.. Mayer	41,834
.. Auferman	175,389
.. Retained in France	566,392
.. Material purchased	415,838
.. Interest on Coupons	139,000
Sundry Expenses	262,930.75
	$2,805,516.75

Also among Epperson's many and diverse memoranda is the following:

Gross Proceeds from the Sale of Bonds:	1869	September 3	26,953,750 fr.
		September 17	8,199,375 fr.
			35,153,125 fr.
		or	$6,825,849.

While no positive totals can be drawn from any of these incomplete tabulations, they indicate that the reports in circulation were by no means exaggerated. But it is quite possible that no one knew or

[79] Frank Stuart Bond, *Statement and Argument Made before the Committee on the Judiciary of the House of Representatives, 44th Congress, 1st Session*, 1876.

would ever know the exact amount and disposition of all the money received from the bond sale.

Ultimately, when Epperson was held responsible for all the company's funds after 1869, he rendered an itemized account listing credits and expenditures in the amount of $1,018,064, all the credits being in gold received from France with the exception of $100,000 loaned to the company by Swenson. Just as Sartre claimed, some of the French money went for stock in the Memphis and Little Rock and San Diego and Gila railroads, for salaries, old debts, and $50,000 for Epperson himself, which he considered as part payment of the commission due on his quadruplicate contract, but which he did not submit for audit.[80] Since Sartre did not include the state of Arkansas bonds, the land certificates purchased from the Texas and New Orleans, or the ninety sections purchased from Swenson for $57,000, the company was not as devoid of assets as he indicated. It was true though that very little was spent on the actual construction and equipment of the railroad. The amount of $13,750 each was paid on two locomotives, the "Epperson" and the "Daniel," track was laid on three miles of road, and an additional twenty-five miles were graded. The two cargoes of iron which arrived in New Orleans, duty and freight unpaid, were attached by John A. C. Gray and A. M. Gentry and sold in New York. Ten locomotives also arrived from France, duty and freight unpaid and their ultimate disposition unknown. The actual returns to the company therefore had dwindled to $1,700,000 in cash, part of which was still in France. The rest of the money, about $1,500,000 outside of commissions and expenses in Paris, was said to have gone into the pockets of certain directors, namely, Frémont and Schmoele.

Auferman must have served as the whipping boy. He was arrested in New York in December and sued for recovery of the money he obtained over and above his commission. Since the cause of action arose in Paris between two nonresidents and neither the bonds nor

[80] Contract, May 19, 1869, between Frémont, Schmoele, Epperson, and Daniel for construction of the railroad, whereby Frémont was to negotiate bonds and operate the road, each to be paid $10,000, and all profits from construction to be equally divided; Acknowledgment, New York, December 15, 1869, Epperson Papers.

their proceeds were brought to this country, there was little chance for recovery, on technical grounds.[81] Schmoele wrote Epperson that Auferman had to pay only $7,000 in cash and that the General had given Gilbert $3,000 of it and the fifteen building lots in the upper end of New York City, estimated at $3,500 each and up, but on which there was a mortgage of $13,000. Fancher would sell the lots at the first opportunity as he held them for the company. They could make Auferman behave because all the papers against him were being kept in Fancher's safe. Mayer had been told to take the Memphis, El Paso, and Pacific's name off his window, door, and sign. And Schmoele advised Epperson to stay out of politics—it wouldn't do to let the Texas radicals think the Transcontinental was a rebel road.[82]

Attention soon focused on the construction of the Transcontinental road, the route of which was to extend from Norfolk to Bristol, to Nashville, via Jackson, Tennessee, to Memphis, to Little Rock. From Little Rock the Memphis, El Paso, and Pacific would run southwest to Texarkana, thence to El Paso, Fort Yuma, and San Diego. When one hundred men began clearing the old grade in September, 1869, the editor of the Clarksville *Standard* refused to believe it until an eyewitness reported he had seen the men at work.[83] In October Epperson published an address to the owners of land in counties through which the railroad would pass. He wanted to buy property along the line at a reasonable price, to be paid for in capital stock of the company and to be made available for the immediate introduction and settlement of immigrants. There was enough money on deposit, he said, to pay for grading the road all the way to Paris, the iron was already in New Orleans, and he had been instructed to contract for the work between Jefferson and the Brazos. Two locomotives and other rolling stock were in New York awaiting Captain Daniel's orders for shipment. Mr. Frémont was still in France with the bonds, awaiting a response to the call for the subscription of lands. The company was indebted to him for all that had been done.[84]

[81] *Flake's Daily Bulletin*, January 6, 1870.

[82] Schmoele to Epperson, January 29, 1870, Epperson Papers.

[83] Clarksville *Standard*, September 4, 1869.

[84] Galveston *Weekly Civilian*, October 6, 1869.

In November, at Frémont's request, Epperson advanced $52,000 for interest on the first mortgage bonds, made the payment of $250,000 for the 10,100 shares of Memphis and Little Rock stock, and transferred to that company 20,400 shares of Memphis, El Paso, and Pacific stock, now held in his name and to be divided equally between himself, Daniel, Schmoele, and Frémont, but on which only he had paid his part.[85] The Texas contractors were then advertising for five hundred hands at $1.00 per day, and one hundred Chinese were expected at an early date, the first of one thousand contracted for with Koopmanschap, a Dutch commission merchant and Chinese coolie importer of San Francisco.[86] In the midst of this flurry of activity, Epperson quietly resigned, as he had planned to do for several months. He had paid the Texas debts and had carried out Frémont's wishes as far as he was able, and was clear, so he thought, of the Memphis, El Paso, and Pacific.

Currently the general public believed that the Memphis, El Paso, and Pacific was a "humbug" and "hallucination"; and the truth was that the company had no transcontinental charter nor any money to speak of. Frémont himself considered the bond sale only a partial success since he had contemplated a return of $8,240,000. His chief interest therefore was to push his Transcontinental bill through Congress and obtain a federal land grant for his embryo railroad. He dared not ask for a subsidy because the people were becoming antagonistic to railroad subsidies. Besides his rivals were already on the ground, and there was going to be a mad scramble to supersede the Memphis, El Paso, and Pacific on the 32nd parallel.

To counter the strong attacks being made by the American and French press Frémont published letters in the Washington *Chronicle* and the New York *Tribune* in which he denied the alleged frauds and asserted that the future of the road was secured in spite of the powerful combination against it.[87] The *Post* was right, he said, in its statement that no American company had hitherto been admitted to quotation

[85] Galveston *Daily News*, November 17, 1869; Statement, Epperson Papers.

[86] *Flake's Semi-Weekly Bulletin*, October 16, 1869; Galveston *Daily Civilian*, November 5, 1869.

[87] *Flake's Daily Bulletin*, January 13, 1870.

on the French Bourse. It was not right in its statement on the means used to obtain their admission. The only real trouble came from a source which his company could not have foreseen and for which it was not in any way responsible. Company officials had been applying to Congress for two years for its authority and aid in establishing their line. In the preceding Congressional session the Memphis, El Paso, and Pacific bill asking for a subsidy had been amended to ask only for a guarantee of interest. On account of the indisposition of Congress to grant moneyed aid the bill was again amended so as to petition only for the right of way. This bill passed the House twice by large majorities at the close of one Congress and at the beginning of another. It was mistaken in Paris for the earlier House bill, which would have granted guarantee of interest for the construction bonds. This mistake reached the knowledge of the company through a French newspaper which had already spread it all over France. It had announced that the bill gave the company's constructions a guarantee of 6 per cent. However, the bonds thus supposedly guaranteed were not on the market and had not been offered for sale. The bonds actually sold on the French market were land-grant bonds which said what they were on their face. Neither brokers nor journals ever said that these had guarantee of interest. The error was confined to claims about the construction bonds, and it was an error of accident rather than intention.

The American legation in Paris had become a recognized bureau of information against the Memphis, El Paso, and Pacific, but the active and malignant hostility of rival railway interests and of certain financial agencies which the company had omitted to employ were the chief obstruction. The bondholders were alarmed, but when correct information was provided in *The Transcontinental*, they continued to hold their bonds and received their interest for July last and January 1st.

"My dates for Paris," he said, "are to the 22nd of December. Up to that time no suit whatever had been instituted against the company except one by a person claiming damages for our refusing to let him have bonds to sell under an alleged contract which the company repudiates."

The last official act of the French government, Frémont said, had been to admit the payment of the taxes on the bonds and to accept the security of Mallet Frères for their continued payment, and this act did not occur until August. This recognition, the direct act of the government, was done through Mr. Magne himself long after all these discussions had been made familiar by the French newspapers.

Shipments of rails had already begun to reach New Orleans; the first ten engines would be ready for delivery by the end of February; the company was about ready to lay the rails on the Texas division; 100 miles of the Memphis and Little Rock were in operation and that line would be completed by July 1; 250 miles would be in operation by the close of the year with an estimated income of over a million dollars. The statement was signed "J. C. Fremont, President."[88]

The following week the New York *Evening Post* published General Cluseret's letter giving more details of the "great swindle practiced on the public of France" and saying that Messrs. Schneider, Rouher, and Magne had countenanced the scheme.[89] Eugène Rouher, the former premier, was the man closest to Louis Napoleon and known as the "absolutist vice-emperor." Pierre Magne was the minister of finance, and Eugène Schneider was the president of the Corps Législatif.

Frémont wired Epperson on February 1, 1870, to procure the vigorous support of all friends in Texas for the bill, to keep out of politics, and to make sacrifices if necessary. "I know," he said, " that above everything else you desire the building of the road. The great point is speedy action." A splendid locomotive and a quantity of rolling stock arrived in Jefferson in the spring, but the Jefferson *Jimplecute* reported that construction would cease as soon as the grading of the first twenty-five-mile section was completed. The land subscriptions were not forthcoming, and the "intelligence" was that all the surplus force had been ordered to Memphis to build the remaining forty-five miles of the Memphis and Little Rock.[90] Everything then depended on the passage of the Transcontinental bill.

To add new vitality and get away from the stigma attached to the old company, the Memphis, El Paso, and Pacific memorial was discarded, and only the name Southern Transcontinental was used in the three

[88] New York *Tribune*, January 10, 1870.

[89] Galveston *Weekly Civilian*, January 20, 1870.

[90] *Ibid.*, March 17, 1870.

new bills which were introduced—two in the House and one in the Senate. HR 1283, introduced in February, 1870, was referred to the Committee on Public Lands and no further action was taken. In March Frederick A. Sawyer of South Carolina introduced SB 660 (similar to HB 1620) in the Senate. It petitioned for incorporation under a federal charter with a land grant and right of way to the Pacific coast. The leading incorporators were John C. Frémont, John A. C. Gray, Enoch L. Fancher, and Marshall O. Roberts. Four other Pacific railroad bills were introduced: the Texas Pacific bill in the House by Roots, two Texas Pacific bills in the Senate by Kellogg, and the Southern Pacific in the Senate by Flanagan. One of Kellogg's bills, SB 647, had the vigorous support of the "Tom Scott" faction. Thomas A. Scott was a poor boy who had worked his way up in the Pennsylvania Railroad until he attracted the notice of Governor A. G. Curtin. He would succeed Oliver Ames as president of the Union Pacific (1871–1872) and would become president of the Texas Pacific in 1872 and the Pennsylvania Railroad in 1874, building an empire which outstripped that of Cornelius Vanderbilt and Jim Fisk,[91] and earning for himself the epithet of the "most hated man in Pennsylvania."

Frémont and his directors worked feverishly to overcome the strong opposition to their Southern Transcontinental bill—SB 660, the one they pinned their hopes on. They already had distributed millions of dollars worth of settlement certificates, stock certificates, and construction bonds to pay for "past and future services to the company and to effect the required legislation in Texas and Washington." Letters written in 1869 and 1870 throw some light on their progress:

D. W. C. Clark, Executive Clerk of the Senate, to Major W. R. Bergholtz

United State Senate Chamber
Washington, June 22, 1869

My dear Major: a few moments since I met Gen. Dent in the lobby. He asked for you and said, "Why the devil don't he come over. We can fix things as he wants them in ten minutes." I told him I expected you last week but could not foresee when you would come. He remarked that he is going West with General Grant early next week. I thought you might like to know

[91] Washington *Daily Morning Chronicle*, June 22, 1871.

this if there remains anything to be fixed by Gen. Grant or Gen. Dent [President Grant's brother-in-law].

D. W. C. C.

Receipt from Colonel Blanton Duncan

Louisville, Dec. 27, 1869

I have received from Col. B. H. Epperson, Pres. of the Memphis and El Paso Pacific Railroad Company various certificates of stock in Washington City during this spring of 1869 amounting to eighty-five thousand dollars, which I distributed according to his directions for the use of the company. I received in the summer other certificates amounting to forty-five thousand dollars for the same purpose, and have distributed them accordingly.

I have received in part pay of services rendered by me to the Memphis and El Paso Pacific Company the amount of one certificate for one hundred thousand dollars stock, and ten certificates, numbers 468 to 477 inclusive, ten thousand dollars each.

Blanton Duncan

Extract, W. R. Bergholtz to Colonel Blanton Duncan

New York, Dec. 31, 1869

Epperson says nobody else has given any receipts for stock received for services, therefore did not want you to do so; it was not required. Gen. F. will go to Washington on the 10th of January to review the field. I saw a letter from Shanks the other day to the General in which he said: "With Duncan we can win; without him it looks very doubtful. He must be fixed so that he will cooperate with us."

General J. P. C. Shanks to Major W. R. Bergholtz

Washington, D.C., Jan. 23, 1870

Major Bergholtz:
My dear friend:

Matters now look better. I cannot explain, but this is true. Hopes have more foundation. Tex. is O. K. So is Arkansas, I understand. More anon. *Today is important.*

Yours truly.
J. P. C. Shanks

General Morton C. Hunter to Major Bergholtz

Washington, D.C., Jan. 29, 1870

Dear Bergholtz:

Your letter just received enclosing clips from newspapers. You must not complain if you do not get letters regularly as you wish. We are all hard at work, and I think doing splendidly. I feel that we will get through Congress all right, and through Texas also. All the Texas men are with us. If we have drawbacks, I will write you. Tell friend Snethen that I received that forty shares of stock all right. If he needs an acknowledgement, I will send it.

All well. Kind regards to Dr. Schmoele, Mr. Snethen, and son, and accept for self.

Your friend,
Morton C. Hunter

W. G. Snethen to William Schmoele

Elizabeth, N.J., Feb. 14, 1870.

Dear Doctor:

Enclosed is a scrap from the Evening Post of yesterday. Report in Tribune today says books will be opened for subscription to the capital stock at an early date. Here, you see, the old thieves are at work again. Gilbert told me that the organization would be made by parties in Gray's interest, with Fremont and his gang left out in the cold. It seems it is Gray and his friends who are outdoors, unless, indeed, this is part of the programme of Mr. Gray, which I can hardly think possible. All will depend on who takes the stock. If Fremont does, he will pay the first installment out of the Frenchmen's money, and, of course, have it all his own way until his brother rogues oust him. It is possible that the Texas people—Throckmorton, Don C. Campbell, and others, are the stockholders, but where can they get the money. I hear nothing from you in relation to your interview with Gilbert and Davenport. Is it not worth the trouble of telling me?

I have got a copy of the bill for you, after almost a quarrel with Mr. Richard Wayne Parker, Cortlandt Parker's son. I receipted for it, for you. It seems that Kinney, the editor of the Newark *Advertiser* managed to get hold of a copy and published a summary, much to Parker's dissatisfaction.

Yours ever,
W. G. Snethen.[92]

[92] New York *Sun*, February 1, 1875.

While lobbying for the Transcontinental bill in the winter of 1870, John A. C. Gray met Nathaniel Paige of Washington as he was coming from Frémont's rooms at the Arlington House in that city. Gray asked Paige to step into the parlor of the hotel and talk with him for a few moments. Paige reported his talk with Gray as follows:

Believing that he was friendly to Fremont and his enterprises, I accepted the invitation, entered the parlor, and was soon engaged in a general conversation concerning Gen. Fremont and the Memphis, El Paso, and Pacific Railroad. He said that Fremont had unfortunately fallen into the hands of a band of unscrupulous knaves, among the chief of whom were Morton and Corwin, and that if he remained under their influence they would not only rob him of a large sum of money but would make sure of the defeat of his bill before Congress. He told me that he had been with Fremont from the very beginning of his railroad scheme on the 32nd parallel and that although he had at one time favored the 38th parallel road, known as the Atlantic and Pacific, he then believed the 32nd was the only one that could be built, the Indian territory being in the way of the construction of the other. He also told me that he was in Paris when Fremont negotiated the bonds of the Memphis and El Paso Railroad, and that he prevented Fremont from being heavily blackmailed while there by a person from New York, who was familiar with all the secrets of the negotiation. That he had saved Fremont several times in New York from arrest, and that it constantly required the exercise of all his skill to keep Fremont out of prison and from the influence of those who would sooner or later surely put him there. At this interview Gray spoke highly of the bonds negotiated by Fremont in Paris, and said legislation by Congress would cure any irregularities in their issue, or any misstatements made in order to secure their sale in France. He said that it was not much of a crime to cheat a French stock speculator, and that if Fremont could only keep in good hands (meaning, I suppose, his—Gray's) he would not be troubled much on account of irregularities.

From the sale of the bonds in Paris Gray turned the conversation to the Land Grant bill before Congress, and asked me what I thought its prospects were. I told him that Fremont felt absolutely sure of the House and also of the Senate, with the exception of the Pacific Railroad Committee; that Senator Howard was bitterly opposed to the bill, and would oppose it to the end. Gray said that Howard could be had for money, and that if Fremont wanted $50,000 to secure his vote, he (Gray) would advance it, and take security upon the iron in New Orleans. In this connection he told me to make the proposition to Fremont. After we had disposed of Howard in this way, in our conversation, I told him that Stewart of Nevada would also be a difficult man to control. Gray immediately replied by saying that Stewart was one of those high-priced political knaves, who must have money in hand, or a sure slice of the job itself, before he would move an inch, and that he would take him in hand himself.

Senator Joseph C. Abbott of North Carolina was also on the Pacific Railroad Committee, and understood to be opposed to Fremont, and in the interest of the Atlantic and Pacific Railroad. Being very well acquainted with Abbott, I called upon him and endeavored to secure his vote for the Memphis and El Paso. He spoke of Fremont in the severest terms, and of Hays, President of the Atlantic and Pacific, in the most flattering—said the latter had sold him stock in the road in Missouri, of which he was President, at one-fourth its real value, from which he had made about $30,000, and asked me if Fremont could do as well by him in the event of his giving his vote and using his influence for his road. A few days after this conversation Abbott called upon me and asked me if I would endorse his note for $5,000 for ninety days. I said yes, and endorsed it, and upon my endorsement had it discounted at the banking house of Lewis, Johnson & Co. At the expiration of ninety days, the note went to protest, and I was called upon to pay it. I went to the Senate Chamber and saw Abbott about it. He said he supposed I would take up the note and charge it to Fremont. I told him there was no such understanding and if the note was not paid within three days, I would denounce him on the floor of the Senate in the presence of his fellow Senators as a thief and a bribe-taker. At the expiration of three days the note was paid.[93]

According to an undated memo written by Frémont, all the purchased material, lands, and other property of the Memphis, El Paso, and Pacific would be turned over to the Transcontinental, and the Transcontinental would assume the interest on all land-grant bonds and one-half million construction bonds issued by the company; the majority of the capital stock of the Memphis, El Paso, and Pacific, not

[93] *Ibid.* The *Sun* printed this statement with the foregoing letters and other data in a broadside on February 1, 1875, as documentary evidence of corruption in the U.S. Congress and the fraudulent manner in which the affairs of the Memphis, El Paso, and Pacific were conducted. The senators mentioned were William M. Stewart of Nevada, Joseph C. Abbot of North Carolina, and Jacob M. Howard of Michigan.

less than $25,000,000, would be turned over to the Transcontinental; the land certificates issued in 1868 would be cancelled; the Transcontinental would pay Paige and Dent $250,000 (nominal value) in land-grant bonds; Colonel Epperson, Major Daniel, and Dr. Schmoele were to be considered among the incorporators of the Transcontinental precisely as if their names had been inserted in the bill; and all stock issued would share pro rata in all benefits of bonds or money secured or obtained by sale of $25,000,000 stock.[94]

As the time for Congressional action drew near, the rival interests circulated charges with abandon. To defend the much maligned Memphis, El Paso, and Pacific and to vindicate his negotiation of the bond sale, Frémont again presented his case in a printed communication addressed to the Honorable J. M. Howard, chairman of the Committee on Pacific Railroads. He said M. J. Paradis, who headed the Bourse, sold all the bonds and was responsible for the advertisements. The misapprehension had grown out of his ignorance of the language and the legislative forms of this country. Paradis "thought" the bill had passed, and "this misunderstanding brought on the violent attacks which took the shape of malevolent misrepresentations." Washburne's interference had then brought the weight of the U.S. government in as an ally to a combination formed against the Memphis, El Paso, and Pacific, and the effect on the Stock Exchange caused the company heavy pecuniary loss and embarrassment. The hostility of Washburne and his slander had resulted in the disfavor of the French government. The Memphis, El Paso, and Pacific had not forfeited its charter; there were about one hundred miles ready for crossties and iron; seven thousand tons of iron and ten locomotives had been purchased and paid for, and the January, 1870, interest had been paid on all bonds at the company offie in Paris.[95]

But when the subcommittee of the Pacific Railroad Committee, consisting of Senators Howard, Stewart, and Rice, met on April 4, 1870, to investigate Senate Bill 660, incorporating the Southern Transcontinental Railway Company, Frémont was ill and did not appear. His

[94] Memorandum labeled "John C. Fremont," Epperson Papers.

[95] Brochure, March 24, 1870, *ibid.*

representatives were R. M. Corwin, Edward Gilbert, and R. C. Parsons, attorneys; James M. Daniel, Samuel W. Morton, and Morton C. Hunter, railway engineers; and B. H. Epperson, former president of the Memphis, El Paso, and Pacific. Others invited to be present were Senators William P. Kellogg of Louisiana, Morgan C. Hamilton and James W. Flanagan of Texas, and Representative William C. Sherrod of Alabama; delegates Richard C. McCormick of Arizona, and J. Francisco Chaves of New Mexico; and Mr. Charles Cobb of the Southern Pacific Railroad Company. The circumstances of the sale of the Memphis, El Paso, and Pacific bonds in France and the actual condition of the charter and franchises of this company were of prime concern. On the basis of the extensive evidence presented in the five meetings, the committee decided, on April 16, 1870, that the Memphis, El Paso, and Pacific Railroad Company had failed to comply with the requirements of its charter and had lost the right to demand any more land from the state of Texas.[96] This meant that the company was considered incapable of building the transcontinental railroad on the southern route.

Whether or not the Memphis, El Paso, and Pacific had lost its reservation was another matter. Supposedly, it had already been terminated by the Reconstruction government of Texas. The Ordinance of August 29, 1868, allowed the heads of families who had settled in the company's vacant lands, to acquire title to the eighty-acre tracts on which they were residing,[97] and the fifth section of Article X of the Constitution of 1869 provided that, "All public lands heretofore reserved for the benefit of railroads or railway companies shall hereafter be subject to location and survey by any genuine land certificates."[98] A special committee, appointed to investigate this question, confirmed the title of the Memphis, El Paso, and Pacific, but recognized the cancellation of its reservation. The Senate Report on June 13, 1870, stated, "from the best examination we have been able to make of the facts and the laws of Texas, our conclusions are that the Memphis, El Paso, and

[96] *Senate Miscellaneous Documents*, 41st Congress, 2nd Session, Serial No. 1408, Document No. 121.

[97] Gammel, *Laws of Texas*, VI, 57.

[98] *Ibid.*, VII, 419.

Pacific Railroad Company is an existing corporation with the right of way across the state of Texas and that it has a valid land grant of sixteen sections to the mile to be selected out of the public lands of Texas, but without special reservation."[99]

On the heels of these reverses, conflicting as they seemed, came the relentless attacks of the company's enemies. A copy of Stephen Sartre's affidavit, alleging fraud and showing the expenditure of the money obtained in France, was circulated in Washington and New York, and the old bond scandal was front page news again. To refute Sartre's charges, copies of a letter, over Epperson's signature, were printed and distributed. The letter said that Sartre was an instrument in the hands of a certain ring which had conspired to fleece General Frémont and blackmail the Memphis, El Paso, and Pacific, and that the statement of finances was false. The company had not spent a dollar for advertisements in French newspapers. Sartre had said this information was submitted by Bergholtz who obtained it from officers of the company. Bergholtz denied this and so did each and every officer, and if Sartre's attorney wanted to publish his client's affidavit in Washington and New York, he could publish what he chose. They would pay nothing to such men.[100]

Sartre's affidavit *was* published in a pamphlet entitled *The Transcontinental Memphis, El Paso and Pacific: How the Money Was Obtained in France under False Pretenses and How It was Squandered.* Since the information was so nearly correct, it could have come only from someone on the inside, and very likely it did come from Bergholtz, who, with Bates, Gentry, and Duncan, was then attacking the company openly in New York. With so much at stake and with intrigue surrounding him on all sides, Epperson, if he wrote this letter, must have considered it his duty to do everything possible to protect the company. It is true that he maintained a firm course and did not abandon Frémont and the Southern Transcontinental. When he and Daniel testified in the Congressional investigation they told nothing that would damage the chances of the bill. Sartre's charges, however,

[99] *Senate Reports of Committees*, 41st Congress, 2nd Session, Serial No. 1409, Report No. 212.

[100] Brochure, May 16, 1870, Epperson Papers.

were printed and reprinted in newspapers all over the country. It was further set forth that the offices of the company in New York were closed under pretext of their removal to Washington where they could not be found and where none of its officers was living.[101] The satire was merciless. "Graphites," in the Louisville *Courier Journal*, ridiculed Ben Butler, Grant, Senator Morton, and

THE PATHFINDER

The most extravagant man in the world, for a small man, not even excepting Ishmail Pasha, is John C. Fremont. When the war began he was made a Brigadier General in the Federal Army and stationed at St. Louis where he proceeded to erect temporary barracks for his troops at an expense to the government for about 4 millions of dollars. He had an idea that war was all glory—that he could travel in a coach and six and put up every night at a first class hotel. He found out his mistake about the time the government found out that, as an officer of the army, he was a remarkable instance of the wrong man in the right place, and he was permitted to hang up his silver-plated arms for monuments, much to the satisfaction of all concerned.

Since the close of the war, Fremont has been engaged in the building of railroads, or rather in the sinking of funds of men who were engaged in trying to build railroads. His heaviest transaction in that line seems to have been carried out by him while acting as president of the Memphis, El Paso, and Pacific and Don't-Care-a-Continental railroad or some such outlandish name as that.[102]

"Hints for Texas Railroad Builders," in the Galveston *Weekly Civilian*, contained excerpts from a work entitled "How to Build a Railroad, by John C. Fremont," which was published by the St. Louis *Times*:

Fremont went to Europe to negotiate $6,000,000 of Memphis and El Paso RR bonds. To realize handsomely on the "promise to pay" of a railroad existing only on paper and on the paper of its advocates, requires *finesse*. It was a trivial undertaking and with the rare acumen of projectors pursuing the glimmering of an idea, the company selected as their agent, Fremont, who, having lunched on a peak of the Rocky Mountains, was once considered eminently qualified for the presidency of a nation, and having

[101] Galveston *Weekly Civilian*, May 19, 1870.
[102] *Ibid.*, June 2, 1870.

proved a military failure, had won a major general's stars and the command of a vast department. The bonds were presented and improbable as it may seem they were negotiated . . . but time passed and no vessels steamed across the Atlantic freighted with Fremont's millions—$4,500,000 in gold —but where was the money. Sartre, a French banker, heard that the company was going to repudiate the bonds. This brought Monsieur to America. He is now in New York where, not only verbally, but by affidavits in the courts he has made most damaging allegations against the distinguished John Charles. He alleges that the illustrious financier's negotiation with him was a fraud and produces evidence of the $4,500,000 gold paid Fremont for $6,000,00 bonds.

Such accusations are a part of the usual and common sufferings of railroad builders, on the patriotic plan of O. P. money, and are not to be heard in the least when success has been attained—that is, when you have got the money. The only thing to be done now is to give a good account of it. Here is the next leaf from the book of "the General who never fought a battle; the Pathfinder who always lost his way; and the millionaire who never had a red," as Frank Blair painted him. The Pathfinder does not deny that he received the money for the bonds; but declares that he devoted it to the interests of the road, in proof whereof he submits the following bilious memorandum:

Sale of $6,000,000 in gold	$4,500,000
Paid for construction of road	300,000
Paid for 7,000 tons of railroad iron (4,000 of which has been seized for duty and freight)	280,000
Paid for 20 locomotives	260,000
Retained to pay duties	300,000
Old debts (said to have been paid by Fremont)	150,000
Controlling interest in Memphis and Little Rock	250,000
Interest reserved to July 1870	450,000
Bankers commissions in Paris	900,000
Pamphlets and Maps	215,000
Senator McDonald [Arkansas] and directors Texas RR Co. for services rendered	150,000
Boilleau, Fremont's brother-in-law, for services rendered	150,000
Office expenses, 3 months, lawyers fees	90,000
	$3,295,000

To the above there should have been added other items, but the Times was unable to obtain them. That paper adds,

Only positive evidence of anything the distinguished financier has sent them is the *iron* at New Orleans, and even that is held for duties and freight. Fremont confesses keeping 300,000 to pay duties. Doubtless the company would like to have him walk up to the captain's office and settle for the iron . . . The fact that European bankers want the bonds paid at maturity does not contribute to the felicity of the situation, and all this troubles the gentlemen of the El Paso Railway.

It was said that Fremont had been arrested and put under bond but there is probably no truth in the report, as we hear nothing more of it.[103]

Not all the publicity was adverse. Some of the New York papers, including the *Sun*, were giving mild support to Frémont because he was asking only for a land grant and not for a subsidy as his competitors were.[104]

Aside from the open political warfare, there was a private conspiracy on foot—of a more sinister variety. Epperson first had wind of it in an anonymous note saying, "I believe Gray is a trickster of the first water —and is possibly at the bottom of your present troubles—Is it not him that has put L[issignol] up to the idea of getting rid of Fremont and all of you and to make a stock jobbing machine of the whole." Swenson, Frémont, and Senator Howard had strangely plaintive letters from Lissignol himself, who was then in the United States. Lissignol asked Frémont for a signed statement showing the use he had made of the millions received in France and urged him to save himself by joining in the scheme to secure the interests of the bondholders and correct the wrong that had been done. In a second letter to Frémont (which he sent to Epperson for transmittal) Lissignol accused Frémont of squandering all the money and said his reputation was such that no Transcontinental bill could ever pass Congress with his name on it.[105] Epperson himself answered this letter on April 24, 1870, and told Lissignol that the company did have some valuable assets and would be able to solve its problems by reorganization. He did not think

[103] *Ibid.*

[104] *Ibid.*, May 26, 1870.

[105] Lissignol to Frémont (undated copies), Epperson Papers.

any Pacific railroad bill would pass Congress without Frémont's support. He was certain Lissignol had fallen into the hands of the company's enemies and was being wrongly and maliciously advised. The course he was pursuing was calculated to ruin the company, and the French bondholders as well, and only the conspirators would profit by it.

To Swenson, Lissignol said that he had just learned that the road in Texas was not built, no lands had been received from the state, and the mortgage was not good. He therefore entreated Swenson to take charge of the Memphis, El Paso, and Pacific bonded debt and take over the Company's assets for the benefit of the bondholders.[106] This then was the heart of the conspiracy. Gray was building it around Lissignol who had been led to believe he could recover the French losses and doubtless had written his letters under Gray's supervision.

Daniel, now living in New York and highly dissatisfied with everything, resigned as a director on May 1, 1870. In all probability he was also contacted by Lissignol, and the drastic step he was soon to take was the result either of Gray's insidious propaganda or of some private motivation. Epperson had made an effort to reorganize the company but Schmoele, to whom he broached the subject earlier in the year, had said he preferred to take the chances as they came. Epperson, then, had to rely on the successful passage of the Transcontinental bill and the reorganization that would follow. Just what they all knew or expected at this time can only be surmised.

On June 3 Frémont received word from Paris that the Despalles suit had been decided in favor of the company and the money was therefore free again. He wrote Epperson that in view of the present political situation in France, "it was just the time for Forbes to intervene." Obviously, he knew what was going on and expected Epperson to understand, though it was his custom to speak in tantalizing riddles. Frémont also said said Dr. Schmoele "declined to act" because he had read Lissignol's letter to Howard and it was not as bad as he expected. It only abused Frémont and urged Howard to see that the bondholders were protected, and was "very carefully worded." As for the Trans-

[106] Lissignol to Swenson, April 26, 1870 (copy), *ibid.*

continental bill, Epperson was not to be alarmed by anything he heard: everything was all right.[107]

Before Gray's conspiracy came to fruition, the fate of the Southern Transcontinental was decided. The reported failure of the Memphis, El Paso, and Pacific, the apparent loss of its reservation, and the exposure of the details connected with the French bond sale nullified all Frémont's efforts and forced him into a tentative compromise with his rivals. The terms of the compromise appear to have been the inclusion of Frémont and his friends as incorporators of the Texas Pacific Railway Company with a representative share of the stock and the formation of a construction company modeled after the Credit Mobilier by Thomas A. Scott and his associates, who would contract to build the railroad for a very large profit. Although the tentative compromise reached in June, 1870, was in the nature of a defeat, Frémont's position was momentarily far from insecure. Some of his friends even regarded it as a great victory. He still had his railroad, with a valid land grant and right-of-way across Texas; and this, with his friend Marshall O. Roberts as president, would insure his future position in the Texas Pacific, which would become the successor of the Memphis, El Paso, and Pacific, take its franchises and grants subject to its liens, and thus do justice to the wronged citizens of France.

When the Texas Pacific bill was taken up by the Senate, it contained a new list of incorporators, submitted by Kellogg as a further compromise. Frémont's name was not on the list. It had been intentionally omitted in committee, but the General had many friends in Congress, among them Sumner, Cameron, Trumbull, and Nye, and his name was added by amendment in the closing hours of the second Session. Senator Jacob M. Howard, who had conducted the investigation in subcommittee, was very familiar with the case of the Memphis, El Paso, and Pacific. Furthermore, he had seen the executive correspondence relating to the French bond sale, made available to the committee by executive order of President Grant. Howard took a firm stand against Frémont and his compromise bill and, in a bitter debate on the Senate floor, exposed all the glaring irregularities of the bond sale.

[107] Frémont to Epperson, June 5, 1870, *ibid.*

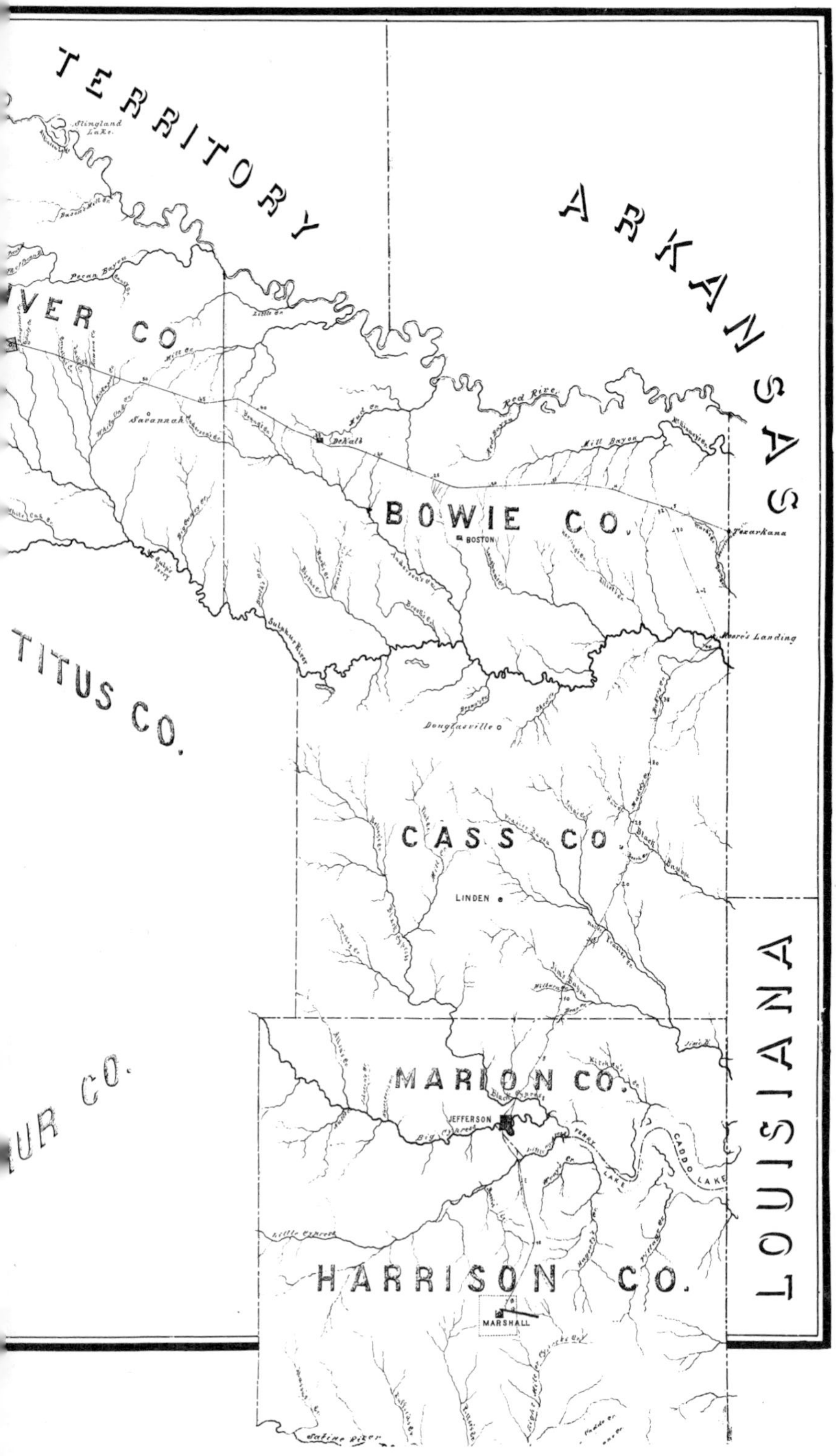

TERRITORY

ARKANSAS

Stingland Lake

Pecan Bayou

VER CO

Red River

Savannah

DeKalb

Mill Bayou

BOWIE CO.

BOSTON

Texarkana

Moore's Landing

Sulphur River

TITUS CO.

Douglasville

CASS CO.

LINDEN

Black Bayou

LOUISIANA

MARION CO.

JEFFERSON

Big Cypress

CADDO LAKE

FERRY LAKE

Little Cypress

HARRISON CO.

MARSHALL

Sabine River

UR CO.

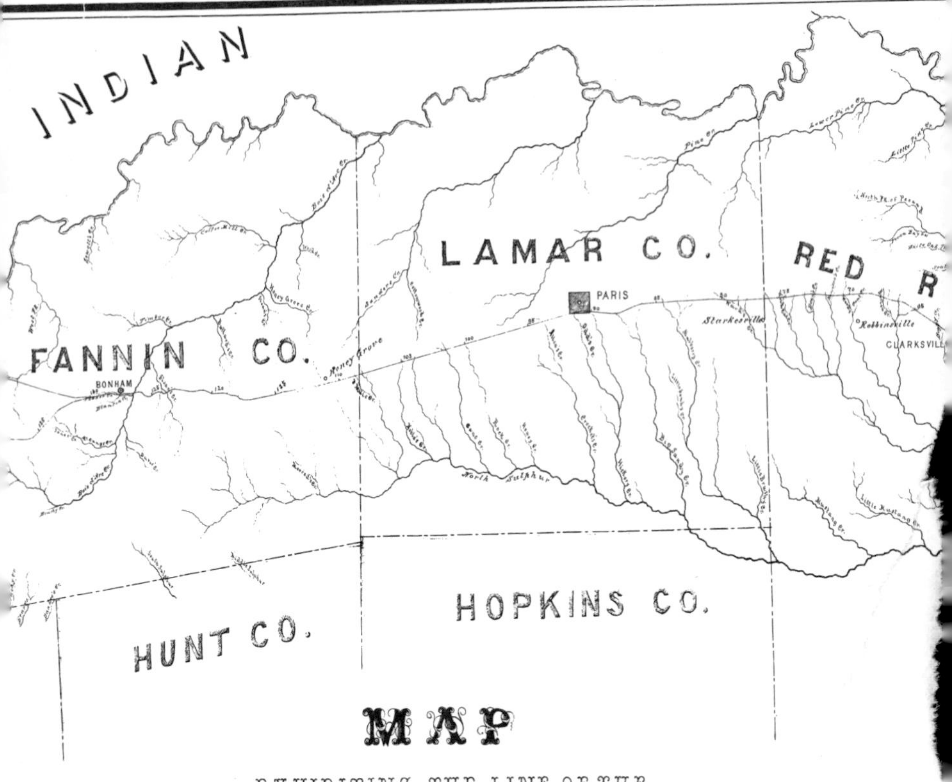

MAP

EXHIBITING THE LINE OF THE

OUTHERN TRANS-CONTINENTAL R.R.

FROM

Marshall to Texarkana

AND

From TEXARKANA & FORT-WORTH.

AUGUST 1872.

SCALE: 5 MILES = 1 INCH.

nap correctly represents
outhern Trans-Continental
a to Texarkana and from
th.

G. M. Dodge
Chief Engr.

Filed in the General Land Office at Austin in accordance with the Act Amendatory of, and supplementary to an Act, entitled, "An Act to encourage the speedy construction of a Railway through the State of Texas to the Pacific Ocean" passed on the twenty fifth day of November 1871, this twentyeighth day of August A. D. 1872.

C. C. Stremme
Chief Draftsman

UPS

THEO. C. LINK, DEL.

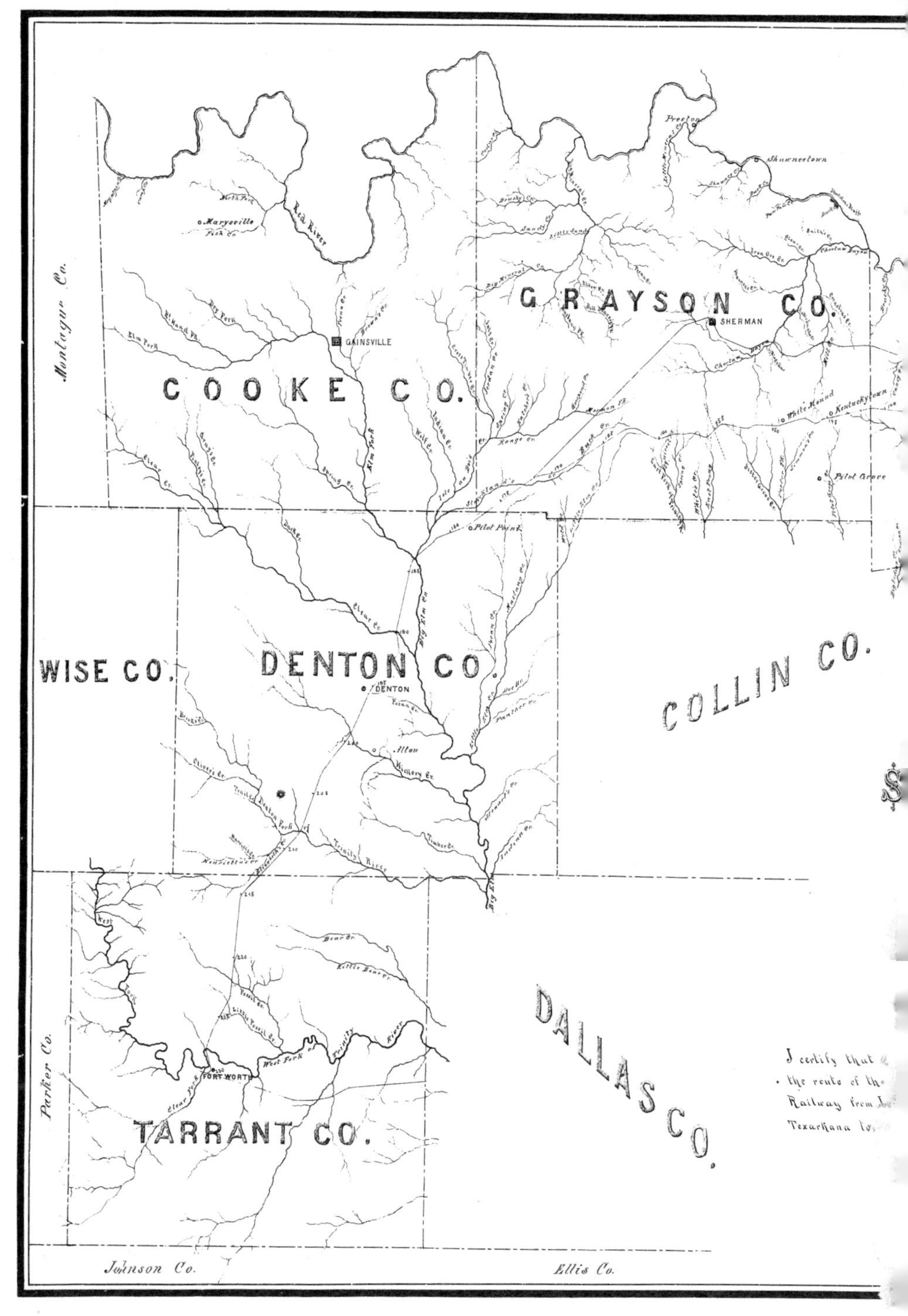

Photo by J. D. Freeman; used courtesy of the Texas Land Office.

Senator Trumbull came to Frémont's defense. He understood that a single party was the purchaser of the bonds and had various notices inserted in the papers in order to sell them for as much as he could get, "so how was General Frémont responsible for that."[108]

Howard said it was inconceivable that Paradis could be guilty. He was only duped by the careful concealment of the adverse facts, such as the loss of the reservation and the lack of a transcontinental charter, and to Senator Trumbull he continued, "Now, Sir, I have no personal feeling of unkindness toward General Fremont; I never had; but when I see him in such suspicious proximity to foul and fraudulent transactions, I feel it to be my duty to pause; I feel it to be my duty as an American citizen not to give a legislative, congressional endorsement to a man however high his character may have been heretofore, against whom there are such causes of complaint for transactions in a foreign country with whom we are at peace and to whom we are bound by ties of ancient friendship, both political and commercial."

Senator Warner at once agreed that Frémont and his associates would give the railroad a bad reputation and probably delay construction. Senator Rice did not think Frémont's name would hurt the bill. Senator Sherman said the Texas Pacific had to have the Memphis, El Paso, and Pacific road and that as long as Frémont did not have control, it was useless to exclude him from nominal interest as an incorporator. Senator Nye insisted there was no cause to "heed the evanescent wail of a disappointed Frenchman" and that the "bursting of a French bubble" was not going to wean him away from a friend. Furthermore, he said, the interest would be paid on the bonds as agreed, and then what would the French accusers have to say. Senator Cameron argued that the passage of the bill would secure the rights of the French bondholders, that they had made a good investment and would only have to wait to make a profit, so why risk blocking consolidation by withholding Frémont's name. The amendment was defeated, but Senator Nye then moved to substitute a list of 124 incorporators: 45 from the original Kellogg bill, 21 from the Sawyer bill, 3 from both, and 55 others, including Frémont. With these incorporators the amendment was

[108] Alice Eyre, *The Famous Fremonts and Their America*, p. 321.

adopted at 11:15 P.M. on June 23, 1870.[109] The bill itself was passed by the Senate four days later.

By this bill, yet to pass the House of Representatives, the Texas Pacific Railway Company was authorized to construct and operate a railroad of five-foot gauge from Marshall, Texas, to San Diego, California. The company was to receive forty sections of public land for each mile constructed in New Mexico and twenty sections for each mile constructed in California, with the condition that the entire project should be completed within ten years. The grant was to be located in alternate sections in a reservation extending twenty miles on each side of a two hundred-foot right of way through the federal public domain. Six branch lines were authorized, and the company would be permitted to consolidate, confederate, or associate with any company or companies who had received grants of land on the right of way from the United States or from another state.[110]

The principal stockholders of the Memphis, El Paso, and Pacific, in conjunction with representatives of the Texas Pacific, promptly petitioned the Texas Legislature to recharter the Memphis, El Paso, and Pacific as the Southern Transcontinental Railway Company. The motive was to strengthen their position with a new charter and franchise, to facilitate the transfer of the old company according to the terms of Frémont's compromise, and to get additional aid from the state of Texas if possible. On July 27, 1870, the Legislature granted the charter which authorized the Southern Transcontinental to purchase the property and franchises of the Memphis, El Paso, and Pacific, to construct a railroad from Texarkana to or near El Paso with a branch line from Texarkana to Jefferson, or to build a joint single line west from the 100th meridian to the state boundary in conjunction with some

[109] *Congressional Globe*, June 22–July 15, 1870, pp. 4732–4770. The senators named were Willard Warner of Alabama, Benjamin F. Rice of Arkansas, John Sherman of Ohio, James W. Nye of Nevada, and Simon Cameron of Pennsylvania and Lyman Trumbull of Illinois.

[110] *United States Statutes at Large*, XVI, 573–579. By a supplemental act, approved on May 2, 1872, the name of the enterprise was changed to the Texas and Pacific Company, to give the road a more national aspect (*ibid.*, XVII, 59–61).

other railroad chartered by the state of Texas, meaning, of course, the Shreveport-Marshall road known as the Southern Pacific.[111] The Southern Transcontinental received no land grant since the Constitution of 1869 prohibited further grants to railroads.

Heading the list of incorporators of the Southern Transcontinental were Frémont and his old crowd: Samuel W. Morton, William Schmoele, Morton C. Hunter, Marshall O. Roberts, and E. L. Fancher, followed by a preponderance of Texas Pacific promoters and only three Memphis, El Paso, and Pacific stockholders from Texas: J. R. Russell, S. D. Rainey, and J. P. Dumas. To make matters worse, Gray's conspiracy had succeeded. The news filtered through that on July 6, 1870, the Memphis, El Paso, and Pacific had passed into the hands of John A. C. Gray, Receiver—immediately recognizable as another of Frémont's henchmen. Texas newspapers retold the old story in gory detail, more facts having been gleaned from the *Advertiser* of Newark, where Judge Bradley heard the receivership case. It was said that Gray's balance sheets were so shocking they had to be suppressed.

When the Southern Transcontinental was organized in New York City on October 31, 1870, Roberts was elected president and H. G. Stebbins vice-president, much to the surprise and discomfiture of General Frémont. The other officers were W. R. Travers, treasurer, J. D. Defrees, secretary, and R. H. Corwin, attorney. Among the twenty-five directors were J. J. Astor, Edwards Pierrepont, J. W. Forney, General B. F. Grafton, General Nathaniel P. Banks, and E. B. Hart, the only Texas men being J. W. Throckmorton, G. H. Giddings, and William M. Harrison.[112] The Clarksville *Standard* called the Southern Transcontinental a swindle and a fraud attempted upon the people of the state, and at a mass meeting in Marshall, Texas, three thousand irate citizens declared they would refuse to pay taxes to support such a road.[113] But it appeared that no road was intended to be constructed by this company itself, for its incorporators and those of the Southern Pacific immediately proceeded to promote the final passage, in the

[111] Gammel, *Laws of Texas*, VI, 542.

[112] Galveston *Daily Civilian*, November 1, 1870.

[113] *Ibid.*, December 9, 1870.

House of Representatives, of the Kellogg bill (S. 647) to incorporate the Texas Pacific Railway Company for the purpose of building a transcontinental railroad along the southern route. The Southern Transcontinental was truly a paper railroad although it was thought for a while that Roberts might actually build it, and although a number of land certificates were later issued to the Texas and Pacific Company under the Transcontinental charter by virtue of a little grading done in 1872 (mainly, the last twenty-five miles graded by the Memphis, El Paso, and Pacific between Jefferson and Clarksville in 1870) and by provision of the Texas Constitutional Amendment of March 19, 1873, which allowed twenty sections per mile to railroad companies.[114]

[114] Gammel, *Laws of Texas*, VII, 676.

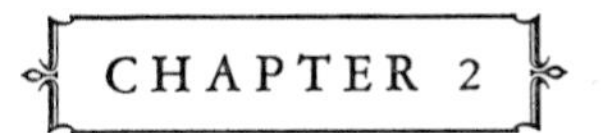

JOHN A. C. GRAY AND THE TEXAS AND PACIFIC RAILWAY COMPANY

Immediately after the Texas Pacific bill passed the Senate, with only the tacit understanding that the French bonds would be honored, the afore-mentioned John A. C. Gray emerged to take the leading role in a long and fantastic sequence of events. Gray, a retired merchant of New York, had been prominent in railroad enterprises and formerly connected with Frémont's business in California, with the Mariposa mine, it was said. In Paris, in the summer of 1869, Gray stumbled on the trail of Frémont's operations when he inquired about sixty bonds that had come into his possession and Washburne told him they were not worth the paper on which they were printed. This knowledge prompted Gray to give Frémont his advice on several occasions, and that advice was found to be very useful. Later, as Frémont's counsel and an incorporator of the Southern Transcontinental, he offered to lobby for the bill, but Frémont did not call on him. However, by keeping in close contact with the affairs of the New York office of the Memphis, El Paso, and Pacific, Gray soon found the means of forcing Frémont to accept his assistance.

(1) Frémont was in need of $50,000 to push his Transcontinental bill; Gray lent him the money, requiring only that Frémont assign him

the company's railroad iron in New Orleans. This occurred in March, 1870.

(2) The officers of the Memphis, El Paso, and Pacific had been discontented for some time. They complained that Frémont had appropriated the money intended for the construction of the railroad; some of the officers had not been paid, and some were suspected of having obtained part of the money received in France; they all felt a certain sense of guilt. When Gray, as a friendly gesture, had them notified that warrants had been issued for their arrests, the offices at 90 Broadway were closed, the furniture sold, and the sign removed from the door.

(3) Gray then went to New Orleans to get his iron. There he met A. M. Gentry, contractor and president of the Texas and New Orleans Railway Company, a very shrewd character, and persuaded him to levy an attachment on the first shipment, probably for unpaid construction work performed by Campbell & Gentry. Gray also met Thomas C. Bates, who was still nursing his alleged claim against the Memphis, El Paso, and Pacific for $300,000.

(4) Recalled to Washington early in April by a telegram from Frémont, Gray rendered efficient service as a lobbyist for the Southern Transcontinental, but all the while he was preparing for the master stroke which would give him control of the Memphis, El Paso, and Pacific, that is, which would place the company in the hands of a receiver, who was to be none other than himself.

(5) In anticipation of the congressional investigation, Frémont had sent to Paris for Emanuel Lissignol, his consulting engineer. Gray took bodily possession of Lissignol and held him in seclusion until he had garnered all the details of the French bond transaction. Gray kept his papers at his home and boarded his witness in Jersey City. Gray's counsel, Cortlandt Parker, incorporated Lissignol's information into an affidavit which Lissignol verified on May 17, 1870. Parker was paid $5,000 for his service; Lissignol was released and sent back to France.

(6) As Thomas C. Bates had already entered suit against the Memphis, El Paso, and Pacific at Rochester, Gray, the company's counsel, advised him to press the claim and obtain a receivership, giving him the information necessary to obtain it. The New York court appointed

a receiver, the son-in-law of Bates's lawyer. Gray persuaded him to resign, paid him his $500 fee, and secured the appointment for himself. The fact that he had once been appointed the company's receiver in the New York jurisdiction helped Gray with his scheme, but from then on it was no simple matter. Although Lissignol's affidavit was to be the foundation of the action, more parties and evidence were needed before Gray could put the Memphis, El Paso, and Pacific into receivership.

(7) Gray contacted Blanton Duncan of Louisville, Kentucky, who was in New York and said to be "breathing vengeance" against Frémont. Duncan was contemplating obtaining a receivership but intended to limit his operations to the local courts. When Gray pretended to believe that Duncan himself should be the receiver, Duncan took Cortlandt Parker to see Forbes, and they convinced him that a receivership was the best means of protecting the French bondholders. Forbes then introduced Duncan to Swenson, who agreed to the receivership but refused to recommend Duncan's appointment, insisting that if the company had mismanaged its affairs, the trustees should leave the appointment of the receiver to the court or to those interested.[1] Since Governor Curtin had gone to St. Petersburg as ambassador to Russia, Forbes decided it would be all right to use his name. The trustees, with the exception of Pollock, were thus made parties to the suit.

(8) In April, 1870, Gray persuaded others to bring suit against the Memphis, El Paso, and Pacific. One was a Mrs. John Ives of Syracuse,

[1] Swenson to Epperson, June 18, 1870, Epperson Papers, The University of Texas Archives. Svante Magnus Swenson, born in Sweden on February 14, 1816, came to America in 1836, settling in Baltimore. In 1838 he migrated to Texas where he became a business partner of John Adriance in the mercantile business, first in La Grange and later in Austin. The business grew until it included banking, land, and cotton. Swenson contracted to sell hundreds of the certificates received by the Buffalo Bayou, Brazos, and Colorado Railway Company, the first railroad in Texas, chartered on February 10, 1850. He purchased many B B B & C certificates himself and located them in northwest Texas, thus becoming the owner of immense tracts of ranch land. In 1870 Swenson was engaged in banking and finance in New York City. He was a lifelong friend of Benjamin H. Epperson. His firm, Swenson & Perkins, handled the accounts of the Memphis, El Paso, and Pacific Railroad.

New York, whose deceased husband had an old claim against the railroad.[2] Another was Frederick A. Lyon, to whom Gray gave three hundred shares of illegally issued stock so he could enter a complaint as a stockholder. Lyon's brother-in-law was an employee of the company and was working with Gray. Gray prepared his bill, Paul S. Forbes, A. G. Curtin, S. M. Swenson, Emanuel Lissignol, and Frederick A. Lyon versus the Memphis, El Paso, and Pacific Railway Company, but he could not bring action in Texas because the officers of the company would resist the petition, knowing that the company was technically solvent. He therefore appealed to Judge Joseph P. Bradley of the United States Circuit Court at Newark, New Jersey. Judge Bradley, who had been recently appointed to the United States Supreme Court but was still holding court in Newark, made two stipulations. The bill would have to be signed by a Texas solicitor, and the president of the company would have to be notified of the process and waive all objection to a hearing out of the circuit limits. After Parker stamped the name of Ballinger, Jack & Mott on the petition, it was filed, accompanied by two letters, written by Gray and signed by Frémont and Daniel! Both petitioned for receivership; Frémont recommended Gray's appointment and authorized Edward Gilbert to appear and waive the objection. The petition was granted without questioning on July 6, 1870.[3]

There were other irregularities connected with the receivership. Frémont was not president of the Memphis, El Paso, and Pacific, a fact which Gray himself had maintained in defending the company against a former suit; Gilbert could not be authorized to waive service without

[2] Land Office records show that Ann Eliza Ives received at least twelve Memphis, El Paso, and Pacific certificates for 7,680 acres of land. The company had assigned some of these certificates to Mrs. Ives for her husband's work as contractor. Gray later tried to force Epperson to pay off the Ives claim, but since he did not succeed, Gray may have paid her with land certificates.

[3] Douglas Campbell, *The Title of the Texas and Pacific Railroad Company to the Property of the Memphis, El Paso and Pacific Railroad Company; Opening Argument of Douglas Campbell, Esq., before the Judiciary Committee of the House of Representatives, April 11, 1878.*

vote of the directors; jurisdiction could not be obtained by waiving service as officers could not be served out of the state; and still other defects too numerous to mention can be found upon further study of the petition. It should be noted here that Gray, on the day before the receivership was granted, advanced Bates $6,000 for the assignment of his claim, on which he (Gray) finally received a judgment of $140,000; and Gray made this judgment the foundation of the foreclosure of the Harrison-Bates mortgage eighteen months later. In the end Gray settled with Bates for $35,000 although they had originally planned to split the amount of the judgment.[4]

It is not altogether difficult to explain Frémont's action. Years later he said he did not even read the statement in the bill. He doubtless realized that he had his back to the wall and had good reason to fear that some of his former officers or influential French bondholders would step in and force a receivership. In such a case he would be quite willing for the assets of the Memphis, El Paso, and Pacific to be resting safely under the protection of the United States Circuit Court, and he was agreeable to Gray's appointment because he expected Gray to continue to be his tool and do his bidding. The idea has been advanced that Frémont also wanted to get rid of Epperson and other Texas stockholders. This was probably true. Epperson said later, under oath, that he knew nothing about the receivership case, and had he known he would have opposed it. Daniel, of course, was anxious to get the company out of Frémont's hands, but it is still difficult to explain his willingness to cooperate under the circumstances, that is, if he even suspected that Frémont was in on the deal and was recommending the appointment of Gray. It is possible that Lissignol persuaded Daniel to ask for a receivership, and that Daniel either did not know who the receiver would be or, if he knew, was convinced by Gilbert that Gray would not favor Frémont. There is, however, another plausible answer.

[4] Douglas Campbell, *Closing Argument of Douglas Campbell, Esq., in Reply to Governor John C. Brown, J. A. Davenport, and Major James Turner before the Judiciary Committee of the House of Representatives, in regard to the Title of the Texas and Pacific Railway Company to the Property of the Memphis, El Paso and Pacific Railroad Company, April 24, 1878.*

Gray had stumbled onto something else in his close watch over the Memphis, El Paso, and Pacific's affairs. In 1867, before the bond issue, Swenson wired Epperson for an affidavit to the effect that there were no liens of record against the railroad. The affidavit was sent, and the bonds were issued and signed by the trustees. But three years later, in 1870, Gray informed Swenson that there was a record of the Harrison mortgage in Paris, the county seat of Lamar County. Gilbert showed him a copy of it and said that Daniel was the man responsible for getting the false affidavit. Swenson was horrified. He wrote Epperson: "If this is true the county clerks of all the counties from Jefferson to Paris have falsely certified that there were no liens in May, 1867, and the trustees have been duped into a similar certificate on the bonds. The serious consequences of which to the Pres^{t}. and Trustees I need not enumerate to you. All I can say is, let me know the truth of the matter. I have lost faith in everyone connected with the RR except yourself—which oppresses me very much indeed."[5] Epperson evidently made light of the situation because Swenson replied that even though the claim was of little or no validity it had alarmed the trustees who were surprised and chagrined that it had not been made known to them before the certification of the bonds. Forbes was upset and had seen him five or six times about it. Swenson said he had spoken to Daniel in "very severe terms and seemed to have made a very strong impression on his mind." No one had heard anything from him in a good while or even knew where he was. Then Gray had told Swenson about another "dirty trick" of Daniel's and Epperson would be appalled when he heard about it. Gray had referred Swenson to Gentry for corroboration, but Swenson said he didn't like the reference, and though he had seen Gentry, he hadn't asked any questions.[6]

Surely Daniel and the trustees themselves were being subjected to strong and not very subtle pressure by Gray and Gilbert. All this happened in the month just before Daniel agreed to sign the following petition for receivership, written—according to Campbell—by Gray himself:

[5] Swenson to Epperson, May 21, 1870, Epperson Papers.
[6] Swenson to Epperson, June 18, 1870, *ibid.*

450 Henry Street, June 24, 1870

Edward Gilbert, Esq.
Counsel for M. El P. and P. R. R. Co.

Dear Sir:

I have information that parties hostile to our company are now moving for the appointment of a receiver, both in Texas and Europe. In the present complicated state of affairs of the road and in view of the fact that our friends cannot be got together in time for consultation as no time is to be lost, I take the responsibility of requesting you to act with promptness, to the end that a receiver may be appointed who will protect the interests of the company as well as those of the creditors.

I am, very truly yours, etc.
J. M. Daniel
Director and Chief Engineer of M. El P. and P. R. R. Co.[7]

Frémont signed his petition for Gray's appointment on July 4, 1870, just two days before the case was presented to Judge Bradley.

Tarrytown, 4th July, 1870

Edward Gilbert, Esq.
69 Broadway, New York

Dear Sir: In view of the temporary embarrassments of the direction of the M. El P. and P. R. R. Co., and the fact that Messrs. Swenson and Forbes, trustees named in the land mortgage, have, in connection with others, commenced, or are about to commence, suit in the United States Circuit Court for the District of Texas, with the view to the appointment of a receiver by Judge Bradley, I write to request you, as the attorney of said company, to appear in any such suit, accepting service therein, and waiving all objections as to the hearing of the case out of the said district; and in view further of the fact that Mr. John A. C. Gray has already been appointed, by the Supreme Court of the State of New York, receiver for that jurisdiction, it seems to me most proper that he should be nominated by you to Judge Bradley, as receiver in his court, and I have to request that you press this appointment to avoid conflict and litigation which might otherwise follow.

Yours respectfully,
J. C. Fremont, President[8]

[7] Campbell, *Closing Argument.*
[8] *Ibid.*

The eminent attorney, Douglas Campbell, said in a subsequent investigation that the Harrison mortgage had been surreptitiously recorded and did not appear in the index or register of records in the office of the county clerk at Paris, Texas. Whatever the truth of the matter, Daniel never lost Epperson's confidence and it was not long until he was back in Swenson's good graces again. Gray, however, had achieved his purpose.

A few days after Gray was appointed receiver, he called on Swenson to get letters of introduction to his Austin friends for J. A. Davenport, whom he was sending to Texas. Swenson told him there was not a more honorable or upright man in Texas than Epperson, and recommended that he take charge of the company's assets there, to which Gray agreed. Although Swenson thought Gilbert was honest, he had a poor opinion of Gray and could not understand how he got the appointment. He was therefore relieved to think that Epperson and Gray would be acting in concert. Later he felt that perhaps this complicated affair would work out after all. Frémont and Gray seemed to be getting along well together, and Snethen was delivering all the papers he had in his possession. At any rate, Epperson had gotten rid of all his associates, good or bad, and there was a "head," a responsible one he hoped, subject to the supervision of the court.[9]

On July 23rd, Gray and his counsel, Cortlandt Parker, went to France for the last $450,000 in gold, which they deposited in England for safekeeping. There was reason for their haste. Not only was France on the brink of war with Germany—the German Army would invest Paris on September 19, 1870—but the Second Empire was rapidly falling apart. With Louis Napoleon gone and his opponents in power the good disposition of the government was certain to alter. It was widely believed that the Emperor and his minister of state had favored the Memphis, El Paso and Pacific enterprise, even to the point of subsidizing some of the newspapers,[10] to promote the sale of the railroad bonds. In view of Louis Napoleon's free trade aspirations, as well as his addiction to sly little gambles, this is not an unreasonable assump-

[9] Swenson to Epperson, July 9, 1870, and July 21, 1870, Epperson Papers.
[10] San Antonio *Daily Herald*, April 4, 1873.

tion. On the other hand, the French government in general did not look with favor on the export of French capital or the emigration of its citizens to America, and although American bonds attracted French investors because they paid higher interest rates than were customary in Europe, these investors much preferred to invest in real estate. Furthermore, French capitalists took all possible precaution before they purchased American securities and even realized the danger of investments which might be complicated by the application of "states rights."[11] It was true though that the authorities refrained from any unfriendly action in this case for a very long time.

As soon as Gray returned from France he made the contract for the transfer of the Memphis, El Paso, and Pacific to the Southern Transcontinental in conformity with his company's charter. The contract was a fair one, but Gray delayed and did not complete it. He filed the original papers of *Forbes et al. versus the Memphis, El Paso, and Pacific* in the United States clerk's office at Tyler, Texas, on January 4, 1871. The receivership was officially recognized in Texas when Judge Thomas H. Duval confirmed them, without new service or appearance, on January 20, 1871.

On January 24, 1871, the receiver reported his proceedings and the information he had discovered, from which the following facts appeared: (1) The company's property and assets to a considerable amount had been sequestered in Paris, in part attached in New York, and in part detained for duties in New Orleans; its offices had been closed and its operations suspended for more than a year. (2) Prior to the late Civil War the company had surveyed a route from the eastern boundary of Texas to El Paso and the commissioner of the Texas General Land Office had officially recognized the said line, and thereby, the limits of the company's reservation had been defined. The company had graded about sixty-five miles by virtue of a contract with Thomas C. Bates, and to secure the fulfillment of Bates's contract the company had in 1860 executed bonds in the amount of $350,000 under a mortgage upon all the lands and property of the company; none of these bonds or any interest thereon had ever been paid but

[11] Henry Blumenthal, *Reappraisal of Franco-American Relations, 1830–1871.*

they had remained on deposit in a New Orleans bank and Bates was engaged in litigation with the company in regard to his claims for construction. (3) Since the Civil War about twenty or twenty-five miles of road had been graded, about three miles of track had been laid and loose rails had been dropped along the line for a few miles farther; ten locomotives purchased in France, together with about 120 tons of railroad iron had been detained at New Orleans for nonpayment of duties, which in the case of the locomotives, exceeded their value; the other railroad iron had been sold or attached in New York for claims against the company. (4) This was the whole extent of the rail operations of the company across the whole northern portion of Texas, an extent of nearly a thousand miles, and in the accomplishment of this result, there had been issued $40,000,000 in stock and about $13,000,000 in bonds and certificates; nothing else remained which the receiver could lay hands on except a few thousand shares of stock in the Memphis and Little Rock and in the San Diego and Gila railroad companies and a residuum of less than 300,000 in cash assets accruing from land-grant bonds sold in France. A more utterly fraudulent concern, a more empty bubble of speculation was rarely to be met with within this highly speculating and fraudulent age. Yet there were franchises and rights and grants of land belonging to the organization, which, in the hands of an honest and energetic association, backed by sufficient capital, could probably pay off the real indebtedness of the company and relieve it and the country of the odium which had been brought upon both. Furthermore, in the struggles for the establishment of rival transcontinental railroads between the Atlantic and Pacific oceans, the franchises of this company might be rendered available to supply a valuable link in one of the lines.

On the basis of Gray's report, the sale of the Memphis, El Paso, and Pacific was confirmed but with orders not to sell to any company other than the Southern Transcontinental without approval of the court.[12]

On January 31, 1871, Gray obtained Judge Bradley's permission to

[12] Forbes *et al. v.* the Memphis, El Paso, and Pacific Company, *et al.* Circuit Court, Western District of Texas, May, 1872 2 *Woods* 323. Also in *Federal Cases Comprising Circuit and District Courts of the United States*, No. 4926, Vol. 9, p. 408.

carry out the contract according to the Southern Transcontinental charter or to sell the company's rights, franchises, and land grants to any other purchaser on the same or "similar" terms, with explicit orders "not to divest the mortgages securing the land grant bonds, and to consider all property purchased with the proceeds of the same as trust property, thereafter to be acquired by the bondholders or payment therefor to be distributed among them."[13] Gray found further excuses to delay the sale to the Southern Transcontinental, for if he had ever intended to fulfill the contract, he had abandoned the idea by this time. He could make a better arrangement with the Texas Pacific, one which would be of less advantage to the French bondholders but more profitable to himself, and to the Texas Pacific as well.

Gray was suddenly a very busy man. The court had also authorized him to clear the title to the reservation, to confiscate and sell all property of the Memphis, El Paso, and Pacific, to obtain from S. M. Swenson and E. L. Fancher the 10,100 shares of Memphis and Little Rock stock they were holding in trust, and to make a division of all assets not otherwise appropriated among the several parties interested according to their rights, specifically mentioning as trust property, not only the capital stock in the Memphis and Little Rock but also that in the San Diego and Gila, and the Arizona Railroad companies. Actually Gray had already begun most of these actions. He had filed suit against Morton C. Hunter and five others on December 1, 1870, to recover certain bonds known as construction bonds which he said had been delivered to them for illegal purposes; and Epperson, on December 8, 1870, had returned 187 first-mortgage construction bonds to Gray. Gray was having Epperson's books audited; he was working on the Bates suit and was preparing to compromise all controversies with Sam Tate, the new president of the Memphis and Little Rock. But when he called on Swenson to surrender the Memphis and Little Rock stock which had been deposited in his bank, Swenson "blazed away" and declared that he would not give it up without a hearing in court.[14]

[13] Order, January 31, 1871, copied from *ibid.*, Epperson Papers.

[14] Swenson to Epperson, February 8, 1871, Epperson Papers. Swenson also owned Memphis and Little Rock stock and bonds. At this time the stock was worth its par value and the bonds were advancing 1 per cent per day. Swenson

Gray obliged by suing Swenson in the Supreme Court of New York. Swenson reported to Epperson: "On yesterday Gray came to see me, we had a long and on my part a plain talk—on his: mere palaver. I insisted that he should dismiss the suit in the State Court—desist from enforcing the decree of the U.S. Court and act frankly toward me, especially in regard to his contract with the So. Transcontl. RR Co., about which there is a mystery and studied avoidance on both sides."[15]

As for the Memphis and Little Rock stock, Swenson "scotched the snake" by filing an answer in which he stated that the stock had been conveyed to the trustees long before Gray's appointment and in which he alleged fraud in obtaining the court order.[16] The mystery surrounding the sale of the Memphis, El Paso, and Pacific, however, was not to be solved in a day. This matter continued to hang fire until everyone grew weary of waiting for something to be done.

Gray, in the meantime, had strengthened his own position by a very bold move. He had filed suit on January 21, 1871, in the United States Circuit Court of the Western District for Texas, to restrain Governor Edmund J. Davis and Land Commissioner Jacob Kuechler from infringing upon the Memphis, El Paso, and Pacific reservation. Kuechler, assuming that the reservation had been terminated, was opening the land to location.[17] The solicitors were Gray and Davenport of New York and A. J. Hamilton, E. M. Pease, and E. B. Turner of Texas. On February 16, 1871, Gray won his case. Davis and Kuechler immediately appealed to the United States Supreme Court. The Texas Legislature appropriated $1,200—$10,000 was requested[18]—to pay for court costs and the expenses of counsel in this suit, and by joint resolution petitioned the Supreme Court to advance the case on its docket and

---

had turned down a broker's offer to buy $25,000 at 72½ and had told him to come back when he could bid 90 (Swenson to Epperson, March 21, 1871, *ibid.*).

[15] Swenson to Epperson, *ibid.*

[16] Swenson to Epperson, April 29, 1871, *ibid.*

[17] Gammel, *Laws of Texas*, VI, 57.

[18] Senator E. L. Dohoney of Lamar County wrote Epperson that he had defeated this motion with the help of the Houston and Texas Central men. Dohoney to Epperson, February 9, 1871, Epperson Papers.

make a decision at as early a date as possible.[19] A favorable decision for Gray would give him control of the Memphis, El Paso, and Pacific with all its rights and privileges restored and would deprive Frémont of the ability to deliver his part of the legislative bargain. It was in this situation that Gray turned his back on Frémont and began to deal directly with Thomas A. Scott, the master mind of the Texas Pacific.

It had been agreed that the Texas Pacific would give Frémont $300,000 in paid-up stock for his interest in the Memphis, El Paso, and Pacific, and $300,000 in bonds for the actual cash expended in preliminary construction. Although this arrangement had been made outside the halls of Congress, it was a gentlemen's agreement, no less, and up to this time Frémont had considered himself relatively secure. Neither he nor Jessie Benton Frémont, now actively concerned with the General's business, realized the strategic importance of Gray's suit, but when he won in the circuit court, Judge Jeremiah S. Black, Jessie Frémont's counsel, was well aware that Gray's increasing power would weaken their position.[20]

The Texas Pacific bill was then before the House of Representatives. Frémont had strong support in Congress, but there was evidence of anti-Frémont sentiment on the outside. One of the General's old Civil War contracts, in which graft was alleged, was unearthed, and the *Herald* had this to say: "The old Memphis and El Paso schemers are here endeavoring to get their job through the house. It is on the speaker's table in the hands of the old Memphis, El Paso, and Pacific managers, giving them the power to throw at least a shadow of legality over their infamous stock transactions in Paris . . ."[21]

In this virtually new bill—it was S 647, but only the enabling act was the same—there was no subsidy, no loan, or pledge of credit. One

[19] Gammel, *Laws of Texas*, VI, 1046, 1050.

[20] Albert V. House, Jr., "Post-Civil War Precedents for Recent Railroad Reorganization, *Mississippi Valley Historical Review*, XXV (March, 1939), 505–522.

[21] Clipping, Epperson Papers. Among the incorporators were: John C. Frémont, M. O. Roberts, E. L. Fancher, Thomas A. Scott, H. D. Cooke, R. C. Parsons, W. T. Walters, Samuel Tate, G. P. Buell, G. H. Giddings, Paul S. Forbes, A. J. Hamilton, W. S. Rosecrans, G. M. Dodge.

of the contracting parties had a land grant from Texas, the other from the United States. The road was to be of uniform gauge and built of American steel or iron. To reduce the amount of the land grant all the branch lines were cut off by amendment: the Kansas Pacific branch from a point in Colorado to El Paso, the Little Rock branch (Dallas to Fulton to Little Rock),[22] the New Orleans branch, and the San Francisco branch at the western end. Construction was to commence on the trunk line simultaneously at San Diego and Marshall. The capital was reduced from $100,000,000 to $50,000,000. The bill passed the House with little opposition, 137–59, 44 not voting, on February 22. When it came before the Senate the next day Senator Sherman made a motion to concur in the House amendments; Senator Howard moved to nonconcur and called for the appointment of a conference committee, which was ordered on February 28.[23] In Conference Committee the House bill was modified so as to allow the New Orleans, Baton Rouge, and Vicksburg to connect with the main line and to allow the Southern Pacific of California, already authorized by the same bill to build a line 700 miles long from San Francisco to Los Angeles, to build 250 miles farther from a point at or near Tehachapi Pass to connect with the Texas Pacific at or near a point on the Colorado River. After a brief debate the Conference report was agreed to on the same day it was presented, March 2, 1871, and the bill passed the House the next day at 3:45.[24] After all, it was generally conceded, it was only fair for

[22] The Fulton to Dallas extension had been added in order to allow the Texas Pacific to get through Texas without assuming the obligations of the French bondholders, letting the road commence at Marshall, run west from there, leaving the first 150 miles from Texarkana out of the line, and making up for the connection by the branch from Fulton to Dallas (Washington *Daily Globe*, March 5, 1871). This was also the purpose of Scott's plan to build to Vinita, Indian Territory, via Little Rock and Fort Smith, and thence due south to Dallas.

[23] The Conference Committee: for the Senate, Howard of Michigan, Kellogg of Louisiana, and Flanagan of Texas; for the House, Wheeler of New York, Logan of Illinois, and Sherrod of Alabama.

[24] Twenty of the incorporators would constitute a quorum when the stock books were opened for subscription in New York; $2,000,000 to be subscribed

the South to have a Pacific railroad. In the North this legislation was hailed as a noble act of generosity on the part of Congress and the Executive to the late insurrectionary states. In Southern California the "San Diego-Texas" road was welcomed with great enthusiasm. In the South it was regarded as a snare and a delusion and called the "Texas Pacific job." It had been introduced by a carpetbagger from New York (Representative William A. Wheeler); it would be a Northern road; it would be a Northern gauge; and it was pointing toward the North.[25]

The news was not favorably received in France. No terms of agreement with the French bondholders had been written into the bill. They placed the blame on Frémont whom they still held responsible for their deception in the first place. Furthermore, there was a restrictive clause that would operate against instead of in favor of the French. According to Section 6, the rights, franchises, and property of purchased roads would vest in the Texas Pacific, and the indebtedness or other legal obligations of such companies would be assumed, but said company should not assume the debts or obligations of any company with which it might consolidate or which it might purchase "to an amount greater than the cash value of the assets received from the same."

A protest was hardly to be expected from war-torn and starving France, where even the American Minister, E. B. Washburne, had become greatly emaciated.[26] The supply of horseflesh had long been exhausted. Mule meat was selling for $2.00 per pound and cats and dogs for $1.50 per pound. Rats were in evidence in some of the markets. No one had believed, after the investment of Paris, that the Germans seriously contemplated bombardment. It was thought that they were

---

and 10 per cent paid; 20,000 shares; seventeen directors; to organize within ninety days (*United States Statutes at Large*, XVI, 573–579).

On April 16, 1871, the Southern Pacific filed an amended certificate of incorporation at Sacramento. The object was to purchase, construct, and operate a continuous line of railroad from San Francisco to San Diego to some point on the Colorado River. The directors were Lloyd Lewis, Leland Stanford, Charles Crocker, C. P. Huntington, Mark Hopkins, Wayne Peter Donahue; capital, $75,000,000 (Galveston *Daily Civilian*, April 19, 1871).

[25] Galveston *Daily Civilian*, March 2, and March 9, 1871.

[26] New York *Times*, February 4, 1871.

trusting in that grim ally famine, but the bombardment had been heavy, and the German army made its triumphal entry in the silent city of Paris on March 1, to remain until the terms of peace were accepted. Grant wired congratulations on the victory to the German king. France was then facing the heaviest indemnity yet known in modern history, certain to lose Strasbourg, Alsace, and part of Lorraine, and soon to be involved in a violent civil war which would leave an additional sixty thousand dead and one-third of Paris in ruins, including the Tuileries and Palais du Quai d'Orsay.[27] Still, and with paper almost as scarce as food, the French press did not fail to make an indignant protest about the railroad bill, in its ragged miniature half-sheets.

R. M. Corwin, meeting Throckmorton on the train from New York, told him he had come down to see if the French were after Frémont in earnest. Corwin was satisfied that "the General was on top of a volcano liable at any moment to burst and blow him to oblivion and dishonor, and all his friends who had upheld him." For that reason he would be glad to place the whole project quietly in Roberts' hands and let the Texas Pacific Company consolidate the Transcontinental and the Memphis, El Paso, and Pacific, assume the French bonded debt, take the reservation, and build the branch road from Dallas to Fulton. Throckmorton warned Epperson that the less he wrote to Washington the better, in case the French bondholders got after them.[28]

Other views were presented by Daniel, who wrote Epperson that Frémont was holding out for millions in Texas Pacific stock and bonds. "He says it is his bill. He knows that if the matter is organized with Roberts at its head his shystering and plundering cannot go on but the profit will be made by building the road in a legitimate way and that does not suit Fremont. He cannot do anything straight. Gilbert and

[27] Both the war with Germany and the civil war led by the Commune terminated when the Treaty of Frankfort was signed on May 10, 1871. The Thiers government took over until May 24, 1873. Thiers was replaced by General MacMahon, who was elected president for seven years. The Third Republic came into being with the Constitution of 1875.

[28] Throckmorton to Epperson, March 9, 1871, Epperson Papers.

Gray say the present bloody revolution in Paris is what now saves Fremont."[29]

Daniel was unhappy about the whole situation. No one knew what Gray was doing or who, if anyone, would build the railroad. He already had told Epperson he was completely worn out with the whole matter, that it was a fret and a "waist" of one's life. Gilbert and Gray would get all the money in Gray's hands, about $700,000, through legal fees and paying off claimants such as Bates and Mrs. Ives. He, Daniel, had advertised his house for sale but did not know for sure where he was going. If the road was ever built he would go back to Texas and settle at Paris.[30]

To encourage the better cooperation of the Southern Transcontinental and the Southern Pacific and their consolidation with the Texas Pacific (created by and under the laws of the national government), the Texas Legislature offered the Southern Transcontinental and the Southern Pacific a subsidy in the form of bonds in the amount of $6,000,000 at 8 per cent, with the option of exchanging them for land certificates of 1,440 acres for each $1,000 bond, or as an alternative the substitution of a land grant of twenty-four sections for each mile of railroad constructed in the event that the state constitution was subsequently amended to permit the granting of public land for railway construction, provided that they agreed on a junction point west of the east boundary line of Shackelford County within six months after passage of the act, and provided the said railroad should be completed to the said junction point by January 1, 1874. The transfer of the rights, benefits, and privileges of the Southern Transcontinental and the Southern Pacific to the Texas Pacific Railway Company were to be made only when the conditions imposed by the act had been fulfilled.[31] In other words, it was mandatory for these two companies to

[29] Daniel to Epperson, March 25, 1871, *ibid.*

[30] Daniel to Epperson, April 6, 1871, *ibid.*

[31] Gammel, *Laws of Texas*, VI, 1623. The date of this act was May 24, 1871. The junction point was changed by the Act of November 25, 1871, to a point within three miles of the junction of the West Fork and Clear Fork of the Trinity River, on the south side of the rivers. It was formally designated as

extend westward from the agreed point of junction by 1874, and the act was predicated on the belief that the Southern Transcontinental Railway Company would succeed by contract to the rights, franchises, and property of the Memphis, El Paso, and Pacific, whose line from Jefferson to the junction point was to be followed as nearly as practicable.

With the passage of this act everything seemed ready for the transfer of the charter and remnants of the old road which were still in the hands of the receiver. Ostensibly, Frémont was the owner of the Memphis, El Paso, and Pacific. He had, however, failed to inspire capitalists with confidence in his management, and he was "unhappily impecunious."[32] His friend Roberts, who was to be the president of the Texas Pacific, had money, and he also owned a controlling interest in the Southern Pacific, now important in the coming alignment of power. But if he really intended to build the road, might he not be outmaneuvered by Scott's proposal to buy the Memphis, El Paso, and Pacific from Gray. Or was it possible that he was a part of Scott's plan to get the Memphis, El Paso, and Pacific and throw Frémont overboard at the same time. It was Throckmorton's opinion that Roberts would not give up since he had entered into the matter; he and his friends would be able to control the Texas Pacific stock subscription, and since he owned the Southern Pacific, he would have the whip hand over Frémont.[33]

Frémont's name headed the list of incorporators of the Texas Pacific bill. The time of the meeting to open the books for subscription would be designated by the first-named incorporator and the six immediately following, namely: Marshall O. Roberts, Henry D. Cooke, John W. Forney, Richard C. Parsons, E. L. Fancher, and Luther R. Marsh, three of whom were supposed to favor Frémont. Slowly beginning to suspect his friends, Frémont threatened not to call the meeting. When he did, it was held at the Southern Transcontinental office in

the Aldredge Survey immediately west of Fort Worth on May 6, 1872 (*Annual Report of the President of the Texas and Pacific Railway Company, May 20, 1872*, p. 11).

[32] Galveston *Daily Civilian*, January 25, 1871.

[33] Throckmorton to Epperson, April 9, 1871, Epperson Papers.

New York on April 15, 1871, but he did not attend. He sent Judge Black to represent his interests. The imposing legal staff availed him little for his subscription was limited to 5,000 shares, which were not listed under his name but that of Judge Charles F. Holly of New York. He had trusted too much in Roberts, who was unanimously voted 11,000 out of 20,000 shares.[34] Had Roberts not abandoned Frémont, the two of them with 16,000 shares could have controlled the company. Now with Frémont virtually out of the picture it remained to be seen who would get the Memphis, El Paso, and Pacific out of receivership and profit by Gray's treachery.

Daniel attended the organizational meeting on May 23. He wrote Epperson:

The enclosed list is the Board of Directors of the T & P RR. The election is just over. There was hard work to get Throckmorton named on the Directory. The NY parties ignoring everyone from Texas. Grafton managed the matter with Roberts and Stebbins. Fremont is totally ignored and has not been present. Neither has Rosecrans, Sedgewick or any of that Washington crowd. Corwin has just dropped in after the election.

Fremont has just come in and is now sitting near me at my back and wishes to know of Hart if the Executive Committee of the Transcontinental meets at 2:00. He looks as usual. Gray has not been about today. I shall go see him immediately and find out all I can . . .[35]

Daniel sent the following printed list of officers and directors, marking the members of the Executive Committee with an X:

M. O. Roberts, President
H. G. Stebbins, Vice-president X
Thomas A. Scott, Acting President X
Edwards Pierrepont, Treasurer X
Moses Taylor
George W. Cass X
W. T. Walters X
William Travers X

[34] Galveston *Weekly Civilian*, April 20, 1871; *Flake's Semi-Weekly Bulletin*, April 29, 1871.

[35] Daniel to Epperson, May 23, 1871, Epperson Papers.

E. B. Hart, Secretary
Henry D. Newcomb
E. W. Rice
Henry J. McComb
John W. Forney
John McManus
John S. Harris
George W. Quintard
J. W. Throckmorton.

According to a later version of this meeting, Roberts really wanted to build the railroad, and having a high opinion of Scott's executive ability, arranged to give him eight directors while he kept nine, but he did not know his man, for Scott immediately purchased two of Roberts' directors, and when they met together, Scott was the master spirit.[36] However it was, the matter appeared to be settled to the satisfaction of all. Everyone felt sure the road would be built and expected the speedy consummation of the sale to the Southern Transcontinental. But Gray, intending to by-pass the Southern Transcontinental and sell to the Texas Pacific, did not execute the contract. Though Gilbert knew why, he was worried. He was afraid the Memphis, El Paso, and Pacific wasn't worth a rush without that reservation and the Texas Pacific would assume they didn't have it as long as the case was on appeal. If they could win "the great case at Washington," negotiation might bring the complicated affair out of the woods. Many of the French bonds were already in New York in the hand of lawyers for prosecution, and Gray would be leaving again for France on June 8th.[37]

Gray's next move was to persuade the French bondholders to agree to a proposal whereby the Texas Pacific would take over the land grant and franchises of the Memphis, El Paso, and Pacific and give them land, instead of money or bonds, in settlement of their claims. In France he issued a circular representing himself as receiver of the United States Supreme Court. The circular listed an enormous amount of company liabilities and very few assets. It stated that an arrange-

[36] Galveston *Daily Civilian*, January 13, 1872.

[37] Gilbert to Epperson, May 30, 1871, Epperson Papers.

ment might be made with the Texas Pacific to obtain land in exchange for their bonds at the rate of about $8.00 an acre or thirteen acres for each $100 bond. The Texas Pacific would receive that part of the assets to which the bondholders were entitled. Most of the French bondholders were peasants who had invested their savings in these securities. They knew nothing of business affairs in America; they heard nothing from the trustees under their mortgages; and they agreed to the exchange. Gray secured the consent of approximately four-fifths of the bondholders. The other one-fifth did not consent.

On his return to America Gray had repeated talks with Edwards Pierrepont, counsel for the Texas Pacific, in regard to the Memphis, El Paso, and Pacific charter and the powers of the receiver to make a sale and conveyance of its corporate property. Roberts had requested Pierrepont's opinion on these points. Pierrepont informed both Gray and Roberts that the Texas Pacific could not complete the negotiations unless the title and franchise of the Memphis, El Paso, and Pacific were free from all liens of record, or in other words, foreclosed to wipe out the mortgages, which, according to the orders of the court, were to be preserved. Gray therefore proceeded to effect this without notice to the court.[38]

During the next six months, as Gray quietly pulled some very tenuous strings, no word was forthcoming to the public or even to those in touch with the railroad hierarchy. Throckmorton, a director of the Southern Transcontinental and the Texas Pacific and also an agent of the Memphis, El Paso, and Pacific, was watching developments at Austin while the Legislature was in session. Roberts was already building the Southern Pacific west from Marshall, but since the Southern Pacific men, Cobb and Hall, hadn't brought any "pewter" with them, Throckmorton thought Scott might have bought them up in an effort to defeat Roberts, or else these two, having deceived him about wanting amendments for his Southern Pacific bill, were trying to keep up their deception until the Legislature adjourned with nothing done, or perhaps they were just trying to hold on to funds wrung out of Roberts

[38] Campbell, *Closing Argument.*

and would let those who had promises make out on promises still. There was definitely a "bug under the chip somewhere," Throckmorton said, and he could "no longer be made a fool of."[39]

By the fall of 1871 it was being publicly aired that Scott and Roberts were arguing. They were said to be having trouble over gauges—broad against narrow—and other matters. The "other matters" were the "broad gauge of debt and double dealing by Fremont" which had saddled the whole concern and the "bleeding of M. O. Roberts of a million dollars for Texas and Washington lobbyism." These were the main troubles.[40] In view of the general state of inertia and conditions in Texas, whose Legislature had a very bad name—it was said it cost more to get a land grant there than the land was worth—the San Diego and Gila Company did not want their property transferred to the Texas Pacific by the Memphis, El Paso, and Pacific, and Rosecrans and Sedgwick had already filed suit in New York to prevent this and also to rescind their former contract with the "bankrupt" company.[41] Too, some thought Scott was not willing to see the road built unless he could manipulate the bonds and make a large sum of money before a spike was driven. California papers were already wondering why work hadn't commenced at the western end. The truth was Scott insisted on having local trade for every mile he constructed, and he was already trying to get released from building at the western end in order to save transportation of iron and material. Grafton, the chief engineer of the Southern Transcontinental, thought he would get the release,[42] as he did by amendments to the T & P bill in May, 1872.

Daniel was then in Richmond, Virginia, where he had taken his family, and was no longer in communication with anybody in New York. In reply to a request from Epperson, he expressed his thoughts on the existing situation. Davenport and Gray, he said, were trying to find out who the old stockholders were and who would own the surplus assets after the Southern Transcontinental had paid off the French bonds. The title to the road certainly lay in the old subscribers, and

39 Throckmorton to Epperson, October 22, 1871, *ibid.*

40 Galveston *Daily Civilian*, November 25, 1871.

41 *Ibid.*, November 7, 1871.

42 Grafton to Epperson, February 19, 1872, Epperson Papers.

Gray, Pierrepont, or anyone else could not get them to surrender nor would they as a mass take any action, but if Gray found out the true state of affairs he would proceed to sell them out on the first mortgage bonds or the Bates draft so he could give Roberts a satisfactory title. It was to their advantage, his and Epperson's, for Roberts to get the Memphis, El Paso, and Pacific, settle with the French bondholders, and build the road, but if possible, he didn't want Gray to swallow the Memphis and Little Rock and about one million dollars in assets and money for the taking.

Daniel evidently had done some detective work before he left New York for he said, "You will see from the enclosed slip that the Court had no right to appoint Gray receiver in the Bates suit."[43]

Swenson was trying to bring about an agreement between Gray and Roberts. Roberts had called on him, and when the subject of the sale came up, Roberts said Gray would not do anything, that he was dealing with the Cairo and Fulton people who were also interested in acquiring the Memphis, El Paso, and Pacific. Swenson then had a serious and cordial talk with Gray, who was mortified by this report. Gray said Roberts was at fault, that he was always equivocating and never of the same mind. He also told Swenson that Tom Scott was going to buy Roberts' interest in the Southern Transcontinental in December but the information was confidential and not to be made public. Convinced then that Scott was more in earnest about building the Pacific road, Swenson considered him the preferred purchaser and sent him word by Gray that the trustees would do all in their power to give him a good title.[44] This was the message Gray had been waiting for. No longer hesitating, he informed the trustees that he proposed to sell the property and franchises of the Memphis, El Paso, and Pacific at public sale by order of the court for the purpose of enabling him to make a

[43] Daniel to Epperson, November 27, 1871, *ibid.*

[44] Swenson to Epperson, December 8, 1871, *ibid.* The Cairo and Fulton Railroad of Arkansas had just been purchased by the St. Louis and Iron Mountain. Thomas Allen and H. G. Marquand, its president and vice-president, were elected to the same office for the new road. Gray could have sold to the Cairo and Fulton, but he said he considered that the Memphis, El Paso, and Pacific would be more valuable to the Texas Pacific.

perfect title to a bona fide purchaser and for the further purpose of protecting the interests of the land-grant bondholders.

Governor Curtin, being in Europe, wrote Swenson on February 27, 1872, consenting to the sale but suggested the trustees bid in the property. Paul S. Forbes, then in Paris, had noted his approval on Curtin's letter, and on the bottom of a copy of it, Swenson wrote a note to E. L. Fancher, one of Gray's lawyers, saying he would provide a bidder for the trustees at the sale to be held by order of the court. Fancher then addressed a letter to John A. Davenport, another of Gray's lawyers, authorizing him to employ attorneys in Texas for the purposes specified in the trustees' letter, but none of these letters said anything about foreclosures.[45]

Things began to move very fast. Marshall O. Roberts resigned as president of the Texas Pacific and the Southern Transcontinental in February, 1872, and announced that he was selling the Southern Pacific to Thomas A. Scott. Roberts' resignation actually occurred in December but was not made known until February. It may have been agreed on at a secret meeting of the Texas Pacific and Southern Transcontinental directors held in New York in June, 1871.[46] The consolidation took place immediately following the sensational news that Roberts had stepped out.

The Texas Pacific, on March 21, 1872, purchased all the assets of the Southern Pacific, including its charter, equipment, and 286 unlocated land certificates. The consideration was three million dollars worth of Texas Pacific land-grant bonds, plus the assumption of the Southern Pacific's $250,000 debt to the School Fund.[47] Nine days

[45] Campbell, *Opening Argument.*

[46] Washington *Daily Morning Chronicle,* June 14, 1871.

[47] Miscellaneous Deeds 371, General Land Office. After the Southern Pacific succeeded the Texas Western, its history grew complicated and its finances incomprehensible. In 1861 twenty-five miles of poorly constructed road had been completed at a cost of $150,000 per mile, and at one time there were two Southern Pacific companies building the same road. In 1886 the company reorganized with Colonel J. M. Waskom as president. In 1868 after a fourth forced sale, Robert B. Hall, a Louisville capitalist, acquired the property. The railroad was then forty-four miles in length from Shreveport to the Marshall railhead. In 1870 the road passed into the hands of Marshall O. Roberts, and

later, on March 30, 1872, the Texas Pacific exchanged $1,000,000 worth of its land-grant bonds for the entire assets of the Southern Transcontinental Railway Company.[48] These assets did not include the Memphis, El Paso, and Pacific as originally planned. Scott would buy directly from Gray, who had already begun his action for foreclosure in the United States Circuit Court of the Western District for Texas, not in the name of the trustees, but in the name of the bondholders, who were the mortgagees, not the mortgagers. His attorneys in New York prepared bills of complaint for the foreclosure of four separate mortgages: (1) the first land-grant mortgage, covering the land along the first 150 miles (1,536,000 acres); (2) the second land-grant mortgage, covering the same amount of land along the second 150 miles; (3) the construction mortgage covering the road, fixtures, franchises, and so on; (4) the mortgage to William M. Harrison for the alleged work done by Bates. This mortgage was set aside by the Memphis, El Paso, and Pacific in November, 1870, in the 8th Judicial District of Texas; but it had been restored by Gray and transferred to J. S. Messenger, the paying teller of a New York bank which Gray controlled.[49]

Gray's attorneys prepared the answers for the Memphis, El Paso, and Pacific, for the trustees, and for John A. C. Gray, receiver. John A. Davenport carried all these documents to Paris, Texas, and had one Texas solicitor, Henry Brace, sign the bill of complaint, and another, R. A. Reeves, sign the answers of the trustees. Henry Brace was from New York. He had gone to live in Paris, Texas, solely for the purpose of executing Gray's orders. The New York firm of Gray and Davenport signed the answers for the Memphis, El Paso, and Pacific. The "Gray" in this firm was John Clinton Gray, the son of John A. C. Gray. On April 30, 1872, the foreclosure papers were presented to the circuit judge of the Western District for Texas. On the next day the

---

when he sold his stock to Thomas A. Scott in 1872, the line extended from Shreveport to Longview, a distance of sixty-five miles, including the twelve-mile branch from Swanson's Landing to Jonesville, relaid by Hall after the Civil War (Andrew Forest Muir, "The Thirty-Second Parallel Pacific Railroad in Texas to 1872" [Ph.D. dissertation], Chapters V–IX).

[48] *Annual Report of the President* (*T & P*), pp. 8–10.

[49] Campbell, *Opening Argument.*

decrees of foreclosure and sale were entered in all four of the actions, and the sale was ordered for June 4 at Paris, Texas. J. W. Throckmorton, the only authorized solicitor of the Memphis, El Paso, and Pacific in Texas, had no notice of these suits or decrees, nor were any of the bondholders notified of the proceedings; Swenson, in New York, also knew nothing of this.[50]

Gray advertised the sale only in Texas. Epperson saw the announcement in an obscure Texas weekly and informed Swenson that the sale would be held on June 4. Surprised that it would be so soon, Swenson immediately instructed Epperson to be present and bid in the property. He was explicit:

> The property must be secured to the French bondholders but how to bid is the question. If no other bidder it is plain enough to buy it for a few hundred thousand dollars, but if others what then. It wont do to let any one else have the property; but at the same time dangerous to go up to millions.
>
> I want you to bear in mind that honor & everything else must prompt us to secure the property to the French bondholders, and you must see to it that there be no mishap to this duty at the sale.
>
> You will be there and if anything happens you will bid in the property as low as you can in the name of the trustees of the land-grant bondholders, A. G. Curtin, Paul S. Forbes, and S. M. Swenson. The intention of the sale is simply to give a good & valid title to a bona fide purchaser upon surrender of the land grant bonds. It is said that Gray has negotiated the same to Mr. Tom Scott but the terms I do not know.
>
> I write in haste but you will not mistake my meaning. Namely to see that the trustees of the land grant bonds become the purchasers in trust for the bondholders of the property, franchise, *etc.*, that are to be sold under decree of court.[51]

Swenson then talked with Gray, who, of course, already had his foreclosure papers and a court decree but no new order from Judge Bradley. Swenson had to agree, reluctant or not, but he told Gray he was sending Epperson to bid in the property. Gray, however, thought that someone not connected with the company should become the os-

[50] *Ibid.*

[51] Swenson to Epperson, May 15, 1872, Epperson Papers.

tensible purchaser of the property, and to effect this they decided on Judge E. L. Fancher, who would send someone to act for him at the sale. On the same day that this agreement was made, May 21, 1872, Fancher executed a deed of trust stating that "he held title to the property and franchises in his name for the purpose of conveying the same as the Court might direct for the benefit of the French bondholders." And on that same day Swenson wrote Epperson to be present at the sale, and in the event that Fancher's representative should be delayed on the road and fail to reach Paris in time for the sale, Epperson was to bid in the property in Fancher's name and see that the U.S. marshal's conveyances were properly made.[52]

Epperson wrote Handley S. Bennett of Paris, a stockholder and former president of the Memphis, El Paso, and Pacific, then a very old man, to represent the company at the sale. Bennett answered on May 27 that he could not be in Paris on that date and hoped Epperson would. Whether or not Epperson was present has not been ascertained. The important thing was that Fancher was Gray's man and worked for him on all occasions, as, for instance, when he was Jessie Frémont's counsel but was really working for Gray. With collusion between Gray and Fancher, the bondholders' interests would not be adequately protected.

Fancher's representative bid in the property and executed official deeds of conveyance covering the following franchises and property.

I. Franchise, rights, and privileges of the Memphis, El Paso, and Pacific conferred by Acts of the state of Texas.

II. All and singular chartered rights and privileges of the Memphis, El Paso, and Pacific, or rights acquired by contract or consolidation.

III. All and singular railroad, roadbed, and tract of said Memphis, El Paso, and Pacific, with all lands, premises, right of way, easements, property, tools, rolling stock, materials, and equipment then owned by the company, and all maps and field notes pertaining to it.

IV. All lands belonging to the Memphis, El Paso, and Pacific on February 14, 1867, and thereafter to May 1, 1872, owned or acquired by the company and all rights to acquire land in the state.

[52] Swenson to Epperson, May 21, 1872, *ibid.* Fancher was at that time the arbitration judge of the Chamber of Commerce of New York City.

V. Land belonging to the Memphis, El Paso, and Pacific on December 23, 1868, and thereafter to May, 1872, conveyed by the five deeds of foreclosure:

(1) John S. Bland, sheriff of Lamar County, June 4, 1872, to party of first part, Enoch L. Fancher

(2) Thomas F. Purnell, marshal of U.S. Circuit Court of the Western District of Texas, June 4, 1872 (the Harrison mortgage—John S. Messenger)

(3) Thomas F. Purnell, August 6, 1872 (the construction mortgage—G. W. Wright)

(4) Thomas F. Purnell, June 4, 1872 (the first land-grant mortgage—Louis Bizion)

(5) Thomas F. Purnell, June 4, 1872 (the second land-grant mortgage—O. Tamin Despalles).[53]

Fancher paid $80,000 for the Harrison mortgage; $5,000 for the construction mortgage; $2,500 for the first and second land-grant mortgages; and $3,000 for some small judgments against the company.[54] The judgments were in favor of some of the original stockholders, and Epperson, in his correspondence with Gray, had insisted on their payment. Besides the charter, franchises, and land grants, Fancher acquired fifty-five miles of graded roadbed, about six miles of line, bridged and tied, on three of which the iron had been laid, three locomotives, and 284 land certificates, according to the statement of President Thomas A. Scott of the Texas and Pacific Company.[55] The 284 certificates must have included the 200 purchased from the Texas and New Orleans and the Memphis, El Paso, and Pacific certificates

[53] Enoch L. Fancher, Trustee, and John A. C. Gray, Receiver of the Memphis, El Paso, and Pacific Railroad Company and Trustee of the Texas and Pacific Railway Company, "Articles of Agreement," *Memphis, El Paso, and Pacific Railroad Company Records, 1856–1877.*

[54] Pierre Fayolle *et al. v.* the Texas and Pacific Railway Company, Equity 6556, Supreme Court of the District of Columbia, November 12, 1883, National Archives, Washington, D.C.

[55] *Annual Report of the Board of Directors of the Texas and Pacific Railway Company, August 10, 1875.*

which had not yet been assigned. Throckmorton had written Epperson about the last 72 Texas and New Orleans certificates which the surveyor Metcalf had just located. They were blank transfers, he said, and if they were not assigned to the company, Gray would steal either them or the land as soon as he got control.[56] William M. Walton's Austin law firm was holding these T & N O certificates on deposit. He too wrote Epperson and said if they could be gobbled legitimately, he would like to gobble part of them.[57]

Gray was now ready to begin his negotiations with the Texas and Pacific. With the foreclosure he had eliminated the Texas stockholders and destroyed the last vestige of Frémont's interest in the Memphis, El Paso, and Pacific. He had settled with Campbell and Gentry for $10,000, and Judge Bradley, in May 1872, had dissolved the injunction obtained by former-directors J. J. Van Nest and James T. Sandford, who charged that they had been defrauded on the grounds that the directors and stockholders had not been consulted about the receivership, that the proceedings were conducted principally in the state of New Jersey when the venue of action was laid in Texas, and that Epperson, Frémont, Daniel, and Schmoele had conspired to get possession of the company's assets and convert them to their individual use, having obtained possession of a large amount of the mortgage bonds for which they had paid in property of the company. Judge Bradley also had refused to recognize the cross bill filed by Roger Fowler, Abraham Rex, and George W. Gerrish, the assignee of Thomas McDowell, claiming they had furnished $50,000 earnest money and had built a portion of the road.[58] In response to detailed instructions from Gray and Davenport, both Epperson and Daniel had given their affidavits to refute these claims. Epperson believed that Frémont was the instigator of the suit by Van Nest and Sandford, whose counsel was Cortlandt Parker, but Davenport wrote Epperson that there was no evidence to support his theory. The Supreme Court had not rendered

[56] Throckmorton to Epperson, April 24, 1872, Epperson Papers.

[57] William Walton to Epperson (n.d.), *ibid.*

[58] Forbes *et al. v.* The Memphis, El Paso and Pacific Company *et al., Federal Cases*, No. 4926; also in 2 *Woods* 223.

its decision on the reservation, but the case had been argued in January, and it was thought Gray would win.

Pending the Supreme Court decision and the settlement to be made with the French, Scott received temporary possession of the railroad, and Gray and Fancher, on October 22, 1872, drew up an indenture whereby all the property and franchises of the Memphis, El Paso, and Pacific would be conveyed to the Texas and Pacific for the sum of $150,000 subject to certain covenants and agreements. In this indenture the French bondholders were offered three propositions. (1) On the tender to the company at its office in New York of any or all the land-grant bonds on the Memphis, El Paso, and Pacific with coupons payable on or after January 1, 1871, attached, the Texas and Pacific would exchange 13 acres of land in the state of Texas for each $100 bond, exclusive of interest and the total not to exceed $5,400,000 in bonds, for which exchange 700,000 acres would be reserved. The bondholders would have the preferential right of selecting choice lands upon the odd surveys of the Memphis, El Paso, and Pacific reservation within ninety days after the delivery of locatable and patentable certificates, to be held in trust for the bondholders. (2) The Texas and Pacific would exchange its own land-grant bonds in the amount of $4,000,000 for the Memphis, El Paso, and Pacific land-grant bonds in the amount of $5,400,000, exclusive of interest, provided that the whole of $4,000,000 in Texas and Pacific bonds was taken. (3) In case of the execution and delivery of a contract for the sale of its first mortgage construction bonds, the Texas and Pacific would give in exchange its land-grant bonds (already secured by a mortgage on record) at the rate of $32 for every $100 of the principal sum expressed in the land-grant bonds, exclusive of interest. Every holder of land-grant bonds was entitled to exchange at his option, according to Articles I, II, or III, with the Texas and Pacific to become the bona fide owner of bonds so exchanged. And, by any of these arrangements, plus $150,000 in cash paid to the receiver, the Texas and Pacific would succeed to a pro rata share of the assets of the Memphis, El Paso, and Pacific Railway Company. At this time negotiations had already been entered into between the Texas and Pacific and John Harold of London, England, Ernest Frignet of Paris, and Robert E. Randall of Philadelphia, Pennsylvania, whereby the second or third proposition might be carried out.[59]

With the Texas and Pacific already in possession of the railroad, the California and Texas Railway Construction Company had gone to work on October 1, 1872. This company, first incorporated as the Domain Land Company in Pennsylvania, had been reorganized on June 17, 1872, for the express purpose of building the Texas and Pacific railroad. On August 6, 1872, the Texas and Pacific stockholders agreed to exchange their shares dollar for dollar for all the paid-in stock of the Construction Company, which then became the owner of the Texas and Pacific Railway Company, whose directors retained only enough of the capital stock to give them a legal basis for operations.[60]

Frémont was now on very shaky ground with the Texas and Pacific. Since the California and Texas Construction Company had taken over the railroad, it was an easy matter for Benjamin H. Bristow,[61] its president, to disregard any gentleman's agreement previously made by Tom Scott. Soon called on for payments on his supposedly paid-up stock Frémont managed to raise only $30,000. Judge Holly wrote him that "Bristow was insisting," and it was then that the Frémonts began to sell their possessions—the Brownstone mansion in New York, the Humboldt library, Audubon paintings, sailboats, and horses, and finally "Pocaho," their fine summer home on the Hudson, which was in Jessie Frémont's name. Bristow kept insisting on payments which Frémont could not make although he continued to hold some bonds for several years.[62]

[59] Articles of Agreement, *Memphis, El Paso, and Pacific Records.*

[60] Samuel B. McAlister, "The Building of the Texas and Pacific Railway" (M.A. thesis).

[61] Grant created the new office of solicitor general for Bristow, but he resigned to accept this highly paid position with the Texas and Pacific. Preferring legal to administrative work, he returned to the practice of law. Grant appointed him Secretary of the Treasury on July 3, 1874 (*Dictionary of American Biography*, III, 55–56.)

[62] House, "Post-Civil War Precedents for Recent Railroad Reorganization," *Mississippi Valley Historical Review,* XXV (March 1939). But not all the Frémont treasures were sold. Many choice books, pictures, and other valuable things were stored in Morrell's "fireproof warehouse" in New York when the

In desperation both the Frémonts filed suits against the Texas and Pacific Company in New York City: Frémont for $125,000 for expenditures and expenses beginning in December, 1869, and ending April 25, 1871; Jessie Benton Frémont for $90,000, the money said to have been loaned to certain parties. Samuel W. Morton had already filed suit against the Southern Transcontinental for expenditures and personal services rendered between January 1870 and March 1871, amounting to $23,000; and against Marshall O. Roberts and the Texas and Pacific for $95,000.[63] By these suits Frémont and Morton hoped to block the proposed reorganization and force the Texas and Pacific to honor its former agreements.

The most paralyzing blow came to the Frémonts on March 27, 1873, when a decree against all parties in the case of the "American Memphis, El Paso Transcontinental Railway for Swindling" was rendered in M. Chevillote's court in Paris. Auferman, Frémont, and Henry Probst were sentenced to five years imprisonment and a fine of 3,000 francs; Crampton to four years and a fine of 3,000 francs; Boilleau, though he returned $150,000 to the company, to three years and a fine of 3,000 francs; Lissignol to two years and a fine of 3,000 francs; Pompinel to one year and a fine of 3,000 francs.[64] General Gustave Paul Cluseret, the New York correspondent of Henry Rochefort's *La Marseillaise*,[65] was exposed by the trials and expelled from France on a twenty-four hour notice.[66] It was reported that Frémont could not be

---

Frémonts left for Arizona in 1878. They were lost when the building burned in 1881 (Dallas *Daily Herald*, December 9, 1886).

[63] Frank S. Bond, *Statement and Argument Made before the Committee on the Judiciary of the House of Representatives, 44th Congress, 1st Session*, 1876.

[64] *Ibid.*

[65] *Flake's Daily Bulletin*, January 28, 1870.

[66] San Antonio *Daily Herald*, February 21, 1870. Rochefort was known as the scandalmonger of the "red-backed" population in France. Cluseret, once a major in the French army, entered the U.S. federal service and fought so gallantly during the Civil War that President Lincoln caused him to be made a general. The coming of peace threw him out of work so he cast himself into the arms of Fenianism and turned up in London as the commander-in-chief of the Fenians who were trying to shatter the tyranny of the Saxons. He appeared as an extreme agitator at Lyons and Marseilles, and in 1871 was a prominent

found. As France had an extradition treaty with the United States, some thought he had taken refuge in Mexico with whom France had no such treaty.[67]

On April 16, 1873, the Supreme Court of the United States announced its opinion sustaining the charter, land grant, and land reservation of the Memphis, El Paso, and Pacific, and enjoining the governor of Texas and the commissioner of the Texas General Land Office from interfering with or infringing upon the company's lands.[68] The decision placed Gray in a commanding position. He alone held title to the land, charter, and franchises of the Memphis, El Paso, and Pacific, which the Texas and Pacific had to have to get across Texas. Scott completed the deal with Gray on June 12, 1873, and it must have been a hard bargain. Long annoyed with Gray's arrogance, Scott made the statement that "nothing would please him better than to witness Gray's destruction."[69]

The conveyance of the Memphis, El Paso, and Pacific and all its assets, including 211½ land certificates, was executed according to the terms of the first proposition set forth in the indenture, but the payment of the $150,000 was delayed. The deed was held in escrow by

---

general under Dombrowski in the Paris insurrection. When the Commune was suppressed and Marshal MacMahon and Thiers entered Paris, Dombrowski was shot. Cluseret, tried for complicity with the Germans, was cleared (Washington *Daily Morning Chronicle*, May 2, 1871). Cluseret had been made a citizen of the United States by an Act of Congress. During the Civil War he had served on the staffs of Frémont and McClellan.

[67] San Antonio *Daily Herald*, April 4, 1873.

[68] E. J. Davis *v.* John A. C. Gray, 16 *Wallace* 203. The United States Supreme Court found that the company had performed all of the conditions prescribed by the Act of February 4, 1846, except those rendered impossible by Texas' entrance in the Civil War. It then held that the provisions of the Ordinance of August 29, 1868, and the Constitution of 1869, insofar as they attempted to abridge the Memphis, El Paso, and Pacific Railway Company's land reservation and grant were null and void, because they were contrary to Section 10 of Article 1 of the United States Constitution which prohibits any state from passing an act which would impair the obligations of a contract.

[69] House, "Post-Civil War Precedents for Recent Railroad Reorganization," *Mississippi Valley Historical Review*, XXV (March 1939).

the Farmers Loan and Trust Company of New York, awaiting this payment, in whole or in part, which would be delivered within twelve months with interest of 7 per cent. All land-grant bonds to be exchanged under the contract would be deposited with the banking firm of Duncan, Sherman & Company of New York until the patents were delivered. The Texas and Pacific would have the option of assigning to the receiver a pro rata share of the Memphis, El Paso, and Pacific assets in lieu of part or full payment of the $150,000.[70] At the time of the foreclosures, 284 certificates were transferred to Fancher. Now there were only 211½. In the process of his trading with the Texas and Pacific, Gray may have been the one who "gobbled" the other 72½.[71]

In his all powerful position, Gray went to work on Epperson, who had refused to pay $123,279, the amount the company owed the receiver according to Gray's audit of 1870.[72] Furthermore, when the trials in France were over, the French court had forwarded Probst's Memphis, El Paso, and Pacific books to Gray, and he had increased the amount to $174,230 because of several errors discovered as well as the $40,900 which Frémont had sent to Epperson in May and June of 1869 and which had not been rendered on the statement submitted to the auditor by Epperson.[73] Gray delegated Henry Brace to make a satisfactory settlement. When Epperson claimed additional allowances, Brace credited him with two judgments, some notes and cash, and a legal fee of $750 and released him on August 4, 1873.[74] Gray wired on August 8: "I hereby notify you that I repudiate the settlement made with Brace as unauthorized by me. I have telegraphed to begin suit

70 "Articles of Agreement," 1–19, *Memphis, El Paso, and Pacific Records.*

71 Throckmorton to Epperson, April 24, 1872, Epperson Papers; William Walton to Epperson (n.d.), *ibid.*

72 Exhibit A, Account Current: May 26, 1869, to January 7, 1870, Epperson Papers.

73 Gray to Epperson, July 21, 1873, *ibid.* In one of Epperson's numerous memoranda, he noted $17,900 as Frémont's salary but did not include it in the audit.

74 Release signed by Henry Bruce, August 4, 1873, in Exhibit A, Account Current, *ibid.*

unless my ultimatum is complied with." Gray had accepted some of the allowances sanctioned by Brace but was demanding payment of the Ives claim in addition to the $40,900. He sued Epperson in the District Court at Tyler and lost his case on April 28, 1875. During the course of this trial, Epperson's lawyer searched the court records at Tyler for Gray's settlement with Frémont but was unable to find it.

Apparently, A. G. Curtin and S. M. Swenson received some compensation as trustees of the Memphis, El Paso, and Pacific mortgages because Swenson wrote Governor Pease on October 1, 1875, that any documents or necessary proof of their services would be furnished, and both expected him "to attend to the matter as soon as possible."[75] Swenson's relations with Gray being somewhat strained, it probably seemed more suitable for Pease to request this compensation, especially since he was one of the company's Texas solicitors.

Epperson had moved to Jefferson in 1875, against the advice of Throckmorton who told him that the town would soon be dead. However, Epperson did not live to see the Queen City of East Texas waste away; he died on September 6, 1878, at the age of fifty-three, from nervous prostration and overwork.[76] In February of that year Epperson had attended a meeting of Memphis and Little Rock stockholders and spent two days examining the books and accounts. He came to the

[75] Swenson to E. M. Pease, October 1, 1875, Pease Papers, Austin Public Library.

[76] Galveston *Daily News*, September 7, and September 13, 1878. Benjamin Holland Epperson was born in Amite County, Mississippi, on November 3, 1824. He entered Princeton University as a junior but left before graduation. He moved to Texas in 1841, studied law, and was admitted to the bar. He was the unsuccessful Whig candidate for governor in 1851 and served intermittently in the Texas Legislature from 1853 until his death. Epperson was a strong Unionist but never a radical, and in 1866, when he was elected to the U.S. House of Representatives, the radical Republican Congress did not permit him to take his seat. Epperson's business interests were extensive and varied. He did not put all his money into the Memphis and Little Rock. Among other things he owned stock in the Southern Pacific of Texas (probably exchanged for Texas and Pacific stock with the merger), Houston and Texas Central bonds, and a plantation in Brazoria County.

conclusion that the property was valuable and that, in the end, it would pay;[77] but in this he was not entirely correct. The Memphis and Little Rock was a short road of five-foot gauge, extending from Little Rock to Hopefield, Arkansas (135 miles). It was chartered on January 11, 1853, sold on foreclosure in 1873 for default on its first mortgage land-grant bonds, reorganized and sold out in April, 1877, when it failed to pay bond interest. The property was purchased on account of the bondholders and conveyed to them on September 29, 1877. It was the following February that Epperson attended the stockholders meeting in Little Rock. Although Poor's *Manual of Railroads* for 1880 showed that the net earnings of the Memphis and Little Rock grew from $116,417 to $303,998 through 1878, 1879, and 1880, Governor Pease sold all his stock and bonds at $.50 in 1879 and Swenson a portion of his at the same price. Then in 1880 the Memphis and Little Rock was purchased by the St. Louis and Iron Mountain and Southern, already owned by Jay Gould. In 1882 it went into the hands of a receiver, previous to its final absorption by Gould's Missouri and Pacific chain in 1886. Epperson, however, had lived to build his own railroad, the East Line and Red River,[78] of which William M. Harrison was president and Epperson a director. Harrison and Epperson were almost the exclusive owners of the East Line road, and they each had $50,000 of paid-up stock in the Texas and Pacific Company.[79] Harrison became a director of the Texas and Pacific in 1875 and continued to hold that position until 1880.

James M. Daniel returned to Paris, Texas, in 1876, after the completion of the T & P main line to Sherman. In 1878, he and his associates chartered and built the city's street railway. It ran from the

[77] Epperson to Swenson, February 22, 1878, Pease Papers.

[78] The East Line and Red River was incorporated on March 22, 1871, and authorized to construct a railroad and telegraph line from Jefferson in Marion County to Sherman in Grayson County, and thence northwest to the western boundary of the state (Gammel, *Laws of Texas,* VI, 1188). This railroad, in 1878, had sixty miles in operation and extended to a point ten miles west of Pittsburg (Galveston *Daily News*, September 15, 1878). The East Line and Red River was acquired by the Texas and Pacific by lease or private sale in 1881.

[79] Galveston *Daily News*, April 17, 1878.

T & P station to and around the square and hauled passengers and freight, small mules being the motive power. The company was capitalized for $20,000, and half the stock was owned by Daniel.[80] Though Paris was his home, Daniel was extensively engaged in silver mining in Colorado and Mexico for twenty-five years. He died in Paris on April 7, 1916 (*The Paris Morning News*, April 8, 1916).

On May 2, 1873, the Texas Legislature had passed a comprehensive act which settled all the complicated legal questions arising from previous legislation and set forth the specific objectives of the successor company. The Texas and Pacific was authorized to construct a branch line from Marshall by way of Jefferson to connect with its main line not more than six miles west of Texarkana. Its main line was to be projected westward from Texarkana to Sherman and thence southward via Denton to the junction point near Fort Worth. The line of the Southern Pacific route was to be extended westward from Longview to the junction point. A single line was to be built westward from the junction point to the Rio Grande near El Paso. The branch line, or eastern leg of the parallelogram, was to be completed by August 1, 1873, the northern leg by July 1, 1874, the western leg by January 1, 1875, and the southern leg by July 1, 1874. Construction west of the junction point was to proceed at the rate of one hundred miles per year. The act provided that if the company should fail to complete any portion of this construction it would forfeit its land grant, except for lands donated for portions theretofore completed. In lieu of all other donations made to its predecessors, the Texas and Pacific was to receive twenty alternate sections for every mile of main or branch line completed in good substantial running order. By this increased land donation, the old Memphis, El Paso, and Pacific reservation between the 100th meridian and the southeast corner of New Mexico was increased to forty miles on each side of the center line.[81]

The California and Texas Construction Company, by the end of

80 Alexander White Neville, *History of Lamar County*, p. 175.

81 Gammel, *Laws of Texas*, VII, 1018. This legislation was permitted by constitutional amendment of March 19, 1873, which allowed the Legislature to encourage railroad construction by making land grants not to exceed twenty sections for each mile constructed (*ibid.*, VII, 676).

October, 1873, had completed 195.3 miles of road, including 11.8 miles of sidings and turnouts, 74.5 miles from Longview to Dallas, 66.2 miles on the Jefferson Division from Marshall to Texarkana, and 42.8 miles from Sherman east to Honey Grove.[82] By that date Scott had more than enough certificates to meet the terms of the agreement with Gray, but he chose to postpone the settlement until he had first located 1,256 certificates for the Texas and Pacific Company: 256 of these certificates were limited to the company's reservation; 1,000 could be located within the reservation or on any part of the vacant public domain. With this wide choice the company made its selections along the future line of the railroad, along the river fronts, in the fertile plains, in timber lands, and in the rich, populous, and productive regions where the road was already built. Surveyors began to make the locations in July, 1873, after they had surveyed and monumented the center line formerly designated by the Memphis, El Paso, and Pacific. At the same time Scott publicly announced that although the Texas and Pacific was in no way implicated with the Memphis, El Paso, and Pacific, he was offering to indemnify the French bondholders. A Paris journal, with obvious irony, commended Scott's judgment and foresight in maintaining American good faith and good credit before the bonds of another American railway should be offered in Europe. The Galveston *Daily News* commented that all the French bondholders understood about the matter was that it was the same road they had put their money into, and they would therefore consider themselves juggled out of it if no return was made to them.[83]

On November 4, 1873, all operations, except the completion of the last 7.8 miles to Texarkana, were halted by the general depression known as the "Panic of 1873,"[84] and the Texas and Pacific was threat-

[82] C. D. Anderson's Inspection Report, November 28, 1873, File 11, Railroad Contracts, General Land Office.

[83] Galveston *Daily News*, July 8, 1873.

[84] A general financial panic was precipitated on September 18, 1873, when Jay Cooke & Company of New York closed its doors, having invested too heavily in the Northern Pacific Railroad. Generally the panic was caused by the reckless development of the country's railroad system beyond its demands and capacity. *The Nation*, on September 25, 1873, ascribed the panic to the "clos-

ened with the forfeiture of its land grant unless construction could be resumed. The company was temporarily protected by the one-year extension granted on April 30, 1874, for the completion of all internal improvements,[85] but without funds or credit little could be done. The contract with the Construction Company had been cancelled in March, 1874, and Scott, working independently, managed to grade about 11 miles west from Sherman and to build about 8 miles west from Dallas by the end of the year. The southern line then extended to Eagle Ford, 27 miles east of Fort Worth, where the western terminus remained for more than two years—to the despair of the citizens of Fort Worth, who organized the Tarrant County Construction Company and tried, without success, to bring the road into the city.[86]

On August 4, 1874, William A. Wallace, vice-president of the Texas and Pacific Railway Company, authorized the commissioner of the Texas General Land Office to deliver one thousand T & P certificates to John A. C. Gray, or to his order. Gray requested that they be delivered to Henry Brace, who requested that they be delivered to Raymond & Whitis, and on August 27, 1874, Raymond & Whitis gave a receipt for certificates numbered 2/257 through 2/1256 and covering 640,000 acres of land.[87] Gray was to locate these certificates within the old Memphis, El Paso, and Pacific reservation, and on completion of the surveys to return the field notes to the Land Office for patenting. The patents would be issued to the Fidelity Insurance, Trust and Safe Deposit Company of Philadelphia and held in trust awaiting the final disposition of the French bondholders. However, Gray had long since conceived another ingenious idea—the formation of a land company to liquidate the Texas property to be transferred to the French. He and others could buy Memphis, El Paso, and Pacific bonds for a few cents on the dollar and become stockholders in the land company

ing of the English markets to American railroad securities under the repeated influence of repeated cases of American rascality such as the Emma Mine fathered by General Schenck and Frémont's swindling Texas enterprise, and the default made by several new roads in the payment of their coupons."

85 Gammel, *Laws of Texas*, VIII, 179.

86 Buckley B. Paddock (ed.), *A History of Central and West Texas*, I, 250.

87 File 11, Railroad Contracts.

he himself would charter, organize, regulate, and supervise behind the scenes.

At this time public confidence in the Texas and Pacific was at a low level, and Scott could not sell his bonds in the United States. Failing also in Europe, he petitioned the federal government for a $60,000,000 subsidy over and above the land grant in Texas and the territories—a subsidy said to be twice the cost of building the railroad.[88] While this legislation was pending those French bondholders who had not agreed to Gray's proposal and who preferred some satisfaction other than land sent representatives to try to force a better bargain with Scott. The group employed Benjamin F. Butler and Caleb Cushing as counsel and the Marquis de Chambrun as agent. Chambrun, then attached to the French legation in Washington, organized a lobby and began a newspaper campaign against Scott's request for congressional aid to the Texas and Pacific. He also threatened to extradite Frémont to France for criminal prosecution.[89]

Under these circumstances a curious thing happened. Frémont, already frozen out of the Texas and Pacific by assessments on his supposedly paid-up stock, joined forces with Chambrun in the campaign against the company. Jessie Benton Frémont deliberated at length on the advisability of following such a course. She investigated Chambrun thoroughly and decided, after consultation with old friends and lawyers, that she would not be compromising her own and her husband's position. The Frémonts had been outmaneuvered in the legal field, but they still had friends in Congress, and they felt that by entering the political arena they could block the subsidy and force a settlement with the Texas and Pacific.

Eastern newspapers objected to the subsidy and joined in the sensational fight against it. Under the headline *Credit Mobilier Eclipsed*, the unfortunate history of the Memphis, El Paso, and Pacific was laid bare in a broadside issued by the New York *Sun* on February 1, 1875. In a subsequent edition the editor, Charles Dana, had much to say

[88] *House Reports of Committees*, 45th Congress, 2nd Session, Serial No. 1822, Vol. 2, No. 238, "Views of the Minority."

[89] House, "Post-Civil War Precedents for Recent Railway Reorganization," *Mississippi Valley Historical Review*, XXV (March, 1939).

about the acts of Judge Joseph P. Bradley.[90] Both Scott and Frémont resorted to letters to the press. In the melee even Washburne, of all people, was charged with receiving $10,000 for his official influence in getting the Frémont bonds on the Paris Bourse. The New York *Herald* printed his denial saying that the charges were false and atrocious, that the parties who put the bonds on the market were furious with him for giving information as to their true character, and that Frémont published a pamphlet on the subject, arraigning him for discrediting a great American enterprise. The *Herald* expressed its firm belief in Washburne's courage, frankness, and patriotism.[91] In Congress the issue was sharply drawn, and almost every member was forced to make a definite stand on the subsidy. Nathaniel Paige reported the congressional situation in his statement to the *Sun*:

> Before the passage of the Pacific Railroad bill in March, 1871, the friends of Thomas A. Scott determined to control the enterprise and throw Fremont out in the cold. This was accomplished by having it understood that after passage of the bill and the organization of the company a construction company would be formed and a contract entered into with the Texas and Pacific Company for building the road, from which very large profits would be made.
>
> After the passage of the bill a large number of members of Congress became directly or indirectly interested in said construction company, and but for the privilege of taking stock in said company never would have voted for the said bill. Gen. Butler took a very large quantity of the stock and was conspicuous in his efforts to secure the passage of the bill; and was also known on the floor of the House as the leader and wire-puller of the Tom Scott faction.
>
> The chief reliance of Scott is now upon the stockholders of the California and Texas Construction Company in the House and Senate. An honest investigation would show that several millions of stock are held by Senators and members or their near confidential friends and relatives; and also that Fremont originally controlled the Senate through stock held by senators in another road.[92]

[90] The Senate, in 1870, had refused to add Bradley's name to the list of incorporators.

[91] New York *Herald*, February 12, 1875 (article and editorial).

[92] New York *Sun*, February 1, 1875 (broadside).

These articles in the press were very hard on Frémont and his wife, and the attendant strain was beginning to take its toll. Just at this time a Washington correspondent wrote:

I saw General Fremont in the lobby of the House yesterday. He is now old and bent. His face is deeply chiseled by the harrowing hand of time. His eyes are slightly bleary; cheek bones stand out as prominent as those of a Sioux chief. Iron gray whiskers, short and stubby, closely trimmed down from the base of the jawbone, grow upon his thin neck. His dark hair is yet a dark iron gray and is worn quite long. It is combed well forward, and hangs down in front of his ears. A well worn beaver, set well upon his head, a bright comforter, a gray tweed light overcoat, and a dark suit of underclothing made up the general articles of his attire. He looks like a whimsical, fussy old man, and little like the hero of the Rocky Mountains, whose pictures during the Presidential campaign of 1856, always represented him with long curls, in the garb of a Western frontiersman, riding apace upon a fiery charger, breathing the smoke and fire of a bloody war. It is said that Fremont is trying to get some allowance for his past services.[93]

The allowance sought may have been for "Black Point," the Frémonts' San Francisco home which had been confiscated in the Civil War, and for which they never ceased trying to get compensation from Congress.

The Texas Legislature, by the Act of March 15, 1875, extended the time for the completion of the construction obligations of the Texas and Pacific Company for a period of six months, provided that within twelve months after the completion of the southern line to Fort Worth, the said company would build the railroad to Weatherford and thereafter proceed with construction at the rate of forty miles per year, or eighty miles each two years, until reaching the Rio Grande; provided further that it would have but six months additional time on that part of the line between Eagle Ford and Fort Worth and between Brookston and Texarkana; and provided further that it would construct and put in running order as much as twenty miles of road between Brookston and Texarkana by November 1, 1875.[94]

In order to resume construction and save its grant, the Texas and

[93] *West Texas Free Press* (San Marcos), April 3, 1875, "Washington Letter."

[94] Gammel, *Laws of Texas*, VIII, 558.

Pacific, on March 27, 1875, again entered into a contract with the California and Texas Construction Company by which it mortgaged its completed line and anticipated earnings. Certain segments of its main line between Brookston and Texarkana and the line between Eagle Ford and Fort Worth were to be constructed for the consideration of $8,000 per mile first mortgage and $17,000 per mile second mortgage.[95] The first and second mortgage bonds were to be exchanged for the old bonds held by the Construction Company in payment for work done before the Panic. "The railway then became the owner of the indebtedness of the Construction Company which was really its own."[96]

In view of the urgent need for the subsidy and in the face of the violent criticism of its supporters, Scott changed his petition to Congress to a request for a guarantee of 5 per cent interest annually for fifty years on $38,000,000, covering costs of $25,000 a mile for the easier construction and $40,000 for the heavier portions of the road. Admittedly, this was a change in form rather than in substance, but it was thought that the Pacific Railroad Committees were in favor of the road and that Scott's bill would pass in spite of the fact that Chambrun's exposure had undermined his legal right to the Memphis, El Paso, and Pacific charter.

Texas and Pacific officials were then dividing their attention between the subsidy in Washington and another time extension in Texas. President Scott and Vice-Presidents Frank S. Bond and John C. Brown appeared before the House and Senate Committees on Pacific Railroads to urge the passage of the company's bill. Collis P. Huntington, then building a southern railroad with private capital, was protesting to the same committees against congressional aid to a competitor building over the same ground. Scott, supremely confident, was leading the fight with all his resources, but he thought Huntington was the hardest block he had yet come up against. When Scott said, "We are beating you," Huntington had replied, "Yes, that is the way I should state it because

[95] J. J. Bowden, "The Texas and Pacific Railway Company Reservation and Land Grant," *Report of the Eleventh Annual Texas Surveyors Association*, p. 53.

[96] McAlister, "The Building of the Texas and Pacific Railway" (M.A. thesis).

you are beating me out of nine things and I shall only beat you in one. You will beat me in demoralizing the press; you will beat me in sending colporteurs over the United States to get petitions to your bill; you will beat me in getting Boards of Trade; you will beat me in this and that, but in building the road, in that one thing I shall beat you." Scott's attack before the House Committee on Railroads on January 19, 1876, was strong, but that of Bond before the Senate Committee on March 10, 1876, was brutal. He accused Huntington and his partners of negligence, mismanagement, fraud, swindling, cheating, bribery, and dishonesty. This intense rivalry between Scott and Huntington developed into a personal and lasting feud which produced reams of scurrilous copy for the newspapers. In the opinion of a Texas editor, if half of what they, or their partisans, said about each other were true, both should have been in the penitentiary.

In the contest between the "King of Thieves" and the "California Charlatan," the old Memphis, El Paso, and Pacific bond scandal was again revived. Frémont's charges against the Texas and Pacific, coupled with the fact that this company had come into possession of the tainted merchandise of the Memphis, El Paso, and Pacific, provided grounds for an investigation by the House Judiciary Committee. When questioned closely about the sale of the bonds in Europe, Frémont told the same story he had told before. His company had sent them to M. J. Paradis of Paris, the head of the Bourse, who put them on the market with a declaration that they were guaranteed by the United States government. He not only did not advise such a declaration, but knew nothing about it until after it was made.[97] Marshall O. Roberts was called before the Judiciary Committee, and "his evidence was a general denial of Frémont's vagaries."[98] Representative Charles Morton furnished the Committee with a list of witnesses to prove that Frémont had paid out $170,000 in money and millions in promises to secure the charter of the Transcontinental road.[99] Frémont testified that he knew of no money being improperly spent to influence the passage of the bill and therefore could not give the Committee a list of the bene-

[97] San Antonio *Daily Herald*, February 23, 1876.

[98] Galveston *Daily News*, March 9, 1876.

[99] San Antonio *Daily Herald*, February 8, 1876.

ficiaries. Ultimately, however, he handed in a list of names which "rattled the dry bones of the Forty-first Congress." He admitted that $290,000 had been distributed among the members to help along his railroad scheme.[100]

Bond, in his appearance before the Judiciary Committee, said the investigation was instituted by Frémont after his attempts at blackmail and extortion had failed and his futile lawsuits had not forced the Texas and Pacific into an adjustment of his improper claims. In defense of the Texas and Pacific, Bond made it very plain that it had been necessary to get rid of Frémont because of his reputation, but he admitted that the arrangement with Gray was advantageous because (1) the price paid, $150,000, for the graded line, iron rails, and locomotives was fair (2) the exchange of bonds for land would encourage immigration (3) the honoring of the so-called French bonds would remove what was generally considered a stain upon American credit and would probably affect the credit of the Texas and Pacific Railway Company in future negotiations, and (4) the company would be able to secure without further litigation a considerable quantity of the most valuable land in the reservation, land that had been covered by certificates or patented to various parties under Article 10, Section 5, of the new state constitution, which, with the quantity reclaimed by certificates in the receiver's possession, would very nearly equal that required to exchange for bonds.[101]

Bond not only retold the facts and figures of the French bond scandal, he presented as evidence against Frémont a copy of M. Chevillote's sentence in the case against the "American Memphis, El Paso Transcontinental Railway Company for Swindling."

Back in Texas, the regular annual bill for a time extension to railroads again came before the Legislature. An amendment was offered whereby the Texas and Pacific would be excepted unless it relinquished its claim to its land reservation. There was strong opposition to the road in Texas at this time as Congress was then considering Scott's proposal to connect with the Atlantic and Pacific, whose unstated

[100] *Ibid.*, March 18, 1876.

[101] Quoting from President Thomas A. Scott in the *Annual Report of the Board of Directors* (T & P, 1875).

terminus on the Mississippi was suspected to be St. Louis—a red flag to all Southerners, who were determined not to let Scott build a feeder line to his Pennsylvania Central Railroad instead of connecting with New Orleans or some other Southern city. The legislative halls reverberated with the heated discussion. Senator A. W. Terrell, never a friend of the railroads, advised the state Senate that the Texas and Pacific had not built the twenty miles from Brookston by November 1, 1875, as required by the Act of March 15 of that year and had therefore forfeited its right to the land reservation.[102]

In his speech, delivered on July 19, 1876, he said (quoting from the summation made by Senator J. P. Douglas, who was on the Committee on Internal Improvements when the Texas and Pacific was first chartered):

> The "Southern Pacific," alias the "Vicksburg and El Paso," alias "Atlantic and Pacific" (and he might have said, alias "Texas Western"), has been chartered with a land grant for more than 20 years and has constructed only about 50 miles of road during that time. This *disreputable old concern has been sold out several times and has changed its name almost as often as it has victimized its friends.* The same and even more may be said of the "Transcontinental," *alias* "Memphis, El Paso, and Pacific." Its reputation for gigantic swindling is co-extensive with two continents, and considering its resources *it stands unrivalled as a public robber.* These rotten old concerns are now endeavoring to don the lion's skin under the new name of "Texas Pacific," but their old acquaintances will recognize them despite their new disguise.[103]

The Austin *Statesman*, normally a supporter of the Texas and Pacific road, but now accused of falling into the arms of the "immaculate

[102] The Constitutional Convention, in session in the fall of 1875, had passed an ordinance on November 23, stating that no company which had begun work in good faith should be considered as having lost any of its rights, privileges, or grants prior to the next session of the Legislature by virtue of lapse of time, provided no cause of forfeiture existed at the time the Act was passed, but since the cause for forfeiture existed before the passing of the ordinance, Terrell considered it to be without effect.

[103] Andrew Forest Muir, "The Thirty-second Parallel Pacific Railroad in Texas to 1872," (Ph.D. dissertation), p. 215.

Huntington," condemned the proposed time extension: "In the name of the people of Texas we ask that this timidity of lawgivers and injustice to the people be no longer tolerated. The contract was made with the Legislature; it has been broken for the sixth time; let the Legislature declare the lands forfeited and no longer tremble in the presence of corporate power."[104]

It was the opinion of the attorney general that the charter rights of the Texas and Pacific had expired but that the charter would remain in force until forfeiture was declared by the state. This left the matter up to the Legislature and no action was taken.

The Texas and Pacific, however, had another deadline to meet. It was trying desperately to build the road to Fort Worth to avoid another breach of its contract before the Legislature adjourned. The track reached Fort Worth at 11:23 A.M. on July 19, 1876—two days after the date called for in the contract. Vice-President John C. Brown and Chief Engineer D. W. Washburne had been on the ground day and night for two weeks, and Contractor Morgan Jones had not changed his clothes or gone to bed regularly during that time. The first train crossed Sycamore Creek on an improvised bridge and came in on a track which left the grade and followed a dirt road almost parallel to the line. The rails were spiked to ties laid on the ground and held in place by very large rocks picked up from the right of way. Lacking cannons, the citizens celebrated by firing anvils they had obtained from a blacksmith's shop.[105] The first passenger train ran on July 23. Two months later it was reported that the train was arriving in Fort Worth some time between midnight and daybreak, the exact time being an unknown quantity to be solved by experimental analysis. It was a common complaint. The old stages were considered more reliable, especially since the train always had to stop along the way while the crew cut wood.

When Thomas H. Murray inspected the road from Dallas to Fort Worth in September he reported that from Dallas for a distance of 2⅓ miles west the track was made of French iron, weighing seventy-two

[104] Austin *Statesman*, July 15, 1876.

[105] Buckley B. Paddock, *History of Texas: Fort Worth and the Texas Northwest Edition*, II, 611, 612.

pounds to the yard, and known as the Frémont iron.[106] This section had been completed with the money raised by a two million dollar bond sale, and it brought the total amount of road constructed to 404 miles, including 179.73 miles between Longview and Fort Worth, 155.12 miles between Texarkana and Sherman, and 69.05 miles between Marshall and Texarkana. For the construction of these 404 miles of track the Texas and Pacific received 8,083 certificates for 5,173,120 acres of land.[107]

[106] The rest of the iron was American, weighing fifty-six pounds to the yard (Thomas H. Murray's Inspection Report, File 11, Railroad Contracts).

[107] J. T. Robison, Report of Commissioner of the General Land Office, October 19, 1916, General Land Office, Austin, Texas. The Southern Pacific had already built the 40 miles between Marshall and Shreveport, completed July 28, 1866, and making a total of 444 miles. The 8,083 certificates did not include those received from the Southern Pacific, the Memphis, El Paso, and Pacific, or the Texas and New Orleans.

CHAPTER 3

A LAND COMPANY IS FORMED

On July 31 of 1876, the Texas and Pacific Company filed in the Texas General Land Office an assignment in trust, conveying to the Fidelity Insurance, Trust and Safe Deposit Company of Philadelphia all of its right and title to, and interest in the 1,000 located land certificates listed in the assignment, and authorizing the commissioner of the General Land Office to issue patents on them. The document was dated March 23, 1876, and was filed in the Land Office in lieu of an "informal transfer" bearing the same date, previously filed on April 13, 1876. The original assignment transferred certificates 257 to 1256 inclusive on the following conditions.

1. The Fidelity Insurance, Trust and Safe Deposit Company would cause patents to be issued in its name on lands located by John A. C. Gray, receiver, within ninety days, on the odd sections in the Memphis, El Paso, and Pacific reservation, these patents to be exchanged for bonds according to the contract of June 12, 1873.

2. The Trust Company would notify Duncan, Sherman & Company, John A. C. Gray, and the Texas and Pacific Railway Company of the receipt of the patents by notice in writing.

3. On tender to the Fidelity, at any time within 30 days after service

of said notice, of at least $4,117,900 in Memphis, El Paso, and Pacific land grant bonds with coupons attached (that amount being then on deposit with Duncan, Sherman & Company or with the receiver), the Fidelity would deliver in exchange for said bonds a conveyance of said lands at the rate of thirteen acres for every $100 bond of the principal sum expressed in the bonds; and an additional 90 days in which to accept the same terms (making 120 days in all) would be granted to parties holding other land-grant bonds. All bonds would at once become the property of the Texas and Pacific Railway Company, and be delivered when and as the exchanges were made. If delivery should be delayed either by the Texas and Pacific or by unforeseen circumstances, the time of said delay would be excepted from the period therein indicated.

4. After the expiration of 120 days, on proof of payment by the Texas and Pacific of all money expended on the contract of June 12, 1873, and properly chargeable thereto, the Trust Company would convey to the Texas and Pacific all the land for which bonds had not been tendered in exchange.[1]

In the second or corrected assignment the mode of transfer remained the same, but substitutions were made in the consecutive run of certificates for which receipt had formerly been given; 67 of the certificates, now already located, were removed from the original listing and replaced by the following: Nos. 2/1257 to 2/1295; 2/1593 to 2/1601; and 2/1603 to 2/1621, all dated October 25, 1874.[2] The 67 certificates removed and retained by the Texas and Pacific covered choice locations, many of them in the Eastern Division, or the "garden region," as Scott himself called it, and around which he had thrown his drag-net. The 67 substituted certificates, like the other 933, were located farther west in the unsettled Brazos and Pecos divisions, in Parker, Palo Pinto, Stephens, Shackelford, Jones, Fisher, Callahan,

[1] Assignment in Trust, March 23, 1876, *Memphis, El Paso, and Pacific Railroad Company Records, 1856–1877.*

[2] Miscellaneous Deeds 383, General Land Office. The other certificates assigned to the Fidelity were: 2/257 to 2/285; 2/288 to 2/298; 2/308 to 2/570; 2/584 to 2/742; 2/748 to 2/912; 2/920; 2/926 to 2/1124; 2/1128 to 2/1232; 2/1239; all inclusive and dated August 27, 1874, making 1,000 in all.

The seal of the Franco-Texan Land Company

Taylor, Nolan, and Mitchell counties with a few surveys overlapping into Denton and Scurry. The French were thus denied not only the first but also the second choice of lands in the reservation, and you might even say the third because when it was discovered that some of the land west of the Brazos was much better than had been expected —in fact some of it was quite good—the patents in this area were withheld from the Franco-Texan, and later, when the Fidelity returned some 70,000 acres to the Texas and Pacific it was these and other selections east of the Brazos which were returned.

In New York, on July 25, 1876, the charter of the Franco-Texan Land Company was drawn up without the participation of the French bondholders who had agreed to surrender their bonds for land and who, presumably, were the only stockholders. On August 7, 1876, John A. C. Gray, who was never in Texas, had the charter filed in the Secretary of State's office in Austin, Texas.

The Franco-Texan Land Company was incorporated under the laws of Texas with a capital stock not to exceed $5,340,000. This amount would be divided into shares of $100 each; the subscriptions would be payable only in patented lands within the state of Texas, transferred by the Texas and Pacific Railway Company for the benefit of the subscriber in exchange for land-grant bonds of the Memphis, El Paso, and Pacific Railroad. The incorporators were H. E. Alexander and S.

Pinkney Tuck of New York and Claiborne S. West and H. C. Withers of Austin, Texas. West was an attorney and H. C. Withers an agent of the Texas and Pacific Company. The thirteen original directors were:

H. E. Alexander, New York City
S. Pinkney Tuck, New York City
Claiborne S. West, Austin, Texas
H. C. Withers, Austin, Texas
C. G. Miller, New York City
Henry Brace, New York City
William M. Walton, Austin, Texas
Joseph Walker, Austin, Teaxs
F. W. Chandler, Austin, Texas
Irving Eggleston, Austin, Texas
John H. Cole, New York City
James H. Fay, New York City
W. H. Willis, New York City

The purposes of the company were (1) the acquisition, by purchase or otherwise, and the location and subdivision of lands, the management and leasing thereof, and the sale and conveyance of same in lots and subdivisions or otherwise; (2) the division of the net proceeds among owners of the capital stock of the company, and the distribution of said lands among the stockholders in exchange for the designated stock on terms to be determined by the company; (3) the promotion of immigration with a view to settlement, subdivision, and sale of any and all lands owned by the corporation.

The principal office for the transaction of business was at Dallas, Texas, but business could also be transacted in New York, Paris, France, or other places suitable to the interests of the corporation.

Stock certificates were to be issued in the name of the holder and detached from a book with stubs.

All dividends out of the proceeds of the sale of the land would be endorsed on the stock certificate at the time of payment. Each share of stock would be received at the Texas office in exchange for land at par, or $100, less the dividends paid, the price of the land being fixed so as to secure a prorata division of the lands or their value among the stockholders; the said stock not to be reissued by the company.

The term of the charter was twenty years, unless dissolved sooner.

A printed copy of the charter and by-laws of the Franco-Texan Land Company, published in Paris, France, with alternate pages in English and French, is to be found in the Texas State Archives. It bears no date, but it appears to be the first edition, that is, it contains the original or unamended by-laws. These by-laws consist of fifty-seven articles, covering the issuance of stock certificates and their liquidation, the administration of the company and duties of officers, stockholders' meetings, and land sales and dividends. Briefly reviewed, they show how Gray contrived to vest all power in the hands of the American directors and to make it as difficult as possible for an individual stockholder to get possession of his land. Subsequent amendments made it even more difficult.

The affairs of the company were to be administered by a board of directors, consisting of thirteen members, at least three of whom would reside in the United States. They would be chosen annually for the term of one year and could be reelected.

The board of directors would choose from its members a president, an executive committee composed of three members (all three residents of the United States, of which the president was an ex-officio member and therefore an American), and a finance committee of five members (all residing in France, of which the vice-president was an ex-officio member and therefore a Frenchman). The executive committee, nominated by the board of directors, would represent the company in the United States and would manage its business there. The French finance committee had no stated purpose or authority.

The board of directors would take care of the general management of the company. It would determine the wages, salaries, and fees of all officers; would name and dismiss the employees and agents of the company; would make all contracts, leases, purchases, and sales of land, and all loans and mortgages; would determine the price at which the property of the company in Texas might be sold and take all proper legal action in prosecution or defense of the company's rights; would prepare the accounts to be submitted to the stockholders' meetings and propose the amount of dividends to be distributed; would fix the order of business at all stockholders' meetings; and would devise the seal of the company. The board's powers for managing the affairs of the company were extensive, and those stated were not restrictive.

The board of directors would meet on the call of the president or vice-president or upon request of the majority of its members. A notice in writing indicating the place, day, hour, and object of the meeting would be sent by mail to each member of the board at least fifteen days prior to the date of the meeting. The notice to directors residing out of the country would be mailed forty days or cabled thirty days prior to the date of the meeting.

At a meeting of the board a majority of the directors would constitute a quorum.

Each director would receive a per diem for attendance at board meetings not to exceed $5.00.

The net amount on hand at the end of every year would be divided as follows: 5 per cent among the directors and 95 per cent among the stockholders; at the expiration of each term, half of the sum of 5 per cent allotted to the directors would be invested in government securities and distributed at the close of the company's transactions among all those who had been members of the board during the life of the company and according to the time they had been members of the board.

The board of directors would elect a president, vice-president, secretary, vice-secretary, treasurer, and vice-treasurer.

The president would preside at all meetings of the board of directors and stockholders; he would sign all contracts and other instruments authorized by the company and countersign all warrants drawn by the treasurer or vice-treasurer; he would have custody of the seal. If the majority of the directors resided in France, the vice-president would perform the duties of president there, signing in France the contracts and instruments authorized by the board of directors and countersigning the warrants to be delivered in France; he would have custody of a duplicate seal which he would have the power to affix to all documents emanating from the company.

The secretary would be an ex-officio member of the executive committee, and would, therefore, be an American. In case a meeting of the board of directors should be held in Paris, the vice-secretary would exercise all the functions of the secretary except to sign new stock certificates.

The board of directors might, whenever necessary, appoint a controller, who would reside wherever the principal office was located. He would serve largely in an advisory capacity, without a vote and independent of the executive committee.

Stockholders' meetings, to be held annually during the month of May, would be called by a notice either sent by mail or published in the newspapers at least thirty days before the meeting. A stockholders' meeting would be competent for the transaction of business when the stockholders present represented one-third of the capital stock of the company. In case this proportion did not attend at the first call, another meeting could be called in the same manner provided in the first case. The proceedings of the second meeting would be valid whatever the number of shares represented.

All resolutions would be decided by a majority of the votes of the members present or represented by proxy. Only a stockholder could act as proxy for another stockholder, and no proxy could represent more than a thousand votes.

No matters would be deliberated, over and above the regular order of business, unless communicated to the board ten days before the meeting and signed by at least ten stockholders.

Each stockholder would have one vote for each share of stock which was registered in his name on the books of the company when they were closed one month prior to such a meeting.

The lands of the company were to be sold for cash or on credit. The board of directors would request the executive committee to make a schedule of the minimum prices at which they might be sold; they could be mortgaged only to provide for indispensable expenses of the company. Dividends could be declared out of the net proceeds of sale or profits arising from any other sources; they would be paid on presentation of the stock certificates at the place indicated by public notice published in Paris, France; the amount and date of payment would be endorsed on the back of the certificate.

Any stockholder would have the right to exchange his stock for land at rates determined by the board of directors and according to the schedule of minimum prices made by the executive committee; the stock would be received at par, less such dividends as may have been paid on said stock. There would always be in Paris duplicate maps and descriptive books of the lands of the company and also a schedule of their respective prices. A stockholder wishing to exchange his shares for land would sign the endorsement on the back of the certificate, and the transfer would be registered on the books of the company and a memorandum made on the certificate. A register was to be kept open at the office of the company in New York for the transfer of the certificates. All the entries were to be transmitted to Paris in order to form a duplicate register, but transfers could be made at the Paris office by application to the vice-secretary. The transfer book would be closed the 1st day of April each year, or one month before the annual stockholders' meeting.

All unclaimed shares of stock, at the expiration of six years and after reasonable notice by newspaper advertising, would become the property of the company and increase proportionally the share of each shareholder.

The by-laws could be amended by vote of the majority of the entire board of directors, but the proposed amendments had to be submitted at a meeting held at least seven days before taking them into consideration. Any article could be temporarily suspended by the unanimous vote of seven directors.

Under the above-described charter and by-laws, Gray issued 42,181 shares of capital stock which he deposited, except those retained by the directors, with Munroe & Company, bankers, in Paris, to be delivered to the stockholders on presentation of the receipts given for their bonds. These shares, or stock certificates, were issued in the following form:

United States of America, State of Texas

This certifies that .... is entitled to .... shares of capital stock of the Franco-Texan Land Company, Nos. .... transferable on the Books of the Company in person or by power of Attorney which may be executed on the back hereof. The holder of this Certificate is entitled to such dividends as may accrue from the sales of the lands of the Company which, when paid, shall be endorsed hereon. This Certificate is receivable at the office of the Company in Texas, at One Hundred Dollars, less such dividends, in payment for the Company's lands at prices fixed so as to secure a pro rata division of the lands or of their value among the Stockholders.

In Witness Whereof the Company has caused the Certificate to be signed by its President and Secretary, this first day of September, 1876, H. E. Alexander, President, S. P. Tuck, Secretary. Principal Office: Dallas, Texas. Branch Offices: New York; Paris, France.

Each certificate contained a translation of the above in French and German. On the right margin of the certificate was written the following: "Incorporated under the laws of the State of Texas; capital stock limited to $5,343,000, in shares of $100 each, issued on the basis of the acquisition by the company of 13 acres of land for each share."

Printed on the back of each certificate was the following:

For value received I hereby sign and transfer unto .... or bearer, the share of capital stock represented by the within certificate and do hereby irrevocably constitute and appoint the Secretary or Assistant Secretary of the within named company my attorney to transfer said stock on the books thereof, dated ....; dividends as follows: Date, amount, signature.[3]

Gray announced in New York in November of 1876 that the agreement of 1873, under which the land-grant bonds of the Memphis, El Paso, and Pacific were to be surrendered to the Texas and Pacific, had been carried out and that a meeting would soon be held to elect a

[3] Franco-Texan Stock Certificate No. 28783, issued to Emmanuel Marie Philibert de Langier de Beaurecueil, September 1, 1876, The University of Texas Archives.

permanent board of trustees to replace the acting officers.[4] When this meeting was held, H. E. Alexander was reelected president and S. Pinkney Tuck secretary. They were reelected in 1877 and again in 1878. New directors were also elected, and in 1878 there were five Americans and six Frenchmen on the board. Also in 1878, William Butler Duncan and Francis H. Grain of New York City and William Watts Sherman of Newport, Rhode Island, "lately composing the firm of Duncan, Sherman, and Company," acquired 758 shares of Franco-Texan stock by virtue of $75,800 of land-grant bonds which they had "subscribed to,"[5] meaning no doubt that 758 bonds had been bought at a very low price from disillusioned French investors and indicating that the Texas and Pacific Company, and Gray and Tuck as well, probably became stockholders in the Franco-Texan Land Company in the same manner.

There was still more than $1,000,000 in bonds outstanding—in the hands of the French "strikers" who yet had hopes of a better deal. Had they all agreed to the exchange, 700,000 acres would have been required to complete the transfer. Scott had reserved 640,000, and Gray, expecting four-fifths of the bondholders to participate, had appropriated 550,000 for his land company. In 1878, when more bonds were surrendered and more land was required, the former deeds were cancelled and new ones made.[6] The Franco-Texan Land Company appears to have received a total of some 567,000 acres from the Fidelity, according to separate deeds recorded in each county. This amount of land represents about 43,500 shares at the rate of thirteen acres for each $100 bond. Since shares numbered up to 47,500 turned up later,[7] additional stock must have been issued.

[4] *Commercial and Financial Chronicle and Hunt's Merchants Magazine*, November, 1876.

[5] Deed Records of Taylor County: I–107, Fidelity Insurance, Trust and Safe Deposit Company to Duncan, Sherman, and Company, September 1, 1876; Duncan, Sherman, and Company to the Franco-Texan Land Company, January 21, 1878; filed August 19, 1891.

[6] *Ibid.*, I–501; M–431; Deed Records of Parker County: Vol. 6, p. 476; Vol. 7, p. 785; Vol. 15, p. 364.

[7] Carbinnier *v.* Franco-Texan Land Company, Cause 215, District Court Records of Parker County.

Tuck went to Dallas to open the Texas office. Finding Weatherford more conveniently located, he conducted his preliminary business there. It was necessary for him to make several trips from New York to Weatherford in 1877 before he was ready to offer the Franco-Texan land for sale.

Gray continued to hold the Memphis, El Paso, and Pacific in receivership. The railway company still had properties to dispose of, and he and Scott were being pressed to make some kind of settlement with the French strikers. When it was discovered that the value of Texas land was far from that which had been represented, a great furor arose in France. On April 21, 1877, the Court of Paris called on Gray for a true estimate of its value, preparatory to rendering a judgment against the company, but he refused to make a definite statement. It did not take long though for the certificate holders to learn that thirteen acres in northwest Texas were worth only four or five dollars and that the largest purchaser up to that time had been the agent of the receiver.

Gray went to Paris in the fall of 1877, and while there he realized that something would have to be done about the pressure from French stockholders, so he temporized by agreeing to a relief measure—an amendment to the Texas and Pacific bill securing a cash payment of fifty cents to all French bondholders whether they accepted land or not. From New York in December, he wrote the Marquis de Chambrun that he intended to complete the arrangement as he regarded it both safe and satisfactory. But he suddenly abandoned the project and returned to France to close his office.

The Texas and Pacific was then making its last effort to secure financial aid from the Federal government. Alexander H. Stephens of Georgia introduced the company's bill into the House in the special session on December 7, 1877. It was a modified version of those which had been proposed before. It allowed $20,000 in bonds per mile for 1,400 miles and $35,000 per mile for 250 miles of difficult or mountain sections, the aggregate not to exceed $38,750,000. The national land grant would revert to the government which would sell the land and apply half the proceeds to the interest payment on the fifty-year 5 per cent construction bonds. The eastern terminus would be located at a point on the bank of the Mississippi not farther north than Memphis, to be selected by a board of commissioners. The company finally resorted to reducing the number of bonds to a straight $27,368 per mile and proposed to mortgage to the government a portion of its future earnings and that part of the line which it would construct west of Fort Worth.

The Southern Pacific (of California) bill was introduced in the same session. Collis P. Huntington was petitioning for the land grant formerly donated to the Texas and Pacific as it was becoming evident that this company would never build west of El Paso, if that far. The terminus was still in Fort Worth, and since the line had not been extended to Weatherford within one year after it reached Fort Worth, as required by the Act of March 15, 1875, the right to receive further land donations from the state had automatically expired on July 1, 1877.

In 1878 the claims of both companies were presented to the Pacific Railroad Committees of the House and Senate. The House Committee heard Frank S. Bond's argument on January 29, 1878. He supported his claims by a strong array of figures and made a severe indictment of the Southern Pacific.[8] Huntington, on January 31, made a forceful presentation of his case and an equally severe condemnation of Texas and Pacific policy and achievements. He called the Texas and Pacific a

"devil fish of a company" and Scott's request for aid a "colossal joke." It was amazing, he said, that this same man who kept an engine standing for three months at Hopewell, New Jersey, and an armed force ready to prevent the crossing of a rival road a few miles west of Pittsburgh to prevent competition with his leased lines, who fought against allowing even an oil pipe in Pennsylvania to cross his railroad and actually compelled the owners to cart oil from one side of the road to the other, and who, at Harrisburg, was trying to prevent the passage of a law allowing oil to flow to Baltimore by the force of gravity, could come there to champion the beauties of competition and condemn the evils of monopoly.[9]

[8] Frank Stuart Bond, *Argument and Statements of Frank S. Bond, Vice-president of the Texas and Pacific Railway, before the Committee on the Pacific Railroad, House of Representatives*, January 29, 1878.

[9] Collis P. Huntington, *Remarks of C. P. Huntington and Argument of James H. Storrs on behalf of the Southern Pacific Railroad before the Com-*

Scott, who arrived late, was allowed fifteen minutes and Huntington ten for rejoinder. Scott made a bitter and personal reply. Huntington admitted that his words were strong but did not retract them. Bond, who had promised he would indulge in no "stable gossip," got the last insulting word by filing a supplemental argument with the excuse that he had prepared it in anticipation of Scott's absence:

> Were Mr. Scott able to be here, he could offer a full refutation of the charges that have been made but in his absence his friends are quite willing to say of this ambitious railway caviller and critic (who has evidently never read La Fontaine's fable of the Frog who wished to be as big as an Ox) that his counterpart, as a witty French writer once said of one of his critics, can be found only in the guardian of an Eastern harem, among those unsexed men filled with envy and malice against other men because of their own impotence.[10]

After the close of the arguments before the Senate Committee in February, the Texas and Pacific bill was reported favorably both in the House and the Senate. Then on March 25, 1878, by joint resolution the House Judiciary Committee was instructed to investigate the Texas and Pacific title to the six hundred miles of road to be constructed between Fort Worth and El Paso and the company's ability to execute a valid mortgage thereon, as that question had not been raised in committee.[11] The investigation was requested by William R. Morrison, who was chairman of the Pacific Railroad Committee of the House and known to be hostile to the bill.

Douglas Campbell of New York,[12] counsel for a group of French

---

mittee on the Pacific Railroads, House of Representatives, Forty-fifth Congress, on the Pending Propositions of the Southern Pacific and Texas Pacific Railroad Companies, January 31, 1878.

[10] Frank S. Bond, *Supplemental Argument and Statements Filed with the Committee on the Pacific Railroad, House of Representatives, February 1, 1878.*

[11] Galveston *Daily News*, March 26, 1878.

[12] Douglas Campbell was reputed to be a fine railroad lawyer, having been retained by the Illinois Central for many years. He was a captain and brevet major of the 121st New York Volunteers during the Civil War. His wife was Harriet Bowers Paige (*National Cyclopedia of American Biography*, XLI, 562).

bondholders, made his opening argument to the House Judiciary Committee on April 11, 1878. In an attempt to prevent the receiver's transfer of all the Memphis, El Paso, and Pacific properties to the Texas and Pacific, Judge Campbell made "an appeal for equity to the innocent parties" who held the valid obligations of the former company. He traced the history of the Memphis, El Paso, and Pacific from the time it was in the hands of Epperson and Frémont until its sale to the Texas and Pacific. He pointed out all the illegalities of Gray's receivership and the foreclosures, a few of which have been mentioned. He enumerated all the assets of the road which had been purchased with the proceeds of the land-grant bonds:

Amount obtained by Gray in France	$450,000
Railroad iron in New Orleans	480,000
State of Arkansas bonds	110,00
Stock of Memphis and Little Rock Railroad	300,000
Stock of San Diego and Gila Railroad	100,000

Other assets included in the transfer and also paid for with French money were 57,500 acres of land bought from S. M. Swenson at 50 cents an acre. The records showed $85,000 expended on land alone. Campbell admitted however that there were offsets, such as the claims of company officers against the funds appropriated by Frémont.

Outside the land-grant bonds and the Harrison-Bates mortgage, which Campbell considered invalid, the debts, according to the receiver's report of 1876, were:

Salary due an engineer	$15,000
One secretary	6,000
Telegraph bill	600
Iron company	25,000

Thus it appeared that the Memphis, El Paso, and Pacific, which was taken over on the theory that it was insolvent, had a floating indebtedness of less than $100,000. But disregarding the alleged receivership and the alleged foreclosures, the French bonds were secured by 1,536,000 acres adjacent to the first and to the second 150 miles of the road, so how then, Campbell asked, could justice be done by giving the owners 640,000 acres in a boundless wilderness, 100 miles west of the point at which the Texas and Pacific had ceased its building operations while that railway company took first choice in a thickly settled region which it never could have obtained except as successor to the rights of the Memphis, El Paso, and Pacific.

Campbell made his plea for all the foreign bondholders, the four-fifths who had accepted Gray's intervention as well as the other fifth who had declined his offer of land, all of whom were trusting in United States courts and had a right to redress. He declared that the Memphis, El Paso, and Pacific was still in existence with all its rights unimpaired, the charter and title of the Texas and Pacific were absolute nullities, the holders of the land-grant bonds were the only creditors, and as creditors their bonds were due, their debt had matured, and their claim covered the surveyed and located route which it was proposed to mortgage to the United States.[13]

Vice-President John C. Brown and J. Alfred Davenport, Gray's counsel, appeared before the House Judiciary Committee the following Saturday. Brown, speaking first, said he would make no detailed reply to Campbell's charges of illegality because the proceedings of the Court showed regularity on their face and the decrees were final and unappealed from. He did not care to go behind the records of the Court. Campbell and Gray could sit there until the middle of August to investigate that, but he had no intention of doing so. Even if all the court findings were void, which they were not, the holders of the land-grant bonds did not have a shadow of a claim west of Fort Worth, and it was idle to talk about it. The first and second mortgages were limited to the land grants, excluding the roadbed, superstructure, and so on; the construction mortgage, dated February 14, 1867, did cover the railroad for a distance of 150 miles with all its track, right of way, easements, and franchises, but all that had been sold and transferred to

[13] Douglas Campbell, *The Title of the Texas and Pacific Railroad Company to the Property of the Memphis, El Paso and Pacific Railroad Company: Opening Argument of Douglas Campbell, Esq., before the Judiciary Committee of the House of Representatives, April 11, 1878.*

the Texas and Pacific solely for the purpose of removing a cloud on the title, not for any rights conferred. It was obvious, he said, that Campbell's attack was a flank movement set on foot by Huntington and his associates to delay the passage of the Texas and Pacific bill and could not conceivably benefit Campbell's clients. Any doubt as to the validity of the Texas and Pacific title could only damage their prospects.

Asked by Senator Frye if his clients would not be benefited by U.S. aid to the Texas and Pacific road, provided the title was valid, Campbell replied that his clients took the position that a creditor was not benefited by the enriching of its debtor if the debtor was so wealthy as to be substantially above the law. However, he did not claim the Texas and Pacific was the debtor of his clients, he claimed that it held their property, and it was certainly not to their advantage to have their property mortgaged to its full value and paid the money to their opponent to contest their case. As for the title, Campbell said that the Texas and Pacific had succeeded in getting it in about as bad a muddle as any title had ever been gotten into. But he was not there to antagonize, and he represented no person or rival corporation. His clients were Frenchmen, he said, living in a distant country, and it was very difficult for them to protect their rights. He held that Congress should not give assistance to the road which was originally theirs until it recognized the rights of the French bondholders and made some provision in the bill, or otherwise, to satisfy their claims.

Following up the question of the French claims, Brown said that land-grant bonds in the amount of $5,064,700 had been filed or registered in the U.S. Circuit Court at Tyler; holders of $4,569,100 of these bonds had given notice of their desire to accept land, and most of the bonds had been surrendered. The Texas and Pacific actually had $4,928,800 in bonds in its possession. It was believed that there were only $100,000 outstanding and unaccounted for. Therefore, the Texas and Pacific should not have its title "beclouded and bedirtied" by such an insignificant claim. "To do this is absurd," he said, "to use the most respectful language I can apply to it."

Brown concluded with an outline of the history of the Texas and Pacific corporation and its legislative title and with the emphatic statement that the company was operating under a direct grant from the state, wholly independent of any judicial proceeding.[14]

Davenport undertook to answer Campbell's charges point by point. First taking up the legal questions, he argued that Frémont was the *de facto* president, the location of the central office was merely directive, six directors were served at Tyler and were present at the proceedings, and the trustees had agreed to the foreclosures. He then denied that the Memphis, El Paso, and Pacific had assets other than its land grant and roadbed. The railroad iron had been disposed of by the company before the appointment of the receiver and its value had been greatly exaggerated; the state of Arkansas bonds and the stock of the Memphis and Little Rock and the San Diego and Gila railroads were worthless, and other land owned by the company was of little value since it was outside the reservation and far removed from railway facilities. The company had paid only $30,000 for the Swenson lands, and the Harrison-Bates mortgage was no longer a question of importance because the Texas and Pacific owned it, valid or not.

Davenport quoted from Gray's reports to the court in 1876 and 1877 to justify the receiver's settlement with the bondholders who had accepted land. Gray had said that the total security contemplated by the "bubble company" was 2,740,000 acres for $10,000,000 in bonds or 27.4 acres for each $100 bond, but he considered 13 acres a fair exchange. Since $7.00 was the average price of the public lands granted by the United States, and since those in Texas were superior in quality and would meet a ready market in view of the rapid immigration to Texas he considered $8.00 a reasonable price. It was true that the Franco-Texan had already made sales of more than $50,000 for something over $4.00, but even that rate would produce $2,200,000, or 5 per cent for the bonds originally sold. The Franco-Texan, however, expected the balance of its lands to command a much higher remuneration. The fact that they were beyond the point of constructed railroad could not be foreseen since those arrangements for exchange were made prior to the Panic of 1873.

[14] John C. Brown, *Argument before the Judiciary Committee of the House of Representatives in regard to the Title of the Texas and Pacific Railway Company, to its Line between Fort Worth and El Paso, April 17, 1878.*

As for Campbell's gratuitous attack on the administration of the receiver, Davenport said the records disproved each innuendo and each derogatory assertion. Furthermore, it was against any possible interest of Campbell's clients, for

> if any bondholder should establish a right to resort to the assets acquired from the Memphis, El Paso, and Pacific, the strengthening of the Texas and Pacific by Congressional aid would increase the bondholder's security and reduce to a certainty the recovery of such obligation as he might establish. The immediate construction of the railroad following the granting of the subsidy would be the one fortunate event which would give the lands of the Franco-Texan Land Company the enhanced value which was so earnestly looked for by its stockholders.

His chief purpose, therefore, was to point out to what extent Congressional aid to the Texas and Pacific would carry out and complete that "beneficent scheme so wisely devised and so skilfully executed in behalf of the Franco-Texan Land Company, and to urge the broadest possible use of discretion and power in that regard."[15]

Major James Turner of Marshall, Texas, an attorney of the Texas and Pacific, replied to Campbell on April 20. Inasmuch as the Texas and Pacific was offering as security the road, the roadbed, its franchise, and certain portions of its future earnings, it needed to be the undisputed owner of a charter from the state of Texas, authorizing the construction of a railroad through Texas on the proposed route, preferably with a reservation. By a very simple formula, Major Turner provided the Texas and Pacific with a triple charter: the company received its exclusive right to the reservation from the Memphis, El Paso, and Pacific; it received its land grant from the Southern Transcontinental, which had no reservation but was allowed twenty sections to the mile; and it derived its authority or franchise to build a road from the Southern Pacific charter, to which there was no adverse claimant.

"This is blackmail . . .," Turner continued. "If Mr. Campbell and

[15] J. Alfred Davenport, *The Title of the Texas and Pacific Railroad to Property Late of the Memphis, El Paso and Pacific Railroad Company: Notes of Argument of J. Alfred Davenport before the Judiciary Committee of the House of Representatives, April 17, 1878.*

his clients have rights, instead of coming here to dig up a lot of filthy, rotten, and fetid scandals, they should go to the courts to have their rights enforced . . . The mortgage was on an intangible right. If no road was built, no lands were received." Yet they came there, he said, to prevent the road from being built, and Campbell came "armed with a club reeking with the filth and slime of the dead, buried, and stinking scandal that characterized the proceedings of Mr. Fremont in France," and he threatened to strike the company down unless it made peace with his clients and paid a debt it never owed. "It may be a harsh term," Turner concluded, "but it looks amazingly like an attempt to levy blackmail."[16]

In his closing argument on April 24, 1878, Campbell alone faced Bond, Brown, Davenport, and Turner, the best talent the Texas and Pacific could muster. He began by reading a letter from Chambrun which disclosed some contradictory information. Chambrun stated that as of that date, the French bonds were owned as follows.

1. The Texas and Pacific, according to figures furnished by Gray and William Butler Duncan, held $4,075,000 in bonds which had been exchanged for land.

2. Owners of $725,000 in bonds had formed a company under the laws of France and their bonds were held in trust by Riggs & Company of New York, or temporarily deposited with the clerk of the court in France, in view of lawsuits pending there. Of that number the owners of $712,000 had received 11 per cent in cash and had released Gray and Fancher from further liability, reserving all other rights.

3. Eighteen land-grant bondholders, with bonds amounting to at least $75,000—more likely $90,000—were formerly represented by Blanton Duncan whose power of attorney had been given to Campbell. They had received nothing in land or money.

4. The Rouen and Berthault bonds amounted to about $32,000, for which Campbell also held power of attorney.

5. The Andrieux bondholders, nine in all, probably held about that same amount.

[16] James Turner, *Argument of James Turner, Esq., before the Judiciary Committee of the House of Representatives, April 20, 1878.*

In the same letter, Chambrun continued,

As for the bonds that have been exchanged for land, I know positively that in a great many instances land in Texas was accepted only because no other option was left, and thus placed between a complete loss and the ownership of lands in Texas, the French bondholders were driven to this last alternative.

But if anyone could imagine that in so purchasing the land-grant bonds of the Memphis, El Paso, and Pacific, the Texas and Pacific has wiped out the dark cloud left hanging over the American credit by the transactions of General John C. Fremont, he would be deeply mistaken . . .

Also, Governor Brown was misinformed about the bonds, Chambrun said, and his error should be corrected for the benefit of the Committee.

Campbell devoted his remaining time to the legislative history of the Texas and Pacific, as embodied in the Act of 1873 and the general railroad law of Texas. According to his argument, the Memphis, El Paso, and Pacific franchise was the only valid and substantial franchise under which the Texas and Pacific could build its road in Texas, and with that point established it then became evident that it was upon the Harrison mortgage, foreclosed eighteen months after it had been set aside and restored *nunc pro tunc* a month after the sale, that the Texas and Pacific founded its title. He had already told how Gray, early in 1870, conceived the idea of wrecking the Memphis, El Paso, and Pacific and obtaining control of its property, making Bates the leading instrument, and how Judge Bradley ignored obvious irregularities; but more incredible than all that, he said, was the role played by Daniel and Frémont:

Here are two men, charged with a crime. A receiver of a company is to be appointed whose first duty it will be to proceed against them for the recovery of money, which, according to the allegations of the bill, they have misappropriated. Into his hands will come the evidence with which it will be his duty to prosecute the criminal, if the allegations of the bill are true. These men recommend to the court a gentleman to whom this delicate mission shall be entrusted, and the court appoints their nominee.

I think it is the first case in the history of jurisprudence when the criminal has been allowed to select his prosecutor.

As Campbell went on to call attention to the documentary evidence supporting his argument, the hearing was brought to a close in the following manner:

BROWN: What limit is there to this discussion. Campbell has brought in many additional facts which seem irrelevant, and I think I should have an opportunity of replying to them, but I do not want to prolong the discussion. But I would like to say this: We have in actual possession $4,215,000 in bonds; we have a contract for the delivery of $716,000 more and $38,000 are in the hands of Duncan, Sherman & Company awaiting an exchange. Those are the facts and the papers will show it and will prove that Chambrun is mistaken.

CAMPBELL: The Marquis de Chambrun says that if the Committee will send to New York he will show the bonds of which he has spoken, in the possession of Riggs & Company; and that is better than the assertions of any of these gentlemen.

CONGER: How large an amount is that?

CAMPBELL: Over $775,000.

BROWN: We have the assignment of Chambrun for $716,000 under his own signature.

CAMPBELL: Can I see that?

BOND: No sir, not now. At the proper time you can.

BROWN: I will submit it to the Committee with my argument.

CHAIRMAN: Either party may present such additional facts and arguments in a printed form, as they may think proper; but the weight which the Committee will give to a document which the counsel refuses to show to the other side is a different question.[17]

On April 29, 1878, Brown restated his former argument in writing and added this conclusion: the intrinsic evidence on the face of these proceedings is overwhelming that the whole object of this investigation is to obstruct the legislation sought by the Texas and Pacific Railway Company. The reply was accompanied by a copy of a document dated April 26, 1877, which showed that L. Lebourgeois, as the director and

[17] Douglas Campbell, *Closing Argument of Douglas Campbell, Esq.., in Reply to Governor John C. Brown, J. A. Davenport, and Major James Turner before the Judiciary Committee of the House of Representatives, in regard to the Title of the Texas and Pacific Railway Company to the Property of the Memphis, El Paso and Pacific Railroad Company, April 24, 1878.*

administrator of a corporation owning $712,000 in Memphis, El Paso, and Pacific bonds, had received a preliminary dividend of 6 per cent, a second dividend of 2 per cent, and that on receipt of a final dividend of 3 per cent, which they acknowledged, they released Enoch L. Fancher and John A. C. Gray and their assigns from further liability, the bonds being retained by the corporation with all other rights reserved,[18] all of which Chambrun himself had stated. The real significance of this document was not that it indicated who did or did not have physical possession of certain bonds, which Brown had to admit were only "constructively" theirs, it was that the Texas and Pacific had been receiving from Gray the dividends on bonds already surrendered and had agreed to let the final payment of $21,360 to Lebourgeois come out of the Texas and Pacific's dividend of 3 per cent provided it would be credited to their account with the Memphis, El Paso, and Pacific. This meant that the Texas and Pacific as holders of $4,215,000 in bonds would be paid $463,350 in dividends by the *bankrupt* Memphis, El Paso, and Pacific, and on bonds which, it seems, should have been cancelled when they were surrendered. As the Texas and Pacific's annual report of 1880 shows a credit of only $314,915 from dividends on these land bonds, it may be that some bonds were traded to Gray and Tuck for certain concessions for land certificates, or for stock in the Franco-Texan Land Company. The French bondholders who were paid money instead of land received $78,320 on $712,000 in bonds, or $11 for each $100 bond. At this point it would seem that those who received land fared slightly better, except for the fact that they did not yet have their remuneration in hand. There were still over $250,000 in bonds outstanding.

On June 4, 1878, the Texas and Pacific bill was laid aside until the next session, and on June 10, shortly before Congress adjourned, it was reported that the Judiciary Committee had made no progress on Hewitt's resolution to investigate "whether Fremont's interest in the El

[18] John C. Brown, *Reply of John C. Brown to Mr. Campbell before the Judiciary Committee of the House of Representatives in regard to the Title to the Texas and Pacific Railway Company, to its Line between Ft. Worth and El Paso.* Filed by leave of Committee, April 29, 1878.

Paso Road accrued to the French bondholders or to the Texas and Pacific Railroad."[19]

In the "battle of the giants," in which immense interests were contained and immense men of iron and brain were engaged, and in which Frémont and the French bondholders played no small part, there was never a victory for any of the contestants. The 45th Congress, on its adjournment in March, 1879, left Scott and Huntington to carry on the fight between themselves; it left the French to their own devices and Frémont with the consolation of a territorial governorship. It was the Washington lobby, the greatest in the history of congressional warfare, that reaped the golden harvest.

For the stockholders in the Franco-Texan Land Company, the arrangement already made with Gray remained the same. He terminated his receivership some time in 1878 and devoted his talents to the management of the land company. Perhaps his last act as receiver was a public sale of Memphis, El Paso, and Pacific property in New York on November 23, 1878. He advertised that under order of the United States Circuit Court he was selling 128,690 acres of land in Callahan, Eastland, Clay, Brown, Stephens, Cooke, Jones, Wilbarger, Dimmitt, and Baylor counties in Texas; also fifteen lots on 132nd Street in New York. The sale was to be held at the Exchange Sale Room, 11 Broadway at noon.[20] This would be what remained of the land purchased from Swenson and that covered by Memphis, El Paso, and Pacific and Texas and New Orleans certificates. Many Texas and New Orleans certificates had been originally located in Stephens and Palo Pinto counties upon the company's reservation, but on March 3, 1874, Gray had appointed J. W. Throckmorton his attorney to lift and float 144 such certificates and cause them to be relocated for the Texas and Pacific upon any of the vacant and unreserved public lands of the state.[21] The vacated tracts were then embraced in Gray's land company to conform with his desire for large blocks of surveys for ready sale.

[19] Galveston *Daily News*, June 11, 1878.

[20] *Commercial and Financial Chronicle and Hunt's Merchants Magazine*, November 23, 1878.

[21] Milam Scrip 1574 (Texas and New Orleans Railway Company), Railroad Scrip Files, General Land Office.

It would be interesting to know the exact figures of Gray's final settlement with Frémont, with the Texas and Pacific, and with the Fidelity Insurance, Trust and Safe Deposit Company, but Gray's books are not available nor are those of the Fidelity, although that company is still in existence. It became the Fidelity Trust Company in 1886, is known today as the Fidelity Philadelphia Trust Company, and its records go back only to 1888.[22] It is certain though that the Texas and Pacific was not to close its account with the Fidelity for some years to come. The two became more closely linked in November of 1884 when the Texas and Pacific was mortgaged to the Trust Company for $6,000,000 for a period of twenty years. It was said that the purpose of the mortgage, which included the rolling stock, track, depot grounds, and lands, was to provide money for the improvement of the road.[23]

Published reports of the Board of Directors of the Texas and Pacific in 1879 and 1880 state that the Fidelity would soon reconvey some 80,000 or 100,000 acres to the Texas and Pacific, representing the lands not taken by the French "strikers." The deed records of Taylor and Parker counties reveal the transfer by the Fidelity of 62,535.52 acres to the Texas and Pacific on February 27, 1885.[24] The land is specifically designated by certificate number and located in the various Texas and Pacific blocks in Taylor, Parker, Jones, Fisher, Nolan, Palo Pinto, Stephens, and Callahan counties. There was also a matter of 10,000 acres surveyed by virtue of fractional or unlocated balance certificates. The Texas and Pacific had assigned the original certificates to the Fidelity for location and patenting, but as there was not always room for a full 640-acre survey, fractional certificates were issued to be located elsewhere. The Fidelity reassigned unlocated balances in the amount of 10,000 acres to the Texas and Pacific on February 28, 1885. The deed is of record in the Land Office because this land could not

[22] Fidelity and Safe Deposit Company of Maryland (Philadelphia Office) to Virginia H. Taylor, November 14, 1963.

[23] Dallas *Daily Herald*, November 29, and December 11, 1884; Deed Records of Parker County, V. 9, p. 52.

[24] Deed Records of Park County, Vol. 15, p. 364; the same deed in Taylor County, M–423.

be patented to another assignee without the Fidelity's authorization.[25] These two deeds account for 72,535.52 acres returned to the Texas and Pacific leaving 567,464.48 acres for the Franco-Texan Land Company.

The last of the French strikers had taken an unexpected step in December of 1878. Their lawyers, ex-Senator Matt H. Carpenter of Wisconsin, Judge Fielding S. Black of Pennsylvania, and Judge Douglas Campbell of New York filed a bill of equity, *Pierre Fayolle et al. versus the Texas and Pacific Railway Company*, in the Supreme Court of the District of Columbia. It was filed on December 12, 1878, shortly after Congress had convened for a second session and just after a motion had been made to bring the Texas and Pacific subsidy bill to a vote.

The complainants in this cause were thirty-nine Frenchmen and one American, a Mr. Hyde of Vermont (Henry B. ?), holding 386 bonds in the amount of $155,100, and other owners of land-grant bonds, the total being about $300,000, none of whom had received any dividend or payment thereon. The bill set forth the whole history of their case, supported by voluminous exhibits, making a printed book of 237 large octavo pages. The petitioners declared that the Texas and Pacific Railway Company had no right or title to, or lien or claim upon any of the Memphis, El Paso, and Pacific property, and prayed for an order or injunction to restrain the Texas and Pacific from selling, conveying, or mortgaging the property upon which these bondholders had a lien for payment, and that the Texas and Pacific be subpoenaed to appear in court to answer their charges and give such relief as should be agreeable to equity and good conscience.[26]

The Texas and Pacific demurred to the jurisdiction of the courts of the District of Columbia, and after argument the court held, first, that it had all the powers of the circuit courts of the United States, and secondly, that the national charter of the Texas and Pacific made the company amenable in all courts of the United States. The plaintiffs then moved for a permanent injunction late in 1879, and it looked as

[25] Miscellaneous Deeds 437, General Land Office.

[26] Pierre Fayolle *et al. v.* the Texas and Pacific Railway Company, Equity No. 6556, Supreme Court of the District of Columbia, November 12, 1883, National Archives.

if the litigation might last for several years. The New York *Sun* considered it a practical step for the French since all the plaintiffs were influential, in England and Holland as well as France, and it was generally thought that they could prevent the sale of Texas and Pacific bonds in Europe until they obtained satisfaction.[27] In the meantime, it was expected that the injunction, if granted, would restrain the company from any disposition of its securities.

The Texas and Pacific filed a second demurrer which was sustained on June 3, 1881. On June 22, no motion to amend having been made but notice of an appeal to the court in general term having been given, the complaint was dismissed. Then on November 12, 1883, the case was argued and the former decree was affirmed, but an appeal to the Supreme Court of the United States was allowed.

Meanwhile, the French were having unfortunate luck with their attorneys. Judge Campbell withdrew from the case on an undetermined date and for undetermined reasons. In February, 1881, Senator Carpenter died, leaving Judge Black to carry on alone. Then, in February, 1883, eight months before the final District of Columbia court hearing, Black too died. James Coleman, Carpenter's law partner, took over the appeal without a fee, merely as a means of clearing up Senator Carpenter's unfinished business. Finding that many necessary papers had been lost or mislaid he was able to proceed only when copies of these papers were furnished him by the counsel of the defense. When the appeal was perfected and the transcript of record was ready to be filed, the deputy clerk of the district court agreed to file it for him in the United States Supreme Court. Relying on that agreement, Coleman closed the Washington office of Carpenter & Coleman and left for Wisconsin. The transcript did not reach the office of the clerk of the Supreme Court until June 12, 1885, one month after the close of the term, and the appeal was not docketed until June 17, 1886.

W. D. Shipman was retained as new counsel on November 9, 1887, by letter from France. He set forth all the reasons for the delay before the Court, but Chief Justice Waite held that the excuses given did not

[27] Galveston *Daily News*, December 21, 1879.

warrant any exception since no attempt had been made to get the transcript on docket until another term had passed and still another had begun. He therefore dismissed the case on February 6, 1888.[28]

Frémont's friends in Congress came to his aid in 1878 and secured his appointment as governor of the Arizona Territory on a salary of $2,000 a year. Jessie Benton Frémont said that she had to leave Arizona because the climate impaired her health and that Frémont gave up his position to join her in New York. When he returned in 1881, penniless in spite of his and Corwin's mining operations, she wrote about their experiences in the West and was able to earn a meager living until public interest declined.

Loyal supporters rallied round Frémont in the North and East, but there was never any sympathy for him in Texas. Even in 1873, when a French tribunal tried and sentenced Frémont as an absconding criminal, presumably on ex parte testimony, the San Antonio *Herald* defended the action, saying that it was done in accordance with the laws of the French Republic to which an American was just as amenable as a Frenchman for offenses committed in that country.[29] And in 1884, when it was proposed to retire Frémont with the rank of a major general and a large government pension, the Galveston *Daily News* could find nothing good to say about him. It saw no plausible reason for thus honoring a man who had been educated at the expense of the United States government, and had made a failure of everything he touched; who, having duped his brother-in-law into assisting him, had succeeded in fleecing a good many innocent people by means of worthless securities and never made any satisfactory explanation of his conduct; who was governor of Arizona Territory for two years but was driven out by intelligent public opinion. Why then, continued the *News*, should the "people of the United States be taxed to pay $10,000 a year to a wild, visionary, perverted creature, living in himself and worshiping his own mental tantrums."[30]

The Frémonts next moved to Washington where, with access to

28 Pierre Fayolle *v.* the Texas and Pacific Railroad Company, 124 *U.S. Reports* 519.

29 San Antonio *Daily Herald*, April 4, 1873.

30 Galveston *Daily News*, April 25, 1884.

government records, the General undertook to write his memoirs. Though he completed and published one mammoth volume, it yielded little or nothing because the first sales had to pay for publication. After so many days of inside work Frémont developed a bronchial ailment and was advised to move to a warmer climate. Wishing to take her husband to California to recover, Jessie Frémont, unmindful of the supreme irony of the situation, appealed to Collis P. Huntington, who was in Washington on railroad business. Huntington regretted that his private car was not available but gave them tickets for the western trip and a generous sum of money for their expenses. In April, 1890, Congress placed Frémont on the retired list as a major general of the Army. He returned East to see about his pension and died from a sudden attack of peritonitis on July 13, 1890.[31]

Frémont's biographers have tended to whitewash his negotiation of the French bond sale. Cardinal Goodwin, the most impartial, says that Frémont was not a scoundrel, no Jay Gould, George Opdyke, Morris Ketchum, or Jim Fisk, but a "loose constructionist," morally careless rather than deliberately criminal in his intentions. Allan Nevins, the most eminent, finds Frémont not dishonest but indiscreet, betrayed by his own precipitancy and lack of circumspection. Alice Eyre, the most partisan, contends that all the misrepresentations were made by the French, and that Frémont's conviction in France had no meaning since he had no representative in M. Chevillote's court. According to Nevins, Frémont did have French counsel—M. Allou—who was not allowed to speak because Frémont had not replied to the summons received in New York ten days previous to the trial. Nevins further states that after a thorough investigation lasting two years, Frémont's name was removed from the list of the accused and then subsequently restored, so he was told, at the instance of the United States Minister Elihu Washburne with whom Frémont had clashed during the Civil War.

Chevillote's decree had a great deal of meaning for the French citizens who were convicted. Emanuel Lissignol committed suicide, and Baron Boilleau spent two years of his three-year sentence in prison. However, according to a report in the New York *Times*, Boilleau

[31] Alice Eyre, *The Famous Fremonts and Their America*, pp. 323–334.

proved to have been a victim rather than an agent of the gigantic fraud. He had married the youngest daughter of Thomas Hart Benton, and her dowry of 700,000 francs had been placed in Frémont's hands. It was not paid until the Memphis, El Paso, and Pacific bonds were on the market and Boilleau had already withdrawn from the project. When the crisis came, Frémont fled to America, and Boilleau was left to bear the brunt of the prosecution. On learning that his wife's dowry had been paid out of the subscriptions of the French bondholders, he gave up the money, but the judge took little notice of his honesty and condemned him along with the rest. The saddest consequence was that Madam Boilleau died from grief while her husband was in prison. Only then was there a change of public feeling about the Baron's case. When efforts were made to obtain his release, the government responded to the first petition. MacMahon pardoned Boilleau in September, 1875, and he had two duels immediately after he was released, having demanded a retraction from two men who had slandered him.[32]

For historians in general the case of the Memphis, El Paso, and Pacific ends with Frémont's defection and the company's absorption by the Texas and Pacific. With reference to John A. C. Gray, little has been said other than "that is another story." Judge Campbell told that story to the House Judiciary Committee, but Gray himself is elusive. As the archconspirator he always remains in the background and leaves a very dim trail, not only in Texas but even in New York. To make his duplicity more complete, on closing his work as receiver, he wrote Frémont, "Throughout the long and careful scrutiny which I have made into the affairs of your Company, I have no proof that would sustain the charges brought against you regarding the fraudulent sale of the Company's bonds in France."[33]

In "Post-Civil War Precedents for Railway Reorganization," Albert House, Jr., makes a study of the Memphis, El Paso, and Pacific receivership, considering that it throws some light on the early development of various techniques and legal processes which came to be an integral part of later reorganization practices. He points out that government lands and subsidies were the prizes which accrued to the re-

32 San Antonio *Daily Herald*, September 21, 1875.

33 Eyre, *The Famous Fremonts and Their America*, p. 320.

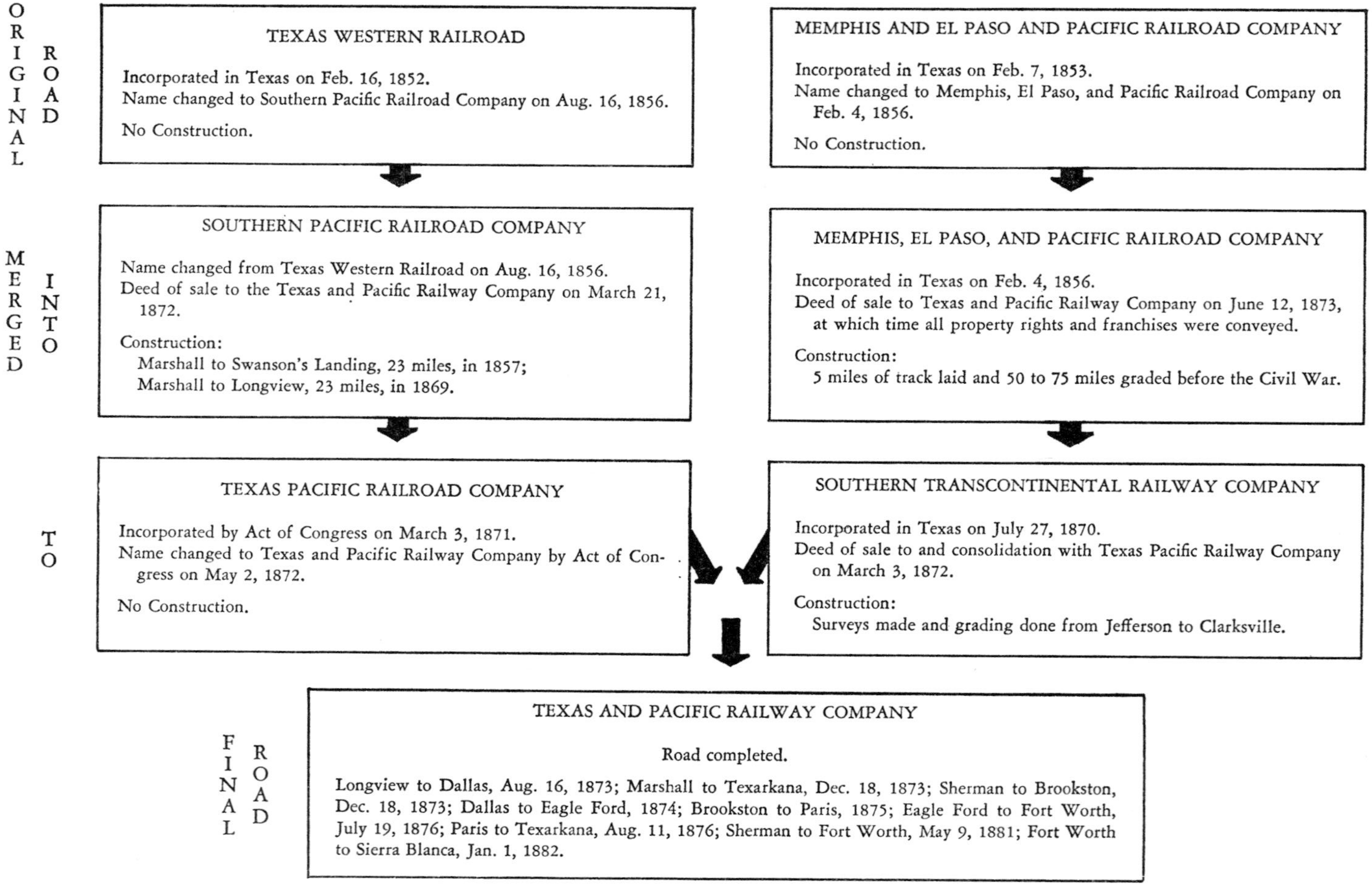

ORIGINAL ROAD

TEXAS WESTERN RAILROAD

Incorporated in Texas on Feb. 16, 1852.
Name changed to Southern Pacific Railroad Company on Aug. 16, 1856.

No Construction.

MEMPHIS AND EL PASO AND PACIFIC RAILROAD COMPANY

Incorporated in Texas on Feb. 7, 1853.
Name changed to Memphis, El Paso, and Pacific Railroad Company on Feb. 4, 1856.

No Construction.

MERGED INTO

SOUTHERN PACIFIC RAILROAD COMPANY

Name changed from Texas Western Railroad on Aug. 16, 1856.
Deed of sale to the Texas and Pacific Railway Company on March 21, 1872.

Construction:
Marshall to Swanson's Landing, 23 miles, in 1857;
Marshall to Longview, 23 miles, in 1869.

MEMPHIS, EL PASO, AND PACIFIC RAILROAD COMPANY

Incorporated in Texas on Feb. 4, 1856.
Deed of sale to Texas and Pacific Railway Company on June 12, 1873, at which time all property rights and franchises were conveyed.

Construction:
5 miles of track laid and 50 to 75 miles graded before the Civil War.

TO

TEXAS PACIFIC RAILROAD COMPANY

Incorporated by Act of Congress on March 3, 1871.
Name changed to Texas and Pacific Railway Company by Act of Congress on May 2, 1872.

No Construction.

SOUTHERN TRANSCONTINENTAL RAILWAY COMPANY

Incorporated in Texas on July 27, 1870.
Deed of sale to and consolidation with Texas Pacific Railway Company on March 3, 1872.

Construction:
Surveys made and grading done from Jefferson to Clarksville.

FINAL ROAD

TEXAS AND PACIFIC RAILWAY COMPANY

Road completed.

Longview to Dallas, Aug. 16, 1873; Marshall to Texarkana, Dec. 18, 1873; Sherman to Brookston, Dec. 18, 1873; Dallas to Eagle Ford, 1874; Brookston to Paris, 1875; Eagle Ford to Fort Worth, July 19, 1876; Paris to Texarkana, Aug. 11, 1876; Sherman to Fort Worth, May 9, 1881; Fort Worth to Sierra Blanca, Jan. 1, 1882.

Historical combinations of the Texas and Pacific Railway in Texas. Chart compiled by Samuel B. McAlister and used courtesy of Mrs. Samuel B. McAlister, Denton, Texas.

organized or successor company in the 1870's and thus caused the lobbies and floors of Congress to be the scene of rival elements, whereas in the twentieth century the battle is in the courtroom and more particularly around the conference table of bankers and lawyers, the stakes centering on underwriting commissions from the sale of securities. House says the sole right of the Texas and Pacific to build through the state of Texas depended upon its ability to acquire and retain control of the old franchises of the Memphis, El Paso, and Pacific. In the struggle, which took place on a national and even international aspect, everything hinged on Gray's federal receivership, made possible by the interstate claims of creditors. The court revealed either a lack of understanding of or an unwillingness to face the realities of the situation by accepting the receiver's explanations as to the fairness and the necessity of the terms of settlement. Even granting that the receivership was necessary to settle the creditor's claims, the sanction of the court was put on an arrangement which failed to protect the rights of many individuals who possessed an equity in the corporation; and ultimately the failure of Frémont and the "unfortunate bondholders" to prevent the receiver's transfer of the Memphis, El Paso, and Pacific properties allowed those properties to pass to more powerful interests already engaged in acquiring a stranglehold on a large portion of American activity. Two other important elements of the struggle, without counterpart in the contemporary picture, were Gray's seeming perfidy and the absence of any vigorous protective committee to look after the interests of the French, or in other words, the negligence of the trustees under the mortgages. House considers this case of "more than ordinary significance because General John C. Fremont was directly involved in the sordid mess, and the successor company was the notorious Texas and Pacific Railroad."[34]

House also mentions that Gray had a land company, and that Throckmorton, who had one too, was competing with him for settlers.

With Gray in full possession, the Franco-Texan Land Company opened for business in Weatherford, Texas, in December of 1877.

[34] Albert V. House, Jr., "Post-Civil War Precedents for Recent Railway Reorganization," *Mississippi Valley Historical Review*, XXV (March, 1939), 505–522.

CHAPTER 4

WEATHERFORD, TEXAS

Weatherford, the county seat of Parker County, was the only real settlement on Texas' northwest frontier in 1877. It was on the route of the wagon trains between Fort Worth and Fort Belknap and the stage lines running west to Fort Griffin and El Paso. The town was situated on the south edge of the Upper Cross Timbers, on the South Fork of the Clear Fork of the West Fork of the Trinity River, in a deep basin enclosed by hills on three sides.

In the county, the average price of land was $3.36½ an acre. Horses were the source of greatest wealth. The largest single business was the cattle trade. Wheat and cotton were the most important farm crops. The old sixteen-mile wide Memphis, El Paso, and Pacific reservation, in which the Franco-Texan Land Company owned 91,602 acres, ran through the county at an angle of 61° 33′ northeast and southwest. The reservation had been steadily infiltrated ever since Land Commissioner Kuechler had erroneously opened it to settlement; the fertile valleys were already taken, and the company's locations made, for the greater part, on the hilltops and the slopes of the steeply undulating prairie.

Weatherford's 2,000 inhabitants occupied an area of 320 acres, with a courthouse square in the center. There was nothing distinctive about the frame buildings, occasionally interspersed with one of stone, brick, or cement, but property values were high, and the town already had two banks, two newspapers, three hotels, eight saloons, twenty-four lawyers, and nine real estate agents. Weatherford was ready for the boom which would come when the Texas and Pacific railroad reached there in July of that year.

According to the editor of the Weatherford *Exponent*, the general state of mind of the populace was such that:

> When the whistle of Carson & Lewis' mill is sounded at noon, the average Weatherford man shuts his eyes and immediately a long train of freight cars loaded with lumber and merchandise comes trooping like a shadow across his enchanted vision, and in his imagination he sees gigantic compresses and grain elevators and nine-story bricks looming up on all the vacant lots, and as he meditates in silence upon the spectral shadows of future reality, he feels in his heart that sweet sense of happiness which only a Weatherford man can feel when that future is so near at hand.[1]

And, with the Houston and Texas Central and the Pacific and Great Eastern chartered to that point, and the Waco Tap almost a certainty, not to mention the climate, the plentiful supply of wood and water and the newly discovered coal fields, who could doubt Weatherford's destiny as the metropolis of the West.

Among the town's leading citizens were Sam H. Milliken, R. W. Duke, W. H. Eddleman, S. W. T. Lanham, Isaac W. Stephens, and A. J. Hood. Milliken came from Ohio and entered the banking business with J. R. Couts on May 1, 1875. He owned more than 12,000 acres of fine farms and eligible town sites. He was developing an addition adjoining the town tract on the north and advertised "residence lots for sale at $40 each, ½ cash; corner lots, $75, ½ cash; balance in two equal payments at 12 per cent interest; prices doubled when work commenced on the Texas and Pacific Railway or Texas Central." By 1882, he was president of the First National Bank and had extensive livestock and industrial interests. His brother, James H. Milliken, was an alderman, a brick manufacturer, building contractor, and deputy

[1] Weatherford *Exponent*, March 31, 1877.

U.S. marshal. He was elected mayor in 1878 and 1880 on the Republican ticket. Another brother, Charles H. Milliken, was first a clerk and later the cashier of the First National Bank.

R. D. Duke was editor of the *Frontier News* until 1861 when he left to serve in the Civil War. On his return, Colonel Duke edited the Weatherford *Times*, and in 1877 was the owner and publisher. He was also county clerk from 1877 to 1883.

W. H. Eddleman, manager of the firm of Ross and Eddleman, Merchants, was on the first board of directors of the Citizens National Bank, was vice-president of the First National Bank in 1886, and president of the Merchants and Farmers National Bank in 1889. In a special edition of the Weatherford *Constitution* on June 24, 1889, he was described as a capitalist. Eddleman moved to Fort Worth in 1905. He was then president of eighteen banks, including the Western National in Fort Worth.

Azariah J. Hood was admitted to the bar in South Carolina in 1846. That same year he migrated to Cherokee County, Texas. He served two years in the state Legislature (1851–1853), moved to Parker County in 1860 and held the office of district judge from 1873 to 1876. In 1877, he was a member of the law firm of Hood and McCall and one of the largest landholders in the county; he was appointed district judge by Governor Hubbard, was reelected in 1878, and served through 1884. It was said that as a judge he was a man of rare ability and the district was to be congratulated on the concentrated talents of its bench; that as a gentleman and a citizen he was kind and courteous and respected by all who knew him.[2] In 1884, when defeated for reelection by R. E. Beckham of Fort Worth, he began practicing law in the firm of Hood, Lanham, and Stephens.

Isaac W. Stephens came to Weatherford with a law degree from Washington and Lee University in 1874. Elected county attorney in 1876, he held that office for four years. Judge Stephens was highly esteemed in Weatherford and all northwest Texas, not only for his ability as a lawyer and public prosecutor but also for his integrity and good citizenship. He practiced law with S. W. T. Lanham from 1880

[2] Fort Worth *Daily Democrat*, September 26, 1879 (editorial).

until 1892.[3] He was appointed associate justice of the Court of Civil Appeals of the Second Judicial District in 1892 and remained in office until 1905.

S. W. T. Lanham of South Carolina joined the Confederate army at the age of sixteen and came to Weatherford as a teacher soon after the war. He studied law while he taught and was admitted to the bar in 1869; as district attorney in 1870, he successfully prosecuted the Indian leaders Satanta and Big Tree, and in 1877, he was practicing law in the firm of Watts, Lanham, and Roach. Lanham was congressman from the 11th or "Jumbo" District for twenty years (1882–1902)—"an able lawyer and a genial gentleman," with a reputation for absolute honesty. He was elected governor in 1902 and served for two terms (1903–1907). Throughout his political career he was so popular that he seldom had an opponent. Edwin Lanham, the author of *The Wind Blew West*, was the grandson of Governor Lanham and Judge Stevens.

One of Lanham's first cases in 1877 was the *State v. Kate Lowe* for "keeping a disorderly house." The county attorney had unguardedly given the lady the alias of "Rowdy Kate" in the indictment, and she was very much offended. In the trial which lasted a whole day, Lanham convinced the jury that her virtue like that of Caesar's wife was not to be questioned, or at least not to be assailed by the county attorney. The result was a verdict for acquittal. It was immediately rumored that Kate would bring action against the county attorney and his witnesses for damages. Fearing that there was some substance to the rumor, the county attorney indicted her again the next day. Her counsel insisted that this was persecution, not prosecution, but unfortunately for "riotous Katherine," neither judge nor jury so regarded it. She was convicted and fined $100. It was said that the defendant, dissatisfied with the compromise verdict, had taken steps to appeal for absolute justice at Austin.[4] The county attorney was I. W. Stephens.

[3] Dallas *Daily Herald*, September 21, 1880.

[4] Weatherford *Exponent*, May 12, 1877. Rowdy Joe Lowe and his wife Rowdy Kate were proprietors of a saloon in Ellsworth, Kansas, in 1869. In Newton, in 1871, Joe shot and killed Jim Sweet in a street fight. Later he and Rowdy Kate became notorious for their establishment in lawless Delano,

There were other prominent men in Weatherford: A. J. Ball, county attorney and legislator; Henry Warren,[5] banker and cattle king; Judges H. L. L. McCall, I. N. Roach, A. T. Watts, and J. M. Richards; J. W. Squyres, justice of the peace; C. H. Cole, immigration agent, and Henry Smythe, the outspoken editor of the *Times*, who was not only sued but caned several times for his offensive language. These citizens, to name only a few, were active, colorful, and cultivated, and Weatherford, thus endowed, thrived on the spirit of individual enterprise. For a frontier town it was strongly addicted to culture, but above all it was beset with growing pains as it strained every nerve and fiber to compete with Fort Worth for the position of gateway to the northwest.

---

across the Arkansas River from Washita. Both were in their element at Preston and Denison, Texas, when the M K & T reached these points in 1872. When Joe disappeared after being involved in a second murder Kate moved on to Weatherford (Harry Sinclair Drago, *Red River Valley,* p. 91). She was living up to her alias in Big Spring in 1886 when John McManus, a brakeman employed by the Texas and Pacific Railway Company, raised a disturbance at her house and received two bullet wounds in return, one in the head and the other in the arm (Fort Worth *Gazette*, June 22, 1886). Wright Mooar, famous buffalo hunter and cattleman, tells of sitting on a jury and refusing to convict Rowdy Kate for vagrancy because he believed her to be a kind and considerate woman. He said she was once in Fort Griffin but died in San Angelo, and it turned out she was "pretty well off" and also a "real church worker" (San Angelo *Standard-Times*, August 23, 1964).

[5] Henry Warren came to El Paso in 1864, a Republican who purchased the confiscated property of Southern sympathizers. He was appointed county clerk on January 5, 1866, and later elected senator of the 11th Legislature from El Paso and Presidio counties but could not get to Austin in time to qualify for his senatorial duties—El Paso was 600 miles away, through territory infested with marauding Indians, and the only means of transportation was by mule-drawn wagons. Warren became a government freighter, and on May 18, 1871, ten of his wagon trains were attacked by Satanta's band. The result of the brutal massacre was that Satanta and Big Tree were arrested and carried to Jacksboro for trial. Warren came to Weatherford in 1872, and in 1877 he bought J. R. Couts's Parker County Bank. He took up ranching, first in Texas, then in Arizona where he was manager and part owner of the Aztec Cattle Company (J. Morgan Broaddus, *The Legal Heritage of El Paso*, ed. Samuel D. Myres; Henry Smythe, *Historical Sketch of Parker County and Weatherford, Texas.*)

1. Benjamin H. Epperson, president of the Memphis, El Paso, and Pacific Railway Company, 1866–1869.

Courtesy of the Bexar Archives.

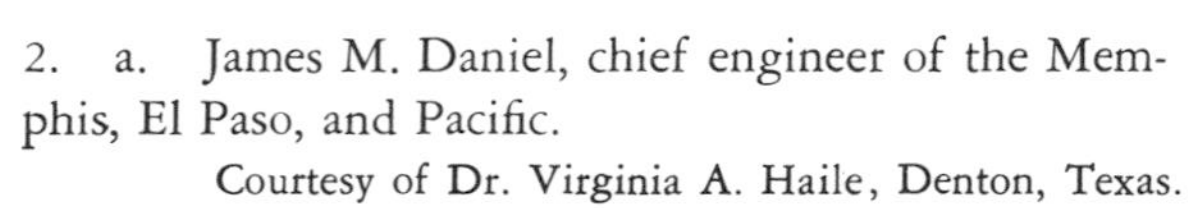

2. a. James M. Daniel, chief engineer of the Memphis, El Paso, and Pacific.
Courtesy of Dr. Virginia A. Haile, Denton, Texas.

b. W. H. Eddleman of Weatherford, capitalist and stockholder in the Franco-Texan Land Company.
Courtesy of the Institute of Texas Cultures.

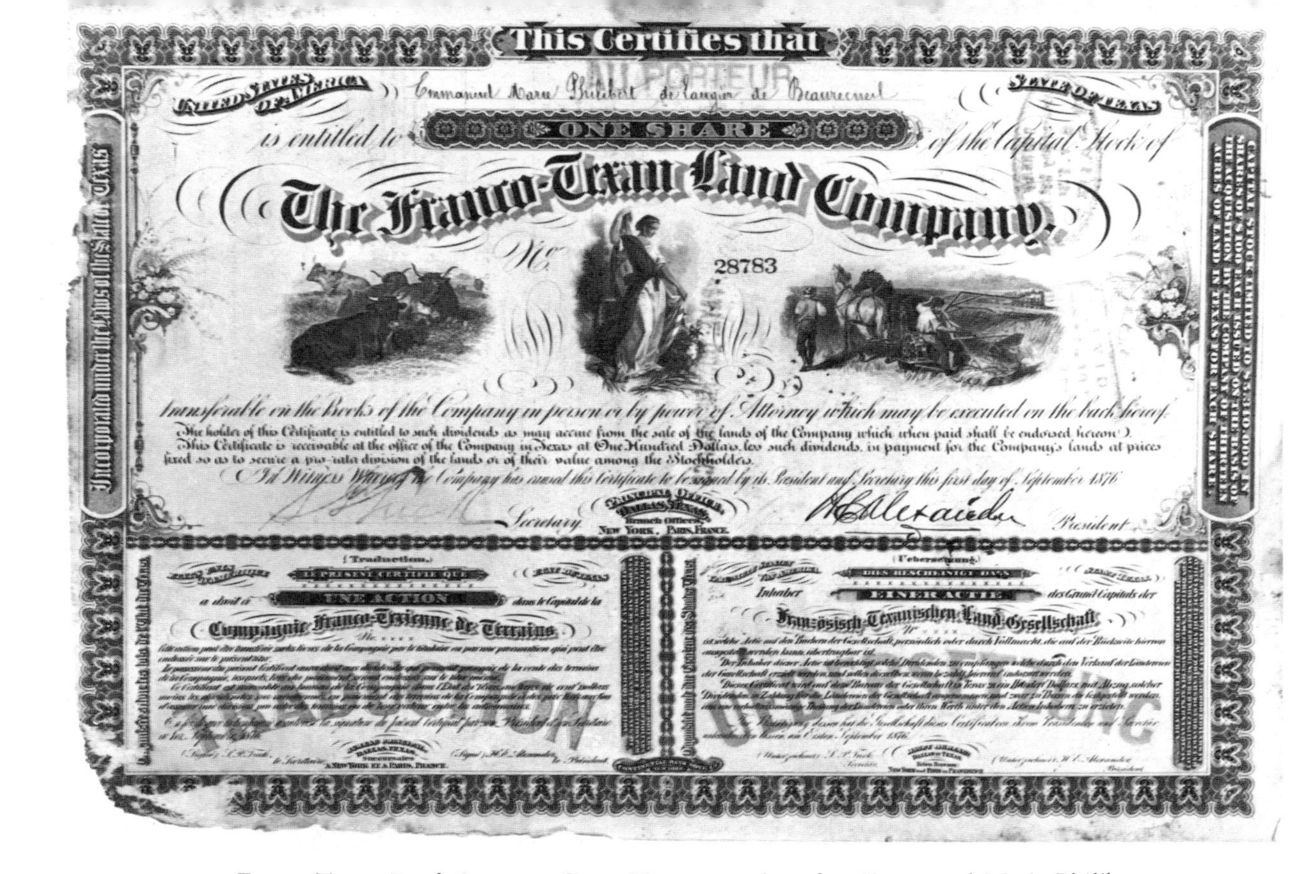
This Certifies that

United States of America

Emmanuel Marie Philibert de Langier de Beaurecueil

State of Texas

is entitled to ONE SHARE of the Capital Stock of

The Franco-Texan Land Company.

No. 28783

transferable on the Books of the Company in person or by power of Attorney which may be executed on the back hereof.

The holder of this Certificate is entitled to such dividends as may accrue from the sale of the lands of the Company which when paid shall be endorsed hereon.

This Certificate is receivable at the office of the Company in Texas at One Hundred Dollars, less such dividends, in payment for the Company's lands at prices fixed so as to secure a pro-rata division of the lands or of their value among the Stockholders.

In Witness Whereof the Company has caused this Certificate to be signed by its President and Secretary this first day of September 1876.

Secretary

New York, Paris, France.

H. E. Alexander President

Capital Stock limited to $5,340,000 in shares of $100 each issued on the basis of the acquisition by the Company of thirteen acres of land in Texas for each share.

Incorporated under the Laws of the State of Texas

(Traduction.)

Une Action

Compagnie Franco-Texienne de Terrains

(Uebersetzung.)

Einer Actie

Französisch-Texanischen Land-Gesellschaft

Traduction

Uebersetzung

3. Franco-Texan Land Company Share No. 28783, issued to Emmanuel Marie Philibert de Langier de Beaurecueil and receivable at $100 at the office of the company in Texas.

Courtesy of the Bexar Archives.

AU PORTEUR

For Value Received, I hereby assign and transfer unto ....
or bearer, the Share of the Capital Stock represented by the within Certificate, and do hereby irrevocably constitute and appoint the Secretary, or Assistant Secretary, of the within-named Company my Attorney to transfer the said stock on the Books thereof.

Dated, ... 27th [illegible] [illegible]

In presence of .... [illegible]

[Traduction.]
Pour Valeur Reçue je cède et transfère par ces présents à * * * ou au porteur l'action du capital social representée par le présent certificat, et par ces présents je nomme et constitue le Sécretaire, ou le Sous-Sécretaire de la Compagnie y mentionnée mon mandataire irrévocable pour opérer le transfert du dit titre sur les livres de la dite Compagnie.
Daté, ce * * * * *
En présence de * * * * * *

[Uebersetzung.]
Für empfangenen Werth cedire und überschreibe ich hiermit an * * * * * oder Ueberbringer, die Actie des Grund-Capitals, die dieses Certificat repräsentirt, und ernenne hiermit unwiderruflich den Secretär oder den Assistent-Secretär der darin genannten Gesellschaft meinen Bevollmächtigten, die besagte Actie auf den Büchern der Gesellschaft zu übertragen.
Datirt am * * * * 18
Als Zeuge: * * * * *

RECEIVED DIVIDENDS AS FOLLOWS:
Reçu dividendes ainsi qu'il suit:
Empfangen Dividende wie folgt:

DATE. DATE. **Datum.**	AMOUNT OF DIVIDEND. MONTANT DU DIVIDENDE. **Betrag der Dividende.**	SIGNATURE. SIGNATURE. **Unterschrift.**
[illegible] 1884	Soixante cents (trois francs)	[illegible]
16 7bre 1886	Un dollar cinq francs	[illegible]
16 7bre 1886	Un dollar vingt cents (six francs)	[illegible]
27 SEPT. 1890	PAYÉ: QUATRE FRANCS.	[illegible]
	PAYÉ: dix FRANCS	[illegible]
	PAYÉ: trois FRANCS	[illegible]
	PAYÉ: cinq FRANCS	[illegible]
	PAYÉ QUATRE FRANCS	[illegible]
8 FEB. 1895	PAYÉ SIX FRANCS	[illegible]
22 FEB. 1896	PAYÉ SIX FRANCS	[illegible]

DIVIDEND
Déclared May 15th 1899
$ 1.15c
PAID

PAID

4. Franco-Texan Land Company Share No. 28783 (back), showing a record of the payment of dividends.

Courtesy of the Bexar Archives.

Land Office in Northern Texas,
rge Hotel), . . . DALLAS, TEXAS.

ds throughout the State of Texas. Pe
of UNQUESTIONABLE TITLES, also
ed to give us a trial.
et rates, and will render property fo
titles, and do everything pertaining to a

style, on short notice and at reasonable

lin, Grayson, Kaufman, Rockwall, John-
pt of the money. Also correct Maps of

REFERENCES

RE,

n

OCERIES

Produce,

Dallas, Texas.

IALTY.

ry produce. Goods delivered to the

HOUSE,

TEXAS.

L IN GALVESTON.

p to a Standard of Excellence Second t
est.

, ACCORDING TO ROOMS.

roprietor.

Extremely Low Monthly Rate

COTTER'S

Don't suffer with Headache any longer.

HEADACHE

—WORK LIKE A CHARM—

PILLS!

Sent by mail, postage paid, on receipt of price—
50 cents. Orders solicited for Drugs, Chemicals, &c

—R. COTTER,—
Manufacturing Druggist,
P. O. Box 327. HOUSTON, TEXAS

PLASTER of PARIS.

—THE—

Franco-Texan Land Co.

LONE STAR

PLASTER OF PARIS FACTORY

A. CHAPTIVE, President; E. CHIFFLET,
Gen'l Sup't and Manager.
Are prepared to fill orders for Plaster of Paris
of best quality at reasonable rates.
E. CHIFFLET,
Fresnay City,
m7-6m Sweet Water P. O., Texas

C. E. VREELAND,
Wholesale Dealer in

PAPER,

Printers' Supplies,

Blank Books, Stationery, Paper Bags,

Twines, Etc., Etc.

407 MAIN STREET, DALLAS, TEXAS.
Printed manilla wrapping paper a specialty,
all sizes and weights, with cuts and cards suitable for any kind ...

5. The Franco-Texan Land Company advertises its Lone Star Plaster factory at Sweetwater in the Dallas *Daily Herald,* from March 7, 1882, through February 2, 1883.

6. a. Henry P. Du Bellet, vice-secretary of the Franco-Texan Land Company and manager of the Société Foncière et Agricole des États Unis.

b. Sam H. Milliken, businessman, of Weatherford, Texas.

Both pictures courtesy of Mrs. Alfred Hammond.

7. George P. Levy, president of the Franco-Texan Land Company (1889–1902), and his wife. Mrs. Levy was the stepdaughter of Dr. C. A. Otterbein.

Courtesy of the Institute of Texas Cultures and Mrs. Alfred Hammond.

The Finest Lands in the World.

500,000 ACRES

That splendid body of lands recently owned by the

FRANCO-TEXAN LAND COMPANY

Extending through Parker, Palo Pinto, Stevens, Nolan, Shackelford, Taylor and Jones counties and comprehending

500,000 ACRES!

Has been bought by the undersigned and are now offered for sale on easy terms. Those lands were specially selected out of

MANY MILLIONS OF ACRES

reserved to the Texas and Pacific Railway and comprehend the very finest lands to be found in Texas.

COTTON, CORN, OATS

Wheat, Fruits and Vegetables

Are grown to perfection. To parties wishing homes in a

Healthy Country

and upon fertile lands we offer special inducements. Address

JAMES B. SIMPSON,

President Inter-State Railway Company.

DALLAS, - - TEXAS.

8. An Inter-State Railway Construction Company advertisement in the Fort Worth *Gazette,* offering Franco-Texan lands for sale, September 30, 1890.

WEATHERFORD.

The Constitution has interviewed a good many of Weatherford's leading business men, and find that all are doing a good business, and from the buyers it learns that goods are being sold cheaper in Weatherford than in any other town in Texas. A careful directory of the city is being prepared for this column, and will be completed in a day or two Of the following a few are estimated, while others are correct, and all will be corrected within the next two or three days:

3 National banks.
1 Building and loan association.
1 Water works system.
1 Electric light system.
1 Mattress factory.
3 Denominational schools.
4 Public schools.
2 Private schools.
10 Churches.
1 Daily newspaper.
1 Horticultural paper.
1 School paper.
3 Weekly newspapers.
1 Steam printing establishment.
1 Exclusive job office.
2 Shoe shops.
2 Real estate and abstract offices.
13 Dry goods stores.
2 Gents' furnishing goods stores.
2 Wholesale grocery stores.
25 Grocery and confectionery stores.
2 Jewelry stores.
1 Shoe store.

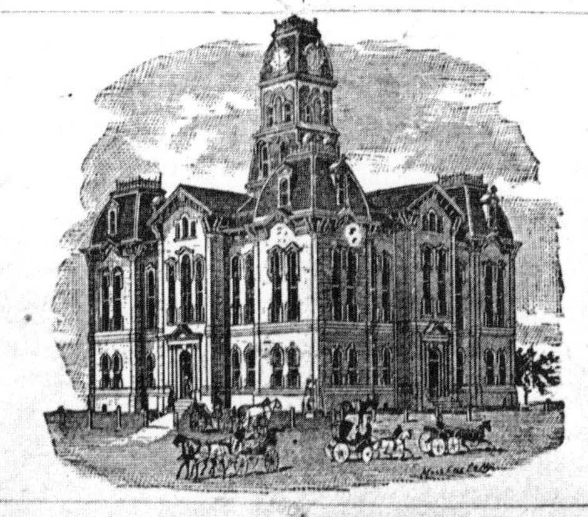

1 Ice factory.
1 Street railway association.
1 Commercial club.
3 Independent railway systems.
1 General offices of railway company.
1 Franco-Texan land company.
1 Castor oil mill.
4 Roller flouring mills.
1 Planing mill.
3 Steam gins.
1 Iron works.
1 Iron foundry.
2 Marble yards.
6 Hotels.
1 Broom factory.
1 Canning factory.
1 Mineral water and blueing factory.
7 blacksmith shops.
1 Candy factory.
4 Butcher shops.
5 Hardware stores.
10 Physicians.
15 Lawyers.
8 Contractors and builders.
4 Livery stables.
4 Wagon yards.
25 To one hundred enterprises not yet enumerated.
3 Lumber yards.
1 Quart dealer in Liquors.
7 Saloons. 4 Grain and feed dealers,
3 Hide and wool buyers.
2 Commission Merchants.
2 Fire insurance agencies.
3 Cotton yards.
6 Cotton buying firms.
1 Chatauqua park and hotel company.
2 Bus lines. 2 Float lines.

9. Weatherford's third and present courthouse, with a list of the city's assets, in which the Franco-Texan Land Company appears as the tenth item (1890).

Courtesy of Fred Cotten, Weatherford, Texas.

10. a. Thomas A. Scott, president of the Texas and Pacific Railway Company (1872–1881) and former president of the Union Pacific and Pennsylvania railroads.

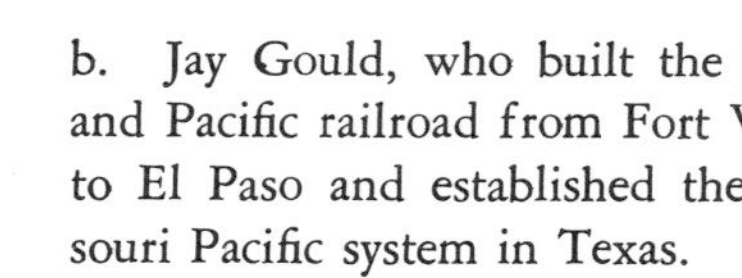

b. Jay Gould, who built the Texas and Pacific railroad from Fort Worth to El Paso and established the Missouri Pacific system in Texas.

c. Marshall O. Roberts, president of the Texas and Pacific Railway Company after its merger with the Southern Transcontinental and the Southern Pacific of Texas.

These three pictures courtesy of the Texas and Pacific Railway Company.

11. Texas and Pacific Engine No. 20, the little wood-burner which pulled the first train into Fort Worth in 1876.

Courtesy of the Texas and Pacific Railway Company.

12. Mrs. Alfred Hammond (de Voisins), the last surviving original member of the French Colony at Weatherford.

Courtesy of Mrs. Alfred Hammond.

13. Views of the Alfred Hammond stock farm and home, a few miles south of Weatherford. The house shows elements of the French influence on the architecture of the region.

Courtesy of Mrs. Alfred Hammond.

14. Belle Plain College, established in 1884 at Belle Plain, the first county seat of Callahan County.

Courtesy of J. D. Freeman.

15. The home of Dr. and Mrs. C. A. Otterbein, who came from Belgium to Weatherford in 1856.

Courtesy of Mrs. Alfred Hammond.

HORSES FOR SALE!

IMPORTED STOCK STABLES,

Two Miles South of Weatherford, on the Cleburne road, Parker County.

Directly Imported from France. Best trotters in the World. Stock still unknown in the United States, and highly estimated by breeders in Europe.

Come and See for Yourselves.
COME ONE! COME ALL!

P. de Bresson, Prop'r.

Stock Visible Every Thursday between 2 and 6 p. m., after and from the 15th of November next.

16. Comte Paul de Bresson advertises the sale of horses imported from France, in the Weatherford Constitution, November 6, 1889.

The Franco-Texan Land Company was introduced to this vibrant community by the following item in the weekly *Exponent*:

FRANCO-TEXAN LAND COMPANY

We have been handed by Sam Milliken a copy of a Paris paper, *Le Conseiler*, containing the report of the directory of the Franco-Texan Land Company. This company is composed of the creditors of the old Memphis and El Paso railroad, which charter and franchises are now the property of the Texas and Pacific line. The debts of the old company were assumed by the present corporation, as well as the charter, and the Texas and Pacific company have been compelled to turn over several million acres of their Texas land grant to the French company to satisfy the creditors of the old Fremont scheme.

These lands are soon to be placed on the market to be sold for what they will bring. The Texas headquarters of the Company have been established at Dallas, and the American headquarters in New York City.

Our townsman, Sam H. Milliken has been elected one of the five directors of the company in America; the other four are H. E. Alexander, J. A. Davenport, S. P. Tuck, New York; W. T. Kimmel, Washington, D.C.[6]

Another land company was no novelty in northwest Texas, and although the slightly inaccurate story branded the Franco-Texan as a foreign enterprise, there is nothing to indicate that it was received with misgiving. Even the aura of scandal seemed to be mitigated by the presence of a local man on the board of directors. Like many other land companies, the Franco-Texan bought, leased, and sold land, but since its primary purpose was to sell, it entered upon that phase of its business immediately. The general order of the day was to encourage immigration by copious advertising in local and out of state newspapers and by circulation of handbills and other descriptive literature. The Donaho & Milliken Land Company, from which Sam H. Milliken had just announced his withdrawal, was distributing a pamphlet entitled *Texas as It Is*; the Texas and Pacific was sending out thousands of maps and circulars, offering an alluring prospectus of the resources of Texas; J. W. Throckmorton was advertising 58,000 acres of first class

[6] Weatherford *Exponent*, April 28, 1877.

land on Elm Creek and beautiful lots in the town of Williamsburg. The Texas Emigration Agency, 321 Market Street, Harrisburg, Pennsylvania, was a cooperative project with a double motive, to sell land and increase the passenger traffic on the Pennsylvania, the Texas and Pacific, and the Houston and Texas Central lines. It entered the competition with a *Description of Northwestern Texas*, by Captain C. H. Cole,[7] to-wit:

OUR CLIMATE

is mild and salubrious. In sunshine the heat is rarely oppressive; the thermometer rarely rises above 96 degrees, and sunstrokes are unknown; none of your hot, sultry weather there; refreshing breezes are always blowing from the South; as their balmy breath, with the fragrance of many flowers, fans your heated brow, you feel as if you were being transposed to some fond elysian shore, where the weary are at rest and your creditors come no more. The nights are delightful; very few of them you'll find uncomfortable sleeping under a blanket or quilt. The greatest country in the world for sweet refreshing sleep; our pretended winter lasts about two months; during this time we may have some four or five Northers, each lasting from one to three days; even the weather is seldom cold enough to produce ice, and snow is rarely seen. No feeding or sheltering is necessary for stock at any time of the year; the grass is green winter and summer.

THE HEALTH

The health of the country is unsurpassed; many who have been afflicted for years have become vigorous after a short residence there, especially those with lung diseases, neuralgia, chills and fever, *etc.*; no malaria with a high altitude; we are clear of the damp mist of the coast. This is no place for doctors or apothecaries to reap a golden harvest by selling and dispensing their drugs to suffering humanity. Our population is increasing, within the last two years especially. Weatherford, the county seat of Parker County, will soon have direct connections with the outward world by the completion of the Texas and Pacific and H. T. Central, which forms a junction at the above-named city, with the T. and P. passing west through Palo Pinto, Stephens, Shackelford, Jones, and thence on to the golden shores of the Pacific.

[7] C. H. Cole was formerly the editor of the Weatherford *News* and had been strongly opposed to the Texas and Pacific Railroad.

INDIAN STORIES, *ETC.*

Don't be scared from a home like this by listening to the many snake and Indian stories you may hear. They are all the *merest bosh.* The red man ceased to tread our broad expanse more than two years ago. Civilization has crowded him out until there isn't a wigwam within one hundred and fifty miles of our line. Ladies and children travel along all over our country without the slightest fear. If the Government continues to offer adequate protection there will be no more trouble in this region. In all candor, we are in no more danger of the red man now than are the money-lenders on Wall Street. Snakes are no more numerous here than you'll find in other States. We haven't one-third as many poisonous snakes as you'll find in Missouri, Pennsylvania, Kentucky, Ohio, and Illinois and many other States that consider themselves by no means snaky to hurt . . .

This invitation to paradise continued for twenty-one pages, accompanied by facts, figures, and testimonials, with two full pages devoted to Parker County, and on the back it gave the railway schedule from Harrisburg, Pennsylvania, to Fort Worth and the points on the four-horse stage line from Fort Worth to El Paso. The text referred to several Texas and Pacific agencies on the route, and at the foot of page 21 it concluded with:

Texas Franco Land Company who have seven hundred and fifty thousand acres of first class land for sale, on easy terms, in Parker, Palo Pinto, Stephens, and Shackelford counties.

Address Davenport & Gray
No. 9, Nassau Street, New York.

On December 1, 1877, the Franco-Texan Land Company announced through a paid ad in the *Exponent* that its Secretary would be at Weatherford from the 5th to the 15 of December, "Prepared to sell the Lands belonging to said Company in the Railroad Reserve in Parker County and counties west. Preference given to actual settlers."[8]

Of the six land sales reported on February 23, 1878, one was that of the Franco-Texan Land Company to A. M. Hempill: 174 61/100 acres for $654.23; and on March 9, seven of the nine real estate transfers were made by the Franco-Texan. They were small tracts sell-

[8] Weatherford *Exponent*, December 1, 1877.

ing from $2.00 to $3.35 per acre. Secretary S. P. Tuck announced on March 16 that the deeds for sales made in the month of December and January were ready for delivery except for sections 17, 67, 161, 163, and 297, which would arrive shortly.[9]

Palo Pinto, the seat of government and the only town in the adjoining county of Palo Pinto, had a population of only 200 in 1877, but immigration had begun on an astonishing scale, and land was selling from $1.50 to $7.00 per acre. Shirley & Ross were agents for the Franco-Texan Land Company and the Texas and Pacific Railway Company. On February 26, 1878, they announced that these two companies owned all the odd-numbered sections in the railroad reserve in Palo Pinto County and the lands were for sale with preference given to actual settlers until April 1, 1878.[10] On May 3, 1878, the following ad appeared:

RAILROAD LANDS
538,135 acres for sale

The Franco-Texan Land Company has acquired title to 538,135 acres of odd-numbered sections in the sixteen-mile Reservation in counties of Parker, Palo Pinto, Stephens, Shackelford, Callahan, Jones, Taylor, Nolan, Fisher, and Scurry. All parties are hereby notified not to settle on same. The Law will be vigorously enforced against anyone found cutting timber or trespassing in any manner on the lands, which are now offered for sale, on time in tracts of forty acres and upwards.

H. E. Alexander, President
S. P. Tuck, Secy.
Weatherford, Texas.

We will receive applications to purchase and give necessary information relative to said lands. Those living on lands must apply and purchase at once. Shirley & Ross, Agents.[11]

The land business seemed to be well under way, not only in Parker and Palo Pinto counties but also farther west, and on November 6, 1878, the Franco-Texan, by amendment to its charter, made Weather-

[9] *Ibid.*, February 23, and March 9, 1878.

[10] *The Western Star* (Palo Pinto), February 26, 1878.

[11] *Ibid.*, May 3, 1878. Massie & Cunningham later took over the agency from Shirley & Ross (*Palo Pinto County Star*, June 27, 1885).

ford its official headquarters in Texas. The amendment had been made at a directors meeting held August 19, 1877, but it was not filed with the Secretary of State until more than a year later.

How much land Gray and Tuck sold or how many colonists they brought in is not known. There is a record, however, of a Franco-Texan colonization project which failed in 1878. In an effort to establish two hundred Russian Mennonites on the company's land in Taylor County, a delegation was brought out to select a suitable site with Samuel L. Chalk as a guide and surveyor. With drivers, cooks, two mule teams, two wagons, and a four-horse ambulance, it was quite a large group. After searching diligently for two weeks, the party failed to find a desirable spot. While most of these people finally settled in Arkansas, a few remained and drifted into northern Callahan County.[12]

There were only two main roads in northwest Texas at this time, the old Butterfield Trail and the Center Line Trail surveyed by the Texas and Pacific in 1874. The Center Line Trail was not really a road, but it could be followed all the way from Weatherford to El Paso, and it became the basis for later roads. A man who went into Taylor County in 1878 still took his life in his hands, and Chalk relied heavily on the Trail while he was guiding the Mennonites and other colonists into the open prairies.

The Franco-Texan was already drawing immigrants from France into northwest Texas though not on a large scale, because the French did not generally emigrate. It was also drawing immigrants of French descent from Louisiana and other central and southern states where their ancestors had settled more than a century before. The company was then advertising land for $1.00 an acre, and one of its brochures pictured a steamboat afloat on the waters of the West Fork of the Trinity. In 1878 the *Sun* reported that eighty-nine Frenchmen had just arrived in New York and were on their way to northwest Texas to form a colony.[13] Some of these colonists remained in Weatherford while others scattered to small settlements in the West—to Belle Plain, Fort Griffin, Breckenridge, and Buffalo Gap.

[12] Abilene *Reporter-News*, May 24, 1932, (50th Anniversary Edition).
[13] Galveston *Daily News*, July 28, 1878.

CHAPTER 5

PARIS, FRANCE

Originally, French citizens had bought Memphis, El Paso, and Pacific bonds as an investment. They had not planned to go to Texas to live. It was now nine years since they first bought their bonds and two years since they had exchanged them for Franco-Texan stock. Most of them either had forgotten about this stock, or considered it worthless. But there were some adventurous souls, like the Du Bellets, who had bought up additional stock and were quite willing to carry on for the captive group of Frenchmen, Algerians, Germans, and Alsace Lorrainers who had put Gray and Tuck in business. Even so, all they had in 1878 was their stock certificates and a copy of the Franco-Texan charter. Gray continued to control the company from New York, while Tuck was in Weatherford selling land at a rapid rate. The French were totally ignored, and Paul Pecquet du Bellet, seeing that drastic reorganization was necessary, planned to effect it by electing General Beauregard president of the company. Beauregard's great name would enable him to accomplish what others could not—in France as well as in the United States. Having already intimated his idea to the General,

Du Bellet took up his correspondence on April 13, 1878, as follows:

Franco-Texan Land Company
3a Rue de la Bruyere Paris, April 3, 1878

My dear friend: 363 St. Claude St., New Orleans

I have just received your kind letter of the 18th of March, and as the postman comes today, I do not want to let him go without acknowledging its receipt. First, some words about the Franco-Texan. The project I spoke to you about, far from being dead, is more alive than ever, and my French board fully decided to entrust the direction of the company in America to you, but as you know we are bound for one year by the elections of last March 29, and we are awaiting the next stockholders' meeting in order to recommend complete and absolute reform of our American company, which, I must say, leaves much to be desired. The board still believes that my trip to America is necessary to effect this reorganization. This point will be brought up at the meeting, supported by the board, and if it is adopted, I do not need to tell you how happy I will be to have you as our new president. Furthermore, I confess that outside of such a decision by the stockholders I do not see any hope, and I do not conceal the fact that our board is very dissatisfied with the domination of those New York gentlemen, and really, that hands off attitude of Yankeedom is fabulous. But with some patience I expect to succeed in my purpose, and I am all the more convinced that a very great responsibility rests on me personally since the great majority of the stockholders are trusting in my efforts. Perhaps I will soon have the opportunity to write you again on this subject, and I will be very grateful if you will kindly consent—as it will help me in the arduous task before me—to write a long report in *French*, giving me your personal and general opinion of the resources of Texas and the probable current value of the company's property in case its affairs should be wisely and honestly administered. Also, give me a few words on what you consider to be the best form of administration. Supported by such a document, I would feel confident of convincing the stockholders *en bloc* because your strength would be added to that I already have. Our lands are situated in Parker, Palo Pinto, Jones, Stephens, Shackelford, Nolan, and Mitchell counties and are within the zone indicated on the enclosed map. They form part of the Memphis, El Paso, and Pacific reservation.

A word now about the Calcassieu sulphur mines. I have not yet received the documents you mention. As soon as I have them, I shall seriously consider that matter and its chances of success (I have just received Professor Nicholson's report, but it is too late to study it).

However, permit me to suggest an idea which I think practical and capable of the best results. Why shouldn't you try to obtain an option from that company for six months or one year. With all the stock of the old company we can then organize a new company under your management and issue some shares and bonds here in Paris, guaranteed by the charter, franchises, and stock of our company. With your well-prepared prospectus, the influence of your name will go far, very far, in assuring our success. If, as you say, the income can be raised to $100,000 per year, it will be easy for us to organize a company with a capital of 3,000,000 francs, which would bear an interest of 16.65 per cent and allow us a profit of 2,000,000 francs, or $400,000 which is legitimate since we would have a much higher interest rate than that of European companies.

Reflect, my dear friend, on this plan which I think is so much better, as I am almost certain of being able to sell our shares or bonds to my own clientele.

Try to get control of the business by the method I suggest, form your new company under the presidency of General Beauregard, and I do not believe I risk too much in saying that I will do the rest in Paris.

Write to De Leon[1] about sending me the documents in question.

On receipt of this letter, please send me a telegram with the simple word "Good," if you think my idea practical.

Awaiting your answer and assuring you of my very sincere friendship.

P. du Bellet

Monsieur Le General G. T. Beauregard

April 16, 1878

Confidential

My dear Beauregard:

If you accept the office which I expect the board of directors to confer on you, I would like to place under your orders as secretary a young relative of ours whose family has been completely ruined by the War of Secession and who is taking care of his two sisters. His name is Edward Brooke; his address is 1113 Main Street, Richmond, Virginia. He is a lawyer by profession and would be glad to come to Weatherford to attend to the business

[1] Edwin de Leon, the Confederate agent sent to France to enlist support and turn French public opinion in favor of the Confederacy.

of our company. He is my wife's first cousin and is a very intelligent and deserving young man.

Because of the position I occupy in the company I would prefer that our relationship is not known until further orders. I shall ask you then, as a favor, to include his name as one of the two persons whose names you telegraph to me as directors. You see that according to our by-laws one can exercise these two functions simultaneously. You could recommend him to us as secretary, and nothing else would have to be done.

Also, if you think it suitable, you may write to him at the above address.

Your very devoted friend,
P. du Bellet

April 16, 1878

Confidential
My dear Beauregard:

Far from having given up the plan in regard to our company, we are now more determined than ever to extricate ourselves from our present situation because our experience in the past year shows that reform is necessary and urgent. Also, I want to have a long and intimate talk with you.

So that there will be no need to recapitulate before the deluge, I remind you that our corporation is made up of 2,900 bondholders owning 41,373 shares covering 536,549 acres of land situated in the counties indicated in one of my preceding letters. In all the Americans own 50 shares ($5,000), and furthermore, they bought them only *to qualify as directors.*

Acting by virtue of the authority given by the old bondholders of the Memphis, El Paso, today our partners, Mr. Gray announced one fine day that the Franco-Texan Land Company was established, and he sent his emissary to us in Paris, a young man 25 years of age, who brought a charter with certain by-laws and some deeds to deliver to those entitled to them. You understand, don't you, that we Frenchmen find ourselves confronted by accomplished facts, without our participation and without our consent to the specific organization which was then imposed on us. So that you can get a better idea of the strange situation in which he has placed us I am sending you by this mail,

1. a copy of the charter and by-laws of the F T L Co.;
2. one of our shares;
3. one issue of the newspaper which contains the report made at our first stockholders' meeting.

It seems to me that in such a simple case as that of liquidating properties which belong exclusively to the French, a charter and by-laws are extremely complicated and offer inextricable difficulties. And consequently, at the very moment the company was organized, under the pretext that a French company could not own real estate in Texas, they bestowed on us a board of directors composed of thirteen members; eight of those members, forming a majority, reside in France. Of the five American members, only one resides in Texas, a Mr. Milliken; two in New York, Mr. Davenport and Mr. H. E. Alexander; another in Washington; and finally, Mr. Tuck, our secretary, who travels from New York to Texas, from Texas to New York, and from there to Paris. Three of the American directors form an executive committee, which, from New York, is supposed to direct and conduct all the operations in Texas, or you see from this that the French majority of the board of directors is subject, with respect to the stockholders, to the executive committee, and, by the vice of that arrangement, is entirely at the mercy of the secretary of the company, who should reside in Texas, without the French board having any effective control over the executive committee or over its own secretary who is also a member of the executive committee.

You see at once how dangerous that situation is for the stockholders and how disagreeable it is for the French board, which I must say, does not begin to understand the necessity of having its president and one of its divisions, the executive committee, in New York a thousand leagues from its principal seat of operations. The outcome of these complications is that up to the present we have not been able to obtain any account of the expenditures in Texas. Now that I have warned you of the dangers which confront us, I am going to enumerate the reforms which I consider necessary.

1. We should dissolve the New York executive committee, which does not seem to have any excuse for being, and replace it with a real president residing in Texas, or as near Texas as possible, who would be the responsible agent of the French board and would have full authority over the secretary of the corporation, who would have to reside in Weatherford.

2. We should reduce the number of American directors to three (See Article 13, Title 3, of the By-Laws), "at least three of whom must reside in the United States."

3. We should modify Article 6 of the charter, which fixes the capital stock at $5,340,000, as follows: "The capital stock of this corporation is composed of land situated in the state of Texas and comes from the old

reservation of the Memphis, El Paso, and Pacific, and can never amount to more than 700,000 acres of land"; and leave all the 2nd paragraph of the same article except the words "of 100 dollars," which it will be necessary to delete and end as follows: "as written below."

Although they have told us many times that according to the laws of Texas, every company is forced to declare a *dollar* capital, I insist on that point because (1) it seems impossible that the Texas law has not foreseen the case of a natural market; and (2) because from the French point of view that modification has a vital importance. Having a seat at Paris we can from one day to the next be called to account by the laws of registry, and in due time it would be necessary for us to pay a certain per cent on the capital declared in our charter instead of a certain per cent on the estimated value of our land, which is our sole capital.

The board is determined to send me to America to have an understanding with you on all these points, and I would have been there long since if it were not for the problem of money which may again delay my departure as we have not had any up to the present time. Counting on your friendship, I am also asking you to study our case and all the questions involved and to send me a memorial which I could submit to my board, and if necessary, at the stockholders' meeting, which I will find some means of delaying until about the end of June.

If the changes suggested cannot be sought from the state of Texas (amendments to the charter) without a vote of the stockholders, I will do what is necessary to authorize the board to ask for them, but in the meantime I will propose reducing the number of American directors to three—these three would be new members, you and two other persons whom you could choose yourself and one of whom would reside permanently in Weatherford as secretary of the company.

It goes without saying, my dear friend, that we do not intend to limit your observations and suggestions to the above plan. On the contrary, the board wants a full study, embracing your views, of a complete and radical reorganization, capable of functioning regularly and of giving satisfaction and security to the stockholders.

I have your first letter before me. If your first estimate has not changed, this business can amply repay anyone who is seriously interested in it, provided that he helps us to make it return as much as possible. And you are certainly the one. You understand that in our situation I do not speak of your emoluments. The sum you mentioned did not appear too large, but not yet having funds at its disposition, the board thought it should first attend to the emergencies. The day that it decides on complete reform that question will again be brought up for discussion.

Let me review. We wish to reorganize everything. Do you agree to co-operate?

We wish to have in America a serious president who is responsible and capable of directing our affairs himself. Do you wish to be, can you be that President?

Perhaps, while waiting for our meeting, it would be advisable to appoint you as controller at once (Title X of our by-laws). Would you accept that position first? If so, we could give you the authority necessary to perform those duties; we would authorize you to receive the necessary amount from our treasurer and would order him to pay you.

As we do not have a moment to lose, I am asking you to send me a telegram immediately on receipt of the present, telling me whether you will accept the controllership. At present it is understood between us that the acceptance of the first office requires the acceptance of the second.

I think I have explained everything. If I have forgot something, the documents I am sending will give you enough information to fill the gaps and suggest some method of carrying out the reorganization which we all desire on that side.

Your very devoted and affectionate friend,
P. du Bellet

Please answer in French. In your telegram you could give me the names of the two persons whom you would like to have as directors.

Paris, May 24, 1878

My dear friend:

I received your two letters relative to our company at the same time I received the one about the Calcassieu. I have informed the Vicomte Fleuriot de Langle and Viscount d'Judy of the part I was to read to them, and since it was very convincing, we are trying to carry out our plan. The stockholders meeting is convoked for the 25th of next June, and we are working for a satisfactory result. I will write you more the first of next week. As you thought, our great obstacle is the financial situation which our executive committee in New York does not seem disposed to improve. They would be willing here to establish the credit you require, but that could be done only by authorizing you officially, after your appointment, to contract a mortgage loan on the property of the company. We are studying these questions, and I believe it will be necessary for the board or the stockholders to decide to send me to America.

Goodbye for the present
and sincerely yours,
P. du Bellet

G. T. Beauregard

Paris, August 9, 1878

My dear Beauregard:

We are always in the same embarrassing situation, and although we have sent our President Mr. Alexander the express order to discount the notes we have in his custody in New York and have asked the resignation of two American directors, we have not heard from those gentlemen. The board is beginning to see that the executive committee is quite determined to hold it down and kill it by starvation.

According to our by-laws the board can make amendments without restriction, and I, on my part, am resolved to abolish the executive committee and replace it with a supervisory committee composed of three members under the control of the president, giving him all the power the board possesses, and to precipitate events, at the next meeting of the board which I have had called for the current 20th, I propose to ask for the revocation of the powers of the executive committee, and with that done, to resign as a member of the board of directors, have you named director in my place, and then to have all the necessary authority delegated to you so that you may represent the company in America as delegate-director until the next stockholders' meeting, which we can then call in order to elect the board of directors which will name you as president.

In the meantime, the board will authorize you to ask Mr. Alexander to deliver the notes which belong to us and to discount them for the use of the company. You would have to go back to New York, you see, so you could have an understanding with our recalcitrant directors and force them, in case of refusal, to execute the resolutions of the Paris board of directors, and you would do that without my going to New York to aid you since we do not have the money and must count on your strength to take what those gentlemen do not wish to hand over to us.

That is my program for the current 20th, and I hope to succeed because our world here is more than tired of the ill-will which reigns in New York and for so long a time has accomplished nothing.

I count on you for the execution of this *coup d'état*. The discounting of the notes will furnish you the means of operation, and the only question left to be settled will be that of your salary, and I hope that the report which you send me will convince the board that the $6,000 you ask will be a necessary expense, well-employed in the interest of the company. That sum at first appeared large to some members of the board, whom I did not try to convince, but the last communications which we had with the executive committee will open their eyes because they are all beginning to believe they will never receive a cent as long as the executive committee is in control.

Such is our situation, such is our program. It seems to me that the Southern California had the upper hand over the Texas and Pacific at the last session of Congress. Since the democrats, in the person of Mr. Morison, are defending, or rather, pleading the cause of the first, I suppose that the Southern California will touch our lands on the west before the Texas and Pacific reaches us on the east. What do you think of the respective situation of those two lines from the debates of the last session?

If I succeed on the 20th, I will telegraph you, and I ask you to be thinking of me at the same time.

Your devoted friend,
P. du Bellet

Paris, August 26, 1878

General Beauregard, New Orleans
My dear friend:

I received your kind letter of the 4th of this month, announcing your intention of returning to the west. I am sending this to the same address, hoping that it will reach you wherever you are. I thank you for your favorable opinion of my report, and for the sake of our stockholders I hope that it has produced the same effect on them as on you because the terrible conspiracy against which I have had to struggle continues its attacks and even goes so far as to question the name that I bear.

I failed in all my efforts to convene the board on the 20th of this month; I was unable to do it. At the time of my sojourn in the country I had only four members out of eight so I lacked a majority. It will be necessary to give up the execution of the plan which I indicated in my last letter. The present members are all on the financial committee, as it is so constituted, and after deliberating it passed a resolution ordering correctional action against our slanderers, and it adjourned expecting to have a board meeting in the course of the next month; at that time I will attempt the *coup d'état* which I have discussed with you and which I sincerely believe is necessary to save the situation. This leads me to mention a Mr. Sam H. Milliken who has been represented to us as a competent man in land affairs, whom we accepted on the board of directors and whom the executive committee wants to remove from the board, demanding his resignation instead of that of Mr. Tuck, which he had thought wise since the functions of director and member of the executive committee were incompatible with those of secretary or vice-treasurer.

Mr. Milliken resides in Weatherford, Parker County. He is a banker and land broker; if I am not wrong, he must have an interest in the newspaper, the Weatherford *Times*, and he quite recently made a contract with the Texas and Pacific Railway Company to construct and bring the railroad to Weatherford. Under the circumstances and in view of the radical changes which we wish to effect in the organization of our company, don't you think it advisable, it is simply a suggestion, to get some true information on Mr. Sam H. Milliken—whether he is a Southern man, has a good reputation, or has any influence in the country. Perhaps it is to our advantage to keep him in the new administration because of the services which he could render to the company as a banker and the supervision he could exercise over the office at Weatherford in your absence, and the advice he might give our secretary even though the latter would be the young man of whom I have spoken. Also, in a large business it would certainly be desirable to always have a competent man on hand. However, my good friend, I repeat that this is a simple suggestion which I offer for your consideration because, if our *coup d'état* is successful we are quite determined to follow your advice to the exclusion of everything else.

Awaiting news from you, I send my warmest regards,
P. du Bellet

P. S. The fact that they seek to oust Mr. Milliken indicates to me that he could be an obstacle to the designs fomented at New York.

Paris, September 9, 1878

M. le General G. T. Beauregard
c/o Mr. W. S. Manin
52 Wall Street

My dear friend:

I have received your letter of the 26th of August from New York. I am glad to hear from you.

Today I gave your message to Mr. Vignaud, and I am going to see M. le Colonel Gerard who has not yet returned the Calcassieu dossier to me.

I expect the admiral in Paris in a few days. We are trying to convene the board early in October in order to proceed with the execution of our plans.

You say you are going to publish your story of our unfortunate war. I suppose you will do that work in English. I suggest that you grant me the privilege of translating it into French with permission to publish it in one of the large Paris newspapers, either in the form of a literary article or as a *variété*, and to make arrangements with a publisher to have it edited. If you accept that suggestion, I would like for you to send me your proofs as soon as they are printed, along with the photographs of the officers of whom you will speak. You should also give me your authorization to that effect.

Goodbye for the present. Waiting your answer, I send my warmest regards.
P. du Bellet

Paris, April 2, 1879

My dear friend:

After a hard struggle for two years and an open battle of three long months, during which the executive committee's delegate, sent to Paris for that purpose, has not ceased to slander and cast suspicion on the honor of such men as Admiral Fleuriot de Langle (the general of the Malroy Division), Vicomte d'Judy, Comte de Lallemand (the old French minister to China), the stockholders decided in my favor on the 31st of March, and I was able to overcome that Northern enemy which has sought every possible means of starving us so as to slaughter us easily on the day of the great combat. More fortunate than the South against Grant, we have baffled the enemy, and we have replaced Milliken with our friend General Debray, to whom I wrote today. And as for yourself, although I realize that your present duties do not permit you to exercise those of a director of our company, you will excuse my use of your name in view of the objective to be obtained and the friendly relations which exist between us. Although my name does not figure in the new roster, I will be the agent who is mentioned in the adopted resolutions. It is time for the mailman. I will write you a longer letter next Friday.

Your devoted friend,
P. du Bellet

Paris, April 4, 1879

General G. T. Beauregard
My dear friend:

I was so pressed for time last Wednesday that I was not able to give you any details on the strange events which developed here during the last three months, and which have just turned out successfully, bringing about the defeat of the famous executive committee. I am now going to fill that gap in order to give you a clear understanding of the situation. As I have told you many times, the executive committee never sent a single cent to Paris. A mortgage of 100,000 francs on the company's land was requested—nothing. An order was given to sell some land at lower prices, at a reduced price to the buyer for a sum of 25,000 francs—nothing. The committee was enjoined to discount the notes given by the first buyers to cover those falling due in Paris and to meet the expenses of the company in France—nothing. And during that time it was defraying its expenses in America with the money taken in, paying out more than the value of the sales made, from which it follows that we existed in France since our formation at the expense of some devoted directors while America was finding the means of getting along well or badly, as unconcerned as if we did not exist. Under these difficult and dangerous circumstances, a Mr. Chardot offered to buy 100,000 acres of land at the rate of 2.50 francs per acre payable in Paris, in cash, without discount or commission, persuaded that the sum of 250,000 for 100,000 acres of land, that is, nearly one-sixth of our property, was a consideration more advantageous to the Company than the pure and simple donation of 1/4 of each section coming to us, as recommended by Mr. Milliken of Weatherford, Texas. The board accepted that proposition subject to ratification by the stockholders who were to meet on December 10, 1878.

That decision was given to the executive committee which then resorted to sending a delegate to Paris, not to bring aid and assistance to the company, but simply for the purpose of fighting the board of directors and putting it under suspicion. That delegate, Mr. Tuck, arrives on the eve of the meeting, and the stockholders vote the measure proposed on December 10 by a very large majority, but, ironically, Mr. Tuck, secretary of the Texas Company, member of the executive committee—that is, an employee of the board, an agent—gathers up at that same meeting some of the members who are always ready for opposition, and he protests the legality of the meeting, saying, in need of a covert explanation, that according to our by-laws it is necessary to have one-third of the stockholders present in order to validate the action taken, or, although we have 42,000 shares, only 39,000 have been taken by those entitled to them, and the others are still waiting to be claimed, something which may never occur. According to our by-laws, those last shares must be returned to the common capital fund if they are not claimed within a period of five years after the establishment of the company. The board had always thought that 1/3 of the capital stock was sufficient for constituting a regular stockholders meeting. But Mr. Tuck declared that it was not sufficient and that 1/3 of the 42,000 shares was necessary. Admiral de Langle let himself be intimidated by Mr. Tuck's legal advice and agreed to re-submit the sale of the 100,000 acres for ratification at a new meeting which was called for January 31, 1879. Mr. Tuck achieved his purpose. He had gained his time. He gathered our enemies around him, that Mr. Leroy Dupree and that Lebourgeois, whose names stand out in my memory. He began a campaign against the board of directors, he organized a cabal which imposed silence on the orators of the board. He did so much and he did it so well that the most violent passions were unchained, the admiral was officially insulted, and the contract rejected by a majority of 200 to 21, a thousand voices expressed. All that was the result of false circulars sent out to the stockholders by Mr. Tuck, our employee, our salaried person. Disgusted with these base plots, the board resigned *en masse*, and it was necessary to call another stockholders meeting to name a new board.

New circulars from Mr. Tuck, inspired by the executive committee and supported by a group of ten stockholders who had been foolish enough to bring off the Yankee joke. My old Southern blood boils before all the insolence, audacity, and bad faith. I accept the fight, I call together a number of stockholders, things I consider most honorable. I inform them of the official reports of the company since its origin, the repeated instructions given to the executive committee by the board, and I point to the circular and the instructions contained therein. And on the 31st of last March, the stockholders, better informed of the acts and intentions of the New Yorkers, voted by a very great majority for the adoption of the resolutions (circular of March 15), suppressing the executive committee by their own *coup* and relieving the members of their functions, and by a very large majority again elected the new board members we presented, in which your name and that of General Debray figure. I did not think I should step aside under that circumstance because, by agreement of the new board, I was assigned to the secretariat and agency at Weatherford where I will probably arrive early in June. For the moment and because of the duties which keep you in Louisiana we are going to name Mister Milliken president of the company, get rid of all the Yankees, and try to tend to our affairs ourselves. I ask you in the name of all your friends in France to accept the position of director which will involve you in nothing more than that. Perhaps you can be a powerful aid to us here, at least till my return to Texas. *Sic fata voluerant* I will soon be en route to America, this time for always perhaps.

Awaiting the pleasure of seeing you in person, accept,
my dear General, my most affectionate regards,
P. du Bellet.

Du Bellet had accomplished what he set out to do, and his articulate account covers a most significant phase of the history of the Franco-Texan Land Company—the elimination of the New York directors. But after telling how Gray and his cohorts were finally deposed, how Sam H. Milliken was elected president, and how he himself was to be sent to Texas as vice-secretary, his letters ceased abruptly, and that fountain of information vanished. Henceforward, no officer seemed inclined to write or even talk about the company's business. And, with the exception of a printed copy of the minutes of a stockholders' meeting in 1892, none of the company's private records have been found, all of which cloaks the slightest fact concerning the company with seeming importance.

Gray and Tuck apparently retired without further protest, leaving their lucrative bonanza in the hands of the French and President Milliken of Weatherford. At this point Henry P. du Bellet appeared on the scene, instead of his father, as vice-secretary of the Franco-Texan Land Company. Without loss of time, the Du Bellets had made arrangements for the company to sell 50,000 acres of its most valuable land—in

Parker and Palo Pinto counties—for $1.00 an acre. The sale was authorized when the board of directors met in Paris on April 25, 1879, just three weeks after Paul Pecquet du Bellet wrote his last letter to General Beauregard. A second company was then formed, the Société Foncière et Agricole des États Unis (the Real Estate and Agricultural Association of the United States), sometimes called the Credit Foncier, of which Henry P. du Bellet was the special agent in Texas and his father, the administrator or manager. Milliken furnished the money, but the sale was made in the name of a third party—Mardoche Lambert, whose address was given as No. 16 Boulevard St. Denis, Paris. After the organization of the Société, Judge du Bellet decided to remain in France and manage the company's business there while his son went to Texas as its agent and also as vice-secretary of the Franco-Texan Land Company.

Though willing to make this sale because they needed money for operating expenses, the Franco-Texan directors had no intention of depleting the company's capital, which was land, by freely allowing the stockholders to liquidate their shares. As a protective measure, at a meeting in Paris in 1879, they had amended a by-law and fixed the price of land at three times its cash value if it was to be exchanged for stock. The board met again in Paris on January 30, 1880, and amended the by-law of 1879. The second amendment further prescribed that if the stockholder lived in America and wished to exchange his stock for land, he would have to deposit his shares with the president in Texas and take a receipt for them. The president would at once forward the shares to the Paris office to be verified by comparison with the stubs. Then on advice of that office the Texas president would convey to the stockholder the amount of land to which he was entitled. The application of the amended by-law proved to be a deterrent to the exchange of stock for land, but in spite of it a number of Frenchmen came to Texas for that purpose or else sold their stock to Americans, and the amount presented for exchange was surprising. The president and the board countered by delaying or by simply refusing to make the exchange, and this move soon threw the company into the Texas courts with disastrous results for the French directors of the Franco-Texan and for those individuals who had invested in the Société Foncière et Agricole des États Unis.

But before the two companies could be put into full operation and even while Paul Pecquet du Bellet was still writing to Beauregard, another development took place. French financiers, inspired by the Société and Franco-Texan enterprises, began to consider the advantages of competing with the British for the American trade. Inasmuch as the French nation consumed 40,000,000 pounds of beef annually and the southwestern states were anxious to supply it, one particularly attractive vista was the beef and cattle trade. For several years live cattle had been shipped from Baltimore to Liverpool in great numbers with very little loss, and the *Labrador* had just made a successful passage to Le Havre with a cargo of fresh beef—45,532 pounds packed in the forepart of the steamer. The run to Le Havre took eleven days; the meat arrived in excellent condition, and 17,648 pounds were sold the next morning in the markets at about thirteen cents a pound.[2] The main problem then was distribution, ultimately to be solved by refrigeration.[3] In the meantime it was expected that Europe would provide a profitable market for American cattle on the hoof.

Leon Chotteau, a French economist and publicist, came to America in April, 1878, with the object of improving commercial relations between the United States and France. These two countries had been very close to reaching a new and satisfactory trade agreement when the Civil War stopped further negotiations. In an address to the New York

[2] Dallas *Daily Herald*, March 6, 1878.

[3] The first successful shipment of beef by refrigerated boat was made by Dr. H. P. Howard of San Antonio, when he fitted out the steamship *Agnes* with a cold storage room and shipped thirty beeves from Indianola to New Orleans in July, 1869. The Texas and Atlantic Refrigerator Company of Denison made the first effort in the United States to transport refrigerated beef over land in 1873 (Walter Prescott Webb and H. Bailey Carroll, *Handbook of Texas*, II, 456). In May, 1877, the first carload of fifty beeves in quarters was shipped in a Tiffany refrigerated car from Fort Worth to St. Louis, but the railroads were not yet supplied with these cars, nor did the shipping of frozen meat become reasonably safe until 1884 (Buckley B. Paddock, *History of Texas: Fort Worth and the Texas Northwest Edition*, II, 533).

Chamber of Commerce, Chotteau proposed an adjustment of the tariff, which, at that time, closed France as an outlet for American cotton and woolen goods, cast iron, hardware, refined sugar, leather goods, and other items. He broached the subject of a commercial treaty and advocated a public discussion in Paris which might help to promote the welfare of the two nations. He was well received in New York, and a committee was appointed in support of the project. Chotteau then left for Philadelphia, Baltimore, and Washington.[4]

In Washington, General Banks presided over a meeting at which the speakers were Chotteau, Senators Hill of Georgia, Eustis of Louisiana, Butler of South Carolina, and Jones of Florida, and Representative Tucker of Virginia. Senator Eustis had a deep interest in the subject since the people he represented were united to the French by tradition, association, language, and a large portion by religion, and he gave the movement his hearty and sincere recommendation.[5]

Chotteau delivered speeches in almost every state in the Union on behalf of his project. He organized committees in Boston, New York, Philadelphia, Baltimore, Washington, Cincinnati, St. Louis, Chicago, New Orleans, Charleston, and San Francisco. These committees were to send delegates to the conference to be held in Paris on August 7, 1878.[6] At the request of the United States, the French government then invited the International Monetary Conference to meet in Paris August 11–30.

Chotteau sailed for Europe on June 18, 1878, and reached Paris in time to attend a picnic in the Bois du Boulogne where four hundred Americans were celebrating the anniversary of American independence,

[4] Galveston *Daily News*. April 5, 1878. According to *La Grande Encyclopedie*, Paris, Leon Chotteau made five trips to the United States between 1878 and 1885. In 1877 he was chosen a delegate of the "free trade clubs," and a committee was formed to secure a Franco-American commercial treaty. Chotteau was never able to fully overcome the protectionist tendencies of the French Parliament, but a general reduction of tariffs was made in 1882. Chotteau is the author of *France et Amerique, mes deux premieres compagnes aux Etats Unis* (Paris: 1879); *Le Traite de commerce franco-americain: documents* (Paris: 1882).

[5] Galveston *Daily News*, April 13, 1878.

[6] *Ibid.*, June 15, 1878.

and to attend a grand concert which was being held at the Trocadero Palace to commemorate that great day.[7]

The Franco-American conference for the consideration of a treaty of commerce met on August 7 at the Grand Hotel in Paris. About forty Americans were present. M. Foucher de Cariel and Mr. Pollock presided for France and America respectively. A preliminary draft of a treaty was presented and referred to a committee of sixteen who approved it the following day. The project proposed the abolition of French prohibitive laws and the reduction of French-American duties from 30 to 50 per cent.[8]

The American members of the treaty commission included Messrs. Appleton of Boston, Limet of New Orleans; Roosevelt of New York; Hodges of Baltimore; Freeman of Philadelphia; Karst of St. Louis; Weston of Charleston; and Young of Atlanta.[9] At another meeting held in Tours on August 17, speeches were made by M. Belle and M. Wilson of the Chamber of Deputies and by Leon Chotteau, Pollock, Appleton, Young, Hodges, and Roosevelt.[10]

A dinner was given to the members of both commissions at the Grand Hotel on August 29, and President Foucher de Cariel telegraphed greetings and best compliments to President Hayes, signed by the French committee. In a toast to the health of the American delegates, he reminded them that Benjamin Franklin came to France in the last century to secure a treaty of commerce.[11]

Opinion Nationale in Paris predicted that although the government had left the task of raising the question of a commercial treaty to private enterprise, it would probably take the matter up when the proper moment arrived.[12] Another Paris newspaper expressed the opinion that possibly within a year's time a French delegation would proceed to America to complete the negotiations.[13]

[7] *Ibid.*, July 6, 1868.
[8] *Ibid.*, August 11, 1878.
[9] *Ibid.*, August 9, 1878.
[10] *Ibid.*, August 18, 1878.
[11] *Ibid.*, August 31, 1878.
[12] *Ibid.*, August 22, 1878.
[13] *Ibid.*, August 31, 1878.

The Monetary Conference closed on August 30 with a banquet at the Continental Hotel, given by the Americans for their European confreres, but the Chambers of Commerce continued their work in the interest of commercial reciprocity. In September, French and American delegates held public meetings at Mâcon, Lyons, Saint Étienne, Nîmes, Montpellier, Avignon, and Marseilles, and adopted resolutions urging the prompt conclusion of the treaty.[14]

When Chotteau returned to the United States in 1879 to advocate the reduction of tariffs, the only city to offer any opposition to the movement was San Francisco, then highly concerned about its wine interests. The State Department, however, denied any probability of the consummation of the proposed Franco-American treaty at an early date, and since all the agitation was coming from private and interested sources and had in no manner received official sanction or even cognizance from either government, it was not thought that the dreams of M. Leon Chotteau and his American coadjutator, Mr. Fernando Wood, would be very speedily realized.[15] But Chotteau was to be heard from again, the next time in Texas.

[14] *Ibid.*, September 27, 1878.

[15] *Ibid.*, October 14, 1879. Fernando Wood, representative of the 9th District of New York, was a Tammany Democrat. He was born June 14, 1812, in Philadelphia, and his early mercantile training enabled him to deal with the tariff question. He was a forcible debater, logical reasoner, personally popular, and thoroughly conversant with parliamentary tactics (*ibid.*, February 15, 1881).

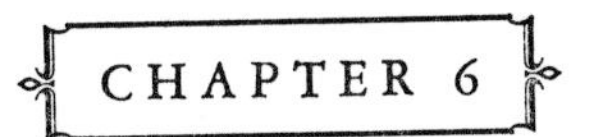

HENRY P. DU BELLET AND THE TEXAS AND PACIFIC ARRIVE IN WEATHERFORD

The Texas and Pacific

Judge du Bellet, though in Paris, appeared to be fully aware of the railroad outlook in Washington and Weatherford. As he had said in one of his letters to Beauregard, the Southern Pacific did seem to have the advantage and "Morison" did not seem likely to lend a helping hand to the Texas and Pacific, which not only had failed to reach Weatherford on July 1, 1877, as expected, but had not yet begun construction on the 28-mile extension from Fort Worth. And what was worse—it was predicted that Huntington, if successful, would build through from California toward the east while northwest Texas remained in status quo—undeveloped still. In this painful situation the people of Weatherford, encouraged and supported by Sam H. Milliken, resolved to build the road themselves. They organized the Parker County Supply and Construction Company and sold stock at $25.00 a share, payable in money, labor, or land; $37,500 was subscribed. The officers of the company were Henry W. Warren, president; T. D. Lewis, vice-president; and W. F. Carter, secretary. It would be an easy matter, they said, after twenty-nine miles of grading was done, to mortgage the road to European capitalists and then buy the iron and rolling stock.

These hopes slowly dimmed as the cost of grading rose to $100,000. It was soon decided to open negotiations with the Texas and Pacific. The assignment fell to Captain Henry Warren, and on September 25, 1877, he left for Philadelphia, having been serenaded at his ranch the night before by friends, who drank all his champagne.[1] In Philadelphia he had an encouraging interview with President Thomas A. Scott, but found that he would have to confer with Vice-president Bond who was in Marshall, Texas. When they talked there later, Bond wanted not only the grading but also the tieing and bridging. This the citizens could not do, but they would be willing, if they couldn't raise the money, "to raise the shovel and the spade," and "agitate the dirt" between Fort Worth and Weatherford. Their determination weakened with the adoption of Baker's Resolution in the U.S. House of Representatives on December 28, 1877, by over a two-thirds vote: "Resolved that the sentiment of the House is opposed to the granting of any subsidies or aid to any private or public enterprises or corporations by endorsement or otherwise, except it be imperatively demanded by the public service." Then, assured by Major Bond that with reasonable assistance the Texas and Pacific would run the road to Weatherford within the year with or without aid from the government, the ambitious citizens determined to make the effort. They finally agreed to do the grading and tieing, and the Texas and Pacific directors approved the contract in Philadelphia on August 14, 1878. The good news was not received in Weatherford until late in October, but the deal was promptly closed in the Parker County Construction Company's office on October 25 and ratified by the Texas and Pacific Company on November 5. The local company was to grade and tie the road from Fort Worth to a point within the corporate limits of Weatherford, work to begin within fifteen days, and to be completed on or before May 1, 1879; the company would receive in payment the 8 per cent interest-bearing bonds of the Texas and Pacific Railway Company, payable within three years from completion of the contract.

[1] Weatherford *Exponent*, September 29, 1877.

The center line having already been located, an engineering crew began to cross section the road as soon as the contract was signed. Late in November, wagons, teams, plows, scrapers, and shovels followed in its wake, joyfully dispatched in a ground-breaking ceremony three hundred yards north of the courthouse. Contractors went to work at both ends of the line in January. The completion date was set as mid-April.

In February, when one-third of the grade was finished, contractors O'Conor and Fields quit work on the east end, and M. S. Hall agreed to take over the whole job on more acceptable terms. He put on 125 teams and 200 men, and the only difficulty was the construction company's need of cash.

In March, Congress adjourned with Tom Scott's bill still on the calendar, "killed," it was said, "by Huntington's gold and contentious southerners." Fort Worth then felt sure that the extension was "busted," and Weatherford knew that more money was necessary. The construction company secured 101 paid-up subscriptions and was able to proceed. Weatherford would have its railroad, and better still, it would be the terminus for perhaps ten years. O'Conor and Fields were paid off, the completion date was moved up to May 1, and it looked as if a July 4th celebration was in order.

On May 3, there were 6¼ miles of grading yet to be done, but that could be finished by June. The unpaid balance of the April payroll, in the amount of $8,000, would be taken care of at once. The tie contract was closed, and the ties would be delivered before September 1.

On May 31, the railroad hands were paid in full; this money and enough to finish the job was obtained on Weatherford securities from the City Bank of Dallas. All doubts and fears about the success of the extension were fully removed. Captain Hall had 600 men at work, and the grade would be completed by July 15.

On July 19, the completion date for the grading was changed to September 1. The ties and bridge timber were in Fort Worth, and, according to Captain Warren, the iron would be laid by September 20. Mrs. Hensley's tract had been purchased for the depot.

On August 23, the grade was still not finished; it would be three more weeks before the track laying could begin at Fort Worth. It was said that the iron and ties would be put down as far as the river so the train could carry material to the bridge. All hands were paid, and a night force was at work under Captain Pat Sheridan.

Suddenly it was the middle of December, 1879. More than a year had passed since the project was begun, and no train had reached the corporate limits of Weatherford, nor had one rail been laid on the roadbed which would be finished within two or three days.

Before the grading was completed, as it finally was on January 21, 1880, the news came that the Texas and Pacific Company had reorganized and contracted to build on to El Paso. Weatherford's dream of becoming the terminus was shattered, but its citizens were not disconsolate. The Texas and Pacific had announced that the first train would arrive on or before March 5, 1880; Weatherford would then be the supply point until the railroad was built several hundred miles west; Fort Worth's obnoxious monopoly was ended, that city was no more than a whistle station. As the track laying would begin by the middle of February, a grand barbecue was proposed to welcome the arrival of the long-awaited locomotive.

On May 8, it was reported that the railroad would be completed the following week, but there was a rumor that no trains would run until the 1st of June. When the Texas and Pacific stopped laying the track with the extension five miles from town, it was more than Weatherford could bear. G. G. Baggerly, the long-suffering editor of the Weatherford *Exponent* and heretofore loyal advocate of the Texas and Pacific, wrote,

> The action of the Texas and Pacific in suspending tracklaying on Weatherford extension when within five or six miles of town for the ostensible purpose of surfacing up the back track is too transparent to deceive any sensible person. It is nothing more than a continuation of mistreatment and bad faith that the company has exhibited toward Weatherford since it contracted to put the road in running order as soon as the Parker County Construction Company should complete the grade. If there has been the least particle of honor in any of their dealings with us we have failed to see it. We may have the road to this point by 1st of June, and then again we may not. It is useless to pay any attention to what they will or will not do.[2]

[2] *Ibid.*, May 16, 1880.

The railroad reached Weatherford at noon on May 27, 1880, and the first train arrived one week later on June 4. It was Weatherford's big day: Flag-draped buildings; vehicles of every shape, size, and variety, bringing thousands of people from miles around, many of whom had never laid eyes on the "great civilizer" before; notables from Dallas and Fort Worth; a speech by ex-Governor Throckmorton; and a grand barbecue. The train left Dallas at 7:30 A.M., stopped for half an hour at Fort Worth, and entered Weatherford at 12:30, traveling the sixty-five miles in 4½ hours. The visitors were met at the depot by Weatherford citizens, delegations of the Knights of Pythias, and the fire department, all headed by the Weatherford band. The line of march led to the barbecue grounds on the side of the hill, where Mayor J. H. Milliken introduced Judge J. M. Richards, who was followed by ex-Governor Throckmorton who made the principal speech of the day —on the past, present, and future of Weatherford. He also paid tribute to the pioneers of that section and to the Texas and Pacific Company. He reviewed the progress of the road and spoke of the great commercial results to follow, along with the future development of the state. The barbecue was delicious and plentiful. After dinner speeches by George Mellersh of Dallas, B. B. Paddock of Fort Worth, and Albert Stevenson and H. S. Moran of the Weatherford bar were appropriate and well received. The celebration ended with a grand ball at the courthouse. Only one thing happened to mar the occasion in the least. The engine ran off the turntable and delayed the return of the excursion train for several hours. It reached Dallas at 2:30 A.M.

After laying the track to Weatherford the Texas and Pacific continued the grading of the road from Sherman to Fort Worth, a section of its main or transcontinental line and the west side of the parallelogram in North Texas,[3] and at the same time began its race to reach El Paso ahead of the Southern Pacific. Jay Gould was at the helm. He and Russell Sage had been admitted to active participation in the company when it became apparent that Scott would receive no financial aid from Congress and that Gould had blocked his eastern outlet by the purchase

[3] The Transcontinental Division was completed to Fort Worth on April 29, 1881 (Galveston *Daily News*, April 30, 1881).

of the International and Great Northern, the St. Louis and Iron Mountain, and the Missouri, Kansas and Texas. Gould and Sage formed a new construction company, the Pacific Improvement Company, to build the road from Fort Worth to El Paso and on to the Pacific if conditions were favorable. By contract of January 16, 1880, it was to start work on or before March 5 and to complete and equip the whole line by 1883. By supplementary contract in October, 1880, the construction company agreed to build to El Paso by January 1, 1882. Scott resigned in Philadelphia on April 12, 1881, and also retired from the board of directors.[4] Jay Gould was elected president of the Texas and Pacific on April 15, 1881, after he bought Scott's interest for $4,000,000.[5] To make the final payment Gould wrote a check for $2,400,000 on an old scrap of paper, said to be the largest check ever written in the history of the United States at that time. Three months before he had made out a check to Thomas Allen in the amount of $2,000,000 for the St. Louis and Iron Mountain. Allen wanted it certified and Gould obliged him.

Huntington, armed with territorial charters and an executive order from President Hayes, was pushing his Southern Pacific[6] eastwardly at the rate of two miles a day. Although Scott had succeeded in getting troops sent to stop Huntington at the Colorado, he had completed his bridge by building after 12:00 at night and thence proceeded on across

[4] *Ibid.*, April 13, 1881. Scott suffered a stroke of paralysis early in May of 1881. He died May 31, 1881. Continued mental strain for a long period as manager of a great enterprise was said to be the cause (Dallas *Daily Herald*, June 1, 1881).

[5] E. B. Wheelock, president of the New Orleans & Pacific, took Scott's place on the board of directors. There were four representatives of Scott's interest still on the board: H. M. Hoxie, general superintendent; George Noble, assistant superintendent; B. K. Jameson; and James H. Scott. Noble, former general superintendent, resigned May 1, 1881.

[6] The Southern Pacific, originally chartered by the state of California, had been authorized by the Federal government to build only to a point at or near the Colorado River: By the Act of 1866 chartering the Atlantic and Pacific (*United States Statutes at Large*, XIV, 292) and by the Act of 1871 chartering the Texas Pacific (*ibid.*, XVI, 573): "the Southern Pacific Railroad of California is hereby authorized (subject to the laws of California) to construct a line of railroad at or near the Colorado River, grants and conditions being the same as the Act of 1866."

the Yuma Reservation. The Texas and Pacific was still in Fort Worth, 600 miles from El Paso. On May 24, 1879, the Southern Pacific track was 185 miles east of Yuma with rails en route to build to Cochise fifty miles east of Tucson and the road completed 155 miles east from San Francisco. Huntington was interviewed that same month in Galveston. Asked when his road would reach El Paso, he said, "I will be at El Paso within two years, and I want to meet somebody there, I don't care much what line it is." Gould was continuing Scott's old feud with Huntington, but it was thought that he and Huntington were in agreement on connecting somewhere in Texas instead of building two parallel lines. However, if Gould entered El Paso first he could force a joint ownership on his own terms and perhaps save his land grant. When the Southern Pacific reached the Rio Grande in the territory of New Mexico on April 12, 1881, Gould filed an injunction suit at Santa Fe, requesting the appointment of a receiver for the Southern Pacific. Huntington countered with a suit in Arizona and built on. With his 3,000 coolies he reached El Paso on May 19, 1881; at that time the Texas and Pacific track was six miles east of Big Spring, about half the distance between Fort Worth and El Paso.

The Southern Pacific could not build beyond El Paso because it had no Texas charter, but Huntington was not without an ace in the hole. He had bought an interest in the Galveston, Harrisburg, and San Antonio Railroad, which he planned to extend from San Antonio to El Paso, thus giving him a connection with New Orleans. He began building at both ends of this road, and the race was on in earnest. There was only one pass leading into the valley of the Rio Grande, at Sierra Blanca, ninety-two miles east of El Paso. The first to build through this pass would have the undisputed right of way into El Paso. Huntington reached Sierra Blanca on November 25, 1881. The Texas and Pacific was then less than twenty-five miles away. Since the Southern Pacific and part of the G H & S A line were already built, and the Texas and Pacific charter would expire on May 2, 1882, Gould had to compromise. On November 26, he and Huntington entered into an agreement (later modified on February 18, 1885) by which (1) the Texas and Pacific would join the Galveston, Harrisburg, and San Antonio at Sierra Blanca, as it did officially on January 1, 1882; (2) the Texas and

Pacific gave up all claims against the Southern Pacific west of El Paso and ceded all its corporate rights in that territory; (3) the two roads, the Texas and Pacific and the Galveston, Harrisburg, and San Antonio would be operated as one continuous line, with the gross earnings divided in proportion to the distance hauled; (4) gross earnings on all traffic between El Paso and New Orleans would be pooled and divided equally; (5) each agreed not to duplicate the other's roads nor to purchase or control a competing road except as authorized by an executive committee composed of Jay Gould and Collis P. Huntington and a third party; (6) at option of the Texas and Pacific it would have a right to perpetual joint use of the Galveston, Harrisburg, and San Antonio from the junction point to El Paso, paying 6 per cent per annum semiannually upon $10,000 per mile, and one-half the cost of maintenance, renewals, and taxes; (7) all disputes would be settled by arbitration.

On December 1, 1881, the Texas and Pacific track connected with that of the Galveston, Harrisburg, and San Antonio at Blanco Junction. The event was reported in the Dallas *Herald* on December 3, 1881:

> Sierra Blanca—December 2. Under the great Blanco Peak on this western range of the beautiful grassy plains, 10,000 square miles in extent, the Atlantic and Pacific took each other by the hand and were entwined in bands of iron at an altitute of 5,000 feet above the sea. Just as the setting sun in all his glory cast his declining rays across the Sierra Mountains the last two spikes on this gigantic alliance were driven . . . 521 days since tracklaying was begun at Fort Worth and 521 miles of track have been laid. Blanco Junction is 91 miles east of El Paso. The lines will be open for general business on the first of January.[7]

Actually, four spikes were driven: one each by Mrs. William Stoll and Mrs. R. E. Montgomery, the daughter of General Grenville M. Dodge, and one each by H. M. Hoxie and D. W. Washburne.[8]

Today the Texas and Pacific trains travel from Sierra Blanca to El

[7] Dallas *Herald*, December 3, 1881.

[8] Fort Worth *Gazette*, December 3, 1881. Grenville M. Dodge was chief engineer of the Texas and Pacific and president of the Pacific Improvement Company. He built the Union Pacific in 1869.

Paso on this joint track. The section of the Galveston, Harrisburg, and San Antonio building from San Antonio met the section building from El Paso, 2½ miles west of the Pecos River on January 12, 1883, and at 2:00 P.M. the last spike—a silver one—was driven on the Southern Pacific's Sunset Route.[9]

After absorbing the Galveston, Harrisburg, and San Antonio, Huntington purchased Morgan's Louisiana and Texas lines, including the Houston and Texas Central. The Morgan lines enabled the Southern Pacific to enter New Orleans and complete the transcontinental scheme. Through cars ran from New Orleans to San Francisco in January, 1883.[10] By this time the Texas and Pacific had a southern connection. Gould bought the New Orleans Pacific, which was already under construction, on June 20, 1881, and completed it on September 12, 1882.[11]

The Southern Pacific was the second transcontinental railroad. The Union Pacific and the Central Pacific met at Promontory Point, Utah, on May 10, 1869. The Atchison, Topeka, and Santa Fe connected with the Southern Pacific at Deming, New Mexico, on March 19, 1881, and then had a connection with St. Louis, but it did not have its own line to the Pacific coast until 1885 at San Diego, in 1887 at Los Angeles, and in 1898 at San Francisco. Henry Villard's Northern Pacific did not reach its terminus at Tacoma until 1887 nor did Jim Hill's Great Northern bring its tracks into Seattle until 1893.[12]

HENRY P. DU BELLET

Nothing has been found to indicate the exact date on which Henry P. du Bellet appeared in Weatherford, but he reached the city in ample time to witness the arrival of the first train. It is certain that he was there on March 29, 1880, because on that date he applied for and purchased two sections of school land in Parker County, a few miles north of town on the Trinity River. On April 7, 1880, he purchased another

[9] *Ibid.*, January 13, 1883.

[10] Galveston *Daily News*, September 25, 1884.

[11] *From Ox-Teams to Eagles*, p. 32.

[12] The Santa Fe did, however, reach tidewater at Guaymas, from Nogales, on October 25, 1882 (Glenn Chesney Quiett, *They Built the West*).

section in the northeast corner of the county. All three applications bear his signature.[13] The United States Census of Parker County for 1880, taken on May 31, lists Henry P. du Bellet as a banker, single, age twenty-seven, born in Louisiana. He and D. Dulong were boarding in the home of S. M. Coker. Dulong was single, age thirty-five, born in France. At that time there were forty Frenchmen living in Weatherford, twenty-five native-born and fifteen from Louisiana.

Not long after his arrival Du Bellet made a formal tender of 2,500 shares of stock to the Franco-Texan, to be exchanged for land. While the application was pending he devoted his time to promoting the Société Foncière et Agricole des États Unis. This was the company which had bought 50,000 acres from the Franco-Texan in the name of Mardoche Lambert, of whom no further trace is found. The record of this sale in Parker County consists of three instruments: a statement sent or brought from Paris, signed by Henry P. du Bellet as vice-secretary, acknowledged before the United States consul on March 18, 1880, and filed in the county clerk's office at Weatherford on April 5, 1880, attesting that the board of directors of the Franco-Texan Land Company agreed to the said sale at a meeting held on April 25, 1879; a deed from the Franco-Texan Land Company, dated December 22, 1879, and filed on January 5, 1880, conveying to Mardoche Lambert of Paris, France, in consideration of the payment of $24,958, a tract of land containing in the aggregate 24,958 acres in Parker County, excepting the right of way for the main line of the Texas and Pacific railway; and a subsequent deed from Mardoche Lambert to the Société Foncière.[14] Du Bellet's statement and similar deeds were recorded in Palo Pinto County. J. H. Baker, then district clerk of Palo Pinto County, refers to these deeds in his diary:

Spent the time mostly from [December] 20–25 recording the transfer of Mordochee Lambert to the "Real Estate and Agricultural Company of the United States," 60 odd pages. Have 27½ recorded. Have worked on it every night. Spent the time from Monday 27–Friday 31 recording the deed

[13] School Land Files 2839, 2840, 2841, General Land Office.

[14] Deed Records of Parker County: Vol. 7, p. 613; Vol. 7, p. 858.

of the Franco-Texan Land Company. It covered 81 pages in a large Record Book, "H." At 15 cents per hundred words the recording amounts to $54.68.[15]

The Société was a corporation organized under the laws of the Republic of France with special reference to business in the state of Texas. It was concerned with all real estate, agricultural, and commercial operations regarding the purchase and improvement of land, public and private, in Texas, and the sale of all products, lands, and other real and personal property belonging to the company.[16] It was incorporated for $1,600,000, and its president was the Comte de Constantin. A number of important Frenchmen had invested in the Société separately and apart from the Franco-Texan, and some were stockholders in both.

On May 8, 1880, Du Bellet published a "Notice to Settlers" in which he advised those who were occuping certain sections in the railroad reservation in Parker County to apply to him for terms of lease and warned that suits would be brought to eject those who did not apply. The notice was undersigned "Henry P. du Bellet, Special Agent of Mr. Lambert. Office, West Church Street, opposite Sikes House, Weatherford."[17]

Du Bellet's application to exchange his stock for land must have been refused because he filed suit against the company in the District Court of Parker County in September, 1880. His 2,500 shares were valued at $250,000, and since this was the largest suit that had ever been brought in the county, it created considerable excitement and interest.[18] The case was dismissed on January 8, 1881, costs to be paid by Du Bellet.[19]

Nevertheless, through the Société, Du Bellet acquired a ranch at Palo Pinto and established his temporary residence there. This quaint little town was located in the heart of the Franco-Texan lands in Palo

[15] Jonathan H. Baker, "Diary of J. H. Baker," Texas State Archives.

[16] Moreau *v.* Du Bellet, 27 *South Western Reporter* 503.

[17] Weatherford *Exponent*, May 8, 1880.

[18] Galveston *Daily News*, September 29, 1880.

[19] Case No. 1452, District Court of Parker County. The file is missing, and only the report in the Civil Minutes is available.

Pinto County. It was situated in a wide bend of the Brazos River about 130 miles around and from 10 to 14 miles across, in timber of live oak, ash, walnut, pecan, mulberry, elm, sycamore, and varieties of cedar. The county was well adapted to stock raising with rich, cheap land, good range, and plenty of water; and it was virtually the cradle of the ranching industry of northwest Texas. Many of Texas' early cattle kings ranched there at one time or another, claiming Weatherford as their home: W. S. Ikard, Charles Goodnight, Oliver Loving, Dan Waggoner, John, William, Jesse, and Jack Hittson, H. M. Kidwell, J. R. Couts, W. E. Hughes, and John N. and E. J. Simpson. In fact, most Weatherford men were ranching in Palo Pinto County or elsewhere in northwest Texas. S. W. T. Lanham and W. K. Baylor had a large herd of cattle on the Clear Fork of the Brazos River, and Kidwell Brothers had one in Yellow House Canyon and another on Double Mountain Fork; Sam H. Milliken and A. S. Simmons had a fine sheep ranch in Palo Pinto, and both J. H. and Sam H. Milliken were Jesse Hittson's partners in the cattle business there; Henry Warren and William Champlin were ranching on the Pease River; Judge H. L. L. McCall in Cottle County; Judge A. J. Hood in Parker; Milliken and Millsap in Stonewall and Fisher; Martin and Milliken in Nolan; and Couts and Simpson in Taylor.

Du Bellet's ranch was west of the town of Palo Pinto, and his brand was BH Fleur-de-Lys on the right side. He evidently bought his cattle from Billy Hittson and added the fleur-de-lys to the BH brand, which Billy Hittson used as his own, apart from the well-known HIT and the Circles Bar. Later Du Bellet had an agent in Sweetwater by the names of Jules Cormier to look after his stray stock.[20]

There is a great void surrounding the activities of the Franco-Texan Land Company in 1879 and early 1880. The Weatherford *Exponent*, available for 1879 and January through May of 1880, yields nothing to clarify the situation, and the dispatches in the widely circulated state papers are silent on the subject. What happened while Milliken was president, other than the sale of land to a few individuals and to the Société Foncière, is not known. He remained in office for only nine

[20] *Palo Pinto County Star*, September 24, 1887.

months. Perhaps the reasons for his short term are to be found only in the minutes of the directors' meeting in Paris, France. At any rate, he ceased to be president in January, 1880, and Du Bellet's services as vice-secretary, if they were ever accepted, seem to have ended at a very early date.

CHAPTER 7

MOVING WEST WITH THE RAILROADS

The Franco-Texan reported several large land sales late in 1880,[1] and though it may be presumed that the company was chiefly active in Parker and Palo Pinto counties in that year, it already had its agents farther west, and business was gravitating in that direction as the Texas and Pacific, the Texas Central, and the Gulf, Colorado, and Santa Fe opened the way into the unsettled regions. On leaving Strawn in Palo Pinto County, the Texas and Pacific cut across the lower southeast corner of Stephens County. In the southeast quarter, where there were no settlements at all, the Franco-Texan owned 100,000 acres of good ranch land, then selling from $3.00 to $5.00 an acre. At Breckenridge, the county seat, William Veale, attorney, and R. H. McNeilly, county surveyor, were the company's local agents. Judge Veale's son, John W. Veale, took McNeilly's place when he became more interested in the coal boom.[2]

At Albany, in Shackelford County, A. A. Clarke, lawyer and land agent, was advertising a "quarter of a million acres of land belonging

1 Galveston *Daily News*, November 18, 1880.

2 Sketch File 10, Stephens County, General Land Office; *Palo Pinto County Star*, January 31, 1885.

to the Franco-Texan Land Company." Clarke's agency must have included not only Shackelford County but also Jones, Callahan, Fisher, and Mitchell counties. In Shackelford the company had title to 85,000 acres covering nearly all the southwest quarter of the county and selling from $2.00 to $5.00 per acre. Albany, the county seat, was situated on a half-section of asylum land owned by H. C. Jacobs. On the north it was adjacent to Franco-Texan Survey 19 in Texas and Pacific Block 11. In 1879 V. G. Frost, the company secretary, and another officer went to Albany and laid off 210 acres in 6-acre tracts, intended as an addition to the town.[3] Because of the Franco-Texan's close association with the Texas and Pacific, this was assumed to mean that the railroad would run through Albany, and considerable excitement was engendered, only to be dissipated when the T & P failed to enter Shackelford County at all. A year and a half later, the railroad committee, of which Clarke was chairman, petitioned the Franco-Texan to donate all or part of Survey 19 to the Texas Central as an inducement to extend its line from Cisco to Albany.[4] The Texas Central built to Albany in December, 1881, the railway company ran out of funds, and the terminus remained there for nineteen years. If the Franco-Texan donated any land, it was not reported, but a tract just north of the depot was known as the A. A. Clarke donation.[5]

Du Bellet's friend, Captain Dulong, appeared in Fort Griffin with Professor Cantagrel in October of 1880. They identified themselves as engineers and capitalists, representing a French company in Paris, which was preparing to establish a copper smelting works at Seymour, the county seat of Baylor County. They had forwarded specimens of copper ore to Paris for inspection, and from their experience in mining and engineering they believed that if the copper mines of Texas were developed they would be a source of immense wealth to the state.[6]

[3] Fort Worth *Daily Democrat*, October 26, 1879.

[4] Fort Griffin *Echo*, April 23, 1881.

[5] *Ibid.*, December 24, 1881.

[6] *Ibid.*, October 16, 1880. A ten-ton portable smelter had been sent to Seymour from St. Louis and hands were employed at $1.50 a day, but no one seems to know who first opened this mine (Galveston *Daily News*, July 31, 1880).

Professor Cantagrel was S. C. Cantagrel, formerly of Dallas and the son of one of the oldest French settlers in the city. He was then a resident of Paris, France, and a member of the Chamber of Deputies. In Dallas, on July 14, 1880, he had delivered a speech in his native tongue at the celebration of the anniversary of the founding of the Republic of France and the destruction of the Bastille.[7]

At Albany an effort was made to establish the Norman horse in Texas. This was considered an important move toward the improvement of native Texan stock. The idea was to increase the size and weight of Texas horses, because they had the activity and the Norman horses had the flesh, nerve, and bone. The Northwest Norman Horse Company brought twenty-seven head direct from France to Albany where the company's stables and offices were located. Some of the large, fine Norman horses cost $800 or $1,000.

At the annual meeting of the Northwest Texas Norman Horse Company, held in Albany in December, 1883, the officers elected were Colonel J. B. Barry (representative from Bosque County), president, and Thomas C. Sterrett of Albany, secretary and treasurer. The directors were J. B. Barry, J. B. Fleming (state senator from Eastland), J. C. Jacobs, J. A. Shelton, T. C. Sterrett, W. E. Cureton, and Kos. Barry.[8] The largest stockholders were the Dillon Brothers of Illinois, the oldest importers of Norman horses in the United States. The company in 1884 had a paid-up capital of $200,000 and owned 100,000 acres of land, all under fence, and 4,000 head of other horses.[9]

Many fine half-breed Norman horses, mostly two-year-olds, were sold within the next few years, but in March, 1890, the pastures were taken over by the Western Loan and Mortgage Company, to be leased and stocked by various firms during the spring.[10] The Norman horse was supplanted in Texas by the Clydesdale and the Cleveland Bay.

After crossing Eastland and Callahan counties the Texas and Pacific

[7] Dallas *Daily Herald*, July 15, 1880.

[8] Dallas *Herald*, August 7, 1883; Albany *Echo*, December 8, 1883.

[9] Galveston *Daily News*, February 3, 1884; Fort Worth *Gazette*, May 20, 1884.

[10] Fort Worth *Gazette*, March 11, 1890.

extended its line all the way across the northern half of Taylor County, just below its north boundary. Two Weatherfordites, J. R. Couts and J. N. Simpson, had been ranching in the northeast corner of this county since 1876. They were making use of the free range and also of three Franco-Texan sections, then unoccupied and adjacent to their headquarters, which were located one and a half miles north of the present Texas and Pacific station in Abilene on a section of asylum land they purchased on July 9, 1879.[11] The site was known as Simpson's Rancho; it was the home of the Hashknife Ranch and the beginning of a great cattle empire. Negotiations were then pending between Simpson and the Texas and Pacific for the building of stock pens and the location of a town which would become the great shipping point of the west. Simpson was offering the railway every alternate lot in this section which he owned.[12]

Couts and Simpson, already being crowded out of their original pastures, were hunting for a new location for the Hashknife herd. John and Sterling Buster, their foreman and bookkeeper, left Weatherford in June, 1880, to cross the plains to the Pecos River. By the advice of the Texas and Pacific engineers and with a map as a guide, they followed the Center Line Trail, but they and their animals suffered greatly for want of water. Seeing a small willow on a sandhill in the distance, they hastened there, dug in the sand for a few feet with their hands, and found water for themselves and their frantic mules. They spent the night by the gracious little pool and then moved on to the Pecos in safety.[13] The little pool grows in significance in view of the fact that Colonel W. H. H. Lawrence and his surveying party encountered more severe tribulations in the sandhills about a month later. They were forced to drink mule blood for several days.[14] And

[11] Blind Asylum Land Files 1726, 1727, 1728, 1729, General Land Office. These four quarter-sections were purchased by E. J. Simpson, J. R. Couts, J. W. Buster, and J. N. Simpson. J. N. Simpson purchased the three quarters belonging to his partners in 1881.

[12] Galveston *Daily News*, September 9, 1880.

[13] Dallas *Daily Herald*, July 4, 1880.

[14] Fort Worth *Daily Democrat*, August 7, 1880.

less than ten days after that, T & P engineers westbound to El Paso, required a company of rangers for protection against the Indians.[15] Exactly a year later, when the end of the Texas and Pacific track was at Carson, fifty miles west of Big Spring, the construction crew was accompanied by a U.S. marshal and a U.S. commissioner to dispense justice to all violators of the U.S. revenue laws, a detachment of rangers to look after the state laws, and a company of the 10th Cavalry (colored) to look after the redskins.[16]

Couts and Simpson rounded up their stock and moved most of it west of the Pecos in October.[17] When the Texas and Pacific accepted Simpson's proposition shortly afterward, he, with C. W. and J. W. Merchant, and J. Stoddard Johnston decided to name the new town Abilene, expecting it to be the counterpart of Abilene, Kansas.

The Texas and Pacific track reached the prospective townsite on or about January 15, 1881. It terminated on a broad and wild prairie, with no wood, water, or stone in sight. By the following Saturday the site was dotted with tents, covering half a dozen dry-goods and grocery stores, a livery stable and stockyard, three blacksmith shops, fifteen eating places, fifteen or twenty saloons, and even a bootmaker's shop and a milliner's store. Immigrants were camped under tents, boards, wagons, and every kind of primitive shelter. Enough lumber for buildings had been hauled in from East Texas, but all were squatters for the time being because they did not wish to make permanent improvements on someone else's land. In early March there were six hundred inhabitants. The track was already laid forty miles to the west and the grade completed something over a hundred miles beyond the southern tip of the Cap Rock.

[15] Dallas *Daily Herald*, July 14, 1880.

[16] Dallas *Daily Herald*, July 13, 1881.

[17] W. E. Hughes of St. Louis, former attorney and legislator from Weatherford, purchased J. R. Couts' interest for $77,500 early in 1881. Hughes and Simpson continued the business as equal partners on a still more extensive basis in Texas and Montana as the Continental Cattle Company (Galveston *Daily News*, January 27, 1881). After E. J. Simpson and Henry Warren established the Aztec Cattle Company in Arizona, Simpson was elected a U.S. Senator from Arizona. The Aztec Cattle Company provided the setting for the famous Tewkesbury Feud.

The station at Abilene was in H. W. Stocking's frontier car, and the train arrived at 11:30 P.M. A correspondent of the Galveston *Daily News*, stepping off into nothing but a sea of white canvas on March 11, 1881, was met by the restaurant drummers who thronged the railroad grounds and proclaimed the merits of their establishments in louder tones than the celebrated George Hawkins of Dallas. One runner called out, "Right this way, gentlemen, for the only shingle roof hotel in the city," and carried the majority of passengers with him. The beds were poor, but there was plenty to eat. Wild turkeys, picked and cleaned, were brought in daily by the wagonload and sold for thirty-five to fifty cents each. One hotelkeeper ordered one hundred turkeys and five antelope for the following Tuesday, the day of the town-lot sale. There was abundant game of all kinds for miles around, except buffalo. They had all been driven two hundred miles further west. None had been killed here for more than four years.

The town was rather quiet. The cowboys visited it frequently but beyond taking a few drinks and dancing a few sets at the "Red Light," they were not demonstrative. Only one murder had been committed, and that tragedy, enacted in the nighttime, was still enveloped in mystery.

On March 15, the day the sale of town lots began, the population aggregated 1,500 persons, and 3,500 visitors were in attendance. With J. A. H. Hossack of Jefferson as the auctioneer, 140 lots sold for $24,500.[18]

In its erratic course, the Texas and Pacific had already by-passed Belle Plain in Callahan County and Palo Pinto in Palo Pinto County and was then abandoning Buffalo Gap and Phantom Hill in Taylor and Jones counties. These four towns were old and distinctive settlements in settings of natural charm, all originally scheduled to be on the line of the railroad and now left to wither on the vine.

Belle Plain, the county seat of Callahan County, was located on the southwest quarter of Section 130, owned by W. H. Parvin, the first postmaster. The northwest quarter was owned by C. W. Merchant,

[18] Galveston *Daily News*, March 16, 1881; Fort Worth *Daily Democrat*, March 27, 1881.

and he and Parvin established the town on August 19, 1877. It was on a clear running stream at the foot of a hill, on a plain said to be shaped like a bell, whence its name. It seems more logical though that Belle Plain simply meant beautiful plain, and obviously no one but a Frenchman would have spelled bell with a final "e," whatever its meaning. Parvin, who came from Pennsylvania, was of French descent, his wife was from Baden, and several Frenchmen were living in or near the town. Two were stonemasons, and they, along with four or five Germans from the unfortunate Eagle Colony in Taylor County, must have constructed the stone buildings predominating there. Belle Plain was abandoned when the county seat moved to the new town of Baird, on the railroad, but some of the old buildings are still standing.

A road connected Belle Plain with Buffalo Gap, which was thirty-five miles to the west and situated in a mountain gap on the Clear Fork of the Brazos, in a beautiful valley of red sandy soil, varying from one-half to two miles in width. W. H. Poitevent was the proprietor of the Galveston House. There was no road north from Buffalo Gap until the Texas and Pacific established Abilene in 1881. The Texas and Pacific also established Clyde, originally a construction camp, in north-western Callahan County, on a quarter-section of school land first purchased by a Frenchman named Harden Blancett on March 5, 1879.[19]

In Jones County, a few settlers had remained in the town of Phantom Hill, a short distance from the ruins of the old Phantom Hill Fort, hoping that the railroad would come that way. Both the fort and the town were situated just within the 56,813 acres assigned to the Franco-Texan Land Company in the southeast corner of the county. There was fine stock range here, water, good soil, and plenty of wood north of the Clear Fork, in a post-oak forest running east and west for twenty-five miles. Allard d'Heur of Paris, France, had exchanged his Franco-Texan stock for land at the rate of $1.00 an acre and was living on his ranch east of the town of Phantom Hill in 1883. D'Heur had also bought the section of school land adjoining him on the south.[20] An-

[19] School Land Files 1134, 1309, General Land Office.

[20] School Land File 1748.

other Frenchman was living or visiting on D'Heur's ranch—a count and French officer whose first name was Louis. He was a pianist and created a sensation at Jones City (Anson) when he was presented to play while there on a visit; surely it was at the Cowboys Christmas Ball first held in M. H. Rhoads Morning Star Hotel in Anson in 1885 and publicized by Larry Chittenden's famous poem in 1892. Ranching east of D'Heur was Conrad Heim who claimed he had been a marshal in the French Army. He had performed valiant service in defense of the city of Paris in the war of 1870 and owned a very fine sword given him by the French government. After the defeat of France, he came to Texas in voluntary exile.

Fletcher Scott, a neighbor, said that he once got Heim on a pitching horse, thinking he would be thrown, but being a trained cavalry officer, Heim proved to be at home on any horse.[21]

In the summer of 1884, D'Heur and a friend by the name of Geer, made a trip to Weatherford, carrying $30,000 in checks and bonds. On crossing Elm Creek in a heavy rainstorm, their buggy washed downstream, and they lost $12,000.[22]

D'Heur was appointed city engineer of Weatherford in 1889,[23] and was later employed in that same capacity by the city of Los Angeles. After leaving Texas he wrote a letter to Fletcher Scott and told him that Heim was then a commander of the French forces in Algeria. D'Heur held fifty or sixty shares in the Franco-Texan Land Company until its dissolution.

Jones City, which became Anson and the county seat of Jones County, was established in 1881 by Martin Duvall and William Bowyer on Section 2, Block 1 (school land surveyed by the Texas and New Orleans Railroad Company). Duvall, a Frenchman from Kentucky, originally a Texas and Pacific surveyor, and later deputy surveyor of the Palo Pinto Land District and county surveyor of Jones County, had built his house on the southeast quarter of Section 2 in 1880. Bowyer, a descendant of a French Huguenot family (Boyer), had settled

[21] *Western Enterprise* (Anson), December 3, 1936, Section 2 (Cowboys Christmas Ball Edition).

[22] Galveston *Daily News*, June 23, 1884.

[23] Fort Worth *Gazette*, July 21, 1889.

on the west half and in 1881 built the first business house, a mercantile store and post office. Other Frenchmen living in Jones County were E. Menielle, a rancher on Cottonwood Creek; F. de la Grandière, owner of a "Livery, Sale, and Boarding Stable," and F. E. Bompart, who took an active part in settling both Taylor and Jones counties. Bompart succeeded Duvall as county surveyor and in 1889 was in charge of Abilene's exhibit at the State Fair, winning the first prize of $500. Another was R. V. Colbert who had an interesting career: He came from Mt. Lebanon, Louisiana in 1883, grubbed mesquite for "Ike Hudson," herded sheep for "Mr. Northington," was a cowboy on the T. Diamond, Horseshoe, and LIL, set type for the *Texas Western* in its early days, and was deputy county clerk under John Ferguson. After holding the office of county clerk for two terms, 1890–1894, he organized the Jones County Bank; he was engaged in the stock business for many years and in 1900 became president of the American Hereford Association.[24]

M. H. and C. C. Compere of Abilene, "Real Estate, Insurance, and Rental Boys," laid out the towns of Compere and Sylvester in Fisher County in 1883, having bought part of the A J Ranch for that purpose when the Kansas City, Mexico, and Orient was surveyed through that point. The Franco-Texan owned some 33,000 acres, lying in a fairly wide strip all across the southern end of Fisher County.

The Texas and Pacific reached Sweetwater in Nolan County on March 12, 1881. This site was originally a store in a dugout on the banks of Sweetwater Creek, where Billie Knight kept a supply of groceries, patent medicines, tobacco, and ammunition for the benefit of the ranchers and buffalo hunters. When James Manning, a deputy surveyor, bought the store and housed it in a wooden shack, Sweetwater was made a United States post office. The Franco-Texan land consisted of 95,000 acres stretching across the northern half of the county, and the company happened to own Section 47, Block 22, embracing that particular spot.

Sweetwater was designated the temporary county seat on December 20, 1880. A year later the Commissioners Court ordered an election to

[24] Emmett Landers, "A Short History of Taylor County" (M.A. thesis), p. 130.

determine whether Sweetwater or Patterson's site, three miles to the west, would be the permanent seat of the county government. By then Sweetwater had moved up on the railroad line and was a tent city, without a single building of rock, wood, or brick. When the soldiers left Fort Griffin in the summer of 1881, some of them came there to live. To induce the voters to cast their ballots for Sweetwater, the Franco-Texan executed a bond for $10,000 whereby it contracted to build a courthouse costing that amount within ninety days and also to furnish a lot for the county jail, if the county seat should be located on Section 47. Sweetwater was chosen on April 12, 1881, but no immediate steps were taken to survey Section 47 or to build the courthouse. On August 8, 1881, the Court ordered the bond forfeited and instructed the county attorney to file suit. There is no record of any court action, and Manning's shack was jacked up and hauled in to serve as the courthouse for a year.[25] When the first session of district court was held in this little picket house, where the merchant had his home, his store, and the post office, Judge T. B. Wheeler sat on a nail keg covered with a buffalo robe.[26]

The Nolan County correspondent reported to the Galveston *Daily News* in June, 1881, that the Texas and Pacific Company had entered into a bond of $10,000 by which it pledged to build a courthouse and donate it to the county.[27] The transactions which followed defy any rational explanation unless the Texas and Pacific and the Franco-Texan were then almost one. The Texas and Pacific sold two lots in June, 1881, and on August 21, 1881, donated two blocks for the courthouse and jail, but the Franco-Texan conveyed no land to the Texas and Pacific until March 18, 1882, when 480 acres out of Section 47 were deeded to the railroad company for $1,060. Then on July 25, 1882, after the town lots were surveyed, the Texas and Pacific re-conveyed one-third of them to the Franco-Texan.[28]

25 R. C. Crane, "Early Days in Sweetwater," *West Texas Historical Association Yearbook*, VIII (June, 1932), 97–123.

26 Dallas *Daily Herald*, April 11, 1884.

27 Galveston *Daily News*, June 19, 1881.

28 Crane, "Early Days in Sweetwater," *West Texas Historical Association Yearbook*, VIII (June, 1932), 97–123.

To add to the confusion, the Franco-Texan president said in May, 1881, that his company owed $450 to the Nolan County people for payment on the courthouse, and Vice-President John C. Brown of the Texas and Pacific, when interviewed on an inspection trip of the railway line in June, 1881, said he was presenting a check for $500 at Sweetwater as a partial contribution for the courthouse.[29] Historian R. C. Crane has said that a compromise was effected whereby the Franco-Texan was to pay the county $700, the lawyer getting $200 of it. Finally, the county issued bonds in the amount of $27,000 to pay for the courthouse, but the jail was built first, under contract to Martin, Byrnes, and Johnston for $8,750, leaving only $22,000 for the courthouse, which was built a year later by J. M. Archer.[30]

By March, 1882, the Franco-Texan Land Company had built the Lone Star Plaster Factory about one mile west of the depot and was preparing to make plaster of paris from the immense quantity of gypsum rock in Nolan and Fisher counties. The company ran an ad in the Dallas *Daily Herald* from March 7, 1882, through February 2, 1883, and the *Herald* carried this news item the first day the ad appeared:

> We almost daily hear of some new enterprise being inaugurated that is calculated to add to the prosperity of this portion of the state. The latest of these is the erection of extensive works for the manufacture of plaster of paris at Fresnay City, a newly located town in Nolan County. This enterprise is set on foot by the Franco-Texian Land Company and is under the management of E. Chifflet who was formerly engaged in the manufacture of plaster of paris in France. The company have ample means to extend their work as the demands of the trade require.[31]

Fresnay City, on the outskirts of Sweetwater, took its name from Victor de Fresnay, a French director and vice-president of the Franco-Texan, whose application for land would be refused by President Duke in 1883. The factory, which cost $30,000 and employed about 150

29 Galveston *Daily News*, May 12, 1881; Dallas *Daily Herald*, June 2, 1881.

30 Nolan County *v.* State of Texas, 83 *Texas Reports* 183; Galveston *Daily News*, June 30, 1881.

31 Dallas *Daily Herald*, March 7, 1882.

hands, had a capacity for working up about one ton of raw material per hour. It was soon turning out a good grade of plaster and appeared to be doing a profitable business.[32] By the end of September, 1882, the company was shipping plaster of paris, cement, and fertilizer (also made from gypsum) in large quantities to various parts of the world.[33] A number of French families came to Sweetwater to work in the plant.

A. Chaptive, the French president of the Franco-Texan, then living in Weatherford, died in November, 1882.[34] The superintendent, Emil Chifflet, and his assistant, Max Guillot, continued to run the plant.

Chifflet, a citizen of France, fifty-two years of age, had moved to Sweetwater from Fort Griffin. He was an alderman and also a land agent of the Franco-Texan. Guillot was from Dallas, where his father, mother, and sister resided.[35] He was twenty-five years old.

The new courthouse lacked only the roof on February 1, 1883. Strangers called it a magnificent building, and citizens of Sweetwater thought it much more elegant than the one in Fort Worth—"a piece of Texas extravagance," they said, but one which spoke well for Sweetwater. Every day the town was full of stockmen and hunters, the latter clad in their comfortable coyote skin suits, and all scurrying about in the wind, in complete harmony with the prairie dogs which had not abandoned the streets. Three recent attempts had been made to burn out the business section of the town, and all parties interested were keeping a vigilant watch.[36]

Chifflet and Guillot also operated the Cattle Exchange Saloon about a block from the depot. They allowed no "rowdyism," and the public considered their place as "high class." There was no bank in Sweetwater, but the stockmen had so much confidence in Chifflet and Guillot that they often left their money in the safe at the saloon, sometimes more than $20,000. Animosity on the part of local competitors, it was supposed, resulted in a raid on Chifflet and Guillot's saloon on a Sun-

[32] Galveston *Daily News*, March 1, and March 28, 1882.

[33] *Ibid.*, September 30, 1882.

[34] *Ibid.*, November 23, 1882.

[35] United States Bureau of the Census: Tenth Census, 1880, figures for Shackelford and Dallas counties.

[36] Fort Worth *Gazette*, February 1, 1883.

day night in February of 1883. When the smoke cleared away after the shooting, Chifflet and Guillot were dead. N. I. Dulaney, one of Sweetwater's leading merchants and the owner of the building, was shot through the leg, leaving a wound that would likely necessitate amputation. One of the raiders was shot in the hand.

Guillot's family in Dallas received the following telegram from Sweetwater on February 26, 1883:

> Mr. E. Chifflet and your son were shot and instantly killed at 8:00. Come immediately.
>
> FRANCO-TEXAN LAND COMPANY.[37]

Max Guillot, born and reared in Dallas, was the son of one of the oldest and wealthiest citizens of that city. His father, Maxime Guillot, arrived penniless in New Orleans in 1847, having left France for political reasons. He began his life in Texas as a government wagonmaker in Fort Worth at $20 a month. When Fort Worth was abandoned as a military post, Guillot went to Dallas where he began building wagons and carriages. He returned to France in 1853 and brought back a wife and four experienced assistants who helped him establish a thriving business at the corner of Elm and Houston streets. Guillot often served as interpreter for Victor Considerant's French colonists when they came across the river from La Réunion. In 1860 John H. Reagan had a carriage built at Guillot's shop. It was lined with imported French damask and decorated with French iron work and trimmings. Guillot also made a buckboard for Governor Lubbock.

On the outbreak of the Civil War the Confederate government sent Guillot to Fort Lancaster to manufacture wagons. Back in Dallas at the close of the war, he built his home at the corner of Live Oak and Harwood. Many prominent people visited in this house, and it was an historical landmark for nearly forty years.[38]

Guillot's son Maxime was a young man of talent and promise. He wanted to enter political life and had gone to the west where he had expected to find fewer rivals in the civic field. He was known to have a kind and charitable disposition, and his friends, in the absence of

[37] Dallas *Daily Herald*, March 1, 1883.

[38] Philip Lindsley, *A History of Greater Dallas and Vicinity*, I, 54–57.

pointed testimony, had no idea what could have led to his death. Private information later revealed that Chifflet and Guillot were shot in the back of the head and presumably were unaware of the presence of their assassins.[39]

Before Emil Chifflet went to Sweetwater, he lived on his wheat farm up on Collin Creek two miles from Fort Griffin. He raised very fine wheat which was ground at one of the Weatherford mills. He also tanned buffalo hides and pelts at the old tannery in Fort Griffin and did a good business when he had a supply on hand. His was the only tannery in northwest Texas, and he employed several helpers.

In December of 1879, Chifflet and a Mr. Linn set out for Mt. Blanco Canyon and the buffalo hunters' camp beyond to get hides and pelts. They found none at Mt. Blanco and left there in a gloomy mood, in view of the absence of comfort on a trip to the prairie in midwinter, and also the improbability of finding any bison. Chifflet was very anxious to shoot at least one buffalo himself, and his favorite refrain, as reported in Mt. Blanco notes on January 2, 1880, was:

> If he dies, I'll tan his skin,
> If he don't, I'll shoot him again.

The Fort Griffin *Echo* announced on May 22, 1880, that Chifflet had on hand and en route from the west enough buffalo hides to keep him employed for three months.[40] By the middle of July, with three men hard at work, he had turned out several hundred fine large robes. One was for his own use, and as fine a piece as had ever been seen on the local market. It contained

> 12 wolfskins bordered with wildcat, in the center of which was a star composed of buffalo with the five radiating points made from the skin of the little animal locally known as the swift. The robe was lined with light red flannel, trimmed and embroidered with blue silk. Mr. Chifflet had refused several offers of fifty dollars for the robe but he preferred to keep it as a pattern for others.[41]

[39] Fort Worth *Gazette*, February 27, and February 28, 1883.

[40] Fort Griffin *Echo*, August 23, November 22, and December 20, 1879; January 10, January 31, May 22, and July 31, 1880; March 26, 1881.

[41] *Ibid.*, March 26, April 30, and May 14, 1881.

The old tannery was sold under execution of a mortgage in March, 1881. It finally came into the possession of H. E. Chapin who tore it down in order to build a cottage on the site. A number of people, having become dissatisfied with the business prospects at Fort Griffin, left in April. Early in May, the troops received orders to move to Fort Clark, and at sunset on May 31, 1881, the flag at the military post came down. Chifflet probably moved to Sweetwater about the same time.[42]

The grand jury of Nolan County returned twelve indictments in connection with the shooting of Chifflet and Guillot. There were two bills against each of six men. They included J. M. Chambers, W. A. Gray, formerly the proprietor of the Palace Saloon in Buffalo Gap, and two brothers by the names of A. J. and Dick Gilstrap. Only these four men were arrested, and Gray, who claimed to be ill, made his escape while held under separate guard by a ranger. Fearing trouble in Sweetwater, Sergeant McNeally took the other three prisoners to jail in Colorado City.[43]

On April 21, 1883, the case of A. J. Gilstrap came up before District Judge Wheeler on a writ of habeas corpus for bail. After a number of witnesses were examined, the court adjourned at 8:00 in the evening to meet again at 9:30 in N. I. Dulaney's room. Having been wounded at the time of the killing he was a material witness for the state but was still confined to his bed. The case was concluded at 10:30 P.M. No bail was granted, and the applicant gave notice of appeal.[44]

A. J. Gilstrap was released on a $10,000 bond late in May. J. M. Chambers and Dick Gilstrap, tried on a writ of habeas corpus before Judge Wheeler in July, 1883, were remanded to jail, but both were released on bond in August after successful appeals.[45]

Dick Gilstrap was tried at Colorado City on October 30, 1883, and given ten years in the penitentiary for killing Guillot.[46]

[42] Dallas *Daily Herald*, March 31, and April 26, 1883.

[43] Fort Worth *Gazette*, April 21, and April 22, 1883.

[44] *Ibid.*, May 22, and July 19, 1883; Galveston *Daily News*, July 20, 1883.

[45] Albany *Star*, November 2, 1883.

[46] Fort Worth *Gazette*, November 29, 1883; Dallas *Daily Herald*, February 4, 1885.

J. M. Chambers, charged as an accomplice in the murder of Guillot, was tried at Abilene in November, 1883. The trial was in progress for a week, and the courthouse was filled with spectators. The eleven attorneys employed, nine for Chambers and two for the state, had a warm fight, with every inch of the ground closely contested. The jury returned a verdict of not guilty. Chambers was held in custody to be tried on a second charge at the next term. The case was continued until February, 1885, when, presumably, it was dismissed.[47]

The case against W. A. Gray, who was finally re-apprehended, was dismissed in April, 1884, at Sweetwater.[48]

Two cases against A. J. Gilstrap were dismissed at Sweetwater in November, 1884. The defendant's lawyers insisted on a verdict of not guilty, but it was refused. The lawyers present were S. W. T. Lanham of Weatherford, H. L. Bentley of Abilene, and F. B. Stanley of Fort Worth, quite an array of counsel for this obscure individual,[49] as were the nine attorneys employed for his partner J. M. Chambers in Abilene.

Thomas Trammell & Company organized a bank at Sweetwater within a month after the shooting of Chifflet and Guillot, and some time in May a large new safe weighing 8,500 pounds was received. By the end of June the Franco-Texan Land Company had built a brick factory which was burning two kilns of brick, one of 70,000 and one of 150,000. The Lone Star Plaster Factory was idle for want of proper management.[50] A ditch six feet deep and two feet wide had been dug

47 Fort Worth *Gazette*, November 29, 1883; Dallas *Daily Herald*, February 4, 1885.

48 Fort Worth *Gazette*, April 19, 1884.

49 *Ibid.*, November 12, 1884.

50 Fort Worth *Gazette*, May 18, May 22, and June 30, 1883. Thomas Trammell is known as the "Father of Sweetwater." His father, Philip Trammell, born near Van Buren, Arkansas, came to Texas in 1852 and entered the cattle business in Navarro County. Thomas, born June 22, 1845, in Arkansas, was reared on the Texas ranch. In 1872 he married Mary Jane Newman, daughter of Martin Newman and sister of John F. Newman of Nolan County. Trammell lived in Navarro County until 1882 when he went to Sweetwater. He soon had large cattle ranches in Texas and New Mexico. In 1889, having acquired the Colorado River Valley Railroad, he made a contract with the president of the Kansas City, Mexico, and Orient to become part of the road from Kansas

around the building, and it was guarded by a watchman named Mc-Ivers. In 1884 it was abandoned and the machinery used for the first laundry in Sweetwater. W. C. Johnson, district clerk, took charge of Chifflet's saloon, married his widow, and squandered all the money she had.[51]

N. I. Dulaney, the wealthiest merchant and one of the most enterprising citizens of Sweetwater, died on January 11, 1890, it was thought from the effects of the old pistol wound accidentally received in the Chifflet Guillot killing.[52]

At last a more cheerful epitaph was written in the Fort Worth *Gazette* on August 30, 1891: "The Texas Plaster Company have bought the old works of the Franco-Texan Land Company at Sweetwater and will enlarge them and put in new machinery. The capacity of the new factory will be fifteen tons per day. Mr. James Quinn of Denver is manager of the new factory. The company have similar interests in Denver, Colorado."[53] There are two large gypsum plants at Sweetwater today: U.S. Gypsum Company and Flintkote Company, and also a cement plant.

The tract owned by the Franco-Texan in Mitchell County, just west

---

City to Topolobampo on the west coast of Mexico. He went to Kansas City and brought Arthur Stilwell to Sweetwater in a buggy and persuaded him to bring the railroad to Nolan County. Sweetwater's "Uncle Tom" was the president of the town's first bank and the first president of the West Texas Cattle Raisers Association (Sweetwater *Reporter*, September 28, 1941, Pioneer and Progress Edition).

[51] Louise Bradford, "A History of Nolan County" (M.A. thesis), pp. 56, 121.

[52] Fort Worth *Gazette*, January 12, 1890. The Dulaney brothers, N. I. and J. D., Sr., went into business in 1877 at Mount Moro in Taylor County where they established a post office and store, hauling building materials from Waco. They moved farther west and operated a store at old Fort Chadbourne, then went to Sweetwater and set up a store in a tent just south of the present Texas and Pacific station. They put in the first lumber yard, and their first carload of lumber was shipped on the first T & P train. They also erected the first stone building. The Dulaney brothers began ranching in the 1890's and had one of the best known Hereford ranches in northwest Texas (Sweetwater *Reporter*, September 28, 1941 [Pioneer and Progress Edition]).

[53] Fort Worth *Gazette*, August 30, 1891.

of Nolan, was a large body of very fine tableland, containing 16,640 acres, between Loraine and Sweetwater. It was grazing country with only a few small streams, but it was believed that if artesian wells could be had, it would make excellent farms. Loraine, originally spelled with two "r's," was first settled in 1881 when the Texas and Pacific track reached Section 47 in Block 25 and the railway company established an experimental farm there.[54] The town was not located on Franco-Texan land, but it was named by a group of Frenchmen who tried out the T & P farm and then acquired land in the vicinity. H. Bouchelle, an employee of the railroad, was one of the chain carriers when Section 47 was surveyed in 1874. Alf H. H. Tolar camped here and cut hay in the open prairie in 1881, while grading a section of the T & P road. When he pitched his tent on the present site of Colorado City, he was the first actual settler. Will Dobbyns of Coleman soon arrived and began printing the Colorado *Courant* in a dugout. Dobbyns had carried his press to Colorado City but had brought no paper. He printed the first issues on brown wrapping paper from A. W. Dunn's store. Tolar purchased the *Courant*, which became the Colorado *Clipper*, and later founded the Abilene *Reporter*. He was elected state representative of the 29th District in 1889.[55]

The ranching industry attracted the "enterprising Frenchman," as well as the "adventurous Englishman, the cautious Scot, and the bold Irishman," to northwest Texas in the 1880's and 1890's. Jules Mapleson of New Orleans was ranching in Jones County, Louis and Eugene Dalmont and the Durants in Taylor; Ford and Beauchamp in Wise; Catlett, Hord, and Malin in Mitchell; Sacre and Richards and Benjamin Hubert in Clay. Mont Dillon had a ranch in Mitchell County in 1881. He built the first rock house in the county and organized the Champion Cattle Company. Pierre Wibaux of Fort Worth sold to the

[54] Galveston *Daily News*, September 30, 1882.

[55] Tolar, of French descent, was a native of Cumberland County, North Carolina. At the age of seventeen he volunteered for service in the Confederate Army. As a second lieutenant he was cited for gallant conduct at Gettysburg. He was a nephew of Major Micajah Autry of Texas revolutionary fame (the Alamo) and had been a resident of the state since 1870 (Fort Worth *Gazette*, October 20, 1884).

Continental in 1881 as did the Millett Brothers of Baylor County. Wibaux acquired extensive holdings in Montana, and he, along with John B. Gillett of Kentucky, helped to bring the Shorthorn into the hearts of the western people.[56] There were Delongs in the Panhandle and in Taylor, Young, and Stephens counties. R. M. Gano (originally Gerneaux) was a prominent stockraiser in West Texas for many years. W. E. Rayner of St. Louis was ranching on 66 sections in King County, and in 1885 the state inspector reported that Rayner owned his land which was fenced and contained no illegal enclosures. In 1890 he established the town of Rayner in Stonewall County. The old courthouse there has been converted into the headquarters of the Baldwin Ranch and is a noted landmark. J. C. Gaynor of the Fond du Lac Cattle Company had a large herd in Fisher County, and L. O. Rumery of Wisconsin bought out O. J. Wiren who went broke in 1888: 160 sections of land, some owned, some leased, for $214,360. A. W. Hudson, Wiren's foreman and a French Canadian, who married E. C. Kellogg's daughter, purchased the south pasture of the Two Buckle (Kentucky Cattle Company) when it went out of business. Two native Alsace-Lorrainers, Mayer Halff of Castroville and Charles Schreiner of Kerrville, had interests in northwest Texas. Both, along with Julius Real, the nephew of Charles Schreiner, are well remembered in the ranching industry today.

In 1878 Jot Gunter, William B. Munson, and John Summerfield secured a contract to locate land for the Houston and Great Northern Railroad. They soon controlled thousands of acres in the Panhandle, and in 1880 they established a ranch, bringing their first herd, branded GMS, from Louisiana. In 1881 Jules Gunter, nephew of Jot Gunter, bought Summerfield's interest and brought a herd from the Indian Territory, branded T Anchor. The Gunters sold to Munson in 1883, and in 1885 he sold about 225 sections and 24,000 head of stock to the Cedar Valley Land and Cattle Company of England. West Texas State

[56] John B. Gillett descended from a French Huguenot family which immigrated to the United States in 1631. He was a breeder of graded stock, and his portrait in terra cotta relief work graces the entrance to the Bank Building of the Chicago Union Stock Yards (Alvin H. Sanders, *History of Short Horn Cattle*, pp. 752–753).

Teachers College at Canyon is located on eighty acres of the original ranch. Jot Gunter went into the real estate business in Dallas and later in San Antonio where the Gunter Hotel and Gunter Office Building were named for him.

There were also the Furneaux, Fuquas, Flournoys, Hilliards, Mal-letts, and Moynes—native Americans of French descent—and not to be overlooked were Dulaney, Wilson, and Maupin of Fort Worth and St. Louis, the largest land and cattle buyers in the West. Colonel M. A. Maupin had mining interests in New Mexico, livestock in Arizona Territory, and horses in Missouri.

Two ranches belonging to Frenchmen, one large, one small, and neither quite in northwest Texas, are worthy of a few words. The Carlin or Las Moras Ranch in Menard County was the "boss" ranch and a landmark in that section in the 1880's. Reuben Ford surveyed this "rancho" at the head of the San Saba River—about 35,000 acres—for E. Carlin of Paris, France, in December, 1876. It was owned by a French stock company and superintended by the North brothers, George L. and William F., assisted by their French cook, H. Caillonett. There were fifteen or sixteen thousand head of sheep on the ranch, all thoroughbreds, a cross between the Cotswolds and the Merinos, which made a large fine sheep. The muttons weighed 160 pounds after shearing; the clip of 1881, marketed in San Antonio, amounted to 70,000 pounds of wool.[57] The ranch was described by Mary J. Jacques in *Texas Ranch Life* as being "beautifully situated, well watered, and near some fine timber." Miss Jacques, an Englishwoman touring the west, visited Las Moras with Kerrville friends in 1891. They received a hearty welcome and enjoyed hot toddies by blazing cedar logs. Their hosts were French, Miss Jacques said, and a partner who was present played the mandolin. The well-constructed rock barns of Las Moras are in use today on a modern ranch. They may be seen on both sides of the old road to Junction about five miles out of Menard.

The Dupuys came to Kimble County from Kentucky in the early 1880's, traveling by boat down the Mississippi River and across the Gulf to Port Lavaca. On July 29, 1881, Joseph Burns of Shelby

[57] Galveston *Daily News*, December 16, 1876, and March 4, 1882.

County, as a surviving soldier of the Texas Revolution, received Veteran Donation Certificate No. 451 for 640 acres, which he immediately sold to George W. Ragsdale for $145.[58] Ragsdale located his land on Kyack Creek, a tributary of the South Llano River, in as beautiful a spot as can be found in Texas. The old road went up the bed of the creek and terminated at the head of a narrow canyon where a roaring spring flows out of the hillside and down amid towering pecan trees that meet overhead. Ragsdale, for some reason, decided to go to Mexico, and he needed a saddle horse. The Dupuys, who were prospecting, traded him one for his 640 acres. They built their home on Kyack Creek, and Mrs. Dupuy had some very fine furniture, bought from the Breckenridges of Kentucky, sent down the Mississippi to Port Lavaca and thence to the Llano in a covered wagon. In 1903 the Dupuys enlarged their ranch by buying four sections of school land up on the Llano divide.[59] In 1930 Mr. and Mrs. Dupuy and her sister, Mrs. Florence Blardone, and Peter Remboldt comprised the French population of Kimble County.

[58] Bexar Donation 1938, General Land Office.

[59] School Land Files 73600, 73601, 73602, 73603 (R. T. and Fannie H. Dupuy).

CHAPTER 8

THE LOSS OF TWO PRESIDENTS

Back in Weatherford V. G. Frost had succeeded Sam H. Milliken as president of the Franco-Texan Land Company, and J. W. Frost had succeeded V. G. Frost as secretary. Little is known of the Frosts except that they were from Palo Pinto and appear to have been related to C. L. Frost, former paymaster of the Texas and Pacific and then vice-president of the Pacific Improvement Company. On February 5, 1881, President Frost made a trip out to Baird with Major H. C. Withers, the depot and town-lot agent of the Texas and Pacific railroad.[1] Two weeks later Frost was awarded the contract to supply wood for the railroad between Dallas and its western terminus.[2]

On April 11, 1881, former Secretary S. P. Tuck of New York came into the Franco-Texan office and told Frost that he had some stock certificates to exchange for land. Frost said he could not make the exchange until he had checked the stubs in the Paris office and that he had no safe in which to keep the certificates while that was being done. When Tuck insisted, Frost said that he had to go to Millsap but would return that evening. Millsap was a new town the Pacific Improvement

[1] Dallas *Daily Herald*, February 9, 1881.

[2] Galveston *Daily News*, February 15, 1881.

Company was building on the railroad about fifteen miles west of Weatherford.

E. P. Nicholson, then a clerk in the Franco-Texan office, was present at the time. Frost left, but Tuck remained, studied the maps and schedules of prices, and made out a written application so as to have it ready when Frost returned. He also wrote out deeds of conveyance to the lands he had selected and a statement for Frost to sign acknowledging the application for the exchange of 996 shares, which he showed to Nicholson, saying that he obtained them while he was secretary of the company. Tuck took his shares and deposited them in Captain Henry Warren's safe with instructions for them to be delivered to Frost on execution of the deeds and then left town.[3]

Frost returned to the office the next morning but refused to sign anything. Some time afterward James Bostic of New York came in to see him. Bostic was the owner of 390 shares of the stock Tuck left in Warren's safe. Originally they were issued to Antoinette R. Bousselet of Paris, France, but had since been assigned to Bostic. This time Frost agreed to the exchange and said he would reserve the land Bostic designated until the stubs in the Paris office were checked. Bostic selected 4,491 acres in Fisher and Jones counties, appraised at $2.96 per acre, or a total value of $13,000. These were choice lands, and the company proceeded to sell 320 acres out of Section 17 and all of Section 19 in Jones County, taking no further action on Bostic's application for the same land.[4]

On May 3, 1881, President Frost departed for parts unknown with $5,500 of the company's funds.[5] Before he left, he let it be known that "he was going to keep out of the noise, that men were always asking him for money, and that he would as soon be in hell as annoyed as he was." Under pretense of paying the $450 which the Franco-Texan had promised to donate for the construction of the Nolan County court-

[3] A. R. Bousselet *v.* Franco-Texan Land Company, Cause 2091, District Court Records of Parker County.

[4] Franco-Texan Land Company *v.* A. R. Bousselet, 70 *Texas Reports* 422; see also File 5902, Texas Supreme Court Files.

[5] Fort Griffin *Echo*, May 14, 1881; Fort Worth *Daily Democrat*, May 4, 1881.

house, he made out a voucher for that amount, forged the secretary's name, drew the money from the bank, and took it with him.[6] Frost's liabilities were no less than $60,000, but as he had a few assets Henry Warren, the company's banker, immediately filed suit for $12,000, and attachments were issued on a large supply of wood Frost had furnished the Texas and Pacific.[7]

Six years later, in October, 1887, Sheriff H. S. Sisk of Parker County received a letter from Greuld Britton and D. A. Peal, formerly of Weatherford but then members of Captain McMurray's company of Rangers, informing him that V. G. Frost, former president of the Franco-Texan Land Company, had been found in Greer County. Sheriff Sisk sent the Rangers a capias, and he soon received a telegram from Captain McMurray reporting that Frost had been arrested and would be delivered to him in Wichita Falls. Sisk brought Frost back to Weatherford and placed him in jail on November 2.[8]

On June 6, 1888, in the district court of Parker County, one of the cases against V. G. Frost for embezzlement was dismissed. In the second case, he made his bond, which was reduced, and was released from imprisonment. The case was continued until the next term of court.[9]

A. Chaptive of Paris, France was appointed to succeed V. G. Frost. An excerpt from the minutes of a meeting held in Paris on May 31, 1881, reads as follows:

> All the efforts of the Paris office remain sterile of results and have not been able to check the ruinous administration of V. G. Frost, an unfaithful agent, who a few months ago had been appointed temporary president and whose flight from Weatherford under shameful circumstances has been announced to us. Although Mr. Warren, the company's banker, has been so obliging as to take charge of affairs for a certain time there is not a moment to lose before sending a director on an extraordinary mission to Texas. The President proposes to allow M. Amelie Chaptive with whom he has conferred to go to America for a sum of 1500 f travel expenses and the sum of 6,000 f salary dating from June 1, 1881.

[6] Galveston *Daily News*, May 12, 1881.
[7] Fort Worth *Daily Democrat*, May 5, 1881.
[8] Fort Worth *Gazette*, November 4, 1887.
[9] *Ibid.*, June 7, 1888.

The company must be protected and defend its property from the greed and bad faith of agents caring little for duty and forgetful of every sentiment of honor.

(Signed) De Fresnay, Vice-President.[10]

Chaptive arrived in Weatherford some time in June of 1881. As it was reported on September 7 that R. W. Kindel had sold his brick residence to a "French gentleman" for $2,800, the gentleman was probably Chaptive.[11] While president of the Franco-Texan, Chaptive acted without a secretary, but he had to have an interpreter. Charles Malcolmson was his interpreter for eight months, and Allard d'Heur, who had no connection with the company but was in and out of the office, often served in this capacity. The staff also included Camille Henry, a clerk, and Barthelotti, a bookkeeper. When Barthelotti went to Sweetwater as one of the company's agents, Julius Royer took his place as bookkeeper.[12]

Chaptive died in Weatherford on November 19, 1882, after little more than a year in office. A dispatch reporting his death stated only: "A. Chaptive was buried here today. He came from France last year."[13] Chaptive was buried in the vault underneath the Catholic Church. In 1945 Bill Tanner, an oldtimer in Weatherford, remembered seeing Chaptive riding into town many times—in his riding habit and short black boots, mounted on a big fine horse, with a pack of greyhounds alongside.

The following year the wife and son of Chaptive, as his heirs, instituted suit against the Franco-Texan to recover $7,441.71, the amount alleged to be due Chaptive for salary, money advanced, and other items and to collect the additional sum of $600 to pay for their return to France. Chaptive's salary as president had been $1,200 a year, and the

[10] Franco-Texan Land Company *v.* Marie Chaptive *et al.*, File 5306, Texas Supreme Court Files.

[11] Fort Worth *Daily Democrat,* September 8, 1881. Parker County deed records show that on this date the Franco-Texan purchased a house from R. W. Kindel and that a few weeks later the company was released from the sale.

[12] Franco-Texan Land Company *v.* Chaptive *et al.*, 3 *South Western Reporter* 31; see also File 5306, Texas Supreme Court Files.

[13] Galveston *Daily News,* November 23, 1882.

company had agreed to pay his travel expenses to and from France. The defendants claimed that he had sold rock from company lands in the amount of $450, had appropriated that sum for his own use, and had also made numerous unauthorized expenditures which were entered upon the books but were not itemized. The case came before the district court on September 11, 1884, and judgment was rendered in favor of the plaintiffs for $384. E. P. Nicholson, the company's attorney, appealed the case, declaring that Marie Chaptive was an alien and had no such rights as she was seeking. The Texas Supreme Court affirmed the judgment of the district court, holding that the latter had balanced the account according to the books, that the entries had been accepted for a long time as the true statement of the corporate transactions, and that there had been conflicting testimony in regard to the $450 received for the rock sold from the company's lands.

The books of the company, presented in evidence in this trial, revealed that Chaptive had made four trips to Sweetwater. On two of them his expenses were $200 each and on the others $100 each. These were the "unauthorized expenditures," and the company claimed that Chaptive had spent the money extravagantly, giving wine suppers, *et cetera.* Allard d'Heur testified that he had accompanied Chaptive on one of the $100 trips and that Chaptive had furnished the wine for a party of eight at the hotel in Sweetwater. D'Heur said he drank a whole bottle himself. He was certain the trip had cost $125. Chaptive had hired two hacks for $20 and they drove half of two days over the company lands looking for deposits of gypsum. The fare to Sweetwater was $7.00. Chaptive had a pass on the Texas and Pacific but he had paid for D'Heur's ticket.[14]

R. W. Duke, the owner of the Weatherford *Times,* was elected president of the Franco-Texan soon after Chaptive's death. Camille Henry was elected secretary, and Charles Malcolmson was promoted to the office of clerk. Instead of returning to Paris, Marie Chaptive and her son Paul continued to live in Weatherford.

[14] Franco-Texan Land Company *v.* Marie Chaptive *et al.*, File 5306, Texas Supreme Court Files.

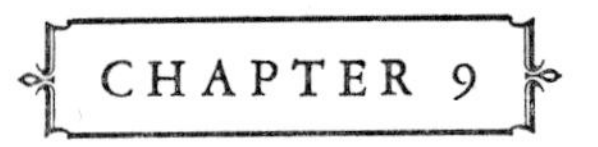

LEON CHOTTEAU COMES TO TEXAS

In 1881 Leon Chotteau made his third trip to the United States. He arrived in Galveston the last week of May, having come by way of New York, Baltimore, Charleston, and New Orleans. He was representing a French company with a capital of 20,000,000 francs, whose object was to import livestock directly to France instead of through England as had been done heretofore. An agent of the company was already in the west making purchases of horses and beef cattle, and the first shipment was to be made in the course of a month. It would be necessary to ship on British steamers until the company could provide a line of its own, especially constructed for the cattle trade. Chotteau expected to form a second company for the importation of manufactured goods of every description. Goods of this type had been prohibited formerly, but under the new tariff going into operation in June they would find a large market in France.[1]

When Chotteau reached Baltimore he had heard from the company's agent in the west. Chotteau thought that livestock, which was to be the chief article of freight, could be bought and placed on board the British steamers at a price low enough to justify the freight rates, which were

[1] Galveston *Daily News*, May 12, 1881.

higher between Baltimore and Le Havre than they were between Baltimore and British ports. If the experiment was successful, the company proposed to build stockyards at Le Havre and keep the horses and cattle there in order to fatten them for the Paris market.

At Galveston, Chotteau was interviewed at his rooms in the Tremont in regard to the promotion of Franco-American trade. When asked if special reciprocity stipulations would be necessary, he said that the new general treaty was better than a special one and that France had removed the tariff restrictions.

Chotteau was also interested in immigration and colonization and intended to organize a company for that purpose, establishing a new route from Marseilles and Bordeaux to New Orleans and then to Texas. The port of Galveston was not included because it did not have a deep enough harbor, the water being only twelve or thirteen feet deep when it should be between eighteen and twenty. The immigrants were to come from Italy and Switzerland and perhaps from Austria, Spain, Southern Germany, and Southern France.

Chotteau exhibited a map and pamphlet in the French language, showing a colonization company with a very large landed interest in Parker County and the county west and stated that he would visit there before leaving Texas. When asked if many Frenchmen would come to Texas, Chotteau said, not many—French people did not leave France very often—but "Texas," he added, "is very attractive to us. Very often we have our monthly dinners and discuss Franco-American affairs, and when we speak of the United States, we always mention Texas. We always keep informed of the situation in Texas."[2]

Chotteau spoke to the members of the Cotton Exchange at noon on May 28. Again he said that a new current of immigration should be formed, that emigrants in the eastern portion of Europe congregated at Avrincourt, a railway station not far from Strassburg, and the exodus should be divided into two portions, one being sent via Le Havre to New York, the other via Marseilles to New Orleans. Texas could have a population of 50,000,000, and such a colonization project would improve Franco-American commercial relations, but the best method for

[2] *Ibid.*, May 27, 1881.

attracting colonists, he insisted, was not articles from newspapers, pamphlets, books, speeches, or advertisements of railway and steamship companies. All that meant nothing, proved nothing. All that was necessary for one conversion was "a soiled piece of paper brought by the mail carrier—to be read by the family." A prospective immigrant "must be asked by a brother or a cousin or a friend already established in Louisiana or Texas." An additional feature recommended by Chotteau was the immigrant's receipt of a deed to his land before he left Europe for his future home in Texas. The immigrant ships would, of course, return loaded with American products.[3]

The question of the importation of Texas cattle into France had been debated in the French Senate on February 3 and 19 of 1881. The French Minister of Agriculture and Commerce, M. Tirard, anxious to pacify the legitimate fears of French farmers, attacked the proposed importation, basing his argument on the report of the English Parliamentary Commission which had visited the United States and Texas in the year of 1880:

> Your attention is called to Texas cattle and the very low price at which they are raised and the probability of their invading our markets. I have proved to you that but a few head of American cattle have been imported to France. I can now give you the assurance that probably no Texas cattle will ever find their way to our country for the very good reason that the cattle of that State are affected with a grave epizootic and endemic disease against which we must very carefully guard our country.
>
> The report of the English commissioners sent to the United States by Parliament thus describes the disease: "The Texas cattle fever (tenian fever) seems to be a very mysterious disease. It is certain that cattle imported into Texas are invariably subject to it and die . . . It exists in a latent state even in cattle of healthy appearance . . . and is contagious to other cattle.

The British report added that like Texas chickens, an exceptionally bad species which were all feet and wings, Texas cattle could be similarly described as all legs and horns.

M. Tirard also gave the lie to a favourable report on the agricultural

[3] *Ibid.*, May 29, 1881.

and mineral resources of the state of Texas, delivered by the French Senator M. Pouyer Quertier.[4]

The Du Bellets, who were also interested in shipping cattle from Galveston to Le Havre, worked diligently to overcome these prejudices against Texas. Henry and his father went to Austin to appeal to A. W. Spaight, the Commissioner of Insurance, Statistics, and History—there was no department of agriculture or bureau of immigration—for an official answer to M. Tirard's attack and also some official action to rid the European public of its unfavourable opinions of Texas. But Spaight was powerless, all he could do was to publish a letter written by Judge Du Bellet and ask for suggestions. The Austin *Statesman* gave the Société Foncière et Agricole des États Unis a boost with an editorial, "Let Us Look after French Immigrants," in which the French were praised at length for their industry and standards of excellence. Furthermore, it said, France was teeming with people and money, and it was only necessary to make Texas known to France in order for the state to draw from it both of these elements.

Henry du Bellet gave the editor a copy of a report on the agricultural resources of Texas made for his company by M. Barral, the secretary of the National Agricultural Society of France. Henry had other business in Austin. He was looking after a corporation bill he had before the Legislature, an amendment to the law empowering corporations to borrow money. It passed the Senate but was killed by the House on March 24.[5]

While Chotteau was still in Galveston, the following notice appeared on the front page of the *News,* "M. Leon Chotteau indicated his intention of visiting Weatherford to see if the Franco-Texan Land Company of that place could not be made available in his colonization schemes. It is unfortunate that some $5,000 of the company's funds absconded, taking the president along too, only a few days ago. The lands, however, are still left."[6]

[4] *Ibid.*, March 30, 1881.

[5] Austin *Daily Statesman*, March 25, 1881.

[6] Galveston *Daily News*, May 31, 1881.

Chotteau went to Weatherford on June 2, and on June 7, the *News* carried this item:

A CORRECTION

Weatherford, Texas, June 4, 1881. At the request of M. Leon Chotteau who has been my guest for several days in Weatherford and in the interest of the company I represent, I hope you will have the kindness to correct the statement published by you in one of your late issues.

M. Chotteau came here to visit the general agent of the Real Estate Agricultural Company of the United States [Société Foncière], and the lands belonging to this French company, and not the Franco-Texan Land Company, with which I am pleased to say neither M. Chotteau nor my company are in any way connected.

Henry P. du Bellet, General Agent.[7]

Du Bellet's letter to the *News* is of special interest because it confirmed his break with the Franco-Texan although it gave no explanation of the cause.

Chotteau's steamship line was the Compagnie General Transatlantique de Francia, and Henry du Bellet was its agent in Texas. In its monthly trips the new line brought hundreds of immigrants to Texas, some with their titles in their pockets, but the number of Texas cattle Chotteau shipped to France has not been ascertained. It is known, however, that "Texans" were exported to France the following year.

Auguste Cerf of San Antonio took a cargo of beef cattle to France in the fall of 1882 and returned with fifty-five Rambouillet bucks from the famous Rambouillet farm in southern France. M. Cerf and the sheep arrived in New York in the steamer *Hermod* in October. During the voyage the steamer experienced such heavy weather that it took nineteen days to make the passage from Le Havre to New York, and the trip to Galveston, on the *Rio Grande,* occupied eight more. Although the sheep were at sea for twenty-seven days, they were in good health and did not appear to have suffered. During the passage they were fed hay and meal and were carried in padded cells and placed in slings when the sea ran very high. These were the first Rambouillets

[7] *Ibid.,* June 7, 1881.

that had been in this country since 1844, and their importation was expected to immortalize the name of Monsieur Cerf among Texas sheep growers. The Rambouillets were alleged to be direct descendants of a flock presented by the King of Spain to Louis XIV in 1786. Monsieur Cerf proposed to cross them with strong Texas flocks. In former experiments the crossbreed gave six pounds of wool worth twenty-five cents and the Mexican ewe two and a half pounds worth eleven cents.[8]

Monsieur Cerf's shipment of forty-four carloads of mutton to the city of Paris in 1881 also brought Texas shippers into direct contact with the Old World and strengthened the stock exportation business. Mutton heretofore had been shipped to Paris from Australia and Buenos Aires. The Texas mutton had been fattened, slaughtered, and shipped in a refrigerated vessel, the cost per car to New York being $150.[9]

Texas cattle were first exported from Galveston to Havana; then from Chicago to England through the Great Lakes, and also from Boston, Baltimore, and New York. The Barrow Steamship Company began to carry cattle to England from the port of Galveston in 1878, and the Monarch Line shipped 7,158 head, a few of which originated in Texas, from New York to London in 1882. This line was specially constructed for carrying cattle. Three decks were fitted with cattle stalls, and the average number carried was six hundred on one trip, the cost per head being £ 7. The ships loaded at Pavonia Ferry, Jersey City, just as the cattle came off the cars, and discharged at Deptford, a few miles below London at the great English stockyards.[10] However, according to reports in the New York *Times* in 1871 and thereafter, few Texas cattle were shipped from New York.[11] Although France and

[8] *Ibid.*, December 8, 1882.

[9] *Ibid.*, July 26, 1881.

[10] *Ibid.*, October 10, 1878; August 18, 1882.

[11] Most of the beef cattle and dressed beef selected for export came from corn-producing states: Illinois, Missouri, Kansas, Nebraska, Iowa (Joseph Nimmo, *Letter from Secretary of Treasury, Transmitting a Report from Chief of Bureau of Statistics in Response to a Resolution of the House Calling for Information in regard to the Range and Ranch Cattle Traffic in Western States and Territories*, 48th Congress, 2nd Session, Executive Document No. 267).

Germany subsequently imported American cattle, export figures do not show what states they came from. But France does not appear to have relaxed her vigilance. When plans were made to take Champion, the famous Texas Longhorn to the Paris Exposition in 1900, the French government objected, fearing "Texas fever."

CHAPTER 10

THE DU BELLET ENTERPRISES

Paul Pecquet du Bellet was in Weatherford in the summer and spring of 1881 to help promote the Société. He left for France on July 16 to look after its business there. Shortly before his departure Henry P. du Bellet purchased 251 lots on which he planned to build a textile mill,[1] and on July 15, 1881, he, Sam H. Milliken, and I. N. Roach incorporated the Weatherford Water Supply Company. The water works system, however, was not installed until October, 1887, and then by the Weatherford Water, Light, and Ice Company, which had other incorporators and officers.[2]

On July 22, 1881, Henry P. du Bellet, S. H. Milliken, and P. F. Brannon incorporated the Weatherford Street Railway. A state charter previously granted to S. H. Milliken and C. H. Cole had been forfeited. A third one was granted on January 28, 1887, to C. H. Milliken, A. S. Simmons, and G. M. Bowie,[3] but the streetcar line was put

[1] Fort Worth *Gazette*, July 15, and July 16, 1881.

[2] D. C. Haynes, president; A. F. Starr, vice-president; R. W. Kindel, secretary and treasurer (Fort Worth *Gazette*, October 21, 1887).

[3] Corporation Charters, Office of Secretary of State, Austin, Texas, Charter Division, Nos. 771 and 1378.

in operation under a city charter in 1889, incorporated by George P. Levy and Henry Warren and financed by a Kansas City syndicate.

The Société Foncière, by a special power of attorney, authorized Du Bellet to sell land in the amount of 100,000 francs and to purchase an equal amount without referring to the board of directors. This power was granted to him on November 10, 1881, in an order signed by the Comte de Constantin, president of the board of directors.[4] The Société's plan was to sell land in large or small tracts and furnish stock, tools, and equipment to the buyer for a certain price, depending upon the amount of land and the number of items supplied. One of many such sales was made to Joseph Baudalt on March 21, 1882.[5] A tract of 328 acres in Parker County, was deeded by H. P. du Bellet, agent, in consideration of a promissory note to the Société Foncière for $6,260.48, the company having advanced the following to the buyer for the purpose of enabling him to move to and improve the land: one house, two plows, one harrow, one ax and handle, two grubbing hoes, two spades, two pitchforks, two mattocks and handles, one bolt, one wagon, one set of harness, one pair of halters, a fifteen-strand wire fence, one doubletree and two singletrees, two belly and back bands, two pairs of trace chains, one saddle and blanket, a forty-eight-foot rope, one whip, and the following livestock: two mules branded $\overset{S}{C}$ on the left shoulder, one draft horse 14½ hands high, one horse 15½ hands high, one brown cow and calf, and one red cow. The 160-acre tracts sold for less—between $3,000 and $3,600, with less equipment. The company would advance further funds for improvement if necessary; the agent would take possession of the land and sell to the highest bidder if the note was not paid. Du Bellet sometimes bought the land back in for the company and sometimes for himself.

A number of individuals in France had given Du Bellet their powers of attorney to purchase and sell land. Among these were the Misses Noémi and Elfrida du Bellet of Paris,[6] for whom he purchased lots in the Millsap, Carter, and Couts additions. The 251 lots he had already

[4] Deed Records of Parker County, Vol. 13, pp. 6–7.

[5] *Ibid.*, Vol. 11, p. 643.

[6] *Ibid.*, Vol. 13, p. 106. Perhaps the Misses Du Bellet were Henry P. du Bellet's sisters.

reported purchasing included these bought for the Misses Du Bellet. He also sold them his own interest in 92 lots, along with eleven cows, four yearlings, and six calves.[7] An undivided one-fourth interest in the same lots was purchased for the Comte de Constantin.[8] Du Bellet also held powers of attorney from M. J. M. Cassagnieu, P. Copin, H. J. Girard, F. Heliot, Ed Hennin, and others.[9]

In early 1882 Du Bellet's activities extended to Mineral Wells, formerly Ednaville, which was twenty-two miles west of Weatherford and seven miles from Millsap, the nearest station on the Texas and Pacific railroad. Ednaville originally consisted of one solitary log cabin located in an eighty-acre tract belonging to Judge J. W. Lynch. Judge Lynch had bought this land from the Franco-Texan Land Company in 1877 and a few years later had drilled a ninety-three-foot well in his yard. After he and his wife had used the water for drinking and household purposes for two months, her rheumatism was cured and so were his eyes which had been diseased for several years.[10] This news quickly circulated over the state, and by the early fall of 1881, the population of the town had increased to twelve hundred; five wells were in operation, and water was selling for 2½ to 5 cents per gallon.[11]

The major portion of Mineral Wells was situated on a section belonging to the Société Foncière et Agricole des États Unis, and Du Bellet, the company's agent, was developing the town. According to "J. M. R." (J. M. Richards of Weatherford) who described the infant wonder in a letter to the Galveston *Daily News*, Du Bellet had acted "with the foresight and business sagacity of a veteran real estate dealer" when he placed the price of the lots at $20 each, spent hundreds of dollars in making improvements for the convenience of the public, and within four months sold over 400.[12]

By late summer of 1882 Mineral Wells was beginning to boom, and

[7] *Ibid.*, Vol. 12, p. 619.

[8] *Ibid.*, Vol. 12, p. 892.

[9] *Ibid.*, Vol. 9, p. 108; Vol. 28, p. 336.

[10] Galveston *Daily News*, August 27, 1881.

[11] *Ibid.*, November 30, 1881; Dallas *Daily Herald*, August 27, 1881.

[12] Galveston *Daily News*, February 4, 1882.

its citizens were seeking a railway outlet. The fifteen hacks running between the town and the Texas and Pacific station at Millsap were insufficient to accommodate the traveling public. Du Bellet, having initiated the railway movement, went to France to get his company's approval to build a railroad from Weatherford, through the company's large body of land in that area, and also a 100-room hotel on the hillside at Mineral Wells.[13] The Société evidently did not approve; it went into bankruptcy on November 4, 1882. The Weatherford, Minerals Wells, and Northwestern was built in 1891 with northern capital. Du Bellet's name does not appear in the list of local supporters, but a friend, Lafayette Fitzhugh of Dallas, helped provide the $52,000 subsidy furnished by Mineral Wells and Weatherford. The little town of Franco, laid out on the line about ten miles from Weatherford, is still in existence.

In October a number of French immigrants arrived to make their home in Mineral Wells.[14] Du Bellet returned from France about that same time, accompanied by Alfred Hammond de Voisins and George P. Levy. De Voisins, a somewhat delicate young man, was an art student and a protégé of Alfred Nobel, who was a close friend of his stepfather, Dr. F. Labadie Lagrave. Dr. Lagrave, an officer of the Legion of Honor, was one of the leading physicians at La Charité hospital in Paris and was several times called to attend Alexander III of Russia. On Paul Pecquet du Bellet's recommendation Dr. Lagrave invested in the Société and gave his stepson permission to come to Texas, thinking a sojourn in the land of sunshine would be good for his health. Levy, a distant relative of the Rothschilds, had first come to America in 1871 as a buyer for a New York firm dealing in laces and had returned to France in 1877 as a member of his company. He too heard about Texas and came to Weatherford with Henry P. du Bellet. Levy brought with him a power of attorney signed by the Comte de Constantin, Rose d'Angier, and Victor de Fresnay, giving him the authority to act in their interests. And since he seems to have had specific instructions to keep an eye on Du Bellet, it was not long before the inevitable break came between them.

[13] Dallas *Daily Herald*, September 1, and September 2, 1882.

[14] *Parker County Journal*, October 5, 1882.

Several other young Frenchmen with money to invest had decided to try their luck in Texas. Among this group, arriving at Weatherford in the early 1880's, were Le Maréchal, Mèchand, De la Grandière, Louis Boret, Henry Clogenson, Joseph la Ravoire, and Allard d'Heur.

Louis Laigle of Paris, France, who arrived in October, 1880, was employed as a bartender in Weatherford. He owned eight shares of Franco-Texan stock and made application to exchange them for land on October 4, 1881. He had been in Paris when the stockholders met in 1879 and had voted his stock by proxy, against the first amendment restricting the exchange of stock for land. When Laigle made his selection he was willing to give three times the cash value of the land, according to the mode of exchange established in 1879, but he demanded the immediate conveyance of the property and declined to deposit his eight shares with the president, as required by the amendment of 1880. The president refused to permit the exchange except in full compliance with the amended by-law. Laigle's counsel, A. J. Ball, then instituted suit in the district court to force a title from the Franco-Texan. H. P. du Bellet was surety on the plaintiff's cost bond. When the case came before the court in the spring term of 1882, Judge Hood handed down an important decision. He decreed that the Franco-Texan Land Company, being a corporation created by the state of Texas, had to comply with its charter and the general laws of Texas concerning private corporations, that the main office of the company had to be located within the state, and that no corporate acts such as stockholders general meetings were legal if carried out in a foreign country. Another question before the court was whether or not the board of directors had authority to adopt rules and regulations which would delay the shareholders in exchanging their stock at the office of the company in Texas. Judge Hood held that the company, having entered into a contract with the shareholders, was not at liberty to break this contract in any way at any time. He ordered that Laigle's shares be filed in the district clerk's office and surrendered to the Franco-Texan for cancellation in exchange for a deed to the land he had selected, 33⅓ acres 3 miles west of Weatherford.[15] E. P. Nicholson, counsel

[15] Galveston *Daily News*, April 11, 1882.

for the Franco-Texan, appealed the case to the Supreme Court. Obviously, if Judge Hood's decision was upheld it would mean much more than giving Laigle judgment for his land. In anticipation of its grave effects, Du Bellet and S. H. Milliken hastened to enter into several private transactions which involved the Société Foncière et Agricole des États Unis and and would soon have to come into the open.

In spite of the pending suit, or perhaps because of it, the Weatherford *Times*, on April 21, 1883, gave the following glowing report on the Franco-Texan Land Company:

> In this day of monopoly and heartless soulless home corporations who are accumulating immense possessions with the view of gaining power and influence in the government, for the purpose of intense selfishness and overriding the rights of the ordinary citizen, 'tis pleasant to look at and contemplate the workings of other companies in our midst which exist for legitimate purposes. The Franco-Texan Land Company owned near a million acres of land in the state, established its principal office in our city, and has been selling its lands to any and everybody who desired to purchase, on five years time, even as small tracts as 25 acres. The easy terms have enabled a great many poor men to purchase homes who otherwise would not have been able to do so.
>
> This company, with our townsman R. W. Duke as its president, Camille L. Henry, its secretary, and E. P. Nicholson, its attorney, is now especially prosperous. Its business is administered with tact and ability and upon true business principles; unpartial in all its dealings. The rich and poor are treated with equal courtesy and consideration. The stockholders are fortunate in having secured the services of such faithful, obliging, and competent officers.
>
> The president and secretary assure us of the healthy and satisfactory condition of the company. Its lands are being sold every day, and it has yet 500,000 unsold.
>
> We take great pleasure in directing the attention of all who want homes or stock ranches, to this company. Any citizen may deal with them, relying with as much confidence upon the officers doing what is just and right as he could upon the integrity of his best nearest neighbor.
>
> We again congratulate the stockholders.[16]

[16] Weatherford *Times*, April 21, 1883.

The following week, on April 27, 1883, the Supreme Court rendered its opinion in the case of the *Franco-Texan Land Company v. Laigle*. It declared that a private corporation could not perform acts of a strictly corporate character outside of the state where chartered. The Paris meeting was declared a nullity, the directors elected by it mere usurpers in assuming to make by-laws for the government of the company. Therefore, the by-law restricting the exchange of stock for land was declared void, and the judgment in favor of Laigle was affirmed.[17]

This decision protected the shareholder, but it made it necessary for the stockholders to meet in Texas, and it placed a cloud on the title to the lands of the Société, which rested on the sale made to Mardoche Lambert at the meeting in Paris in 1879. The following day 53 tracts belonging to the Société were put up for sale by the tax collector of Parker County. It was then revealed that Milliken, while president in 1879, had lent Du Bellet the money to purchase the 50,000 acres from the Franco-Texan and that the Du Bellets had organized the Société. On July 9, July 21, and December 27, 1882, Henry P. du Bellet had executed notes to Milliken on behalf of and in the name of the Société and had given deeds of trust to secure their payment. When the notes were not paid on January 9, 1883, suit was brought in the federal court, and service of process made upon Du Bellet as agent. On May 16, 1883, Du Bellet borrowed more money from Milliken and gave a new note in the name of his company. A second suit was brought, and judgments were rendered in both suits on June 8, 1883.[18]

Meanwhile, everyone concerned continued to be active and seemingly prosperous. In March Levy bought several lots and 10,000 acres from the Société. In May Sam H. Milliken fulfilled his subscription of $50,000 for the building of a textile mill. Henry P. du Bellet, H. E. Swain, and A. S. Simmons had already subscribed $35,000, and $15,000 was added by Carson & Lewis, C. B. Rider, and J. W. Hedrick, making the amount necessary to start the machinery. Northern capitalists had pledged another $50,000 to put the mill into full

[17] Franco-Texan Land Company *v.* Louis Laigle, 59 *Texas Reports* 339.

[18] Societe Fonciere et Agricole des Etats Unis *v.* Milliken, 135 *U.S. Reports* 304.

operation. Milliken himself began the construction of a three-story building to house the First National Bank.[19] In July, R. W. Duke, the Franco-Texan president, opened the Duke House at Mineral Wells— "a newly furnished and elegant hotel, a rara avis in its way . . . in its appointments and conveniences none could excel the Duke House at the justly celebrated Lone Star watering resort."[20]

That same week the editor of the *Times* had the pleasure of visiting the new residence of Colonel Henry P. du Bellet on College Hill, North Main Avenue, one mile from the courthouse in Weatherford. This large, commodious, and convenient house was 77 feet above the level of the public square, and the view was one of "surprising grandeur." A verandah, ninety-one feet long, surrounded the first story; it was ten feet wide in front and nine on each side. On the first floor there was a hall eight feet wide and twenty-two feet long, with library and billiard room on the east side, sixteen by twenty-two and the Colonel's chamber on the west, sixteen by eighteen with a four by six closet and connecting bathroom seven feet square. A hall, six by twenty-one, divided the rear portion of the structure. The dining room, in the rear, was fourteen feet square and contained an elevator from the large kitchen and another seven by fourteen chamber below. A spacious stairway led from the rear hall to the second floor where there were three rooms, each twelve by sixteen, and one twelve by twelve. There were many large closets in this splendid residence which was "the finest in the city or vicinity." Water ran through pipes in the three stories, supplied by a tank containing thirty-nine barrels and connected with the well and pump and run with a very successful windmill. The house was built by architect W. F. Glassie.[21] There were stables too, with living quarters for the groom, Charles Barbier, and his wife Marguerite, and by the first of the year Du Bellet would have a telephone, as would S. H. Milliken and the Franco-Texan Land Company, along with the other twenty-three members of the Weatherford Telephone Exchange.[22]

[19] Fort Worth *Gazette*, May 16, 1883.
[20] Weatherford *Times*, July 7, 1883.
[21] *Ibid.*, July 7, 1883.
[22] Fort Worth *Gazette*, January 30, 1884.

Du Bellet left his ranch at Palo Pinto in charge of Joe Cunningham, and with his wife—he had married Kittie Clara Shaw of Weatherford on February 8, 1883—returned to Weatherford to live in his new home.[23] Also living in this same house were his friends George P. Levy and Alfred Hammond de Voisins. Levy was then in the sheep business, having acquired a 1,900-acre farm in Parker County and fine Rambouillet stock from A. Cerf in San Antonio.[24] De Voisins had gone out to Throckmorton to stay at the Hittson Ranch, where he was learning the ranching business.

On August 12, 1883, Du Bellet wrote De Voisins that he was glad the sojourn was proving useful and the strenuous life had not upset his health. He would send the "powder for the bugs" at once and would have written sooner had he not been "up to his ears" in liquidating the Société. Most of "les cowboys," he said, were fine young men, of course a bit rough, but one could associate with them without discredit and to do one's job intelligently was never degrading. He had broken with Levy and would explain this later. The two of them, Du Bellet and De Voisins, would work together in the future for the best interests of both.[25]

Du Bellet's differences with Levy came to a head when Levy sued the Société in the District Court to obtain a good title to his land, Du Bellet having claimed the existing title was invalid because it did not bear the seal of the company. The payment of the Société's debt to Milliken began on August 6, 1883, when James D. McKee, United States marshal, came from Dallas to sell 19,000 acres in Palo Pinto County and 726 lots in the town of Mineral Wells, all belonging to the Société and known as the Lambert lands, to be sold by a decree of the federal court, foreclosing the mortgage lien of $28,000. The people were of the opinion that Milliken would bid the land in at a price few men could pay, and therefore the attendance was light. Marshal McKee called the sale promptly at 10:00 on the morning of the 6th. No one

[23] *Palo Pinto County Star,* February 14, 1885; Parker County Marriage Records, 1874–1886.

[24] Dallas *Daily Herald,* June 1, 1883.

[25] Du Bellet to De Voisins, August 12, 1883 (letter in possession of Mrs. Alfred Hammond, Weatherford, Texas).

was there to represent Milliken or the company, and as quite a few were afraid the titles would be worthless, only eleven tracts sold, at a very low price. While the sale was dragging along, James H. Milliken and George P. Levy drove up in a buggy. Milliken jumped out and asked the marshal at what price he was selling. On being told Milliken immediately ran the bid up to $1.00 an acre.

Milliken, it seemed, had either miscalculated the time or overslept, and therefore lost the first eleven tracts. He said he would not let the sales stand because of the inadequate price and asked the purchasers to let the land be sold again. They concluded that their titles would be good and refused.

On the 9th, Du Bellet served notice on the first bidders not to trespass on the land as he intended to file a motion to set the sale aside. The purchasers said they would employ the best counsel in the state to make the sale stick if Du Bellet filed such a motion. Marshal McKee insisted that the sale was just as legal as any sale ever made by a marshal in the northern district of Texas, and the general opinion was that a heavy lawsuit might be expected.[26]

On August 15, notice of a similar sale was posted on the bulletin board in the county courthouse of Weatherford. This sale was to be carried out in September, also under an execution issued out of the United States district court at Dallas in the case of Sam H. Milliken versus the Société Foncière et Agricole des États Unis. It took forty-eight pages of legal length paper to describe the lands to be sold. The sale took place on the 5th, 6th, and 7th of September. Sam H. Milliken, the owner of the judgment, was the purchaser though there was some spirited bidding. Eight or ten thousand acres were sold at an average price of $1.25 an acre.[27] Another such sale was held on April 4, 1884, when Milliken acquired 63 lots in Carter's addition for $315.[28] All this created a sensation in Palo Pinto and Weatherford, as well as a severe strain on Du Bellet's relations with the Millikens.

About that same time the Studebaker Company filed suit against J. H. Milliken and Du Bellet to collect payment for wagons valued at

[26] Fort Worth *Gazette*, August 13, 1883.

[27] *Ibid.*, September 6, 1883.

[28] Deed Records of Parker County, V. 15, p. 559.

$1,600. These wagons, destroyed by fire the previous year, had been bought on credit and secured by a note signed by Milliken and Du Bellet. When the Studebaker Company entered suit, Milliken filed a protest, claiming that Du Bellet was meant to be the principal although it was not so stated in the note.[29] The Studebaker Company was granted a judgment for $1,788.84 against Du Bellet and Milliken in 1883, and in 1889 received $63.50 and an interest in some 300 lots in the Carter addition.[30]

The bankrupt Société came back onto the scene in December of 1884. Henry P. du Bellet, its "late president," was reported to be in Weatherford in connection with the company's business.[31] A few weeks later, the following notice appeared in the Dallas *Herald*:

> Liquidation of the Societe Fonciere et Agricole des Etats Unis. Sale by auction at the Palais de Justice, Paris, on Saturday, January 17, 1885, at 2:00 P.M. in one lot, of a property situated in Parker and Palo Pinto County in the State of Texas in North America, consisting of land, farms, and building plots at Mineral Wells and Weatherford.
>
> Upset Price, $10,000
>
> Address U. Delihu, 24 Blvd. St. Denis, and M. Edmond Moreau, advocate and judicial liquidator, 21 rue de Hauteville, Paris.[32]

This must have represented an effort on the part of the Société to salvage the remnants of its property in Texas. Whatever the outcome of the sale, nothing more was heard from the Société until six months later, when its representative, Edmond Moreau of Paris, applied to the Federal circuit court of Dallas to set aside the former judgments in favor of Milliken and the sales made thereunder.[33] Milliken filed general and special demurrers, which were sustained, and the application was dismissed.

[29] Studebaker *v.* Milliken and Du Bellet, Cause 1792, District Court Records of Parker County.

[30] Deed Records of Parker County: Vol. 14, p. 189.

[31] *Dallas Daily Herald*, December 18, 1884.

[32] *Ibid.*, January 4, 1885.

[33] Fort Worth *Gazette*, June 7, 1885.

Moreau and his attorneys, Harcourt and Ball of Weatherford, then applied to the United States Supreme Court for a review and rehearing of the judgments, claiming that H. P. du Bellet had no authority to receive process on behalf of the company, that the 10 per cent attorney's fee provided in the notes was a cover for usurious interest in the amount of $1,179.08, taken and received by Milliken, and that Milliken, by his management, prevented fair competition and discouraged other bidders so that he could purchase all the said property. The Supreme Court held that by Texas laws, in suits against any incorporated company, the citation could be served upon the local agent representing the corporation within the county in which the suit was brought; that no specific art of wrongdoing appeared in the averment from which the court could deduce misconduct; and that, assuming the matter of usurious interest to be true, the defendant had waited two years and two days, and more than one year after all the sales had been made, before challenging the validity of the proceedings, with no cause for the delay being shown.[34]

If, as indicated, Du Bellet made out no notes to Milliken until 1882, or until it looked as if Judge Hood's decision might invalidate the sale, then Milliken was able to collect on a very shaky claim, but once the forced sales were made and Milliken took the land it was evident that the Société had little hope for recovery, except perhaps from Du Bellet, who, in the interval between 1879 and 1882, had been operating on the Société's money. He was sued later by both Milliken and the Société and emerged unscathed. He sold his three sections of school land for $800 in April, 1885, probably because he needed cash, but he was by no means stranded. He still had his ranch, and the following year his own land company. When he opened his agency, his office was with Harcourt and Ball, Counsellors at Law. He advertised splendid farms for sale, lots in the Millsap addition, and ten acres on Galveston Island. He would also trade for sheep.[35] Milliken sued Du Bellet in 1887 for $1,900 due on his land west of Palo Pinto and for $1,300 owed Milliken by the Société. The case was dismissed on November

[34] Societe Fonciere et Agricole des Etats Unis *v.* Milliken, 135 *U.S. Reports* 304.

[35] Weatherford *Times*, June 26, 1886.

14, 1887.[36] In 1889, Du Bellet was still busy liquidating the Société.

There was a large fire in Weatherford on January 3, 1884,[37] the second time that buildings in the same spot had burned, and then on March 1, 1884, between 12:00 and 1:00 in the morning, the courthouse caught fire. It was held in check until 4:00 when the upper floor burned through. The whole building immediately went up in flames and burned down in about an hour. The county court records burned, but several heroic gentlemen saved those of the district court, though in slightly damaged condition, or so it was reported.[38] There were some differences of opinion as to where and how the fire originated. Some said it started from the stove in the district court room and was an unavoidable accident. Others said it started in the county clerk's office and was the work of an incendiary. Judge Hood called the grand jury to investigate.[39] Whether or not the district court records burned very few previous to 1884 are in existence today, and much information about the early days of the Franco-Texan Land Company has been lost.

36 S. H. Milliken *v.* the Societe Fonciere et Agricole des Etats Unis, Cause 2396; and Civil Minutes, Vol. 4, p. 127, both in District Court Records of Parker County.

37 Dallas *Daily Herald*, January 4, 1884.

38 Fort Worth *Gazette*, March 2, 1884.

39 *Ibid.*, March 6, 1884.

CHAPTER 11

MORE TROUBLE IN WEATHERFORD

The Franco-Texan president, R. W. Duke, made a business visit to Palo Pinto early in April of 1884. He informed the *Gazette* correspondent that the vice-president of the company was coming to Weatherford from France in May or June, and they would inspect the company's holdings in ten western counties. The correspondent commented that the price of the company's land in Palo Pinto County was too high and said he would endeavor to get it put within reach of a poor man.[1]

Vice-President Laurent Goybet arrived on June 8 with an interpreter, and the stockholders of the Franco-Texan met the next day to elect officers for the ensuing year. After meeting for three days, they elected a board of directors and reelected R. W. Duke president and Charles Malcolmson secretary.[2] This was the first stockholders meeting held in Texas. Since one-third of the stock had to be represented for this meeting to be legal, either the Texans had managed to purchase an immense number of shares or else Goybet was representing a very large number of French shares by proxy.

[1] Fort Worth *Gazette*, April 13, 1884.

[2] Dallas *Daily Herald*, June 10 and June 13, 1884.

Shortly after this meeting, on September 1, the Franco-Texan received its greatest accolade in the newly established Weatherford *Sun*. The company was hailed as the most important institution in Texas, perhaps in the United States. It had acquired 800,000 acres of land since its organization in 1876, and was under the efficient control of three men—"the popular president R. W. Duke, who was located in Parker County when the buffalo was the only visitor to the site; C. Malcolmson, the well known and talented secretary and treasurer, and Edmond O'Bierne, the experienced accountant," all of whom were able and energetic men, the type Texas needed for the development of its resources. The *Sun* also said that L. Goybet of Paris, the vice-president of the company, had recently visited Weatherford to inspect its property on behalf of the French shareholders and had been completely satisfied with its management and future prospects.[3]

President Duke made his grand assault on the company's holdings early in 1885. Acting without the authority of the Board and waiving the vendor's lien, he sold twenty-six sections to an associate, Wyly G. Martin, who, in turn, conveyed them to his partners, S. H., C. H., and J. H. Milliken. The consideration was $9,920 in cash, Martin's note for $950, due one day after date, and J. H. Milliken's note to Martin for $40,000 bearing 10 per cent interest from date. An unusual and illegal feature of the promissory note executed by J. H. Milliken to W. G. Martin or bearer was the provision making it collectible in horses of a certain brand at $30 a head.

On the day Duke acknowledged the deed, February 20, 1885, Wyly G. Martin conveyed to J. H. Milliken a half interest in thirty-three sections, and on March 10, 1885, Duke, as president, conveyed to Martin and Milliken eight other sections for the consideration of the reconveyance to the company of seven sections of the land conveyed to them by the first deed.

Once the facts of this sale became known, the company declared it invalid, and subsequent purchasers, or "innocent buyers," claiming through the deed from Duke to Martin, ultimately brought suit against the Franco-Texan. The Texas Supreme Court and the Court of Ap-

[3] Weatherford *Sun*, September 1, 1884.

peals upheld the company in its attempts to recover the land. In three cases which were appealed from the district court of Taylor County, Duke's action was labeled as attempted fraud.[4]

On March 17, 1885, Henry P. du Bellet, acting as agent for Antoinette R. Bousselet (or her assignee James Bostic), requested the exchange of her stock certificates and selected other lands in Jones and Fisher counties to replace those which had been sold. He also presented ten more shares for exchange and selected lands in Fisher County valued at $223 according to the scheduled price. In the meantime, the company had declared a dividend of $1.00 a share, so an additional $400 was claimed for Miss Bousselet, making the value of her shares $39,360. This was the second dividend, the first one having been for $.60. President Duke refused to make the exchange, and "A. R. Bousselet" instituted suit in the district court to secure a deed to the land that had been selected and a judgment for damages plus the amount of her dividend. The case would come before the court in the fall term.

Now that the Franco-Texan had been more or less thrown into the hands of the Texas stockholders, it was certain that local factions would compete for control of its profitable business. The first effort was made by Jesse J. Hittson and R. E. Montgomery, who, as stockholders, filed suit against the company, petitioning for the appointment of a receiver. It was said that if appointed the receiver's bond would be something like $2,000,000. The suit must have been a serious threat because the Franco-Texan employed E. P. Nicholson, A. J. Hood, Albert Stevenson, and Harcourt and Ball to resist the application. On April 25, 1885, District Judge R. E. Beckham refused to appoint a receiver.[5] This suit was filed again in February, 1886, continued, and then dismissed on August 21, 1886.[6] The appearance of R. E. Montgomery in the suit is interesting. Formerly of Council Bluffs, Iowa, he had been

[4] Fitzhugh *et al. v.* Franco-Texan Land Company, 16 *South Western Reporter* 1078, and 81 *Texas Reports*, 306; Clayton *et al. v.* Franco-Texan Land Company, 39 *South Western Reporter* 645; Franco-Texan Land Company *v.* McCormick, 85 *Texas Reports* 416.

[5] Galveston *Daily News*, February 8, and April 26, 1885.

[6] J. J. Hittson *et al. v.* the Franco-Texan Land Company, Cause 2081; Civil Minutes, Vol. 3, p. 578, both in District Court Records of Parker County.

an agent of the Texas and Pacific and was then connected with the Decatur and West Texas Railroad, which was backed by the Fort Worth and Denver. He was also in charge of the Land Department of the Fort Worth and Denver, with headquarters in Fort Worth, and was married to the daughter of General Grenville M. Dodge, chief engineer of the Texas and Pacific and president of the Pacific Improvement Company.

On July 15, 1885, the city of Weatherford was shrouded in gloom. At 9:00 that morning James H. Milliken shot and killed James Lee, his young partner in the firm of Milliken & Lee, then engaged in building the courthouse—a horrible cold-blooded murder that does not bear describing. The cause was reported to be a difference in their adjustment of accounts. Fred Desmith, Milliken's brother-in-law and J. J. Hittson's bookkeeper, with Milliken at the time, was tried as his accomplice, but the case against Desmith was dismissed. A year and three months later Desmith was dead, killed by John Hayes, foreman of the Hittson Ranch in Throckmorton County.[7] S. W. T. Lanham, Milliken's lawyer, finally saved him after a change of venue, continuances, and two hung juries, the majority for conviction in both instances. In the interlude, the town was rocked by such low drama as threatening letters, a witness who jumped his bond, the perjury of one, and the intimidation of another. The feeling in Weatherford grew so intense that the case could not even be discussed.

In 1887, when the second trial opened at Granbury, it was almost impossible to get a jury. Only four men served out of a special venire of sixty. In 1888 it was reported that the judge had urged the jury to reach an agreement, but no further account of the trial is found in the newspapers nor is there any record in the district court at Granbury, except of the appearance of three bondsmen. There is an entry in the index, but the corresponding information has been erased, and a search of the minute books reveals no report.

The Desmiths, Fred, Frank, and their sister Mrs. J. H. Milliken, were Belgians. Their uncle was Dr. Charles A. Otterbein, also a Belgian, who came to Texas in 1856. Frank Desmith, very popular in

[7] *Fort Worth Gazette*, November 27, 1886.

Weatherford, died at the age of thirty-one on December 18, 1884,[8] from an incurable illness, and Mrs. Milliken later committed suicide.

The Milliken name and fortune suffered mightly in this affair though both were already on the wane. In 1882 J. H. Milliken had been deposed as mayor for the flagrant violation of a city ordinance prohibiting the renting of houses to prostitutes and had publicly announced that he preferred that type of property to any other because the rents were higher.[9] He did not try for reelection, and the Democrats elected a mayor and four out of five aldermen, with great rejoicing over the victory as the city had formerly been controlled by Republicans.[10] J. H. Milliken suffered serious financial losses under his contracts to build the Callahan and Parker county courthouses. Sam H. Milliken resigned as president of the First National Bank early in 1886, and the controlling interest passed to A. F. Starr, W. H. Eddleman, and W. W. Davis. C. H. Milliken remained in the bank but not as cashier.[11] The Millikens, however, did not give up their attempts to control the Franco-Texan Land Company or at least to keep up their connections and participate in the spoils. The three brothers, with President Duke and later President Levy as a friend and ally, remained a formidable threat.

Before the Bousselet case came to trial, the second annual stockholders meeting was held in Weatherford, at 9:00 A.M. on July 30, 1885. President Duke took the chair and called the meeting to order. Judge Hood and W. K. Baylor were appointed inspectors, and the meeting adjourned until 3:00 P.M. On reassembling the inspectors reported the following stockholders present, each being entitled to one vote per share:

R. W. Duke, 1001 shares
E. B. Ross, 1001 shares
John H. Lewis, 1001 shares
W. K. Baylor, 1079 shares

[8] *Ibid.*, December 19, 1884.

[9] Milliken *v.* the City Council of the City of Weatherford, 54 *Texas Reports* 388.

[10] Galveston *Daily News*, February 24, and April 6, 1882.

[11] Fort Worth *Gazette*, February 8, 1886.

A. J. Hood, 1251 shares
N. B. Johnson, 1001 shares
J. W. Squyres, 1001 shares
R. J. M. McKenzie, 1001 shares
Ed O'Bierne, 1001 shares
W. Malcolmson, 1001 shares
H. McDermott, 1001 shares
L. W. Christian, 1001 shares
C. Malcolmson, 1001 shares
C. Henry, 8 shares
H. P. du Bellet, 4 shares
A. d'Heur, 2 shares

As these 13,355 shares represented one-third of the total of 39,388 shares (amounting to 399,510.20 acres), a quorum was declared present. Announcing that the meeting was duly organized, President Duke addressed the stockholders:

On occasions of this kind it has been the custom of the President to submit an annual report setting forth the operations of the Company during the past 12 months, the present condition of the same, and its further prospects. On this occasion we will simply submit in lieu thereof a few remarks relative to the past conduct and the future prospects of the Company I have the honor to represent. Corporations, like individuals, must yield to the forces of surrounding circumstances. Various causes combined during the last twelve months have had a tendency to affect seriously the operations of this Company. First, the short crops of last year. This section of our State, where the lands of the Company lie, was visited by a long and disastrous drought which cut short all kind of production; add to this a financial crisis throughout the country which alarmed the institutions to withhold their usual favors and facilities from the people and thus made money very scarce and high and land buyers very few. Added to this, the long and unusually severe winter of 1884–5 with the snows, sleets, and frosts, caused thousands of cattle to die, and the spring found the survivors of those Hibernian storms emaciated, weak, and very poor, so that no money could be realized from them for months. It is not surprising then that the land sales of our last fiscal year have not come up to the measure of other years. But, gentlemen, we enter upon this fiscal year under more favorable auspices. A generous earth and favorable season have abundantly rewarded the agriculturist with a Benjamin's Mess. All our staple products, cotton, corn, wheat, and other cereals have and are contributing in all their potency to a change of times. Our fine crops will bring immigration, immigrants will want lands, and we are here to supply all such wants. Money will be plenty and seeking investment, and we confidently look to the fiscal year upon which we have just entered for unexampled thriftiness and prosperity.

Thereupon Judge Hood presented for consideration a code of by-laws, and along with the original charter they were read by the secretary. The proposed or amended by-laws were adopted by a vote of 13,344. Title II, Articles 5 and 6, concerned with the transfer of stock, provided that the shares of stock, in the first instance having been issued in the name of the original owner, could only be transferred by the signature of such owner, duly acknowledged and authenticated, and such transfer had to be duly registered on the books of the company; but after a share of stock was sold, transferred, and registered, if such transfer was made to bearer, the title to such share might pass by actual sale and delivery without any formal written transfer. Hence, the lively traffic of Franco-Texan stock certificates in Weatherford. The actual owner then only had to have the share or shares of stock registered in the company's books before he would be allowed to vote as a stockholder.

Two commissioners were elected to examine the books and accounts and report to the stockholders: Henri Colont and Louis Thesio. The new directors elected were R. W. Duke, Charles Malcolmson, J. W. Squyres, Baron d'Ailly, Baron d'Acfeuille, D. Mouracin, De Lens, Herman Fleury, Laurent Goybet, General de Villers, Andre Jacquier, Miollan, Pinasseau. The officers: R. W. Duke, president; L. Goybet, vice-president; C. Malcolmson, secretary and treasurer; Pinasseau, vice-secretary; A. Jacquier, vice-treasurer.

The last act of the meeting was the adoption of a new mode of exchanging shares of stock for land. Lands of average value could be exchanged at the rate of ten acres for each $100 bond, but when lands of below average value were selected, the amount of acreage received would be proportionly increased, and when above average, the amount would be decreased. The owners of shares in all cases would be required to deposit them with the secretary at Weatherford and, at the same time, to make a written application for exchange, designating the lands desired so that they could be inspected and appraised. The old schedule was no longer a basis of exchange.[12]

The new mode of exchange was expected to block A. R. Bousselet's application for land. In September the company answered her charge, stating that she had never made a written request for exchange, as was required, and that the land in question was choice and worth more than $2.96 an acre, according to a new schedule set up at the stockholders meeting on July 30, 1885. District Judge R. E. Beckham gave a verdict and judgment in favor of Antoinette R. Bousselet for the tracts of land designated for exchange and for the $400 dividend. Hood, Lanham, and Stephens, counsel for the company, appealed the case to the Texas Supreme Court, and in 1888 the district court's decision was affirmed.[13]

At the July stockholders meeting President Duke had received 11,142 out of 13,355 votes, but within a month he was removed from office by the board of directors. Judge A. J. Hood was appointed to succeed him on October 3, and Edward Gonthier of Paris arrived in Weatherford soon afterward as special delegate and acting secretary. When notified he was no longer secretary of the company, Malcomson refused to recognize Gonthier's authority. Duke contested Hood's appointment and refused to give up the books and seal of office. For a period of two and a half months he claimed he was still president of the company.[14]

On December 12, 1885, a notice appeared in the Abilene *Reporter*, signed by Duke, Malcolmson, and O'Bierne. It accused A. J. Hood and Edward Gonthier of attempting to usurp the office of president and secretary and warned all persons not to transact any business with "these gentlemen." O'Bierne was quoted as saying that Duke was the lawful president, that he had all the books in his possession and in-

[12] Franco-Texan Land Company *v.* A. R. Bousselet, File 5902, Texas Supreme Court Files.

[13] Franco-Texan Land Company *v.* A. R. Bousselet, Cause 2091, District Court Records of Parker County; also reported in 70 *Texas Reports* 422, and 7 *South Western Reporter* 761.

[14] Fort Worth *Gazette*, October 27, and November 21, 1885.

tended to keep them. On the same day this notice appeared Duke finally surrendered the keys, books, and seal of office to Judge Hood.[15]

On January 5, 1886, Sheriff Baylor served a writ of sequestration on Charles Malcolmson for books, papers, maps, and other items belonging to the company. Malcolmson up until then had politely refused to give up the books in his possession. On January 6, Malcolmson filed or tendered a replevy bond of $1,200 for the property taken from him, but Sheriff Baylor refused to accept the bond until he invoiced the "outfit," since a replevy bond had to enumerate everything that was replevied.[16] On inventory some $30,000 in notes and paper were found, also 287 shares of floating stock. The company then dismissed the sequestration suit and instituted suit by injunction and mandamus in the district court. In addition to the suit for the seized property, the company sued Malcolmson for $20,000.[17]

On January 17, 1886, the following letter signed by Malcolmson appeared in the Fort Worth *Gazette*:

> To Whom It May Concern: I hereby warn and give notice to all parties owing money or promissory notes given for land or lease not to pay money to A. J. Hood or Edward Gonthier upon any indebtedness due the Franco-Texan Land Company as neither Hood or Gonthier have any right to receive the same, they not being officers of the said company. But in order to save interest, parties indebted to said company had better deposit their money in their own names with one of the banks in Weatherford, and thus set apart the money to meet their indebtedness, whenever they can be satisfied that said company has fully authorized some person to receive it.
>
> C. Malcolmson
>
> Secretary and Treasurer Franco-Texan Land Company.[18]

On the next day, an anonymous letter appeared on the editorial page of the *Gazette*. It was a reply to the Weatherford correspondent who had reported all the foregoing events in his regular column, indicating that Hood and Gonthier were the legal representatives of the Franco-Texan.

[15] *Ibid.*, December 13, 1885.
[16] *Ibid.*, January 7, 1886.
[17] *Ibid.*, January 14, 1886.
[18] *Ibid.*, January 17, 1886.

THE FRANCO-TEXAN LAND COMPANY

The correspondent who furnished the notes published in the Gazette of the 14th instant was not fully informed of the facts. They are shortly as follows: Hood and Gonthier who seek to obtain control of the company took out a writ to get possession of the papers and property from C. Malcolmson who is the secretary and treasurer, appointed by the shareholders, and whose term of office does not expire until July next. They gave bond for $1,000 so as to bring the matter into a smaller court but Mr. Malcolmson at once obtained a writ of replevin giving bond for $2,000, and obtained repossession of the effects seized which remain in his charge and had never actually passed into that of the self-elected claimants above named.

The business value of the papers will probably be considerably above the nominal bond and having been inventoried by the sheriff, are also under his official control for production by Malcolmson before the proper courts.

The best of the paragraph seems to be a romance made up of extracts from an injunction prayed for by Hood and Gonthier and which they no doubt wish they may get. Malcolmson had no suit for damages, nor is he in any way involved in the difficulties stated from the fact that everything is ready to be produced when required by the competent tribunals. A seizure has however since been effected through the exertions of the acute and active gentleman who is emulating the fable by transforming himself from a French frog into a Texas bull, and additional bond for a considerable amount has been given with the result of a seizure of some empty cases, which it is not likely will be replevied.[19]

The Weatherford correspondent answered in his regular column that if the "unknown and self-justified person" responsible for the item in the *Gazette* had been very anxious for the facts to become known to the public he could have easily given them to the correspondent who had received his information from the president of the company.[20]

On January 27, 1886, capiases were issued by the justice court in five cases against C. Malcolmson, former secretary and treasurer of the Franco-American Land Company and two against H. McDermott, his brother-in-law, for embezzlement. Malcolmson was charged with col-

[19] *Ibid.*, January 18, 1886.
[20] *Ibid.*, January 19, 1886.

lecting money due the company and appropriating it for his own use and benefit. It was alleged that McDermott collected money due the Franco-Texan when he was not an officer of the company. Deputy Sheriff Robert C. Ross arrested Malcolmson and McDermott and placed them under $500 bond in each case for their appearance in the justice court for preliminary examination.[21] J. H. Milliken and C. H. Milliken were Malcolmson's bondsmen.

On February 15, accountant Edmond O'Bierne and his family registered at the Palace Hotel in Abilene, preparatory to making that city their future home.[22]

A. J. Hood, the new president, announced on July 3, 1886, that the annual stockholders meeting would be held at 9:00 A.M. on July 30, at the principal office of the company in the city of Weatherford. This meeting lasted for two days. Judge Hood was reelected president and L. Goybet of Paris, France, vice-president. Thirteen board members were elected, ten of whom resided in France and three in Weatherford: Judge A. J. Hood, I. W. Stephens, and J. W. Squyres. By a change in the by-laws considerably more power was vested in the president. This was done to avoid the trouble caused by some of the former secretaries. The meeting passed off quietly and harmoniously, and it was reported that there was no doubt as to the legality of the proceedings as had been charged at previous meetings. The business of the land company, "the largest in the state," was expected to be more profitable to the stockholders in the future, and under the supervision of Judge Hood, it was certain that the company's affairs would be conducted in a strictly businesslike way.[23]

The civil suit against Malcolmson ended in the district court in September, 1886, with a verdict for the plaintiff. It had been instituted to recover possession of $30,000 worth of personal property consisting of promissory notes, money, books, patents, deeds, and general office archives. The decision in favor of the Franco-Texan Land Company was said to be a source of satisfaction to the officers and stockholders,

[21] *Ibid.*, January 28, 1886; Dallas *Daily Herald*, January 28, 1886.

[22] Fort Worth *Gazette*, February 15, 1886.

[23] *Ibid.*, July 31, and August 2, 1886.

and a great relief to many citizens of Parker and other western counties who had purchased land from the company but for the past nine months had been deprived of their proper papers.[24]

Malcomson was also indicted for embezzlement in the district court of Parker County. He was tried on June 7, 1887. The trial lasted for four days, and the jury, which was out for two days, found him guilty. He was sentenced to two years in the penitentiary.[25] Attorneys A. T. Watts, E. P. Nicholson, and L. F. Smith appealed his case to the Circuit Court of Appeals.

According to court records, the books of the company showed that the secretary and treasurer was short in excess of $500 when he went out of office. It was proved that he used $385 of the company's money to buy a span of horses and harness, which he afterwards sold to Jasper N. Haney for $150 and the cancellation of some of his private debts. It was also proved that after President Duke was removed from office, Secretary Malcolmson joined him in the conveyance of a tract of land to C. H. Milliken in consideration of certain shares of the company's stock. The land conveyed to Milliken was nine sections in Nolan County, and the consideration was 520 shares of capital stock in the company. The transaction was considered fraudulent because it violated the by-laws of the company and because the deed was executed after Duke ceased to be president of the company. Malcolmson appealed the case on the grounds of injury by the introduction of inadmissible evidence (*i.e.*, the land sale had nothing to do with the material facts of the case and his reputation had been damaged by the evidence). The judgment was reversed and remanded by the Court of Appeals, Judge J. Willson dissenting. It was his opinion that the testimony relating to the land and stock transaction threw some light on the charge of embezzlement, a fair inference from the evidence being that ex-President Duke, Milliken, and the defendant were promised a fair division if the scheme should succeed, all of which tended to show that the secretary was not guarding the interests of his company as it was his duty to do, but was scheming to defraud it, and that such tendency was pertinent

[24] *Ibid.*, September 14, 1886.

[25] *Ibid.*, June 12, 1887.

and relative to the issue.[26] After repeated continuances the case against Malcolmson was dismissed in 1890.

Just as all the turmoil of the summer of 1886 ended, the redoubtable S. P. Tuck again filed suit to force the Franco-Texan to exchange his stock for land. In February, 1887, Tuck was ordered to give bond for costs. On May 17, 1887, he filed a supplemental petition, and on January 27, 1888, the Franco-Texan moved for a continuance.[27]

The 996 shares of stock Tuck had left in Henry Warren's safe included the following:

(1) 390 shares issued to Antoinette R. Bousselet—James Bostic, assignee;
(2) 215 shares to Leon Dounat;
(3) 48 shares to Benoit Chalimbord;
(4) 343 shares issued to Raymond, Guerin, Gerard, Bernard, Corriard, *et cetera*—James Bostic, assignee.

Seventy-six of the shares listed under (2) and (3) were to be assigned to Tuck, the remainder being unassigned. In some cases these shareholders or their assignees received land in exchange for stock certificates, and in others they did not. For instance, Antoinette R. Bousselet (or her assignee James Bostic) had to resort to the district court, but Adelaide Corriard received 2,290 acres (160 shares) in Taylor County on April 11, 1881, without any apparent difficulty. And Benoit Chalimbord, whose stock had been in Tuck's hands, finally lost his case in the district court in 1892.[28]

In at least a dozen other cases filed against the Franco-Texan between 1880 and 1890, nominally by Frenchmen for the purpose of forcing the exchange of stock for land, the same curious pattern is observed. Louis Ranger of New York broke down in the course of his two-day trial and took a voluntary non-suit. A. J. Ball and H. P. du Bellet were sureties on his bond. On a second attempt he received

[26] Malcolmson *v.* the State of Texas, 8 *South Western Reporter* 468.

[27] S. P. Tuck *v.* the Franco-Texan Land Company, Cause 2162, District Court Records of Parker County.

[28] Benoit Chalimbord *v.* the Franco-Texan Land Company, Cause 2169, District Court Records of Parker County.

3,132 acres in Taylor, Jones, and Noland counties.[29] Harcourt and Ball presented A. Carbinnier's petition on June 29, 1888, and the court was occupied with it for four days. Late in the evening of July 2, the jury rendered a verdict in favor of the plaintiff. Carbinnier recovered land valued at $12,595: 1,259½ acres priced at $10 per acre; and also $358.50 in accrued dividends. He had 128 stock certificates, Nos. 28466–28494 and 45824–45923 inclusive. For some reason, perhaps because he had not recovered on three of his certificates or because the price of the land was too high, a new trial was asked for on July 4, 1888, and the motion was sustained.[30] The case of Victor de Fresnay, a vice-president of the Franco-Texan, who brought suit for the exchange of 216 shares of stock for land, was removed to the federal court on August 16, 1883. Before it was tried, the company gave De Fresnay a deed for 1,565 acres in Parker County. The following year De Fresnay tried to exchange another 190 shares for which he claimed 1,790 acres valued at $6,742, but the case was dismissed on February 2, 1885.[31] Others who filed suit and received judgment for their land were Jean Baptiste Colpart and Jean J. Colpart—90 shares for 971.42 acres; L. T. Delort—29 shares for 258.27 acres; and L. E. Jardin—34 shares for 324.71 acres.

The Franco-Texan, however, was more often the plaintiff than the defendant. The company filed and refiled hundreds of foreclosure suits against purchasers of Franco-Texan land and kept the lawyers and courts of Weatherford well occupied from year to year.

Judge Hood was reelected president in 1887, and A. J. Hood, Jr. was elected secretary. By a notice dated September 23, 1887, and published in consecutive issues of the Palo Pinto *Star* for the remainder of the year, Judge Hood warned that delinquent purchasers could avoid forfeitures and suits only by making payment at once. He was reelected president in 1888, and at the annual meeting of the Franco-

[29] Lewis Ranger *v.* the Franco-Texan Land Company, Cause 2083, District Court Records of Parker County; U–162, Deed Records of Taylor County.

[30] Fort Worth *Gazette*, July 3, 1888; Carbinnier *v.* the Franco-Texan Land Company, Cause 2215, District Court Records of Parker County.

[31] Victor de Fresnay *v.* the Franco-Texan Land Company, Causes 1896 and 1966, District Court Records of Parker County.

Texan stockholders on April 4 and 5, 1889, Judge A. J. Hood, George P. Levy, and John Pit were elected American directors. Judge Hood was reelected president; H. Merlin of Paris was elected vice-president; John Pit of Weatherford, secretary and treasurer; L. Guillet of Paris, vice-secretary.[32]

Judge Hood resigned in July, 1889, and was succeeded by George P. Levy. Judge Hood was not in ill health and he was not retiring from public life. He had been president for almost four years, the most peaceful and reputable period of the Franco-Texan's existence, but it has been said that when Levy became president and general manager he found its affairs in a chaotic condition and that he put the company back on its feet. The statement was made in a biographical sketch of Levy's life, written in 1895, and was probably based on information received from Levy himself.[33] It is true that few dividends were paid while Judge Hood was president, but then Judge Hood sold very little land, which is the best evidence that he was not engaged in swindling the company. He had good reasons for resigning as will be seen. More likely it was Judge Hood who put the company back on its feet, and when Levy took over as president, everything was in good order for his rapid rise to power in Weatherford during the next seven years.

[32] Fort Worth *Gazette*, April 10, 1889.

[33] *History of Texas: Together with a Biographical List of Tarrant and Parker Counties*, p. 427.

CHAPTER 12

GEORGE P. LEVY

George P. Levy lost his fine sheep as the result of a severe norther and late freeze, and his 1,900-acre farm was sold for $1,640 to George E. Cooper at public auction, under execution in favor of Eugene E. Rich, on December 1, 1885.[1] He then tried the grain business, and again had hard luck when his barn was completely demolished by a windstorm. In 1886 he formed a partnership with Paul Lavigne of New York, who came to Weatherford to invest in real estate. The new company had a capital of $10,000 and soon made contracts for large shipments of corn, hay, bran, and other feed in Texas and New Mexico.[2] Levy had married Emily C. Schoover, the stepdaughter of Dr. Otterbein, on December 17, 1885,[3] and in the fall of 1887, he bought Du Bellet's residence and spent $1,500 for improvements, making it the finest home in the city.[4] The following week he purchased fourteen acres about 1⅜ miles south of the courthouse, near the future site of

[1] Fort Worth *Gazette*, December 2, 1885.

[2] *Ibid.*, July 11, 1886; November 19, 1887.

[3] *Ibid.*, December 17, 1885.

[4] *Ibid.*, October 12, 1887; March 16, 1889.

the Presbyterian Female Seminary: the consideration, $100 per acre.[5] In 1890 Levy became president of the Weatherford Street Railway Company; in 1891 he was made a director of the Merchants and Farmers National Bank; and in 1892 he was elected mayor.[6] He was reelected mayor in 1894 and was a member of the Board of Trade and the Commercial Union Club. In 1899 he was vice-president of the Western National Bank of Fort Worth, established by W. H. Eddleman.

Levy went to Paris in the spring of 1889 to superintend the display of a large exhibit, already shipped, which would represent the numerous resources of Parker County and the city of Weatherford at the World's Fair. Parker had been the best or banner county at the Dallas State Fair in 1888, and the U.S. Department of Agriculture had sent a special agent, Colonel James R. Binford, to Weatherford to gather an exhibit for the Paris Exposition. It was thought that Levy, having been in charge of the agricultural products at Dallas, and also being a native of France, could put the exhibit properly before the people who would visit the Exposition.[7]

One special feature of Weatherford's exhibit was jute plants and fiber in different stages of growth and development. The jute crop had been successfully grown on a twenty-acre experimental farm in Parker County, owned by the Franco-Texan Land Company and established at the instigation of J. Juvenet, a grower of native jute in Louisiana. Notes on jute culture, written by Levy and R. E. Bell, and 10,000 pounds of jute seed had been distributed to farmers at cost by the Weatherford Native Jute Rope Manufacturing Company, which was chartered by the city of Weatherford with a capital stock of $25,000, the directors being A. F. Starr, C. D. Hartnett, R. H. Foat, Paul Lavigne, George P. Levy, and the First National Bank.[8] Jute had been tried out in Midland, Hays, Comal, and Dewitt counties, where it had grown in spite of the drouth. Fort Worth and Galveston had already

[5] *Ibid.*, March 25, 1889.

[6] Weatherford *Constitution*, August 15, 1890; January 21, 1891; Weatherford *Enquirer*, April 28, 1892.

[7] Fort Worth *Gazette*, February 12, and April 10, 1889.

[8] *Ibid.*, January 6, January 21, and July 19, 1888.

introduced the manufacture of coarse jute fabrics, and it remained only to build factories for the manufacture of finer fabrics from the staple, such as carpets, table covers, and blankets.[9]

When Levy returned from Paris in December, he reported that he was especially proud of Parker County's exhibit, which had won a gold medal. At the fair he met the Honorable S. P. Tuck of New York, one of the U.S. commissioners and former secretary of the Franco-Texan Land Company. Tuck told him that he had many inquiries about Parker County and that if the exhibit had been a little larger it would have resulted in a vast amount of good to the country. "But as it is," he said, "the benefits will be very great. There are prospectors here from all over the world and not a few of them have examined the Parker County exhibit with amazement and favorable comment."[10]

If Mr. Tuck had revisited Parker County on the turn of the decade he would have found it experiencing a slow and steady growth. The total population of the county was 21,682. That of its capital city was 3,369.[11] The big boom had not come, but Mr. Tuck would have been pleased to see that Weatherford was no crossroads hamlet. It had mills, factories, cotton gins, streetcars, electric lights and waterworks, a new courthouse, three colleges, and two railroads and a contract for a third. And it had the perennial Franco-Texan Land Company, then accorded thirteenth place in a published list of the city's 108 assets.[12] Surely Mr. Tuck inquired about the Franco-Texan when he and Levy met in Paris, and perhaps they discussed Mr. Tuck's suit against the company, which was still pending in the district court of Parker County.[13]

About that same time, two of Weatherford's citizens were enjoying

[9] *Ibid.*, April 30, 1889.

[10] Weatherford *Constitution*, December 25, 1889.

[11] United States Bureau of the Census, *Eleventh Census, 1890; Report on the Population of the United States*, Vol. 11, Part I. This figure does not tally with the estimate of 7,000 made by the editor of the Weatherford *Constitution*, who considered that the city of Weatherford should have included more of Precinct 1.

[12] Weatherford *Enquirer*, December 31, 1891.

[13] Tuck's case was discontinued in 1893 by agreement of both parties (Civil Minutes, District Court Records of Parker County, Vol. 6, p. 105.

individual strokes of good luck. They were winners in the Louisiana State Lottery. L. H. Frey, a local jeweler and ranching partner of the Millikens, had won $5,000 and J. J. Coe $15,000 in June of 1889. A reporter, having heard that Mr. Frey had received $5,000 in cash on Ticket No. 38847, called on him for confirmation. Mr. Frey cheerfully replied that he actually received the money and the First National Bank had collected it for him without exchange.[14] Coe and six others had bought a lottery ticket together. They each received $2,141.10. Coe was a member of Sheppard's bridge force, then working at Palo Pinto.[15]

The Louisiana State Lottery's half-column ad, displaying the facsimile signatures of G. T. Beauregard and J. A. Early, appeared regularly in the Weatherford *Constitution.* General Beauregard died in New Orleans on February 20, 1893, not long after Louisiana made the sale of lottery tickets illegal. It has not been learned whether the General and his friend X. B. Debray ever served as directors of the Franco-Texan. Paul Pecquet du Bellet said they were elected directors in 1879, at the same time Milliken was elected president. If either of them ever served, it would have been between 1879 and 1883, during the period when the stockholders meetings were held in France and there were so few Texas sources of information about the company. However, the fact that Du Bellet's letters to General Beauregard were found in the Spanish Archives of the General Land Office, where Debray was employed as translator, indicates that they may have served or contemplated serving at some time or possibly owned stock in the company.

On the surface, things appeared to be going well for the Franco-Texan by the end of 1889. At a meeting held the last week of December, a dividend of 4 per cent was declared. The by-laws were amended and thirteen directors were elected for the coming year—ten from France and three from Weatherford: George P. Levy, A. J. Hood, and I. N. Roach. Levy was reelected president.[16]

Now almost a household word in Weatherford, the Franco-Texan

[14] Fort Worth *Gazette*, July 3, 1889.
[15] *Palo Pinto County Star*, June 21, 1889.
[16] Weatherford *Constitution*, January 8, 1890.

became the victim of a new type of fraud—false agents who collected payments on the company's outstanding notes. On April 9, 1890, the board of directors found it necessary to publish a notice warning all parties whose notes were in possession of the Franco-Texan Land Company to pay only on delivery of the original notes and not to accept any receipts signed by any officers or agents, as such receipts would be repudiated.[17]

Levy went to France again in May, 1890. He took his family along and stayed all summer. He returned to Weatherford on August 13, and on August 15, the *Constitution* reported a large real estate deal:

> Yesterday the Franco-Texan Land Company filed 39 deeds of conveyance in the County Clerks office, transferring their entire landed property in Parker County to the "Inter-State Railway Construction Company." The deeds were forwarded from Dallas by Colonel J. B. Simpson.
>
> The Inter-State Railway Construction Company is a Texas institution, but is doing business under a charter obtained in Arkansas, such companies not being charterable in Texas. The number of acres conveyed and the amount of aggregate consideration were not obtainable this morning but both were very large.
>
> It is not known whether the Franco-Texan Land Company will go out of business or not, but this sale of their entire real estate in this county would seem to indicate some important change.[18]

Four days later the Franco-Texan made the front page. Colonel George A. Knight, United States marshal for the Northern District of Texas, had come from Dallas on August 9 to serve an injunction on its officers, restraining them from disposing of any of the lands, notes, or other assets of the company. The order was issued by Judge Don A. Pardee, circuit judge of the federal court, on application of James H. Allen, to have the company placed in the hands of the receiver. On August 13, Judge Pardee had issued subpoenas to the defendants in Weatherford, Galveston, Abilene, and Sweetwater. The case was to be tried on the first Monday of October in the federal court at Dallas, to

[17] *Ibid.*, April 9, 1890.

[18] *Ibid.*, August 15, 1890.

determine whether or not the injunction would be made perpetual or would be dissolved.

Levy was quoted as saying that on August 1 he returned from France where he had been in consultation with the principal stockholders of the company as to whether or not it should accept an offer to sell all its land. He also said that he had, on August 4, made deeds to the entire lot of the lands belonging to the company, amounting to 350,000 acres situated in Palo Pinto, Stephens, Callahan, Shackelford, Jones, Taylor, Fisher, Nolan, and Mitchell counties, and since the company had nothing for sale, it was not in the least molested by the injunction.

James H. Allen, so Levy said, had acquired some Franco-Texan stock from parties in France, who considered it almost worthless. A dividend had been declared on the stock, but since Allen had not presented it within the time prescribed by the by-laws, the dividend was automatically forfeited. When the company refused to pay the dividend to Allen, he obtained the temporary injunction.[19]

The Austin *Daily Statesman* carried the same story under the heading, "Too Late with his Injunction, A Stockholder in the Franco-Texan Gets Beautifully Left."

But Allen was not yet left. Within a few days he had put another obstacle in the way of the "Great Land Trade." The Weatherford *Constitution* reported that after the court granted Allen's petition for an injunction, he had amended it, alleging fraud in the sale of 350,000 acres of land at $1.75 an acre when it was worth $3.00 in cash, and making Simpson and the Arkansas members parties in the suit. It was understood that the purchasers paid $80,000 cash and were to pay the balance in six yearly payments. Information received from the secretary of state of Arkansas showed that the Inter-State Railway Construction Company was composed of James B. Simpson of Dallas, Texas, and Calvin Huffman, Sol F. Clark, E. O. Clark, and P. C. Dooley of Arkansas. Only fifty-three deeds had been filed for the record in Parker County whereas there were six hundred in all, scattered over the various counties mentioned in the suit.[20]

[19] *Ibid.*, August 18, 1890.
[20] *Ibid.*, August 21, 1890.

James H. Allen v. the Franco-Texan Land Company

Case in Equity No. 181, *James H. Allen v. the Franco-Texan Land Company et al.* was a long array of facts and figures which belied Levy's statements to the press and dispelled all doubts that he was depriving the company of its land like many others before him had done. Levy, however, had a better system. He had dummy directors in France who gave him a free hand. He then controlled the stockholders meetings in Texas by means of proxies obtained in France. Levy had purposely set out to get control of the company in this manner, and it was when he returned from France with a large number of these proxies, some of them false, that Judge Hood had resigned as president. Judge Hood had no wish to be president in name only, and the fact that he remained on the board seems to indicate that although he could not prevent Levy's usurpation of power, he was determined, if possible, not to allow him absolute control. But by means of mutual cooperation between the French directors and the Texas men who were furnished with stock or proxies, Levy soon had his system so well established that it looked as if no one could challenge it. He was willing to dole out a few dividends from time to time but he refused to give up any land without some profit to himself. Allen had then brought suit to put the company in receivership or else compel Levy to give him a fair exchange of land for stock. Undoubtedly though, it was Du Bellet, Allen's agent, who was responsible for locating and buying a large amount of stock in France and using it to force Levy's hand. Not to be outdone, Levy had resorted to the sale of all the company's property in spite of Judge Pardee's restraining order, and Allen then amended his petition to allege fraud.

The complaint, consisting of forty pages, was brought against the Franco-Texan Land Company and George P. Levy, F. Applegate, A. J. Hood, and I. N. Roach of Weatherford; Henry Sayles and Thomas O. Anderson of Abilene; and K. R. Seaton of Sweetwater, on behalf of James H. Allen and all stockholders who desired to join in the suit. In full detail and authoritative tone it proceeded to cite some amazing facts.

After a full account of the origin and history of the company and an examination of its charter, it was averred that Allen and John H. Traylor[21] purchased 4,023 shares of capital stock at face value of $100 each between April 26, 1889, and November 1, 1889; the said stock having an actual value of $50,000, and being formerly owned by 175 Frenchmen whose names were listed;

That Allen and Traylor deposited the said shares of capital stock with F. Applegate, secretary of the Franco-Texan, in Weatherford on November 26, 1889, for registration in the books previous to the December meeting but that Applegate and Levy refused to transfer the shares upon the books although Levy paid them a dividend of $78 on each share, as endorsed on the back of said shares; and that on June 3, 1890, John H. Traylor had transferred all his right, title, and interest in said stock to Allen;

That the Franco-Texan Land Company, since its organization had been controlled by a small number of stockholders in France in cooperation with the officers of the company in Texas, the stockholders in France manipulating the meetings in Texas by the use of false proxies, in order to get themselves elected directors; that no directors meetings had ever been held in Texas, that they had all been held in Paris, France, where such meetings were recorded in the French language; that there had always been a vice-president, vice-secretary, and vice-treasurer in Paris, that the annual salary of the vice-president was $2,000 and that of the vice-secretary $1,000; that the ten French directors were paid a per diem of $5.00 while engaged in the discharge of their duties and a commission of 5 per cent on all sales and leases of land; that two auditors residing in France were selected at each meeting at an annual salary of $200,

21 John H. Traylor had sold and surveyed land in Hood, Palo Pinto, Parker, and other western counties in the 1870's. He was sheriff and tax collector of Hood County in 1881 and senator from the 13th Senatorial District in 1883. He moved to Dallas in 1887 and became mayor in 1898. (*Handbook of Texas*, II, 797).

and that the directors in France rented an office and provided a porter at an annual cost of $800 per year, paid by the company;

That at the last stockholders meeting in Weatherford on December 26, 27, 28, 29, and 30 of 1889, George P. Levy was allowed 15,297 votes by virtue of pretended proxies, some signed by stockholders in France but without the signatures being any way attested, acknowledged, or proved, and others without any evidence that the signers were stockholders; that almost all of the proxies were made in blank; that most of them, if not all, were fabricated in France—all of which were in possession of the company and which it was notified to produce in the hearing of this cause;

That the entire number of shares represented at said December meeting was 19,196, including the proxies, and therefore Levy controlled the majority of the votes cast; that Levy said he had just returned from France and had been instructed to have the following thirteen directors elected for the ensuing year:

George P. Levy	Parker County
A. J. Hood	Parker County
I. N. Roach	Parker County
Comte de Mas Latrie	France
G. Rendu	France
Amaury Salmon	France
Baron de Biancourt	France
Alfred Girardin	France
Comte de Verchere	France
Dunican	France
Noel	France
Henri L. Merlin	France
L. Caen	France

That of the ten directors then residing in France only De Mas Latrie was an original stockholder, all others having purchased a small number of shares for the purpose of manipulating the affairs of the company to their own interests and against the interests of the majority of the stockholders;

That from September 1, 1876, to December 26, 1889, the company had sold 166,692 acres of land at the average price of $3.50 per acre, or a total sum of $538,422; that less than $100,000 had been paid in dividends, and that the remainder had been in part absorbed by payment of salaries, commissions, and expenses, and a large part squandered by the directors and officers of said company;

That there were still outstanding about 35,000 shares of capital stock, covering 375,000 acres of land; that there were cash and land notes on hand amounting to $125,000; that, as provided by the charter and by-laws, each share of stock on a general average would be entitled to 10.57 acres of land and $3.57 in money;

That A. J. Hood and I. N. Roach, two of the three resident directors composed the Advisory Board, and that on March, 1890, John H. Traylor, for himself and James H. Allen, made application to George P. Levy to exchange 556 shares of the capital stock of the company for certain designated lands, and President Levy, either acting alone or in conjunction with the Advisory Board, determined the proportionate amount of land for each share of stock to be 5.017 acres and refused to allow them any part of the money and notes then in the hands of the company, and claimed that the designated land was involved in litigation or had been leased to other parties and could not be exchanged; that the lands said to be available for exchange were inferior to those he refused to exchange, and that Traylor was compelled to accept the least desirable lands at a rate far in excess of their value; that Levy refused to give Traylor a warranty deed or make any other valid quitclaim to the land he was compelled to accept;

That on January 27, 1890, George A. Cook purchased 60 shares of the company's stock, then owned by Henry du Bellet, and on deposit in the company's office at Weatherford; that these shares of stock had originally been issued to Leopold Duval and were numbered 422 to 481 inclusive; that Cook purchased the shares from Du Bellet for the purpose of exchanging them for 510 acres of land in Palo Pinto County, known as Survey No. 89 in T and P Block No. 3; that on January 31, 1890, Cook presented his application to Levy for the exchange of his stock for the above-described land; that Levy accepted the application on condition that Cook pay $150 in money;

That on January 31, 1890, three groups of 20 shares each, originally issued to Anatole Hallez, Alfonse Martel, and J. B. Vallanson, and already registered for exchange, were claimed by other parties; that Article 6 of the by-laws provided that no transfer should be made at either office so long as any dispute existed as to the ownership of any certain shares;

That Levy accepted Cook's 60 shares but kept them as his own property, and in making the exchange for Cook, he transferred the disputed shares to Cook's name; and that when Cook paid the sum of $150 on February 1, 1890, Levy executed a deed for Cook's land with covenants of general warranty;

That on February 3, 1890, George P. Levy conveyed to R. H. Foat, by general warranty deed, two tracts of land in Nolan county; all of Section 33 in Block 23 (640 acres) and all of Section 45 in Block 23 except the NE ¼ (being 480 acres); that said conveyance for 1,120 acres of land was made in exchange for 175 shares of stock but no description of such shares was given in the deed;

That on the same day, February 3, 1890, R. H. Foat conveyed said 1,120 acres to George P. Levy, and on the same day Levy conveyed an undivided one-half interest in the same land to K. R. Seaton;

That the said 1,120 acres were situated near a depot on the Texas and Pacific railroad and adjoined land of the railway company on which Station Vista (now Roscoe) was located, and that on February 3, 1890, the said 1,120 acres of land were worth $15 an acre but had already increased to $25 an acre; that the said pretended exchange was made at the rate of 6.40 acres per share for land worth $15 an acre; that said deeds were in possession of George L. Levy and K. R. Seaton, and they were notified to produce them upon hearing of this cause;

That George P. Levy conveyed to D. L. Cunningham 80 acres out of the section in Palo Pinto County formerly refused to George A. Cook, in exchange for 13 shares of stock which Levy himself sold to Cunningham, three of these shares being the same three

(Nos. 479–481), which were originally issued to Leopold Duval and the same three which George A. Cook had heretofore exchanged for land;

That on May 3, 1890, Levy issued to M. Marx, a general warranty deed for 9,595 acres in exchange for 1,243 shares of the stock of the company, and to Henry Sayles a similar deed for 3,373 acres in exchange for 430 shares;

That according to the by-laws no exchange of land in an amount exceeding 10,000 acres could be made without being submitted to and approved by the board of directors; that M. Marx, Henry Sales, T. O. Anderson, and George P. Levy on that same day, May 3, 1890, formed a syndicate for the purpose of securing title to the lands thus conveyed to Marx and Sayles for much less than their actual value and that Levy, Sayles, and Marx conspired to make the purported exchange, which was in truth one transaction, in violation of the company's by-laws;

That the affairs of the company were virtually subject to the unrestrained control and management of George P. Levy, who, since his appointment as president, had been constantly making sales, leases, and conveyances of land for his own interests and the interest of his friends and favorites; that Levy was then in France, his second visit within twelve months, and his object was to purchase and secure in his own name a large number of shares of capital stock at nominal cost so that on his return with such shares he could make exchanges on the books of the company as would secure to himself and his friends the title to all the valuable and desirable lands then belonging to the company, thereby defrauding the other stockholders of the company; also that Levy was trying to secure the appointment of a receiver for the company in France, which would be an irreparable injury to the stockholders;

That Allen's shares still remained on deposit with the company and that although he had made application in writing on June 14, 1890, F. Applegate, the secretary, refused to take any action whatsoever;

That the December meeting was held in violation of the by-laws which set the regular time of the stockholders meetings as the first Tuesday in April; that the meeting was held at that time to prevent legitimate stockholders from presenting their certificates for exchange and to enable Levy, through the pretended directors in France, to preserve his control of the company; that Levy did control the action of said meeting by refusing to allow Henry P. du Bellet to vote 530 shares of stock although Levy recognized the said stock and paid Du Bellet a dividend on each share a few days afterwards; that also at said meeting Levy refused to allow John H. Traylor to vote his 3,138 shares and a few days later recognized said stock as valid and paid the dividends thereon; that a minority report of the committee on credentials, showing the full status of those shares, was voted down; and that a copy of that report marked Exhibit A was attached and the company was notified to produce the original on hearing of this cause;

That at the December meeting Levy claimed to own only 1,804 shares of stock and that at the same time he had either sold or furnished to other parties at least 1,989 shares on which he had allowed 7.50 acres per share of the company's most valuable land and on which he had executed general warranty deeds, all made since January 1, 1890, including in addition to those already mentioned:

200 acres to W. T. Reeves, Sr., for 31 shares;
440 acres to G. W. Rivers et al. for 69 shares;
114 acres to D. Q. Murphree for 16 shares;
40 acres to C. B. Rains, Jr., and J. P. Owens for 12 shares;

and sales to other parties unknown to Allen, but that in every instance Levy had secured an interest in such land;

That the Franco-Texan had failed to accomplish the purpose for which it was organized, the speedy distribution of its lands and their proceeds among the stockholders, having been in operation for fourteen years and having disposed of only 160,000 acres out of 548,000; that the shares outstanding and uncancelled were owned by a large number of persons scattered over the Republic of France and the Empire of Germany and such shareholders had lost all interest in the affairs of the company and considered their shares worthless and would decline to join in any action pertaining to the company;

That the by-laws of the company required a majority of the directors to constitute a quorum and that since ten of the thirteen directors resided in France, neither I. N. Roach or A. J. Hood, if disposed to aid in securing proper corrective action, would have any power to secure such action;

That at the meeting held in Weatherford in December, 1889, W. H. Eddleman, R. H. Foat, Ira B. Taylor, T. A. Wythe, Steve Maddux, M. V. Kinnison, H. P. Dorsey, C. Otterbein, C. D. Hartnett, Albert Stevenson, and Paul Chaptive were present and participated in said meeting although they were not stockholders, Levy having placed shares temporarily in the hands of said parties, all of whom were his friends, thus securing representation for the pretended proxies and keeping control of the meeting; that Levy claimed the shares owned by Allen and Traylor had not been transferred to the company's books; that Levy, upon demand of some of the stockholders, produced a book which was partially made up and claimed that he had brought it from France a few days before the meeting and that no other stockbook was kept at the Weatherford office;

That three or four stockholders joined Traylor and Allen in requesting relief for these irregularities but all action was refused and by-laws were adopted vesting unlimited authority in the president for the management of the affairs of the company and the disposition of its property and assets;

That under the by-laws, special stockholders meetings could be called only by the board of directors, and when such meetings were called, forty days notice was required by publication in Paris, France, and Weatherford, Texas; and that under the by-laws the board prescribed the order of the day for both general and special stockholders meetings and no outside subject or matter could be considered unless at least ten shareholders had given notice to the board at least thirty days prior to the meeting, for which reason Allen saw no possibility of relief from the wrongs and injuries already specified by or through any action of Levy or said board of directors or stockholders meetings;

Therefore, Allen requested that F. Applegate be required by court decree to register his (Allen's) stock upon the books of the company, that all officers of the company be restrained by a writ of injunction from making use or disposing of any land, money, notes, and other assets of the company, and that a receiver be appointed to take possession and control of all said land, money, notes, and other assets and all the record books and papers of the company;

That the deeds of conveyance made to M. Marx, Henry Sayles, R. H. Foat, and K. R. Seaton be cancelled and the lands reconveyed to the company;

That the lands of the company be sold under the orders of the court and the proceeds arising from the land, notes, and other assets be equitably distributed among the stockholders;

That if the court should decline to order the company's land sold, Levy should be required to make a just and equitable exchange of Allen's stock.

Attached to this complaint were two affidavits, one by James H. Allen and one by Henry P. du Bellet, and Exhibit A, which contained the minority report of the Credentials Committee. Watts and Aldridge of Weatherford were Allen's solicitors.

After the announcement that the Franco-Texan had sold all its holdings to the Inter-State Railway Construction Company, Allen alleged in the amendment to his bill of complaint that the deeds of conveyance were not made by Levy until after the restraining order had been issued by Judge Pardee, that they could not have been signed on August 4 and acknowledged before Lafayette Fitzhugh on August 6 as indicated because Levy had not then returned from France and did not return until August 12; and that although Levy claimed a cash payment of $80,000 was made to him on August 4, no such payment was made until after Levy had been served with notice of the restraining order, forbidding him to make the sale. Attached to the amendment was the affidavit of Henry P. du Bellet stating that he was the agent of James H. Allen. The statement was notarized by W. A. Kemp of Dallas County, Texas.

Before the federal court convened for its hearing of Allen's complaint against the Franco-Texan Land Company, the case was dismissed on motion of the complainant. On September 17, 1890, Allen declared himself fully satisfied with the compromise settlement made with the defendants.[22]

With Allen and Du Bellet paid in full there was smooth sailing ahead for Levy and his friends, two of whom were Sam H. Milliken and R. H. Foat. Milliken's name was not mentioned in the suit, but he was behind the scenes with President James B. Simpson of Dallas. Simpson was also an agent of the Scottish American Mortgage Company (owner of the Prairie Cattle Company), headquarters in Glasgow, which had refinanced loans for struggling farmers who had purchased Franco-Texan land on terms, the interest often running as high as 15 per cent.

Beginning on September 29, 1890, the Inter-State Railway Construction Company ran a mammoth ad in the Fort Worth *Gazette* for five consecutive days, announcing the sale of 500,000 acres of Franco-Texan land. And on January 21, 1891, the following ad appeared in the Weatherford *Constitution*:

LAND FOR SALE
(The Franco-Texan Lands)
Seventy five tracts in Parker County and Thousands of Acres in Other Counties These Lands Are Unsurpassed for the Production of Cotton, Grain, Fruits, & Vegetables
APPLY TO INTER-STATE R'Y CONSTRUCTION CO.
Sam H. Milliken, Mgr.
503 Elm Street, Dallas, Texas.
Or at the office of the Franco-Texan Land Company, Weatherford.[23]

Here was Sam H. Milliken selling the Inter-State Railway Construction Company's land from the Franco-Texan office in Weatherford. But the Franco-Texan had not gone out of business. After settling James H. Allen's suit out of court in 1890, the company had immedi-

[22] James H. Allen *v.* the Franco-Texan Land Company, Case in Equity No. 181, V. 3, U. S. Circuit Court, Dallas, Texas.

[23] Weatherford *Constitution*, January 21, 1891.

ately released the Inter-State from some of its purchase obligations. What it all amounted to was that since the pretended sale to the Inter-State had failed to accomplish its purpose, the Franco-Texan retained part of the lands it was supposed to have sold and both companies continued in business. The Inter-State, however, had acquired a large block of Franco-Texan land for much less than its actual value. Real estate transfers printed in the Weatherford *Enquirer* on September 1, 1892, included the following:

Inter-State Ry. Construction Co., part of Section No. 377 to R. H. Foat	$2,316.65
Inter-State Ry. Construction Co., 640 acres out of Survey No. 379 to R. H. Foat	2,443.00
Inter-State Ry. Construction Co., 640 acres out of Survey No. 453 to R. H. Foat	2,443.00
Inter-State Ry. Construction Co., 602.08 acres out of Survey No. 359 to R. H. Foat	2,378.30

The price per acre of these tracts in which the number of acres is given was either $3.81 or $3.95, and the Inter-State Railway Construction Company bought them from the Franco-Texan at $1.75. Mr. Foat was by then a director of the Franco-Texan, and he probably considered the land a bargain at this price.

And listed on August 25, 1892, was:

Henry P. du Bellet et ux to T. A. Price, 184 acres out of the W. J. Mays survey and 220.97 out of No. 187 $3,500.00,

or $8.94 per acre. Du Bellet, temporarily residing in Dallas at the A. C. Daniel Hotel, was a notary public and president of the Texas Guaranty Company. He went back and forth to Weatherford to attend to his land business.

Du Bellet had been sued by Edmond Moreau, the receiver of the Société Foncière et Agricole des États Unis in the District Court of Dallas County on May 1, 1891. Moreau alleged that Du Bellet had fraudulently represented himself to be the agent of the company and that he had collected money for the company and appropriated it for his own use. Moreau petitioned for an order requiring Du Bellet to bring the books and papers of the company into court and also an injunction restraining him from assigning or negotiating the notes and papers of the company. A temporary injunction was granted, but it was later held that according to Texas law, a receiver did not have the authority to act in his official capacity outside the jurisdiction of the court by which he was appointed. Since Moreau was appointed by an order of a court of the Republic of France, he had no standing in the courts of the United States or in the state of Texas and could not sue in France or elsewhere. The case went to the Court of Civil Appeals on May 30, 1894, and the judgment was affirmed.[24]

Du Bellet's Dallas address in 1893 was the McLeod Hotel. On November 14, 1893, he had become the U.S. consul at Rheims, France, and on that date he appointed A. J. Ball of Weatherford his attorney to sell any and all property he might own or any property belonging to Noémi and Elfrida du Bellet. In 1894 Du Bellet was still listed in the Dallas City Directory, with Rhines, France, as his address.

Mayor Levy

Levy had made another extended trip to France in January, 1891, doubtless in search of additional Franco-Texan stock. In 1892 he was requested to be a candidate for mayor of Weatherford, by petition containing seventy-five names headed by that of L. W. Christian, one of the city's prominent citizens. Other candidates were J. B. Hutcheson and F. A. Leach, and both had strong followings. The Weatherford *Enquirer* supported Levy, saying that he was one of the main agitators of the first street railway line, was president of the Franco-Texan Land Company, a large taxpayer, a progressive and a liberal, who would serve the city without compensation, solely for the honor of the position and the chance to work for the improvement of the whole town.[25]

Levy was elected by a majority of 135 votes, and on April 7, 1892, under the headline "Mayor Levy," the *Enquirer* wrote:

> George P. Levy is a Frenchman and a large property owner and president of the street car company was the cry raised against him, and notwith-

[24] Moreau *v.* Du Bellet, 27 *South Western Reporter* 503.
[25] Weatherford *Enquirer*, February 25, 1892.

standing the fact that free hacks placarded with the old Knownothing cry, "America for Americans," were passing to and from the polls all day, he was elected by such a handsome majority that none can doubt that Weatherford does not believe it a crime to be a Frenchman.

Weatherford, like America in the early days, received Frenchmen and French money to help her in her early struggles, hence she has a warm place in her heart for the French, and she is also cosmopolitan enough to think that a foreign born citizen is just as good as any other citizen. The result of the election has much in it to encourage all of the progressive element of Weatherford, and the Enquirer opines that Levy will make Weatherford an excellent mayor.[26]

On the night that Levy was to take the oath of office, E. P. Nicholson, alderman and former attorney of the Franco-Texan Land Company, offered an objection. He questioned Levy's eligibility to hold office because it was not certain that he was a citizen of the United States and because he could not be released from bond as the city treasurer, although he had withdrawn his name, until the books had been examined. An investigating committee was appointed, and on April 28, it reported that Levy was legally a citizen, having been a resident for ten years, and that he would be responsible on F. Applegate's bond only until April 11 when the treasurer's new term began. H. W. Kuteman, Levy's counsel, argued in his favor for thirty minutes, and Nicholson argued against him for an hour. When the final vote was taken, Levy won 6 to 1.[27] He took office on May 4, 1892.

H. W. Kuteman began his association with the Franco-Texan Land Company as an attorney and possibly as a stockholder. Before coming to Weatherford in 1882, he had lived at Quitman where he was a law partner of James S. Hogg. In the early 1890's he was a member of the Commercial Union Club and president of the Board of Trade. He specialized in criminal law, but being a good businessman, he made profitable investments, and by 1906 was able to retire and spend his time handling his private affairs—ranch properties, farm lands, and vendor's lien notes. In 1908 he acquired a controlling interest in the

[26] *Ibid.*, April 7, 1892.
[27] *Ibid.*, April 28, 1892.

First State Bank, later the Parker County National Bank, and he also established banks in other towns.[28]

In 1934 his daughter, Ina Kuteman Hill, married Douglas Chandor, the famous portrait painter whose works included paintings of the Prince of Wales, Herbert C. Hoover, Sam Rayburn, Mr. and Mrs. Winston Churchill, and Franklin D. Roosevelt. Chandor's very fine portrait of President Roosevelt now hangs in the Senate Chamber of the State Capitol in Austin, and the Chandor Gardens are one of Weatherford's showplaces today.

A Stockholders Meeting in 1892

A stockholders meeting was held in Weatherford on December 13, 1892. Those present were George P. Levy, president, F. Applegate, secretary, Alfred Gerardin, R. H. Foat, M. V. Kinnison, W. H. Eddleman, Ira B. Taylor, and Charles A. Otterbein.

The president appointed M. V. Kinnison, Ira B. Taylor, and Charles A. Otterbein to the Credentials Committee. This committee reported the following stockholders entitled to take part in the meeting:

George P. Levy	238 shares
F. Applegate	71 shares
M. V. Kinnison	5 shares
R. H. Foat	37 shares
C. A. Otterbein	30 shares
H. P. du Bellet	1 share
Ira B. Taylor	20 shares
W. H. Eddleman	30 shares
A. Gerardin	25 shares
George P. Levy	11,098 proxies

Total number represented 11,555.

The number of existing shares was 33,494. Since one-third of this number was necessary to hold a stockholders meeting, it was announced that a legal quorum was present.

Each member of the committee was then voted the sum of $10 for services rendered.

[28] G. A. Holland, *History of Parker County and the Double Log Cabin*, pp. 198–199.

The president presented the following account of receipts and expenses for the company in Weatherford from December 1, 1891, to December 1, 1892:

RECEIPTS	
Balance in the bank on December 1, 1891	$13,388.91
Sale of Lands	740.50
Notes Paid	49,580.86
Interest on deferred payments	3,193.03
Interest on Bank Deposits	718.18
	$67,621.48

EXPENSES	
Paid to Inter-State Railway Construction Co., part of the total sum for leasing lands sold to it by the Franco-Texan	$ 889.96
Registration of titles and deeds	48.20
Discount on notes paid in advance	202.80
Court costs and fees	677.74
Taxes for 1891	240.09
Dividends paid in Weatherford office	3,319.92
Officers salaries	2,919.98
Commissions for recovery of debts	2,460.62
Commissions to agents for sale of lands	8.30
Credentials Committee for meeting of 1891	30.00
Telegrams	25.80
Office expenses	105.15
Office rent	150.00
Printing	10.50
Travel Expense	460.00
Land surveys	38.75
Lawyers fees for James B. Simpson	1,580.75
Remitted to Paris for dividends	23,521.81
Balance in Bank	30,931.86
	$67,621.48

The report was approved by the stockholders. The president then explained that the sale en bloc to the Inter-State Railway Construction

Company had not produced the good results expected, the president of that corporation having had some very bad luck and having compromised the situation of the company—an incident which could not have been foreseen but which prevented the payment of its obligations. President Levy thought it best not to act hastily and take back the lands. He proposed that the Franco-Texan appoint him *fidéicommissaire* to take all the unsold lands, effect their sale, collect the money, and apply it to the sum the Inter-State owed the company. All expenses involved in the transaction would be charged to the Inter-State, and the $1,580 paid to Simpson would of course be recovered. This sale had been made on conditions of absolute security, not an acre of land had been lost nor was there any danger of losing any. The Franco-Texan was safe and had a great future. A dividend of five francs per share was recommended.

R. H. Foat moved that the company authorize the dividend of five francs per share, totalling $26,840. The motion was seconded by Mr. Taylor and adopted unanimously. This dividend, which was the seventh, would be paid after February 2, 1893, at the Weatherford office or at 24 rue de l'Arcade, Paris.

R. H. Foat then moved that the company authorize the transfer by the Inter-State Railway Construction Company to George P. Levy of all its unsold lands in order to protect the interests of the Franco-Texan in said lands. The motion was seconded by Dr. Otterbein and unanimously adopted.

Two French auditors were elected: Georges Lemarquis and Henri Colont; and a new board of directors chosen: George P. Levy, R. H. Foat, C. A. Otterbein, and S. H. Milliken of Texas; De Mas Latrie, E. Villot, Henri Merlin, Alfred Gerardin, E. Renevey, E. Salmon, M. Chaize, Leon Caen, and A. Salmon of Paris.

Levy was reelected president; F. Applegate, secretary; Henry Merlin, vice-president, and L. Thesio, vice-secretary.

Also presented at this meeting was the general audit of the company's accounts for the year of 1891, submitted and approved by the two French auditors on November 16, 1892. The point was made that the accounts balanced according to the figures furnished by the Weatherford office, but these of course were accepted on good faith, and comparisons were made in favor of the current administration. In 1886 the receipts amounted to only 163,049 francs; in 1887 these fell to 15,927 francs, and in 1888 to 5,731 francs, while in 1891 they amounted to 576,108.50 francs. In 1889 the dividend was only 594 francs, in 1890 it was 125,000, and in 1891 it was 346,000. These figures spoke for themselves and were the result of the prudence and activity of the president and board of directors.

A copy of the minutes of this stockholders meeting was printed in French and distributed to the stockholders in France, along with the report of the administrative council which authorized the transfer of the Inter-State lands to George P. Levy.[29]

James B. Simpson, the so-called president of the Inter-State Railway Construction Company, was a leading citizen of Dallas and the head of at least a dozen business enterprises. He was president of the 4th National Bank of Dallas, and in early 1892, when he foresaw the approach of financial troubles, resigned as president of that institution. Within a few weeks he was publicly accused of absconding with $300,000 in cold cash. On February 5, 1892, he was in Kansas City advertising Texas land for sale, but when the bank story broke he had gone to Hot Springs, Arkansas, where he said he was "recuperating." The stringency of the money market had brought on a crisis and attachments for large amounts were run on his business enterprises by creditors without giving him a chance to meet his obligations. "Had I been given a little more time," he said, "I could have met all demands and there would have been no trouble." He insisted he was not guilty of fraud and would return to Dallas to face all charges. The Fort Worth *Gazette* described Colonel Simpson as a typical Texan, small of stature, neatly dressed; he wore a soft felt hat and possessed a face of remarkable determination and intelligence. "His every action was that of a man of cool calculation and of iron nerve."[30]

In Dallas on February 18, 1892, Simpson was arrested on an affidavit sworn out by Thomas F. Bennie, representative of the Scottish

[29] A copy of the printed minutes of the meeting held in Weatherford on December 13, 1892, is in the possession of Mrs. Alfred Hammond of Weatherford.

[30] Fort Worth *Gazette*, February 13, 1892.

American Mortgage Company, of which Colonel Simpson was agent. Bennie said Simpson had embezzled $28,000. Simpson admitted that he had lost money speculating in real estate, but asserted that he had intentionally wronged no one and expected to pay his creditors. He was released on $5,000 bond given by J. B. Adoue, president of the National Bank of Commerce, and M. L. S. Robertson.[31]

For this reason, Levy said, it was best that he take over Simpson's obligations instead of letting the company take back the lands. According to releases signed by Levy and recorded in Taylor, Parker, and other counties, the Inter-State paid some of the promissory notes. Whether or not the sale had been pretended, it was now allowed to stand at the price of $1.75 per acre. Levy could sell the land himself, pay the notes, and make an enormous profit, and possibly a large commission.

Both R. H. Foat and Levy made trips to France in early June of 1893. Foat returned in July, but Levy stayed until October. They must have been trying to put the company into receivership or at least to get possession of the outstanding stock before someone else did. In any case, Levy continued to be president for three more years, or until the day before the Franco-Texan charter expired by limitation on August 6, 1896.

The Liquidation of the Franco-Texan Land Company

Levy resigned on August 5; W. H. Eddleman *et al.* petitioned for receivership in the district court of Parker County on August 10; and the court appointed Levy receiver and Harry W. Kuteman master in chancery on August 12. The papers connected with this cause (No. 3305) make up a file four or five inches thick. The original petition is missing, but from Levy's testimony it appears that the suit was brought by W. H. Eddleman of Weatherford and S. Kahn and H. Merlin of Paris, France: Eddleman owning 140 shares, S. Kahn 700, and H. Merlin 500. Out of 29,743 shares, 5,000 had been cancelled for collateral, leaving a total of 24,743. There were no American directors at this time. All had resigned, and none, including Levy, pro-

[31] *Ibid.*, February 19, 1892.

fessed to own any stock. The total assets of the company were represented as $588,054.60, all in notes except for several lots in Rockport and Fulton, valued at $8,331, and some land in controversy in Taylor, Nolan, and Fisher counties.

As receiver, it was Levy's duty to sell all the land and convert all the notes into money and divide it pro rata among the stockholders within a period of three years. By 1899 he had made very little headway in liquidating the company's assets. Many notes had been cancelled, 146,429 acres had been deeded back to the company, and new notes made. Therefore a time extension was necessary, and on application to the Legislature, the company was granted an additional three years (until January 1, 1902) in which to conclude its business.[32]

Levy made two trips to France, in 1900 and 1901, in an effort to get all the stock into court for the payment of dividends. During his absence from May 24, 1900, to October 15, 1900, and from May 21, 1901, to September 30, 1901, F. Applegate, the former secretary of the company was appointed co-receiver and was empowered to make deeds, covenants, and conveyances when approved by the master in chancery.

On July 19, 1901, before Levy had returned from his second trip to France, T. M. Wadsworth, a large landowner in Parker County, filed his second petition as intervenor, requesting a valid title to 11,522 acres on which he had paid $3,456 down. District Judge J. W. Patterson had overruled Wadsworth's first objection in which he claimed a shortage and petitioned for relief because he had heard that the company was going to sell the notes and go out of business, leaving him nobody to fall back on for his title.[33] In his second petition Wadsworth charged that the receivership was illegal since no directors had ever made an appearance in the cause; no shareholder had joined in the application except Eddleman if he was one; Levy's appointment had never been ratified; not all the stockholders had received dividends, the residence of many being unknown; only 22,000 shares had been pre-

32 Gammel, *Laws of Texas*, XI, Special Laws of the 26th Legislature, 1899, Senate Bill 149, p. 1.

33 T. M. Wadsworth *v.* F. Applegate *et al.*, Cause No. 3821, District Court Records of Parker County; Civil Minutes, *Ibid.*, Vol. 8, p. 148.

sented for dividends, and some 3,000 shares were still in Levy's hands. Wadsworth's solicitors were A. H. Culwell and McCall & McCall.

F. Applegate, being sworn for the intervenor, testified:

I am one of the defendants in this suit. I was secretary of the Franco-Texan Land Company for a number of years before its dissolution. George P. Levy was the president of the company. He was not president at the date of the dissolution. Our charter expired on the 6th, and he closed up the business on the 5th. He had no stock at that time. He had owned stock but had disposed of it before the expiration of the charter. He was president of the company and director too. He resigned everything. I have no copy of his resignation. I suppose it was sent to the Paris office. He was in possession of the property of the company up to the 5th when he resigned and then he had nothing further to do with it. It was just turned over to me. I never inquired into why he resigned. I suppose it was to be appointed receiver. He had stock at one time in the company. The by-laws required as long as he was president of the company to have stock in the company. I don't know how much he had. Sometimes little and sometimes more. What he had he sold to parties in France. If he sold to Mr. Eddleman I did not know it. I don't know what amount of shares of stock Mr. Levy owned in the company at the date of dissolution.

CROSS[-EXAMINATION]

I was sued in 1896 as defendant for the possession of the property. I will state that I had possession of the property at the time I was sued and held it until Mr. Levy was appointed receiver when I turned it over to him. I then had no further interest in the property of the company. Afterwards I was under the employment of Mr. Levy as bookkeeper and have since held that position. I was appointed co-receiver with limited power on account of the temporary absence of Mr. Levy in France. My appointment expired on the 15th of October. I was appointed co-receiver twice, this year and last year. While I was co-receiver Mr. Levy was absent in France. It was expedient that someone under the circumstances be appointed co-receiver with power to make deeds and transact business for the company. I don't say that I could do what others could do, but I was familiar with the business and had no trouble in doing it. It would have been hard for another man to have done the business because it would have been hard for him to have familiarized himself with the lands, *etc.* in three months, and he could not have done it. I am not really a defendant in this suit. I thought I was out of possession a long time ago. The property was turned over to Mr. Levy on the 12th as receiver. During the time between no business was done, the things were locked up. I had no authority to do anything until Mr. Levy was appointed receiver. The company could not do anything until he was appointed receiver. I think the condition of the affairs of the company demanded that a receiver be appointed. Not a very big amount of money was on hand at the time the receiver was appointed. It was dull at that time but a good deal of money came in that fall and winter. There was a large amount of notes outstanding. At the time I was appointed co-receiver of the company I was not interested in the company only that I was bookkeeper. I had no adverse interest to the plaintiffs or anyone else. I had nothing to do with the property except as bookkeeper. I surrendered all the property to the receiver.

CROSS[-EXAMINATION]

After Mr. Levy resigned his office of president I had the property in charge until someone could be appointed who could take charge. The amount in the bank was in the name of the Franco-Texan Land Company till the 12th, then to George P. Levy. Nothing was done before Mr. Levy's appointment as receiver. Business was stopped till the receiver was appointed. We could not do anything. I was in possession as secretary. I attended to the locking up of the books and other things in the safe. There was no one else to do it. Levy was out and the things locked up and I did not turn them over to anyone until Levy was appointed receiver. I did not own any stock at the date of the dissolution. I sometimes bought a share or two and then sold it. I was simply secretary. I was not required to own any because it was an appointive office.

RECROSS[-EXAMINATION]

I had the key to the office and the things were turned over to Mr. Levy on the 12th. I would not have turned it over to anyone who did not have full authority. I knew that a receiver was going to be appointed and when that was done he would take charge and till that was done I had no authority to turn it over to anyone.

RE-DIRECT[ION]

I don't know that counsel told me that the directors had charge and control of the affairs until someone should be appointed receiver. There were no directors in America on the 6th of August, 1896. They had all resigned before that time, according to my understanding, and I don't think there were any in France. It required three directors to be here in Texas. I don't know that it is a fact that there were 13 directors and all but three were French [or that], 3 or 4 should be in Texas. It is my opinion that most of the men who acted as directors had no stock. They might own stock one day and then sell it. It was just like a share of anything else and could be transferred. The stockholders were not here at the date of the dissolution. The French stockholders practically owned all the stock except a few thousand shares and they dictated. I was appointed co-receiver this year on the 25th of May. I acted as co-receiver until the 1st of October. My powers were prescribed. I have no copy of the resignation of Levy. My understanding was that the whole directory resigned to take effect at the same time. I could not swear to it. I had so much business to attend to that I did not pay much attention to it. I don't know if the whole directory resigned who did accept their resignations. I did not know that it was necessary for anyone to do it. I don't think there was a directory at the time of the expiration of the corporation. I think they had all resigned before the charter had expired. Mr. Levy was a director by virtue of his office of president. The directors are elected by the stockholders and the president by the directors and they had a vice-president in Paris. I don't know as a fact that the directors resigned.

Kuteman, being sworn for the defendants, testified:

I will state that I was somewhat familiar with the affairs of this corporation at the date of its dissolution by operation of law, and since that time. At that time I was acting as attorney for the receiver and was afterwards appointed by Your Honor as Master in Chancery. It was thought that a Master in Chancery was not necessary; afterwards you thought it best that I be appointed. I attended to the winding up of the business . . . The three Texas directors were not stockholders. It was a kind of a subterfuge, to comply with the law about local directors; no stock was owned but the circulating stock, and they did not act as directors. None of them had assumed to act for some time before the expiration of the charter in any manner or had been concerned about it any more than an entire stranger. Mr. Levy was appointed at my instigation because he was the best party for it. Nearly all the stockholders resided in France, and it was impossible to get them to come to this country to give good evidence. He, being familiar with the French language, had gotten to go to France and see them about the matter. He has been over to France two or three times to declare dividends and get these stockholders before the court. During his absence Applegate was appointed co-receiver to carry out the business of the company in leasing and selling lands, only however with the approval of the Master in Chancery and Your Honor knows he has complied with it. I further state that the 29,000 shares of stock, all of it, is before the court. It is in this shape: 22,000 shares have been presented for their dividends. They are here subject to inspection. I am willing for counsel to examine them, and they show that all these stockholders have received their pro rata stock. There are 2,800 shares that I can't say about. They have been filed with the receiver but he has not sent here yet all the shares. This administration has been pending ever since 1896. The affairs of the company have just been wound up. There are a few lots in Rockport and part of the land in Jones County and one or two matters that are in controversy in Nolan County and one in Taylor County. These will have to be settled in some way. Also, the lands have been sold. I suppose $100,000 has been turned over to the stockholders and no one of them has ever made any claim about it. None of the pretended directors have ever presented any stock for payment. No shares are on file with the clerk. The 2,800 shares of stock I understand are over with Levy in France. They are filed with him as receiver. There were 29,000 shares of stock at the time the receivership was instituted. Five thousand shares were held as collateral and they were taken up and cancelled, leaving 24,000 shares, of these 22,000 are over in the bank and Levy has 2,800 [*sic*]. There is no secret about the matter; there is no scheme. We had no idea of anyone being a party or receiver. This corporation has been run by a French directory. They were in France and a part of Africa. Three directors were held over here. I don't know the reason for having three directors here. I think they were trying to comply with the law. Those directors over there wrote to me to give them my opinion as to how this corporation should be wound up, and I investigated it with the expectation of finding that the directors should wind it up. Levy had no stock at the dissolution of the corporation. The Texas directors as a matter of fact had no stock at the time of the dissolution and even before that. I expect, he, Levy, got rid of his stock in order to be appointed receiver. I presume that I told him that if he had stock he could not be. The stock shows that dividends have been paid. There have been 6, 7, or 8 dividends since the receivership. Mr. Applegate was appointed co-receiver as a matter of expediency because he was familiar with the affairs of the company. I suggested it to the court in the absence of Mr. Levy. It would have been almost impossible for a man not familiar with the affairs of the company in two or three months to learn how to make the deeds, and he had experience. Mr. Applegate at the appointment of receiver turned over all the property and was subsequently selected by Levy as bookkeeper and did the clerical work. He made his appearance here in court in the receivership and has never made an adverse claim to receiver. We discussed it and it was finally decided that he should be appointed co-receiver. The court talked it over with me. He was no party to the suit technically speaking. He has never been technically dismissed. The receiver was appointed and he turned the assets over to him just as soon as he qualified as receiver. There was more in his hands than in Levy's. He had the keys to the office. He might have had a key and might have locked up the notes for all I know . . . The stock belongs to the stockholders and when it was wound up I supposed it would be cancelled . . . No director of the old Franco-Texan Land Company has ever objected to the receivership or to its management.

Kuteman then offered the order for Levy's appointment and his bond and oath as evidence that Levy was authorized to terminate the affairs of the company under the orders of the court.

On November 19, 1901, Eddleman filed a supplemental petition praying that R. H. Foat, Charles Otterbein, and Sam H. Milliken be made parties to the suit, to remove the cloud on the title cast by Wadsworth.

On November 21, these directors, who were said to have resigned, filed an answer ratifying and approving the appointment of the receiver and all his acts.

On November 23, in "Conclusions of Law and Fact," Judge J. W. Patterson formally stated that Sam H. Milliken, Charles Otterbein, and R. H. Foat had been elected directors at the last meeting in 1895 and that none of said directors was acting at that time although they had previously held one share each for the purpose of qualifying as directors. Judge Patterson found that since the appointment of the receiver 5,000 shares of stock had been cancelled, that there were about 24,000 shares outstanding, and that all except 550 had been filed with the master in chancery for the purpose of receiving the money belonging to the owners of said stock. Judge Patterson authorized Levy to give Wadsworth a deed to the land he had purchased if he wanted it, and concluded with the statement that W. H. Eddleman had acquired title and possession of about 22,000 shares of said outstanding stock.

Finally, on January 15, 1902, the master in chancery approved and filed Levy's report. It was a balanced account showing the disposition of the company's assets since 1899. The most significant items were:

Dividends paid in 1899 and 1900 in Paris	$112,800.25
Dividends paid to Eddleman in 1901 on 23,006 shares	123,215.80
Dividends paid to Eddleman in 1902 on 23,133 shares, to R. S. Stanhope on 16 shares, and to A. S. Flanay on 2 shares	116,210.00
Dividends on 109 shares paid to G. A. Holland	738.55

Land received by Eddleman on January 15, 1902:		
Jones County	5,238.96	acres
Palo Pinto County	24,754.88	"
Nolan County	22,789.13	"
Taylor County	4,394.50	"
Stephens County	17,374.58	"
Parker County	9,718.91	"
Fisher County	7,076.31	"
Shackelford County	1,760.00	"
Mitchell County	5,600.00	"
Total	98,707.27	acres

Other items of interest appearing in the report were:

Kuteman's fee as master in chancery	$2,500.00
Kuteman's additional legal fees	1,750.00
Levy's fee as receiver	2,333.28
Levy's monthly salary as receiver	291.66
Levy's expenses to Paris in 1900	1,000.00
Expenses of Paris office for 9½ months, 1898–1899	603.40
Cash on hand in Paris office, 1898–1899	1,129.35
Amount of Levy's bond	100,000.00

On May 17, 1902, Levy petitioned to be discharged as receiver. He reported 168 shares still outstanding. The owners, he said, could not be found after repeated advertising, but the Merchants and Farmers National Bank was the custodian of a sufficient amount for their payment, and his bonds and sureties were therefore vacated.

Kuteman was not then released. On May 6, 1903, he submitted 50 shares of stock for payment of dividends—40 originally issued to Pierre Dupree and 10 to Henry Giffard, in the amount of $637.50. He did not state to whom the dividends were paid.

On June 20, 1903, he approved the payment on 6 shares to Allard d'Heur.

On April 3, 1905, he reported $3,154.44 in dividends paid to W. H. Eddleman on 300 shares.

On October 15, 1905, he reported $4,367.64 in dividends to C. C. Littleton, G. A. Holland, Allard d'Heur, and Mrs. C. E. Condere of Dallas. On this date Kuteman was discharged.

W. H. Eddleman, it will be noted, received some $242,000 in dividends plus 98,707.27 acres of land, which, combined, must have approached three quarters of a million dollars or more in value. Levy's report gives no clue as to how so much land and virtually all the Franco-Texan stock came into Eddleman's possession, nor does it explain why the French stockholders would be willing to surrender their stock certificates when there were still more and larger dividends to be paid and more land to be disposed of. In this regard a letter was written on October 1, 1910, by A. Linol, attorney of the H. Cahn Bank, 28 Boulevard St. Denis, Paris, France, to Alfred Hammond of Weatherford. The French consul at Galveston had recommended Hammond as the best source for reliable information on the Franco-Texan receivership. Linol said that in 1896, the Cahn Bank sent in for liquidation 1,754 shares of Franco-Texan stock, 958 shares belonging to C. Cahn, and the rest to clients of the Bank. These shares were sent in at the same time Levy sent in his. Levy then returned to France in 1900 and settled with Cahn and the bank's clients for twenty francs per share, deducting the sum of two francs each for his trouble and work, that is, eighteen francs net. This represented the conversion value of the claims sent to him in 1896. Levy himself told Linol that he exchanged these 1,754 shares for 59 notes signed by purchasers of the company's lands, their total value being $10,691.97.

Levy then sold these notes to a Mr. Eddleman for a lump sum a good deal lower than their nominal value which meant that he received for the transaction only twenty francs per share. Levy's brother was one of the managers of the Cahn Bank, and Levy advised the exchange instead of awaiting the distribution of funds after the liquidation. In the end, the shares that had not been exchanged received a dividend of 32 francs when only 20 francs were received in proceeding as Levy advised. Linol therefore wanted information on the following points:

1. Wasn't it true that the Franco-Texan Land Company bought back the 1,754 shares with the notes Levy had in his office signed by the Inter-State Railway Construction Company which had bought the land and had been bankrupt since 1892?

2. Could an agent accept in good faith the notes undersigned by a company in bankruptcy as payment for shares which had a definite value?

3. The Franco-Texan balance sheet on January 13, 1895, showed assets of 2,180,686.95 francs and should have returned 67 francs per share for the 32,388 shares representing the company's capital. The sum of $10,691.67 which Levy said he received was insufficient.

4. Hadn't Mr. Levy collected on a large part of those notes between 1896 and 1900 instead of at the time he claimed to have exchanged them?

5. Could it be positively established that Levy made the pretended sale of those notes to Mr. Eddleman in 1900? Also what had become of $130,000 which the receivership had not distributed and which was reserved for the 10,000 shares not represented?

Mr. Levy had not been a faithful agent, Linol said. He had collected more than twenty francs for each share, and Linol wanted Levy to pay him the difference. Levy had returned from Texas with a fortune of two million francs ($400,000), and if Linol obtained a judgment against him he would pay Hammond for his assistance.[34]

So much for Levy and his misrepresentations to the French, including his own brother. Was it then so easy a matter to have these transactions approved by the district court of Parker County? The pattern,

[34] Letter in possession of Mrs. Alfred Hammond of Weatherford.

of course, was set when Levy, the president of the company was appointed receiver, when Kuteman, Levy's counsel was appointed master in chancery, and when Applegate, the company's secretary was appointed co-receiver. There was little doubt that Levy's figures would be accepted.

The $100 stock certificate reproduced in the illustration section provides a different picture of the distribution to the stockholders of the company's assets. It was issued to Emmanuel Marie Philibert de Langier de Beaurecueil on September 1, 1876. The amounts and dates of each dividend appear on the back of the certificate, the last two being paid in 1899 and 1900. As they were the only two paid after 1896, they contradict Kuteman's statement that "6, 7, or 8" dividends had been paid since that date. The 1899 and 1900 dividends listed here were for $1.15 and $2.00 respectively, and they fail to add up to Levy's alleged total of $112,000 paid on 24,780 shares. No dividends of $5.00 and $10.00, such as those received by Eddleman and others in 1901, 1902, 1903, and 1905, are shown, but, since the certificate appears to be uncancelled, perhaps it would have been due another and larger dividend if it had fallen into the right hands.

This $100 certificate was transferred to "Bearer" on July 21, 1890. It changed hands four times, William Dumery being the last owner. The total of dividends paid through the years was $13.35. As a $100 certificate was originally good for thirteen acres, the French had paid $8.00 an acre for their land. It was therefore impossible for them to receive face value for a stock certificate unless the land had been held until the average price per acre in northwest Texas had risen as high as $8.00, or, that is, until after the company's charter had expired. Nor did they have a chance to recover by coming to Texas to exchange certificates for land because, according to the by-laws of the company, the number of acres redeemable was always reduced as the price of land rose, and almost invariably an ordinary shareholder had to sue the company before he could get possession at any price. Only the Frenchman or the American who could buy a stock certificate for a few cents on the dollar and re-sell it for a higher price or trade it in for ten acres of land could make a profit, and this could not be done without the right contacts in Weatherford, for the directorate of the Franco-Texan

Land Company habitually evolved into a select circle of the president's friends and favorites. If the French tried to dictate, it was because they had the mistaken idea that since they owned the stock they could manage their business themselves. No doubt they tried, but in the end they were defeated because they were forced to rely on the president in America—the man on the ground—who could always give them token recognition and still find ways and means to deceive them.

I. W. Stephens, Judge Hood's law partner in the firm of Lanham, Hood, and Stephens, was a director of the Franco-Texan in 1886–1887, the year Judge Hood was elected president. It is possible that he was still on the board in 1887–1888, but he was not on it in 1889, and it is likely that he resigned. Judge Hood and Judge Stephens, in addition to being officers of the Franco-Texan, had, with Governor Lanham, handled countless cases for the company, and they probably knew more about its affairs than any other persons, except Levy and Du Bellet. Edwin Lanham, the grandson of Judge Stephens and Governor Lanham, perhaps better known as the author of *Double Jeopardy*, wrote a novel entitled *The Wind Blew West* many years ago. It was a fictional version of the dramatic days when Weatherford's hopes of becoming a great railway center faded away, with elements of the Franco-Texan story woven into the plot. He received *first hand* information from Judge Stephens, who wrote him this letter on January 30, 1934:

In reference to the Franco-Texan Land Company, you might be able to get the story, which is an interesting one, from the office of the Fidelity and Safe Deposit Company located either in New York or Philadelphia, as this was the channel through which the details were handled by the operators from General Fremont and John A. Scott [*sic*] down to the Franco-Texan Land Company charter. In brief, General Fremont promoted the sale of the bonds to the French peasants on the faith of the grant by the state of Texas of a large body of land to the old Memphis-El Paso and Pacific Railroad Company, the predecessor of the T & P Railway Company. These bonds were based on representations of the value of the land which were enormously exaggerated and the transaction was often referred to as the "Fremont Steal." The bondholders, being unable to collect their money, were finally driven to the necessity of taking these lands in lieu of bonds, the substitution being handled through the Fidelity and Safe Deposit Company above-mentioned. The Franco-Texan Land Company was chartered in pursuance of this arrangement to make a distribution of these lands amongst the bondholders, either by selling the land and dividing the money or by exchanging lands for their stock in the Franco-Texan Company in a manner provided in the charter.

These French peasants sustained further losses due to the fact that they were again deceived and misled when these lands became valuable by the representation that they were still of very small value, and thus holders of these shares in the Franco-Texan Land Company were induced to sell their shares of stock at a very low price, and to consummate the scheme, which was carried on through the cooperation of people in France and Weatherford, large quantities of shares were obtained and exchanged for land at a price which was much less than what the land was worth. One of the gentlemen who profited by this enterprise was a banker at Weatherford who was said to have picked up one or two hundred thousand dollars and was so elated over it that he chartered a special car and carried his friends through the Yellowstone Park and other places, all at his own expense.

This could have been one of five or six bankers in Weatherford but probably not S. H. Milliken or W. H. Eddleman because they both picked up much more than that.

Edwin Lanham says he received further information in conversations with his grandfather and that "in his memory" there were several persons living in Weatherford who had been lured to Texas by the Franco-Texan Land Company. According to the U.S. Census, there were still ten native-born Frenchmen living in Parker County in 1940.

CHAPTER 13

MRS. ALFRED HAMMOND OF WEATHERFORD

This brings us to Mrs. Alfred Hammond, née Amélie Grandjean, the last surviving member of the original French colony in Weatherford. Mrs. Hammond was not actually a colonist. She came to Texas on a visit in 1902, but she married Alfred Hammond de Voisins who came with Du Bellet on his return from France in 1882, just as Levy had done. After deciding to remain in Weatherford, De Voisins had shortened his name to Alfred Hammond to escape the never-ending question, "How do you spell De Voisins?"

Mrs. Hammond, now eighty-six years old, has a marvelous command of the English language, but through the years she has retained a French accent that is strong and undiluted. She did not know Du Bellet. He left before she arrived. Her husband, however, had lived in Du Bellet's home, and he told her much about his activities in Weatherford. Levy had also left when she arrived, but he returned several times and she herself made a visit to France in 1908, and she knew him well.

Du Bellet was extremely handsome, she said, with black hair and dark blue eyes; but he was unpopular with the Americans because of a tendency to be overbearing, and with the French as well because he took advantage of the newcomers and often "beat them out" of their land. Levy, though no less interested in acquiring land, was suave, affable, and ingratiating. He won over the people of Weatherford and was able to control the Franco-Texan Land Company for thirteen years, and although it was Paul Pecquet du Bellet and his son Henry who evicted John A. C. Gray and his New York friends from the company—a notable feat for which they deserved much credit—Mrs. Hammond's admiration for Levy was undimmed. She was glad that he defeated Du Bellet in the end; he was "perfectly charming," she said.

Though not aware of the specific occasion, Mrs. Hammond remembers her husband's telling her that Levy once said, "Alfred, I signed deeds for three days and nights, I couldn't lift my arm when I finished." It was of course when he was making out the deeds to the Inter-State Railway Construction Company in 1890. Another of Mrs. Hammond's very pertinent recollections was: "Alfred told me they burned three wagonloads of Franco-Texan records"—"Real wagons," she said, "not carts"—with Judge Hood's consent she thought. If so, perhaps it was for the honor of the city.

According to Mrs. Hammond, many of the French were disappointed in Texas. It was not the utopian country they had been led to expect. Most of those who came were farmers, and they found the land very different from France, a difference to which they had to become reconciled because they were too poor to return. A question raised more than once on arrival was "What is the matter with the trees?" Dust-laden and sparse, they bore no resemblance to France's verdant forests. Other Frenchmen, those who had money, came and stayed until the novelty wore off or until they had made more money.

One of the wealthy class was the Comte de Bresson, with whom Alfred Hammond was associated. On January 26, 1889, Dr. Lagrave wrote Alfred Hammond that the Comte Paul de Bresson was coming to Texas and the two of them, working together, could count on his assistance—not his advice alone, but also his resources. De Bresson imported and raised thoroughbred horses on a stock farm two miles southeast of Weatherford, said to be the finest in Texas. The De Bresson stables with their high-pitched roof, thick stone walls, and sturdy beams are still standing; although the present roof is not the original one. In the fall of 1889 De Bresson took his beautiful chestnut sorrel blooded mare Ribaude and his celebrated stallion Scotland Glory II to the Dallas Fair.[1] Mrs. Hammond said that Dr. Lagrave sent Alfred a thousand dollars, and he invested it in Scotland Glory II. In October of 1889 M. Haentjens and M. Talvende of Paris were visiting at Comte de Bresson's farm.[2] Another visitor from Paris was Hubert Vitalis, a distinguished writer who was making the American tour for pleasure and data. He spent a few days in Weatherford with his friend A. J. Lamarque.[3]

Mrs. Hammond knew Lamarque, also Marguerite and Charles Barbier, Du Bellet's groom and his wife, who moved to Mineral Wells and grew quite prosperous there. And Dr. P. G. Legrande, president of the Northwest Texas Medical Society, and Henry Clogenson, who became a photographer for the Dallas *Morning News.*

One story Mrs. Hammond told about Levy occurred in New York. He once recognized or thought he recognized a Frenchman from Weatherford working in Delmonico's as a waiter. The first time Levy saw him he said nothing, and neither did the waiter. On the second encounter Levy asked to see his hand, and, just as he expected, a slightly stubbed finger established his identity. When Levy evinced great surprise to find him working there, the answer was that he liked good food and clothing just as Levy did. Mrs. Hammond was not positive but she thought this was Joseph la Ravoire.

Levy had crossed the ocean thirty-nine times, she said. It would be forty when he returned to France for the last time. In 1910 Levy was living in the Chateau du Cauffry, near Cantigny, in the Department of Oise. He died in Paris after the first World War.

Mrs. Hammond was very fond of Levy's son Pierre and had many pictures of him as a child and adult. Born in Weatherford in 1886, Pierre had been sent to France at the age of eleven to be educated. He returned to Texas in 1905, worked in the Western National Bank in Fort Worth, and then became manager of the Interstate Theaters in

[1] Weatherford *Constitution*, October 16, 1889.

[2] *Ibid.*

[3] *Ibid.*, February 19, 1890.

Fort Worth and Arlington. Pierre Levy in fact provided Fort Worth with entertainment from the Nickelodeon era to the age of Technicolor. He was the first to introduce Charlie Chaplin on a screen in Fort Worth and pioneered by providing sound effects, live musicians, and raising admission to a dime. Besides Charlie Chaplin, Levy's favorite film stars were Geraldine Farrar and Carol Lombard. Theirs were the only two photographs on the walls of his office above the Palace Theater. Levy ran the Hippodrome for ten years, bought the old Strand, and then the Palace. He sold all three to the U.S. Amusement Company in 1919 and signed an agreement that he would not go into any phase of show business for five years. He spent two of these years in France. Returning to Fort Worth he went into the oil business, and in 1934 he went back to his first love, show business. That year he became manager of the seven Interstate Theaters of Fort Worth and later the two in Arlington. During that time he brought to Fort Worth not only the finest movies but excellent roadshows starring Katharine Cornell, Helen Hayes, Alfred Lunt, and Lynn Fontanne. Pierre Levy died of a heart ailment in 1939, at the age of fifty-three.

Mrs. Hammond said that in 1902 Paul Pecquet du Bellet was living in a fine house just off the Champs Élysées in Paris. In 1907 Kate Louise Noémie du Bellet[4] published a book entitled *Some Prominent Virginia Families*, and in 1918, Henry P. du Bellet translated for publication in the United States René Louis Jules Radiguet's *The Making of a Modern Army and Its Operations in the Field*. But by 1920 apparently all the Du Bellets in Paris had died. According to district court records of Parker County, Howard Rhea, in 1919, recovered from the unknown heirs of C. H. Milliken, the Comte de Constantin, and Misses Noémi and Elfrida du Bellet certain lots in the Millsap Addition, and in 1919 and 1920 B. W. Akard and others recovered from H. P. du Bellet and his wife Clara P. du Bellet, both deceased, and their unknown heirs certain real estate in Weatherford. In an earlier suit, in 1905, the Weatherford Cotton Mills had recovered valuable property on which they had been paying taxes and which they were

[4] Or Louise Pecquet du Bellet. She was the granddaughter of Henry W. Moncure of Richmond and the great granddaughter of Colonel John Ambler of Jamestown.

occupying in peaceable and adverse possession, the Comte de Constantin having died in 1903, leaving children and heirs but their residence unknown. H. P. du Bellet as agent had sold this land in 1899, 1900, 1901, and 1902, and the money had been received as proved by drafts payable to him and showing his endorsement.[5] So the cotton factory projected by Du Bellet in 1881, like the waterworks and the street railway, became a reality, but only after his departure.

Mrs. Hammond recalled stories of Frenchman's Lane on the road to Jacksboro. There was a long stretch of seepy ground often impassable even in dry weather, and as a French farmer always had a team of heavy draft horses ready to assist travelers, the rumor went around that he was keeping the road well watered.

Alfred Hammond remained in Weatherford until his death in 1920. He had not always had an easy time in Texas, and Nobel had sent him five or six hundred dollars on several occasions, in addition to a $10,000 legacy. Today, Mrs. Hammond can quote beautiful passages from Nobel's letters to her husband. These letters were in her possession until 1945 when they disappeared under rather strange circumstances. In 1948 she sold her farm and her Limoges china to C. Wyatt Hedrick, a noted architect and engineer of Houston, Texas. The five-room farmhouse built by her husband may be seen today—of French style, with a porch around three quarters of the house, decorated with wooden grill work and carved railings, a high pitched roof with wide eaves, a stained glass door, carved interior cabinets, and the kitchen in a room unattached to the house.

The Joussomes lived on the farm across the road from the Hammonds. They succeeded in growing luscious grapes but found no ready market for them. The vineyard was later wiped out by drouth. Louis Joussome, seventy years old in 1960, recalled that he learned English from the girls who attended the Seminary on top of the hill out on South Main. He was only thirteen months old when he arrived in Weatherford in 1889. The Otterbeins, who lived in town, were quite

[5] Weatherford Mills *v.* Unknown Heirs of Comte de Constantin, Cause 4017, District Court Records of Parker County; B. W. Akard *v.* Unknown Heirs of H. P. du Bellet, Cause 5550, *ibid.*; C. A. Walker *v.* J. C. Hurd, Cause 6140, *ibid.*

well off financially. Dr. Otterbein hunted birds with his dogs, and Mrs. Otterbein, a sculptress and artist, had painted the murals in the large hall of their house. In Belgium Dr. Otterbein had been the editor of a newspaper by the name of *L'Abeille*, but he had to seek political refuge in Texas when he voiced the opinion that the French-speaking population of Belgium should be annexed to France. The Laudes, Armand and Emile, were rock masons and contractors from the Ohio valley. They built courthouses in Palo Pinto, Kaufman, and Parker counties and the First Methodist Church in Weatherford.

Mrs. Hammond has been featured as "Woman of the Week" in the Weatherford *Sun* and is a thoroughly delightful person. She could not say how many Frenchmen had come to Weatherford though she was certain that the Franco-Texan Land Company stimulated interest in Texas and caused many to come either to visit or to stay.

CHAPTER 14

THE FRENCH IN TEXAS

The number of French immigrants in Texas reached 2,730 in 1890. This number included foreign-born Frenchmen with both parents French or one parent French and the other a different nationality. At the same time there were 1,682 native-born with the same characteristics, 2,318 with French fathers and native mothers or French mothers and native fathers, and 1,990 with French fathers or French mothers, the nativity of one or the other not known, making a total of 8,720 persons with one or both parents French. The Census of 1890 also enumerated 293 French Canadians, the first time for an entry under this heading. The increase in northwest Texas was evident from the newspapers of the previous ten-year span, especially in Weatherford and Abilene where names like Jacquette, Chevalier, Dubois, Manger, Lallier, Brevard, Montford, Giraud, Anceline, Lamont and Huville appeared often in the daily news. In Parker County the French colony numbered 77 including 14 French Canadians. According to state totals, the number of foreign-born Frenchmen in Texas in 1860 was 1,883; in 1870, 2,232; in 1880, 2,653; in 1890, 2,730; in 1900, 2,025; in 1910, 1,811; in 1920, 2,544 (including 609 Alsace-Lorrainers); and in 1930, 1,803. And on that last date the "French white stock" in Texas numbered 10,185 (including both foreign- and native-born with one or both parents French).

The French population of Texas was preponderantly urban and very small when compared to the many Germans, Austrians, English, Irish, and Scotch who came to Texas in the same periods (in 1890, for instance, there were 44,843 foreign-born Germans in Texas). There were reasons for the consistently small number of French immigrants. France was a republic, the French loved her soil, revered her memories, and gloried in her past and present greatness; in general, they did not wish to leave their native country. The conditions that did cause them to leave were political adversity, resulting in voluntary exile more often than not, and times of undue stress and hardship such as the German attempt to nationalize ceded territory after the Franco-Prussian War in 1870, when 26,000 Alsace-Lorrainers left for America,[1] or the terrible destruction of home and field in World War I, which caused the largest increase in French immigration to the United States. In the 1840's it was a combination of the failure of the liberal revolution and the generous colonization laws of the Texas Republic which brought the first 647 French immigrants to Texas.

In 1885, when there was a general lag in all immigration to Texas and so few Frenchmen that a statistical report listed them under "others," the Dallas *Herald* regretted their conspicuous absence since it was known that the French were thrifty and industrious, a class much to be desired in the development of Texas. This immigration lag lasted throughout the 1880's. Texas was not receiving a representative share of immigrants from foreign countries or other states, at a time when she had urgent need of a larger population. The state did nothing, supposedly because there was a provision in the Texas Constitution prohibiting the appropriation of public money for the maintenance of a bureau of immigration for any purpose related to bringing immigrants into the state. To meet the emergency, towns, cities, and counties formed immigration societies to advertise their respective localities, and

[1] In the general exodus through the years the number of emigrants from Alsace-Lorraine totalled at least 360,000, most of them going to western France. The highest number claimed is 645,000 (Ruth Putnam, *Alsace and Lorraine: From Caesar to Kaiser, 58 B.C.–1871 A.D.*, p. 191).

the movement had to be financed locally. It helped, but in the field of immigration and settlement the railroads played the most important part. In 1880 the Southwestern Immigration Company was chartered, with W. W. Lang of Falls County as president; James H. Raymond of Austin as secretary; and H. M. Hoxie of the International and Great Northern, George Noble of the Texas and Pacific, and W. W. Lacy as the executive committee.[2] Colonel Lang in 1881 published and distributed a 255-page booklet entitled *Texas: Her Resources, and Her Capabilities*, and he and W. L. Kingsbury, the agent of the Sunset Route, made trips to England and Germany as early as 1878 to recruit immigrants. Colonel Lang resided for four years in Europe (1881–1885) with headquarters at Hamburg, and during that time entire German villages emigrated to the United States.

The Texas and Pacific also had its own land department. J. W. Throckmorton, the first T & P land commissioner, resigned within a year and was succeeded by his assistant, W. H. Abrams.[3] Among its special agents were E. H. Sabin, the colonizer of Odessa, and John E. Ennis, who sold 12,000 acres to the notorious Earl of Aylesford at Big Spring. Another was J. R. Mulkey, a talented artist and writer, also engaged by the *Daily Graphic* of New York and the Louisville *Courier Journal* to sketch and describe a number of western states. He arrived in Austin in January, 1885, and in his special car near the ticket office, he gave a reporter the following information:

> I have been in Texas four months and have illustrated El Paso, Colorado City, and Abilene. I also took nine different views of a round-up that I witnessed near Colorado City. Besides this work I am also interested in immigration, being assistant secretary of the Southern Immigration Association and have within a little while secured four colonies for Texas—one of them from France.

[2] On July 6, 1880 (Galveston *Daily News*, July 29, 1880).

[3] Abrams was a graduate of Monmouth College, Illinois, and had been connected with the land department of the Union Pacific from 1866 to 1873. After succeeding Throckmorton he served as land commissioner for the Texas and Pacific until its lands were alienated. He then became president of the Texas and Pacific Land Improvement Company and held that position until his death in April, 1926 (Samuel B. McAlister, "The Building of the Texas and Pacific Railway" [M.A. thesis]).

An immigrant could buy a ticket at Hamburg that will land him at Castle Garden for $14 and after reaching New York the trip across the continent can be made for $30. The Gould system will meet the cheap transportation by a similar reduction in rates and carry immigrants destined for Texas at a lower cost than ever before. The country along the line of the Texas and Pacific has a wonderful future before it. The colony from France that was mentioned a minute ago will devote its attention to the cultivation of fruits.

Can fruits be successfuly grown there. Yes, undoubtedly west of Fort Worth, all the way to El Paso they can grow English walnuts, pears, peaches, German prunes, apricots, nectarines, and many other fruits and garden vegetables. In this lies the future of all that region, not in raising of cereals and cotton.[4]

A railroad could not pay dividends on through trade and travel alone. It had to have local patronage. Therefore, the controlling motive of the land department was to secure immigrants, but with an empire of land to sell, the aim was twofold. Besides the usual practice of calling attention to the advantages of the country through which the railway line would run, the Texas and Pacific had immigrant houses at Fort Worth and Baird and furnished shelter, fuel, water, and a stove free of charge while prospective settlers looked over the country. Although concentrating its efforts on securing Germans and Swedes, as they were considered splendid industrious farmers, inured to work and used to the plow, the Texas and Pacific established a Portuguese colony on an experimental farm near Clyde in 1882. The Portuguese colony was a great success for about three years, having supplied Abilene and the surrounding area with fruits and vegetables each summer and having made fine wheat crops each spring, averaging eighteen bushels to the acre in 1884.[5] Then, stricken by the terrible drought of 1885–1886, the Portuguese colonists gave up and returned to California where they had been recruited.

Since the Texas and Pacific established and owned the town of Pecos, it must have been responsible for another instance of French immigration to Texas reported in November, 1891. A party of forty-

[4] Austin Daily *Statesman*, January 22, 1885.

[5] Galveston *Daily News*, July 4, and June 7, 1884.

seven winemakers, direct from the winemaking district of southern France, arrived in Galveston on the S.S. *Concho* on November 1 and left for Pecos. This was the first of a colony of five hundred who proposed to locate in West Texas for the purpose of cultivating grapes for winemaking. Recognizing the fact that the El Paso grape was the equal if not the superior of the French product and being informed that West Texas soil was adaptable for grape growing, they had decided to come to a new country and help develop a practically unknown industry. The winemakers were a thrifty and intelligent group of people, and it was expected they would aid materially in making West Texas a famous wine-producing country. Captain Bolger of the *Concho* said they were the most respectable lot of immigrants he had brought to Galveston in many months, and he thought the people of Texas should induce more of them to come here to help settle the grape-growing counties. A number of others of the same class were to arrive on the next steamer from New York.[6]

One might wonder what future awaited the French winemakers in Pecos and what they thought on entering the alkali desert once described as "not fit for flesh, fish, or fowl, worse than the dry Tortugas a regular Gehenna, more lonesome than the Arctic Circle, hotter than the equator, and dryer than a powder horn." Deep artesian wells dug by the Texas and Pacific in 1881 eventually made Reeves County one of the largest grape-producing counties in the state, and grape culture became an important industry in Texas, due primarily to the arrival of thousands of European immigrants who transplanted their native custom of vine growing in Texas. Thomas V. Munson of Illinois and of French descent was the father of the grape-growing industry in Texas. He and his brother William Benjamin Munson had moved to Denison, Texas, to enter the real estate business. Thomas Munson, however, devoted his time to improving the American grape. He began by hybridizing and created some three hundred new varieties, among which were the Carmen, Extra, and Beacon. He was also responsible for shipping grapevine cuttings from Texas to France and saving the French vineyards from destruction by the grape *phylloxera.*

[6] Fort Worth *Gazete,* November 9, 1891.

Among his many awards and honors, Munson received the French Legion of Honor, which was conferred on him in Denison by a special delegation from the Republic of France.

In connection with the subject of French immigration to Texas another project should be mentioned, one faintly akin to the Franco-Texan Land Company or at least born of the same parent, the railroads. The promoter was a man who perhaps got the idea of bringing Frenchmen to Texas through his former association with the Memphis, El Paso, and Pacific Railroad and as a contractor with the Texas and Pacific. He was Morgan Jones, president of the Fort Worth and Denver and the Wichita Valley railroads. In 1881 John Adamson, the immigration agent for the Fort Worth and Denver, brought Frenchmen from the Ohio and Mississippi valleys, but it was in 1890, as president of the Wichita Valley that Morgan Jones made an effort to get French immigrants from outside the United States in preference to all others. He appointed M. C. Machet, a native of France, as the company's immigration agent. Machet's plan was to go among his people in Canada, France, and Belgium, and tell them of the attractions of Texas and the opportunities to be offered. The Frenchmen he would bring would be those who considered forty acres a good sized farm and would till every acre of it. Only those who had enough money to support themselves for some time would be asked to come. Machet inspected a tract of 150,000 acres in Archer County, near Dundee, and found the land to be such that he could recommend it to his countrymen. The sugar beet grew well in that section, and the French thoroughly understood beet culture. Mr. Davis, the ticket agent, and Mr. Machet were busy for several days preparing a conservative circular. Thousands of Frenchmen would be glad to come to Texas if they understood what they could do here. When the first colony was located and the members found that it all was just as represented, there would be no trouble in bringing many others over to Texas. The Fort Worth Chamber of Commerce also wanted to locate some of these frugal and industrious people within the confines of Tarrant county.[7]

Morgan Jones brought Frenchmen to the Wichita Valley and also

[7] *Ibid.*, June 3, 1891.

to the Panhandle, to Henrietta, Clarendon, Clairemont, Bellevue, Dumont, Dumas, Seymour, Lefors, Arden, Benjamin, Harrold, and Benvanu (Bienvenu). No numerical reports from Jones have been found to indicate to what extent he carried out his project, but after 1890 when the French Canadians were listed for the first time, the increase was noticeable up to 1930 when there were 452 foreign-born and 1,345 native born French Canadians in Texas, making a total of 1,797 persons of French Canadian extraction.

If the prodigious work of the railroads in recruiting immigrants was one atonement for their monumental sins, long since a subject of public discussion and long since forgiven, then the same might be said of the Franco-Texan Land Company. In spite of the unpleasant ramifications, the legal injustices, the fraudulent practices, and heartbreaking stories, it brought to Texas hundreds of French immigrants who contributed their industry and thrift, their skill and genius for perfection to the development of the frontier. But the analogy ends there because the Franco-Texan was never publicized. While much has been said about lesser enterprises, never has one with such an unsavory reputation received so little attention. Perhaps in its early stages the focus was on the national scandal which produced it, and during its later stages those involved, having no desire to divulge its secrets, possessed the means of keeping them well covered or confined to their own inner circle. However, someone usually ferrets out such stories, and in this case it was Dr. R. C. Crane who, having first encountered the Franco-Texan Land Company in his work as a lawyer at Roby and Sweetwater, began his research in the court records of Nolan and Parker counties. Dr. Crane made the Franco-Texan Land Company the subject of an address to the West Texas Historical Association in Wichita Falls, in which he presented a synopsis of the background of the company and the general facts of its dissolution in 1896, with comments on its affairs in Sweetwater: the building of the courthouse, the establishment of the first gypsum plant in Texas, and the shooting of Chifflet and Guillot. His address was published in the form of a brief sketch in the *West Texas Historical Association Yearbook* in 1949, and since that time no further investigation appears to have been made of the company's long life in Texas.

The Texas and Pacific, though never failing to condemn Frémont and the Memphis, El Paso, and Pacific, had little or nothing to say about the operations of the Franco-Texan Land Company. The following simple statement, accompanying a frank résumé of the French bond scandal, was made by William J. Powell, a Texas and Pacific surveyor and land man in 1944: "The affairs of the Franco-Texan Land Company were badly managed and the holders of the bonds who had surrendered them in exchange for land realized little benefit from the management and sale of the lands by the company." He might have added that the Memphis, El Paso, and Pacific, empty bubble that it was for the French bondholders, the future stockholders of the Franco-Texan Land Company, furnished the Texas and Pacific with a charter, franchise, land reservation, and right of way across Texas, and more assets than have ever been admitted, that it was the French who paid the first installment on the building of the Texas and Pacific railroad, and that at this point the national government erred by not requiring a guarantee of the French interests written into the Texas and Pacific bill. If this had been done, Gray's ingenious plan would never have been sanctioned as a workable or even legal solution. The French bondholders would have received either money or railroad bonds which they preferred, and there would have been no Franco-Texan Land Company. But as it was, Scott's failure to give the French due satisfaction and his and Gray's continued manipulation of the Memphis, El Paso, and Pacific bond account were instrumental in bringing about Scott's loss of the subsidy, his ultimate defeat by Huntington, and the acquisition of his railroad by Jay Gould. It was fortunate for Texas that Gould had the resources to construct the final six hundred mile segment of the Texas and Pacific to El Paso without government aid, even though Huntington had said he would build it if he had to. In 1881 Gould also completed the International and Great Northern to Laredo, where he connected with the Mexican National to Mexico City. And only recently the nineteenth century cry of "On to Topolobampo" has been fulfilled by the completion of the Chihuahua-Pacifico Railway which departs from Ojinaga, opposite Presidio, Texas, and connects with the Mexican Central at Chihuahua and the Mexican Pacific at Los Mochis, with a short branch line to the port of Topolobampo. This road, originally the dream of Arthur E. Stilwell and dedicated officials of the Kansas City, Mexico, and Orient (sold to the Santa Fe in 1928), was completed in November, 1961, after being in process for nearly a century. The final link, through the bottomless canyons and high sierras of Chihuahua and Sinaloa, was the work of French engineers who used concrete ties in its construction.

Political conditions between 1850 and 1875 almost made a myth of the historic friendship of France and the United States. French politicians were fearful lest the young western giant upset the European balance of power. Americans in general disliked "Emperor" Napoleon, and though he never recognized the Confederacy, the United States government was displeased with his professed sentiment for the Southern cause, and with the French occupation of Mexico as well. French public opinion was divided during the Civil War, but Southern leaders were certain France would send the desperately needed aid. When it did not come, the South was alienated too. The French in turn were deeply hurt by the Administration's strongly pro-German sympathy in the Franco-Prussian war, though they admired and respected E. B. Washburne who never left his post and did everything in his power to relieve the suffering in Paris. Gradually, with the advent of the Third Republic and with Grant out of the White House, the strain was eased somewhat. President Hayes sent President Jules Grevy and the Marquis de Lafayette[8] and his family signed invitations to the Yorktown Centenary, to begin on October 6, 1881, one hundred years from the day that the allied forces of France and America occupied the first parallel of the breastworks of the Yorktown fortifications, with the French fleet lying off the harbor. Lafayette died in March, shortly after receiving the invitation, and the following October General Boulanger represented France at the elaborate celebrations planned with the assistance of Leon Chotteau. On July 4, 1884, when the citizens of France presented Bartholdi's Statue of Liberty to commemorate the 100th year of United States independence, neither president attended the unveiling which was held in Gauthier's workshop with little fan-

[8] Oscar Thomas Gilbert Motier de Lafayette, son of Washington Georges Motier, Marquis de Lafayette, son of Marie Joseph Paul Yves Roch Gilbert du Motier, Marquis de Lafayette, of Revolutionary War fame.

fare. Prime Minister Ferry, who was ill, sent his message to be read by a delegate. De Lesseps spoke for the Franco-American Committee and Ambassador Morton for the United States. The statue, supposed to be shipped in July, did not arrive in New York until June of 1885. It could not then be installed because the United States had not collected enough money to complete the pedestal. A campaign launched by Joseph Pulitzer of the New York *World* finally produced $101,091, 80 per cent of which was contributed in amounts of less than $1.00. The dedication took place on Bedloe Island on October 28, 1886, and President Cleveland, in the presence of French and American notables of the day, expressed the proper gratitude to his country's oldest friend.

Whether or not the Franco-Texan affair was a manifestation of severely strained Franco-American relations or merely a frayed end of the greatest era of corruption and lawlessness the United States has ever known, it added a substantial and not unsalutary episode to the history of "the French in Texas,"—to La Salle, St. Denis, Champs d'Asile, Jean Lafitte, Castroville, La Réunion, Icaria, and Alfonse de Saligny and the pigs.

In Weatherford today the little Texas and Pacific station looks forlorn, and all the French except Mrs. Hammond have moved away. The Kuteman Building built by Allard d'Heur burned not long ago, but if you look you will find the footsteps of the French—Du Bellet Street, the De Bresson stables, the Methodist Church, and many houses in town and county, bearing the unmistakable traces of French architectural style. If not immediately aware of these signposts in Weatherford, you will undoubtedly sense the pervasion of some indefinable charm, characteristic of few other nineteenth-century Texas towns.

BIBLIOGRAPHY

MANUSCRIPTS

Akard, B. W., *v.* Unknown Heirs of H. P. du Bellet, Cause 5550. District Court Records of Parker County, Weatherford, Texas.

Allen, James H., *v.* The Franco-Texan Land Company, Equity No. 181, Vol. 3, U.S. Circuit Court, Dallas, Texas. Federal Records Center, Fort Worth, Texas.

Baker, Jonathan H. "Diary of J. H. Baker." Texas State Archives, Austin, Texas.

Blind Asylum Land Files. General Land Office, Austin, Texas.

Bousselet, A. R., *v.* The Franco-Texan Land Company, Cause 2091. District Court Records of Parker County, Weatherford, Texas.

Bradford, Louise. "A History of Nolan County." M.A. thesis, The University of Texas, 1934.

Carbinnier *v.* The Franco-Texan Land Company, Cause 2215. District Court Records of Parker County, Weatherford, Texas.

Chalimbord, Benoit, *v.* The Franco-Texan Land Company, Cause 2215. District Court Records of Parker County, Weatherford, Texas.

Civil Minutes, Vols. 2–12. District Court Records of Parker County, Weatherford, Texas.

Colpart, Jean Baptiste, *v.* The Franco-Texan Land Company, Cause 1670. District Court Records of Parker County, Weatherford, Texas.

Colpart, Jean J., *v.* The Franco-Texan Land Company, Cause 1669. District Court Records of Parker County, Weatherford, Texas.

Confederate Army Service Records. Texas State Archives, Austin, Texas.

Corporation Charters. Charter Files in Office of Secretary of State, Austin, Texas.

Crane, R. C. Crane Papers. Hardin-Simmons University Library, Abilene, Texas.

De Fresnay, Victor, *v.* The Franco-Texan Land Company, Causes 1896 and 1966. District Court Records of Parker County, Weatherford, Texas.

De Lort, L. T., *v.* The Franco-Texan Land Company, Cause 2165. District Court Records of Parker County, Weatherford, Texas.

Donation Land Files. General Land Office, Austin, Texas.

Du Bellet, Henry P., to Alfred Hammond (de Voisins), August 12, 1883. Letter in possession of Mrs. Alfred Hammond of Weatherford, Texas.

Du Bellet, Paul Pecquet. SEE Pecquet du Bellet, Paul.

Eddleman, W. H., *et al. v.* The Franco-Texan Land Company, Cause 3305. Court Records of Parker County, Weatherford, Texas.

Epperson, Benjamin H. Epperson Papers. The University of Texas Archives, Austin, Texas.

Fayolle, Pierre, *et al. v.* the Texas and Pacific Railway Company, Equity No. 6556, Supreme Court of District of Columbia, November 12, 1883. National Archives, Washington, D.C.

Fidelity and Safe Deposit Company of Maryland (Philadelphia Office), to Virginia H. Taylor, November 14, 1963.

Franco-Texan Land Company *v.* Marie Chaptive *et al.*, No. 5306. Texas Supreme Court Files, Austin, Texas.

Franco-Texan Land Company *v.* A. R. Bousselet, No. 5902. Texas Supreme Court Files, Austin, Texas.

Franco-Texan Stock Certificate No. 28783. Emmanuel Marie Philibert de Langier de Beaurecueil, September 1, 1876. The University of Texas Archives, Austin, Texas.

Hittson, J. J., *et al. v.* The Franco-Texan Land Company, Cause 2081. District Court Records of Parker County, Weatherford, Texas.

Jardin, L. E., *v.* The Franco-Texan Land Company, Cause 2166. District Court Records of Parker County, Weatherford, Texas.

Landers, Emmett. "A Short History of Taylor County." M.A. thesis, Hardin-Simmons University, 1929.

Lanham, Edwin, to Virginia H. Taylor, April 2, 1963.

Linol, A., to Alfred Hammond de Voisins, October 1, 1910. Letter in possession of Mrs. Alfred Hammond of Weatherford, Texas.

McAlister, Samuel B. "The Building of the Texas and Pacific Railway." M.A. thesis, The University of Texas, 1926.

Milliken, S. H., *v.* The Societe Fonciere et Agricole des Etats Unis, Cause 2396. District Court Records of Parker County, Weatherford, Texas.

Miscellaneous Deeds. General Land Office, Austin, Texas.

Miscellaneous Scrip. General Land Office, Austin, Texas.

Muir, Andrew Forest. "The Thirty-second Parallel Pacific Railroad in Texas to 1872." Ph.D. dissertation, The University of Texas, 1949.

Parker County. Deed Records. Weatherford, Texas.

———. District Court Records. Weatherford, Texas.

———. Marriage Records, 1874–1886. Weatherford, Texas.

Pease, Elisha M. Pease Papers. Austin Public Library, Austin, Texas.

Pecquet du Bellet, Paul, to General P. G. T. Beauregard. Ten letters, April 3, 1878–April 4, 1879. Spanish Archives of the General Land Office, Austin, Texas.

Powell, William J. "The Texas and Pacific Railroad and Its Land Grant." Typescript article in the private collection of G. D. Huddleston, Houston, Texas.

Railroad Contracts. General Land Office, Austin, Texas.

Railroad Scrip Files. General Land Office, Austin, Texas.

Ranger, Lewis, *v.* The Franco-Texan Land Company, Cause 2083. District Court Records of Parker County, Weatherford, Texas.

Red River County. Marriage Records, 1845–1877. Clarksville, Texas.

Robison, J. T. Report of Commissioner of the General Land Office, October 19, 1916, attached to Railroad Scrip Index. General Land Office, Austin, Texas.

School Land Files. General Land Office, Austin, Texas.

Sketch Files. General Land Office, Austin, Texas.

Spaight, Ashley W. Spaight Papers. The University of Texas Archives, Austin, Texas.

Studebaker *v.* Milliken and Du Bellet, Cause 1792. District Court Records of Parker County, Weatherford, Texas.

Swink, G. W. Report to Randolph Lawrence, Secretary of State Land Board, October 30, 1885. General Land Office, Austin, Texas.

Taylor County. Deed Records. Abilene, Texas.

Tuck, S. P., *v.* The Franco-Texan Land Company, Cause 2162. District Court Records of Parker County, Weatherford, Texas.

United States Bureau of the Census: Tenth Census, 1880. "Free Inhabitants of Callahan, Dallas, Parker, and Shackelford counties." Microfilm, Texas State Archives, Austin, Texas.

Wadsworth, T. M., *v.* F. Applegate *et al.,* Cause 3821. District Court Records of Parker County, Weatherford, Texas.

Walker, C. A., *v.* J. C. Hurd, Cause 6140. District Court Records of Parker County, Weatherford, Texas.

Weatherford Mills *v.* Unknown Heirs of Comte de Constantin, Cause 4017. District Court Records of Parker County, Weatherford, Texas.

BOOKS AND PAMPHLETS

Abstract of All Original Texas Land Titles; Comprising Grants and Locations to August 31, 1941. 8 volumes. Austin: Bascom Giles, 1942.

Annual Report of the Board of Directors of the Texas and Pacific Railway Company, August 11, 1874, with *Supplemental Report, March 29, 1875.* Philadelphia: Review Printing House, 1875.

Annual Report of the Board of Directors of the Texas and Pacific Railway Company, August 10, 1875. Philadelphia: McLaughlin Brothers, 1875.

Annual Report of the Board of Directors of the Texas and Pacific Railway Company, August 8, 1876. Philadelphia: McLaughlin Brothers, 1876.

Annual Report of the Board of Directors of the Texas and Pacific Railway Company, August 14, 1877. Philadelphia: Review Publishing and Printing Company, 1877.

Annual Report of the Board of Directors of the Texas and Pacific Railway Company, August 13, 1878. Philadelphia: Review Printing House, 1878.

Annual Report of the Board of Directors of the Texas and Pacific Railway Company, August 12, 1879. Philadelphia: Review Printing House, 1879.

Annual Report of the Board of Directors of the Texas and Pacific Railway Company, August 10, 1880. Philadelphia: Review Printing House, 1880.

Annual Report of the President of the Texas and Pacific Railway Company, May 20, 1872. New York: George W. Wheat & Company, 1872.

Biographical Encyclopedia of Texas. New York: Southern Publishing Company, 1880.

Blumenthal, Henry. *A Reappraisal of Franco-American Relations, 1830–1871.* Chapel Hill: University of North Carolina Press, 1959.

Bond, Frank Stuart. *Address to J. R. West, Chairman of United States Senate Committee on Railroads, March 10, 1876.* Philadelphia: n.p., 1876.

———. *Argument and Statements of Frank S. Bond, Vice-President of the Texas and Pacific Railway, before the Committee on the Pacific Railroad, House of Representatives, January 29, 1878.* Washington, D.C.: n.p., 1878?.

———. *Argument and Statements of Frank S. Bond, Vice-President of the Texas and Pacific Railway Company, before the Committee on Pacific Railroads of the U.S. Senate, February 15, 1878.* Washington, D.C., n.p., 1878.

———. *Argument before Senate Committee on Railroads, February 1, 1876.* Washington, D.C.: n.p., 1876.

———. *Statement and Argument before Committee on Pacific Railroad, House of Representatives, January 19, 1876.* Washington, D.C.: n.p., 1876.

———. *Statement and Argument Made before the Committee on the Judiciary of the House of Representatives, 44th Congress, 1st Session.* Washington, D.C.: n.p., 1876.

———. *Supplemental Argument and Statements Filed with the Committee on the Pacific Railroad, House of Representatives, February 1, 1878.* Washington, D.C.: n.p., 1878.

———. *Who Shall Build a Southern Transcontinental Railway on the 32nd Parallel of Latitude: Reply of Frank S. Bond to Collis P. Huntington, January 3, 1876.* Philadelphia: Review Printing House, 1876.

Broaddus, J. Morgan. *The Legal Heritage of El Paso*, ed. Samuel D. Myres. El Paso: Texas Western College Press, 1963.

Brown, John Calvin. *Argument before the Judiciary Committee of the House of Representatives in Regard to the Title of the Texas and Pacific Railway Company, to Its Line between Fort Worth and El Paso, April 17, 1878.* Washington, D.C.: T. McGill, Printer, 1878.

———. *Argument before the Senate Committee on Pacific Railroads, February 22, 1878, in Behalf of the Texas and Pacific Company.* Washington, D.C.: Thomas McGill & Company, 1878.

———. *Argument before the Senate Committee on Railroads, February 7, 1876.* Washington, D.C.: n.p., 1876.

———. *Statement and Argument before the Committee on the Pacific Railroad, House of Representatives, January 19, 1876.* Washington, D.C.: n.p., 1876.

———. *Reply of John C. Brown to Mr. Campbell before the Judiciary Committee of the House of Representatives in Regard to the Title to the Texas and Pacific Railway Company, to Its Line between Ft. Worth and El Paso,* Filed by leave of Committee, April 29, 1878. Washington, D.C.: n.p.

Campbell, Douglas. *The Title of the Texas and Pacific Railroad Company to the Property of the Memphis, El Paso and Pacific Railroad Company: Opening Argument of Douglas Campbell, Esq., before the Judiciary Committee of the House of Representatives, April 11, 1878.* Washington, D.C.: Thomas McGill & Company, 1878.

———. *Closing Argument of Douglas Campbell, Esq., in Reply to Gover-*

nor John C. Brown, J. A. Davenport, and Major James Turner before the Judiciary Committee of the House of Representatives, in regard to the Title of the Texas and Pacific Railway Company to the Property of the Memphis, El Paso and Pacific Railroad Company, April 24, 1878. Washington, D.C.: Thomas McGill & Company, 1878.

Clark, Ira G. *Then Came the Railroads.* Norman: University of Oklahoma Press, 1958.

Clayton *et al. v.* Franco-Texan Land Company. *South Western Reporter,* Vol. 39, p. 645. St. Paul: West Publishing Company, 1897.

Cole, C. H. *Description of Northwestern Texas.* Pamphlet, n.p., 1877.

Congressional Globe, June 22–July 15, 1870.

Connor, Seymour V. (ed.). *A Biggers Chronicle.* Lubbock: Texas Technological College, 1961.

Convention Journal, 1866. Austin: Southern Intelligencer Office, 1866.

Cox, James. *Historical and Biographical Record of the Cattle Industry and the Cattlemen of Texas and Adjacent Territory.* St. Louis: Woodward and Tiernan Printing Company, 1895.

Dallas City Directory, 1891–1892; 1893–1894; 1894–1895. Galveston: Morrison & Fourmy, 1891–1895.

Davenport, J. Alfred. *The Title of the Texas and Pacific Railroad to Property Late of the Memphis, El Paso and Pacific Railroad Company; Notes of Argument of J. Alfred Davenport before the Judiciary Committee of the House of Representatives, April 17, 1878.* New York: B. H. Tyrrel, 1878.

Davis, E. J. *v.* John A. C. Gray. *Cases Argued and Adjudged in the Supreme Court of the United States; Reported by John William Wallace,* Vol. 16, p. 203. Washington, D.C.: W. H. and O. H. Morrison, 1873.

Dictionary of American Biography. 20 vols. New York: Charles Scribner's Sons, 1928–1936.

Drago, Harry Sinclair. *Red River Valley.* New York: Clarkson N. Potter, Inc., 1962.

Eyre, Alice. *The Famous Fremonts and Their America.* Revised Edition. Boston: The Christopher Publishing House, 1961.

Fayolle *et al. v.* The Texas and Pacific Railroad Company. *United States Reports,* Vol. 124, p. 519. New York and Albany: Banks and Brothers, 1888.

Fitzhugh *et al. v.* Franco-Texan Land Company. *Texas Reports,* Vol. 81, p. 306. Galveston: Clarke and Courts, 1892. *South Western Reporter,* Vol. 16, p. 1078. St. Paul: West Publishing Company, 1891.

Forbes *et al. v.* The Memphis, El Paso, and Pacific Company *et al.* Circuit Court, Western District of Texas, May, 1872. *Federal Cases Comprising Circuit and District Courts of the United States,* No. 4926, Vol. 9, p. 408. St. Paul: West Publishing Company, 1895. Also reported by the Honorable William B. Woods, Circuit Judge, 2 *Woods* 323.

Ford, Gus L. (ed.). *Texas Cattle Brands.* 2nd Edition. Dallas: Texas Centennial Exposition, 1958.

Franco-Texan Land Company: Procès-Verbal de L'Assemblée Générale des Actionnaires, December 13, 1892. Paris: Imprimerie de la Presse, Ch. Simonot [1893].

Franco-Texan Land Company Charter and By-Laws (in English and French). Paris: T. Symonds, 1876.

Franco-Texan Land Company *v.* A. R. Bousselet. *Texas Reports,* Vol. 70, p. 422. Austin: Hutchings Printing House, 1888; *South Western Reporter,* Vol. 7, p. 761. St. Paul: West Publishing Company, 1888.

Franco-Texan Land Company *v.* Chaptive *et al. South Western Reporter,* Vol. 3, p. 31. St. Paul: West Publishing Company, 1887.

Franco-Texan Land Company *v.* Louis Laigle. *Texas Reports,* Vol. 59, p. 339. Austin: State of Texas, 1884.

Franco-Texan Land Company *v.* McCormick. *Texas Reports,* Vol. 85, p. 416. Austin, Texas: Ben C. Jones & Company, 1893; *South Western Reporter,* Vol. 23, p. 118; Vol. 23, p. 123. St. Paul: West Publishing Company, 1894.

From Ox-Teams to Eagles. Dallas: The Texas and Pacific Railway Company, n.d.

Gammel, H. P. N. *The Laws of Texas, 1822–1897.* 10 vols. Austin: Gammel Book Company, 1898.

Goodwin, Cardinal Leonidas. *John Charles Frémont: An Explanation of His Career.* Stanford, California: Stanford University Press, 1930.

Haney, Lewis. *A Congressional History of Railways of the United States.* Madison: Democrat Printing Company, 1910.

History of Texas: Together with a Biographical List of Tarrant and Parker Counties. Chicago: The Lewis Publishing Company, 1895.

Holland, G. A. *History of Parker County and the Double Log Cabin.* Weatherford, Texas: Herald Publishing Company, 1937.

House Reports of Committees. 37th Congress, 2nd Session. Serial No. 1142, Vol. 1, No. 2; Serial No. 1143, Vol. 2, No. 2. Washington, D.C.: Government Printing Office, 1862.

House Reports of Committees. 45th Congress, 2nd Session. Serial No. 1822, Vol. 2, No. 238. Washington, D.C.: Government Printing Office, 1878.

Huntington, Collis P. *Remarks of C. P. Huntington and Argument of James H. Storrs on Behalf of the Southern Pacific Railroad before the Committee on the Pacific Railroads, House of Representatives, Forty-fifth Congress, on the Pending Propositions of the Southern Pacific and Texas Pacific Railroad Companies, January 31, 1878.* Washington, D.C.: Judd and Detweiler, 1878.

Jacques, Mary J. *Texas Ranch Life.* London: Horace Cox, Windsor House, 1894.

La Grande Encyclopédie. Paris: Société Anonyme de la Grande Encyclopédie.

Lindsley, Philip. *A History of Greater Dallas and Vicinity.* 2 vols. Chicago: The Lewis Publishing Company, 1909.

Loving, George B. *The Stock Manual: Containing the Name, Post Office Address, Ranch Location, Marks and Brands of All the Principal Stockmen of Western and Northwestern Texas, Showing Marks and Brands on Electrotype Cuts as They Appear on the Animal.* Fort Worth, Texas: George B. Loving, 1881.

Loving Brand Book. Austin, Texas: The Pemberton Press, 1965.

Malcolmson *v.* State of Texas. *South Western Reporter,* Vol. 8, p. 468. St. Paul: West Publishing Company, 1888.

Memorial of the Memphis, El Paso, and Pacific Railroad Comp'y of Texas, Praying for a Grant of Public Lands, and a Loan of United States Bonds, to Aid in Constructing a Continuous Line of Railroad and Telegraph from Jefferson, in Texas, to San Diego, in California, by Way of El Paso, with Authority to Make Such Railroad Connections as to Reach San Francisco, Guaymas, Memphis, and Virginia City on the Harbor of Norfolk, or Any Other Point on the Atlantic Coast, and Washington City, under the Title of the Southern Transcontinental Railroad. Philadelphia: King & Baird, 1868. Bound with *The Transcontinental Memphis, El Paso and Pacific Railroad.*

Memphis, El Paso and Pacific Railroad Company Records, 1856–1877. Fifteen Pamphlets, n.p.: n.p., n.d.

Milliken *v.* the City Council of Weatherford. *Texas Reports,* Vol. 54, p. 388. St. Louis: The Gilbert Book Company, 1881.

Moreau *v.* Du Bellet. *South Western Reporter,* Vol. 27, p. 503; St. Paul: West Publishing Company, 1894.

National Cyclopedia of American Biography. 42 vols. New York: James T. White & Company, 1898.

Neville, Alexander White. *History of Lamar County*. Paris, Texas: The North Texas Publishing Company, 1937.

Nevins, Allan. *Fremont: The West's Great Adventurer*. 2 vols. New York and London: Harper and Brothers, 1928.

Nimmo, Joseph. *Letter from Secretary of Treasury, Transmitting a Report from Chief of Bureau of Statistics in Response to a Resolution of the House Calling for Information in regard to the Range and Ranch Cattle Traffic in Western States and Territories*. 48th Congress, 2nd Session, Executive Document No. 267. Washington, D.C.: Government Printing Office, 1885.

Nolan County *v*. State of Texas. *Texas Reports*, Vol. 83, p. 183. Galveston: Clarke and Courts, 1892.

Paddock, Buckley B. (ed.). *A History of Central and West Texas*. 2 vols. Chicago and New York: The Lewis Publishing Company, 1911.

———. *History of Texas: Fort Worth and the Texas Northwest Edition*. 4 vols. Chicago and New York: The Lewis Publishing Company, 1922.

Pecquet du Bellet, Louise (Kate Louise Noémie). *Some Prominent Virginia Families*. Lynchburg, Virginia: J. P. Bell Company, 1907.

Pecquet du Bellet, Paul. *The Diplomacy of the Confederate Cabinet of Richmond and Its Agents Abroad*, ed. William Stanley Hoole. Tuscaloosa, Alabama: Confederate Publishing Company, 1963.

Poor, Henry V. (ed.). *Manual of Railroads of the United States, 1869–1886*. New York: H. V. and H. W. Poor, 1869–1886.

Proceedings of the First Biennial Meeting of the Stockholders of the Memphis, El Paso, and Pacific Railroad Company, Held at Paris, May 10, 1858 (n.p.: n.p., n.d.). A copy appears in File 4, Railroad Contracts, General Land Office.

Putnam, Ruth, *Alsace and Lorraine: From Caesar to Kaiser, 58 B.C.–1871 A.D.* New York and London: G. P. Putnam's Sons, 1915.

Quiett, Glenn Chesney. *They Built the West*. New York: Cooper Square Publishers, 1965.

Reed, S. G. *A History of Texas Railroads and of Transportation Conditions under Spain and Mexico and the Republic and the State*. Houston: The St. Clair Publishing Company, 1941.

Report of Explorations and Surveys to Ascertain the Most Practicable and Economical Route for a Railroad from the Mississippi River to the Pacific

Ocean. Senate Documents, 33rd Congress, 2nd Session. Document No. 78, 11 vols. Washington, D.C.: Beverly Tucker, Printer, 1855.

Sanders, Alvin H. *History of Short Horn Cattle.* Chicago: Sanders Publishing Company, 1918.

Scott, Thomas Alexander. *Statements of Mr. Thomas A. Scott and Judge Baker before the House Committee on Pacific Railroad; January 13, 1875.* Washington, D.C.: n.p., 1875.

———. *Argument of Thomas A. Scott, President of the Texas and Pacific Railway Company, before the House Committee on the Pacific Railroad; January 19, 1876.* Washington, D.C.: n.p., [1876?].

———. *Argument of Thomas A. Scott before the Committee on Railroads of the U.S. Senate; February 7, 1878.* Washington, D.C.: n.p., 1878.

Senate Documents. 33rd Congress, 2nd Session. 11 vols. Document 78. Washington, D.C.: Beverly Tucker, printer, 1855.

Senate Executive Documents. 41st Congress, 2nd Session. 3 vols. Serial No. 1406, Document No. 59. Washington, D.C.: Government Printing Office, 1870.

Senate Miscellaneous Documents. 41st Congress, 2nd Session. Serial No. 1408, Documents No. 96 and No. 121. Washington, D.C.: Government Printing Office, 1870.

Senate Reports of Committees. 41st Congress, 2nd Session. Serial No. 1409, Report No. 212. Washington, D.C.: Government Printing Office, 1870.

Smythe, Henry. *Historical Sketch of Parker County and Weatherford, Texas.* St. Louis: L. C. Lavat, Printer, 1877.

Societe Fonciere et Agricole des Etats Unis *v.* Milliken. *U.S. Reports,* Vol. 135, p. 304. New York and Albany. Banks and Brothers, 1890.

The Transcontinental, Memphis and El Paso Railroad. Washington, D.C.: Printed at the Congressional Globe, 1870.

The Transcontinental Memphis, El Paso and Pacific: How the Money Was Obtained in France under False Pretenses and How It Was Squandered. New York: E. Wells Sackett, 1870.

Turner, James. *Argument of James Turner, Esq., before the Judiciary Committee of the House of Representatives, April 20, 1878.* New York: Benjamin H. Tyrell, 1878.

United States Bureau of the Census. *Seventh Census, 1850; Report of the Superintendent of the Census.* Washington, D.C.: R. Armstrong, 1853.

———. *Eighth Census, 1860; Population of the United States,* I. Washington, D.C.: n.p., 1864.

———. *Ninth Census, 1870; Statistics of the Population of the United States,* I. Washington, D.C.: n.p., 1872 .
———. *Tenth Census, 1880; Statistics of the Population of the United States,* I. Washington, D.C.: n.p., 1883.
———. *Eleventh Census, 1890; Report on the Population of the United States,* Vol. 11, Part I. Washington, D.C.: Government Printing Office, 1892.
———. *Twelfth Census of the United States; 1900,* Vol. I, Part 1. Washington, D.C.: Government Printing Office, 1901.
———. *Thirteenth Census of the United States; 1910: Population,* III. Washington, D.C.: Government Printing Office, 1913.
———. *Fourteenth Census of the United States; 1920: Population, Texas.* Washington, D.C.: Government Printing Office, 1921.
———. *Fifteenth Census of the United States; 1930: Population,* III, Part 2. Washington, D.C.: Government Printing Office, 1932.
United States States Statutes at Large, XIV, XVI, XVII, ed. G. P. Sanger. Washington, D.C.: Government Printing Office.
Wallis, George A. *Cattle Kings of the Staked Plains.* 2nd Revised Edition. Denver: Sage Books, 1964.
Webb, Walter Prescott, and H. Bailey Carroll. *Handbook of Texas.* 2 vols. Austin: The Texas State Historical Association, 1952.
Williams, T. Harry (ed.). *Hayes: The Diary of a President.* New York: David McKay and Company, 1964.

NEWSPAPERS

Abilene *Reporter-News*, May 24, 1932 (50th Anniversary Edition).
Albany *Echo*, 1882–1884.
Albany *Star*, 1882–1883.
Austin *Daily Statesman*, 1880–1890.
Austin *Statesman*, July 15, 1876.
Buffalo Gap *Weekly News*, January 28, 1882.
Clarksville *Standard*, 1856–1860, 1868–1869.
Dallas *Daily Herald*, 1878, 1880–1887.
Dallas *Herald*, 1856, 1878–1887.
Flake's Daily Bulletin (Galveston), 1869–1871.
Flake's Semi-Weekly Bulletin (Galveston), 1869–1872.
Fort Griffin *Echo*, 1880–1883.
Fort Worth *Daily Democrat*, 1876–1882.
Fort Worth *Gazette*, 1881, 1883–1892.

Galveston *Daily Civilian*, 1869–1872.
Galveston *Daily News*, 1869–1885.
Galveston *Weekly Civilian*, 1869–1871.
New York *Herald*, February 12, 1875.
New York *Sun* (Broadside), February 1, 1875.
New York *Times*, February 4, 1871.
New York *Tribune*, January 10, 1870.
Palo Pinto County Star (Palo Pinto), 1882, 1885, 1887, 1889.
Parker County Journal (Weatherford), 1882.
San Angelo *Standard-Times*, August 23, 1964.
San Antonio *Daily Herald*, 1870, 1873–1876.
Sweetwater *Reporter*, September 28, 1941 (Pioneer and Progress Edition).
Washington *Daily Globe*, March 5, 1871.
Washington *Daily Morning Chronicle*, 1871.
Weatherford *Commercial*, March 14, 1882.
Weatherford *Constitution*, 1889–1891.
Weatherford *Democrat*, October 17, 1960.
Weatherford *Enquirer*, 1891–1892.
Weatherford *Exponent*, 1877–1880.
Weatherford *Sun*, September 1, 1884.
Weatherford *Times*, 1878, 1883, 1886.
West Texas Free Press (San Marcos), April 3, 1875.
Western Enterprise (Anson), August 24, 1933 (50th Anniversary Edition); December 3, 1936 (Cowboys Christmas Ball Edition).
Western Star (Palo Pinto), 1878, 1887.

PERIODICALS

Armstrong, A. B. "Origins of the Texas and Pacific Railway," *Southwestern Historical Quarterly*, LVI (April, 1953), 489–497.

Bowden, J. J. "The Texas and Pacific Railway Company Reservation and Land Grant," *Report of the Eleventh Annual Texas Surveyors Association Short Course* (October 8, 9, 10, 1962), pp. 45–62.

Commercial and Financial Chronicle and Hunt's Merchants Magazine, November, 1876.

Crane, R. C. "Early Days in Sweetwater," *West Texas Historical Association Yearbook*, VIII (June, 1932), 97–123.

———. "The Franco-Texan Land Company," *West Texas Historical Association Yearbook*, XXV (October, 1949), 101–103.

Freeman, Bert M. "Fremont's Arizona Venture," *The American West*, I (No. 1, Winter, 1964), 9–19.

House, Albert V., Jr. "Post-Civil War Precedents for Recent Railroad Reorganization," *Mississippi Valley Historical Review*, XXV (March, 1939), 505–522.

Rejebian, Ermance V. "The French Colony in Dallas County," *Southwestern Historical Quarterly*, XLIII (April, 1940), 472–478.

Traxler, Ralph N., Jr. "The Texas and Pacific Railroad Land Grants," *Southwestern Historical Quarterly*, LXI (January, 1958), 359–370.

———. "Collis P. Huntington and the Texas and Pacific Railroad Land Grant," *New Mexico Historical Review*, XXXIV (April, 1959), 117–133.

INDEX